Chernyshevskii's What Is to Be Done?

Chernyshevskii's What Is to Be Done?

A REEVALUATION

Andrew M. Drozd

NORTHWESTERN UNIVERSITY PRESS / EVANSTON, ILLINOIS

Northwestern University Press
www.nupress.northwestern.edu

Printed in the United States of America

10 9 8 7 6 5 4 3 2 1

ISBN 978-0-8101-2852-1

The Library of Congress has cataloged the original, hardcover edition as follows:

Drozd, Andrew Michael, 1963–
Chernyshevskii's What is to be done? : a reevaluation / Andrew M. Drozd.
p. cm. — (Studies in Russian literature and theory)
Includes bibliographical references and index.
ISBN 0-8101-1739-8 (alk. paper)
1. Chernyshevsky, Nikolay Gavrilovich, 1828–1889. Chto delat'? I. Title.
II. Series.
PG3321.C6 C625 2001
891.73'3—dc21
00-011680

∞The paper used in this publication meets the minimum requirements of the American National Standard for Information Sciences—Permanence of Paper for Printed Library Materials, ANSI Z39.48-1992.

In memory of my mother

Contents

Preface

Any study of Chernyshevskii, especially his literary works, is greatly complicated by textual problems because there are few authoritative texts available. Although Chernyshevskii's *Polnoe sobranie sochinenii* (*PSS*) has long been used as the basic source by most scholars, it is somewhat untrustworthy.[1] Some of Chernyshevskii's literary works were handled in roughshod manner, so that the *PSS* version is sometimes quite different from the manuscript version.[2] Fortunately, however, with regard to *What Is to Be Done?* a scholarly text is available. In 1975 Soviet scholars published a completely new edition of the novel as part of the *Literaturnye pamiatniki* series.[3] This edition is by far the most definitive one available and is also valuable in that it contains the rough draft of the novel.[4] It is this edition that is used as the basic reference point for the present work.

Although there is a checked, scholarly edition of *What Is to Be Done?* available, there will always be some problems with the study of the novel. We cannot say for certain that the published version of the novel actually corresponds fully to what Chernyshevskii wanted to say. All that remains is the manuscript of the rough draft and the published version of the novel that appeared in the journal *Sovremennik*. The fair copy and the proofs have not been preserved. Thus, it is simply impossible to say for certain who or what is responsible for any of the differences between the rough draft and the published version. Without the manuscript that Chernyshevskii sent to his publisher for comparison, we simply cannot say for certain whether Chernyshevskii himself, his colleagues at *Sovremennik*, or even the censor is responsible for the differences. We do have some contemporary evidence that the novel appeared in print without many cuts or changes.[5] However, when the novel was being prepared for publication the tsarist authorities did not even allow Chernyshevskii to read, much less correct, the proofs. Numerous mistakes may have crept into the novel without Chernyshevskii's own knowledge. Thus, we will always be faced with a text that is, in a certain sense, not authoritative.[6] However, even with the possible distortions that may have crept into the text, it remains evident that the novel is quite literary in its construction and should be reevaluated in those terms.

The thesis of the present work is that Chernyshevskii's novel has consistently been misread by both his detractors and his admirers, in large part because of a refusal to treat it as a literary text. If *What Is to Be Done?* is treated first and foremost as literature, however, the reader is forced to draw conclusions that differ greatly from those traditionally offered. The introduction provides the reader with the necessary background materials to approach the novel. In chapter 1 we examine Chernyshevskii's views on aesthetics, how they were perceived by contemporaries, and the relevance of that for understanding the novel. Chapter 2 undertakes an analysis of the structure and composition of *What Is to Be Done?* In particular, I analyze Chernyshevskii's use of language and the complicated relationship between the narrator and his characters. I also discuss in detail the meta-narrative aspects of the work. After the literary nature of the novel has been explored, we turn to an analysis of the novel's political content. In chapter 3 I reexamine several oft-discussed topics, particularly love, feminism, and the theories supposedly expounded by the text. In chapter 4 I undertake a challenge against the traditional interpretation of Rakhmetov as Chernyshevskii's ideal. In this regard, I attempt to show how the text itself gives many clues that Rakhmetov is rejected, not endorsed, by the author. I then proceed to a discussion of the philosophy of revolutionary asceticism and Chernyshevskii's attitude toward it. In chapter 5 I subject Vera Pavlovna's co-op and her dreams, long a popular topic of discussion among scholars, to a reexamination. Finally, in the conclusion I analyze the often-ignored winter picnic scene and discuss the question of Chernyshevskii's "message" as it appears in the novel.

The present work uses several conventions when making references to the novel and Chernyshevskii's other works. For purposes of quotation, Michael Katz's translation, which is based on the *Literaturnye pamiatniki* edition, is used.[7] References to it are given within the text by means of the page number in parentheses: (203). In quotations from the English translation I do change Katz's system of transliteration to the Library of Congress system, which I use throughout the text.[8] References to the original Russian text, using the *Literaturnye pamiatniki* edition of 1975, are indicated by use of the initials LP and the page number in parentheses: (LP 303). References to Chernyshevskii's other works, which appear in his collected works, the *Polnoe sobranie sochinenii,* are given by the volume number followed by a colon and the page number in parentheses: (10:230). When available, I have used translations of Chernyshevskii's works for quotations. In particular, I quote from Chernyshevskii's publicistic articles as they appear in the collection *Selected Philosophical Essays.*[9] Although the translations that appear in that collection are often less than satisfactory, I rely on them because the collection is a ready resource in most university libraries. Whenever translations of Chernyshevskii's works are unavailable, I have provided my own translations for purposes of quotation and have done the same for quotations from the works of other Russian authors and scholars. Finally, although many works were consulted for this study, only those actually cited in the text are listed in the bibliography.

I would like to thank those people who have helped me to see through the revision and publication of my doctoral dissertation. In particular, Michael Katz and Dennis Reinhartz were kind enough to read the dissertation and make valuable suggestions for revision as well as encourage publication. I would also like to thank the anonymous reviewer at Northwestern University Press for detailed comments and suggestions for revision. I am indebted to the staff at the Inter-Library Loan office at the University of Alabama for procuring materials necessary for further research. I am grateful to Andrei Korobkov for graciously serving as my native Russian informant. Finally, I would like to thank Emily, Alex, and Lindsey for being a continuing source of inspiration.

Chronology of Chernyshevskii's Life

All dates given are in Old Style.

July 12, 1828
Nikolai Gavrilovich Chernyshevskii is born in Saratov.

1846–50
Chernyshevskii attends University of Saint Petersburg.

March 1851
Chernyshevskii returns to Saratov to work as a teacher of Russian literature.

April 29, 1853
Chernyshevskii marries Olga Sokratovna Vasil'eva.

May 1853
Chernyshevskii returns to Saint Petersburg with intent to pursue academic career.

1853–62
Chernyshevskii's publicistic career at the "thick journal" *Sovremennik* (*The Contemporary*).

May 1855
Public defense of Chernyshevskii's master's dissertation, *The Aesthetic Relations of Art to Reality*.

1855
Publication of Chernyshevskii's *The Aesthetic Relations of Art to Reality*.

1856
Publication of Chernyshevskii's review of the young Tolstoi in *Sovremennik*.

1860
Publication in *Sovremennik* of Chernyshevskii's "The Anthropological Principle in Philosophy."

July 7, 1862
Chernyshevskii is arrested.

December 14, 1862
Chernyshevskii begins work on *What Is to Be Done?*

March–May 1863
What Is to Be Done? appears in *Sovremennik*.

May 19, 1864
Chernyshevskii's civil execution.

May 20, 1864
Chernyshevskii is sent to Siberia.

1864–66
Chernyshevskii serves in forced labor in the Kadainskii mine in Siberia.

1866–71
Chernyshevskii serves in forced labor at the *Aleksandrovskii zavod* in Siberia.

1872–83
Chernyshevskii lives in exile in Viliuisk, in Siberia.

1883–89
Chernyshevskii is transferred to exile in Astrakhan.

1888
Chernyshevskii publishes his critique of Darwin, "The Origin of the Theory of the Beneficence of the Struggle for Existence," in *Russkaia mysl'*.

June 1889
Chernyshevskii is allowed to return to Saratov.

October 17, 1889
Chernyshevskii dies in Saratov.

Chernyshevskii's What Is to Be Done?

Introduction

> If one were to ask for the title of the nineteenth-century Russian novel that has had the greatest influence on Russian society, it is likely that a non-Russian would choose among the books of the mighty triumvirate—Turgenev, Tolstoy, or Dostoyevsky. *Fathers and Sons? War and Peace? Crime and Punishment?* These would certainly be among the suggested answers; but . . . the novel that can claim this honor with the most justice is N. G. Chernyshevsky's *What Is to Be Done?*, a book few Western readers have ever heard of and fewer still have read. Yet no work in modern literature, with the possible exception of *Uncle Tom's Cabin,* can compete with *What Is to Be Done?* in its effect on human lives and its power to make history. For Chernyshevsky's novel, far more than Marx's *Capital,* supplied the emotional dynamic that eventually went to make the Russian Revolution.
>
> —Joseph Frank, "N. G. Chernyshevsky: A Russian Utopia," *Southern Review,* New Series 3, no. 1 (1967): 68

PREVIOUS SCHOLARSHIP ON *WHAT IS TO BE DONE?*

Both Chernyshevskii himself and his novel have generated considerable commentary since the work first appeared in 1863. Because the body of literature, especially that in Russian, is so large, I do not intend to provide a point-by-point discussion of each individual work.[1] Rather, the discussion will be limited to a general outline. The secondary literature is so extensive primarily because Chernyshevskii was one of the icons of the Soviet regime from its very beginning to its collapse. Lenin's admiration and love for Chernyshevskii are very well known.[2] Because there was little danger of Chernyshevskii's falling out of favor with the Soviet elite, Chernyshevskii was *always* a safe topic for Soviet scholars.[3] As a result, publication on Chernyshevskii became a veritable industry during the Soviet era.[4]

The parameters of the Soviet interpretation of Chernyshevskii were determined by Lenin.[5] *What Is to Be Done?* was Lenin's favorite novel and he was convinced that it was a great literary work because of its influence on the revolutionary movement.[6] In addition to Lenin's various statements G. Plekhanov contributed much to the future Soviet study of Chernyshevskii. Plekhanov began his work with an article in *Sotsial-demokrat* in 1890, shortly after Chernyshevskii's death. Plekhanov's work on Chernyshevskii culminated with his monograph published in 1910.[7] Plekhanov admired *What Is to Be Done?* for its contribution to the revolutionary movement, but interpreted it as an artistic failure. In all his writings, Plekhanov consistently viewed the novel as a transparent tract that had little artistic merit.[8] For the most part, Chernyshevskii was valued by the Bolshevik and early Soviet political figures not for his contributions as a writer of fiction, but for those in the political arena. Only Lunacharskii made any attempt to argue that *What Is to Be Done?* was to be valued in terms of literature.[9] Thus, although the novel was highly valued in terms of its "content," the question of "form" was all but ignored.

During the 1920s the systematic study of Chernyshevskii and his novel in the Soviet Union by actual scholars took root. In Chernyshevskii's hometown, Saratov, scholarship on the writer began to blossom. The works of A. P. Skaftymov, for example, have become standard reading for any student of Chernyshevskii.[10] Although later scholars have challenged him on many points, Skaftymov was the first to explore such essential questions as the relationship between Chernyshevskii's novel and George Sand's *Jacques*. However, regarding the basic evaluation of the novel *What Is to Be Done?* Skaftymov repeated the formulations given by Plekhanov and gave the novel a very low grade in terms of artistic merit.[11]

The year 1928 brought a flood of works devoted to Chernyshevskii in one form or another as part of the celebration of the one-hundredth anniversary of his birth. Many of Chernyshevskii's previously unpublished documents appeared in print, as did numerous commentaries, scholarly works, and memoirs of contemporaries. With the publication of this material (which continued into the early 1930s) the stage was set for a truly exhaustive study of Chernyshevskii by Soviet scholars. However, Soviet studies of Chernyshevskii soon entered what can only be termed a dark age. There was no lack of studies of Chernyshevskii or of publication of his works during the Stalin years.[12] Indeed, from this standpoint it might even be termed a golden age. But, in terms of quality, cheap sloganeering and ritual citations from Lenin replaced any serious attempt at analysis.[13] In terms of the study of Chernyshevskii's fiction as fiction, this period was absolutely sterile: the focus was entirely on Chernyshevskii's politics.[14]

After Stalin's death, the situation began to change and Chernyshevskii's fiction began to receive serious attention. Articles by S. A. Reiser and B. Ia. Bukhshtab opened new avenues of discussion of *What Is to Be Done?* by subjecting previously accepted beliefs to critical analysis.[15] Likewise, the appearance of full-length works such as those by Verkhovskii and Lebedev marked a major step forward in the study of Chernyshevskii's fiction.[16] However, the majority of the works of this period operated well within the established tradition, with the critical, exhaustive work remaining a rarity. It was not until the late 1960s that a truly qualitative leap in the study of Chernyshevskii's fiction was taken. At that point Soviet scholars began to study topics such as the position of the author within Chernyshevskii's novel, the genre of the work, and so forth. The newfound emphasis on the study of Chernyshevskii's fiction as fiction began to blossom in the 1970s. During that time, both *What Is to Be Done?* and *Prolog* were studied not as mere cloaks for Chernyshevskii's political views, but as works of fiction operating within the established tradition of Russian literature. As a result, Chernyshevskii's fiction as a whole, including his youthful attempts at writing, became a topic of serious study.[17] The journals *Russkaia literatura* and *Voprosy literatury* devoted many articles to Chernyshevskii's fiction during that period, making the study of it common fare. In 1978, the one-hundred-fiftieth anniversary of Chernyshevskii's birth, those and other journals were literally inundated with works dealing with Chernyshevskii's fiction as fiction.[18]

During the 1980s the level of scholarship on Chernyshevskii's fiction in the Soviet Union reached its height, far outpacing that of the West. Using Bakhtin's notions of chronotope, Soviet scholars provided several bold analyses that, whatever their individual merits, were unanimous in the assumption that *What Is to Be Done?* should be read as literature.[19] The appearance of *glasnost'* seemed to promise much for the study of Chernyshevskii as Soviet scholars began to move away (slowly) from the traditional restrictions placed upon them by Lenin's formulations. The collection *"Chto delat'?" N. G. Chernyshevskogo: Istoriko-funktsional'noe issledovanie,* for example, was distinguished both by the lack of traditional sloganeering and by ample documentation of assertions.[20] It is perhaps ironic that *glasnost'*, however, and the subsequent collapse of the Soviet Union have virtually ended the study of Chernyshevskii in Russia. Because Chernyshevskii was so worshipped by the Bolshevik founding fathers, he has been thrown out of favor along with them. It is unlikely that much new scholarship will appear in the near future, nor are any further editions of Chernyshevskii's works likely to appear.[21] It is unfortunate that as scholarship on Chernyshevskii was reaching an incredibly high level, it was doomed to such an inglorious death.

The study of Chernyshevskii and *What Is to Be Done?* in the West has never occupied the scholarly profession to the extent that it did in the former Soviet Union.[22] Western scholarship on Chernyshevskii has often been marred by ideological considerations and, on occasion, outright laziness and sloppiness. Few scholarly studies of Chernyshevskii's work appeared in the West before World War I.[23] After the establishment of the Soviet Union and the subsequent canonization of Chernyshevskii by the regime, Western scholarship slowly began to turn its attention to Chernyshevskii, accepting Soviet claims that Chernyshevskii was a direct forerunner of Bolshevism in the process.[24] With the onset of the cold war the attitude toward Chernyshevskii in Western scholarship became increasingly hostile and often quite unfair.[25] Chernyshevskii was studied in the West primarily in relation to the evil of Bolshevism, with study of his fiction often not considered worthy of effort unless in relation to its influence on the Russian revolutionary tradition.[26] Western scholarship viewed Chernyshevskii as scornful of art and as turning to fiction only as a cover for his ideology.[27] Thus, *What Is to Be Done?* was not treated as fiction, but solely as a sociopolitical document important for the understanding of the genesis of Russian radicalism. Most commentary rarely analyzed the novel itself but was concerned with explaining the source of its immense popularity in nineteenth-century Russian society and with linking it to Socialist Realism.[28] The one exception to this trend is Francis Randall, who in 1967 did attempt to defend the novel on literary grounds.[29] His argument was subsequently rejected, notably by nonliterary specialists on Chernyshevskii. William Woehrlin, who provides an otherwise valuable study of Chernyshevskii, rejects Randall's argument, dismissing the novel as incoherent.[30] N. G. O. Pereira is even more explicit, stating that "it is precisely and only as a social document or tract that Černyševskij's novel does have great importance."[31] This disparaging view of Chernyshevskii remained predominant among most Western scholars until the end of the 1970s and, indeed, to this very day.[32] Although some reevaluation began to take place in the 1960s and 1970s, these changes took place in the nonliterary sphere, with most scholars continuing to disregard Chernyshevskii as a writer of fiction.[33]

In addition to the ideological considerations and the deep-seated prejudice against Chernyshevskii as a writer of fiction, another factor contributing to the negative perception of *What Is to Be Done?* in the West has been the notoriously bad translations of the novel into English.[34] The Vintage 1961 edition, in particular, was so badly cut and distorted, that, as Katz states, "the result bears the vaguest resemblance to Tucker's flawed translation of a translation and almost none to Chernyshevskii's original novel."[35] Finally, one can point to a certain amount of laziness by Western scholars that has hindered a reevaluation of Chernyshevskii's novel. As Randall noted in the 1960s, although many Western Slavists have a negative opinion of *What Is to Be Done?* few have actually read it.[36] When Western Slavists are forced to read the novel, as in the case of those studying Nabokov's novel *The Gift*, scarcely one seems to have read the novel in the original Russian; instead most seem to have relied on the flawed English translations.[37]

Only circa 1980 did any kind of a change occur in Western attitudes regarding Chernyshevskii's novel.[38] Since that time several literary scholars have turned their attention to *What Is to Be Done?* What distinguishes this newer scholarship is both a freedom from traditional stereotypes and a willingness to treat the novel on its own terms.[39] Perhaps the biggest contribution to the field has been a new, scholarly translation of the novel into English produced by Michael Katz.[40] Some Western literary scholars have begun to realize that *What Is to Be Done?* is much deeper, more literary, than previously thought. In what is perhaps the final irony, this process is finally taking place in the West just as his homeland is preparing to consign him forever to the dustbin of history.

THE PUBLICATION OF *WHAT IS TO BE DONE?*

Chernyshevskii had been in prison for about six months when he decided to write *What Is to Be Done?* In late 1862 he asked the prison commandant, A. F. Sorokin, for permission to write a novel.[41] The request was granted and Chernyshevskii began work on December 14, 1862. Realizing that, if his trial and sentencing were to take place, he would probably be unable to publish his work, Chernyshevskii worked intensely on the manuscript.[42] After completing the first two chapters of the novel, Chernyshevskii submitted them to the investigative commission in charge of his case in January 1863. Those chapters were held by the investigative commission for ten days and then sent to the chief of police on January 26. The manuscript was then passed on to the journal *Sovremennik* and was promptly lost by the editor, Nikolai Nekrasov, in a cab. Nekrasov reported the loss to the police, an advertisement was placed, and the manuscript was returned in short order.[43]

On February 12, 1863, Chernyshevskii sent chapter 3 to the commission, with continuations following on March 26, 28, and 30. Chernyshevskii finished the novel on April 4, 1863, and sent the ending to the commission on April 6. The entire novel was completed in a span of less than four months. While Chernyshevskii continued his work on the novel, the first chapters had already appeared in *Sovremennik*. The first two chapters, approved by the censor on February 15 and March 14, appeared in the third issue on March 19, 1863. The third chapter, approved on April 20, appeared in issue number four on April 28. The last two chapters came out in the fifth issue, on May 30, 1863, after having been passed by the censor on April 27 and May 18.[44]

This short summary of the basic information in no way conveys the very absurdity of and the controversy over the writing and publication of *What Is to Be Done?* Scholars have long argued over how this most dangerous novel ever saw the light of day when its author was safely in the government's hands. Indeed, the government had every opportunity to prevent the novel's very creation, much less its publication, but somehow *What Is to Be Done?* slipped through. Incidents such as Nekrasov's loss of the initial manuscript only add to the aura of mystery that surrounds this text. To explain such an improbable combination of circumstances, many conjectures have been put forward. The most popular is that the appearance of *What Is to Be Done?* was purely the result of a bureaucratic oversight. Joseph Frank sums up this position succinctly when he states that the novel's appearance was "the most spectacular example of bureaucratic bungling in the cultural realm during the reign of Alexander II."[45] Key to this explanation is the notion that the authorities paid very little attention to the novel as Chernyshevskii turned in the various parts. The chief evidence for such an interpretation comes in a diary entry of one N. Ia. Agafonov. In 1878, almost fifteen years after the events in question, he recorded the words of the censor, Vladimir Nikolaevich Beketov: "The novel was censored by Beketov and Fed. Iv. Rakhmaninov, who, being calmed by the fact that the manuscript had passed through the filter of the Third Section, looked it over superficially and blindly signed their names, without eliminating a single word. That's how it was published."[46] Supporters of this explanation often add that the censor, with typical bureaucratic mentality, trembled upon seeing the official stamp of the investigative commission (headed by Prince Golitsyn) and passed the novel for publication without even reading it.[47]

This interpretation is the one that is generally repeated by scholars, both Russian or Soviet and Western. Whatever variation there may be, these explanations all have in common some amount of bungling on the part of the tsarist authorities. Tsarist bureaucrats were incredibly literal upon many occasions and no doubt the element of rank consciousness was very strong. There is much in this version that is tempting. It does seem clear that State Councilor Dmitrii Ivanovich Kamenskii, a member of the investigative commission and the first official to see the novel, was primarily concerned with the text as it related to Chernyshevskii's criminal case. Seeing nothing particularly criminal in the first two chapters, in which a mother and daughter squabble, he passed it on to the censor in full confidence that the latter would take care of things.[48] Yet this explanation is far too simplistic. As Joseph Frank, a supporter of this explanation, admits, "These facts explain how the first installment was published; but why the remainder slipped through the censorship net, even after the revolutionary drift of the work was clear for all to see, still remains a mystery."[49]

Among the many facts against this explanation is that the government authorities did indeed read the novel and read it closely. For example, Osip Antonovich Przhetslavskii, a member of the Council of the Minister of Internal Affairs on Book Publishing, read and commented extensively on the manuscripts.[50] In his second report he gives an extensive plot summary and evaluation of the novel's supposed utilitarian philosophy. It is simply not possible to argue that the novel was passed without being read.[51] The contention that the censor passed it out of fear upon seeing the stamp of the investigative commission has more weight to it. But as Naumova argues, such an explanation (that is, a mix-up) is a bit naive: Beketov probably used this claim to defend himself. An oversight by the censor would be believable if the novel had been given to the censor all at once.[52] However, the novel was written and published in installments; the government had time to stop the appearance of the other installments if it chose to do so. Its inactivity was certainly not due to ignorance or ineptness.

A possible explanation for the government's inactivity, put forward by Richard L. Brown, bases itself upon the close relationship between the censors and the men at the "thick journals."[53] Brown notes that the censors were usually far from bungling, simple-minded individuals, but rather well-educated men who often shared the views of the editors and writers to whom they were assigned. Brown posits that many questionable works may have slipped through because of this close relationship and that "literalness" or "bungling" was a sort of self-defense mechanism by the censors. There is indeed much to support Brown's argument in regard to Chernyshevskii's case. As Smolitskii has noted, the censor, V. N. Beketov, had a very close relationship with both the writers at *Sovremennik* and the editor, Nekrasov. He was usually present at the various dinners given by Nekrasov for the staff of the journal. Chernyshevskii was present at those dinners and often found it his part to entertain Beketov.[54] In addition to this personal relationship, Beketov liked to parade his liberalism. According to Nekrasov, Beketov was the very best censor. It was because of him that many articles appeared that otherwise might not have passed.[55] Thus, Beketov was in a very difficult situation and may have found himself under considerable pressure to let the novel through.[56] The one factor that works against Brown's argument in this particular case, however, is that everybody knew that Chernyshevskii was a marked man. Any kindness in his direction was a sure path to harsh reprisal. It seems very unlikely that Beketov would have taken such a responsibility upon himself unless he felt very confident that his superiors would not be displeased.

Another possible explanation may simply be in the fact that Chernyshevskii was extremely successful in his attempts to mystify the censors. As Soviet scholars have always stressed, Chernyshevskii took great pains in hiding his intentions and views and did everything possible to confuse the government censors.[57] It does seem clear that his practice of sending the novel out in installments was a technique designed to get the novel passed.[58] Perhaps he had the incident of Turgenev's *A Sportsman's Sketches* in mind when doing this.[59] In addition, Chernyshevskii also resorted to techniques such as sending out a note to Nekrasov and Pypin in which he stated his intention to write a continuation of *What Is to Be Done?*[60] Chernyshevskii never undertook such a project and it seems clear that this was part of his campaign to convince the authorities that the novel was just a harmless romance.[61]

These and other facts, which will be discussed later, leave no doubt that Chernyshevskii did everything possible to fool the censors. However, it would perhaps be too much to explain the passing of the novel as solely due to Chernyshevskii's cleverness. Rather, some believe that the government, simply assuming Chernyshevskii would be an utter failure as a creative writer, let the novel pass in the hopes that he would embarrass himself and the radical left as a whole.[62] However, when quite the opposite turned out to be the case, the government attempted to cover its tracks, placing all the blame on the lowly censor.

There are indeed some indications that the novel was published due to conscious calculation by the government authorities. First, Chernyshevskii was safely in the hands of the authorities who had total control over him. He had to ask permission to write the novel and it was the authorities who supplied him with the necessary materials (such as writing paper). This fact is most curious in that it was the only right or request that was respected by the authorities during his entire imprisonment. At that very time, Chernyshevskii was denied even the most basic rights, such as visits from his wife. One wonders how the authorities, who were so determined to keep Chernyshevskii isolated and harmless, could have even considered letting him submit a novel for publication. In addition, when Chernyshevskii began his hunger strike and wrote numerous letters to protest his conditions, he was threatened with retribution. But the threat of preventing his work on *What Is to Be Done?* never seems to have arisen. One definitely gets the sense that the authorities wanted him to write the novel. Another fact that tends to corroborate this supposition is that although the government allowed him to write and publish the novel, it did not allow him to read and correct the proofs.[63] That is, it seems as if the government wanted as faulty a version as possible to appear in print.[64]

Finally, the government had ample opportunity to prevent the later installments from appearing but took no action. It was only after the novel had appeared as a whole and the young generation received it with adoration that the government took stern measures. The Third Section blamed the censor for the novel's appearance, although the censor in return claimed that the Third Section had already approved the novel before he passed it. The censor, conveniently a low-level functionary, was sacked and the novel was, of course, outlawed.[65] It seems likely that the only explanation of this curious circumstance was indeed a miscalculated plot on the part of the government.[66] For example, although the censor in charge of *Sovremennik* was indeed sacked, there are indications that the sacking was done only for cosmetic purposes. Despite the "oversight" of allowing such a dangerous work in print, the censor, when forcibly retired, did receive his full pay and a full pension.[67] The one weakness of this explanation, however, is that it gives perhaps too much credit to the government.[68]

Finally, a modified version of this explanation has been developed most recently by A. A. Demchenko, who argues that the government intentionally let the novel be published as a mere public relations ploy, rather than as a plot to embarrass Chernyshevskii. That is, by allowing Chernyshevskii to write and publish the novel, the government hoped both to forestall any public demonstrations in support of him and to grant itself an aura of impartiality and humaneness.[69] Despite the many creative explanations proposed, we will probably never know the entire story of this episode. And, although the story of the novel's publication is indeed intriguing, to focus on it too much is to ignore study of the novel itself.

THE AFTERMATH OF *WHAT IS TO BE DONE?*

The appearance of *What Is to Be Done?* sent a shock wave through Russian society. Despite the government's ban on the novel and attempts to recall all issues of *Sovremennik* containing it, *What Is to Be Done?* circulated widely among the Russian youth and became its bible.[70] Manuscript copies passed from hand to hand, and several émigré editions were published and smuggled into Russia.[71] Unlike previous Russian literature, *What Is to Be Done?* managed to tap the psyche of the Russian youth and move it to action. Numerous young Russians called themselves followers of Chernyshevskii and professed to act in his name, with some in the 1860s actually using the term *Chernyshevtsy* to refer to themselves.[72] As one contemporary, Aleksandr Mikhailovich Skabichevskii, has described it, *What Is to Be Done?*'s influence on the Russian youth was simply phenomenal:

> We read the novel almost like worshippers, with the kind of piety with which we read religious books, and without the slightest trace of a smile on our lips. The influence of the novel on our society was colossal. It played a great role in Russian life, especially among the leading members of the intelligentsia who were embarking on the road to socialism, bringing it down a bit from the world of drama to the problem of our social evils, sharpening its image as the goal which each of us had to fight for.[73]

E. N. Vodovozova confirms Skabichevskii's account of the novel's influence:

> At the present time it is difficult to imagine what immense influence this novel had on its contemporaries. It was discussed not only in meetings specially arranged for this purpose, but it was a rare gathering that went by without arguments and discussions about this or that question touched upon in it.[74]

Not only Chernyshevskii's admirers, but also his detractors noted the overwhelming popularity of the novel. Professor P. Tsitovich of Odessa University, for example, remarked that every schoolgirl and student was "considered a dunce if she was not acquainted with the exploits of Vera Pavlovna."[75] Katkov, the editor of *Russkii vestnik,* sounded a similar note when he said of the younger generation that they took *What Is to Be Done?* as a revelation "like Moslems honor the Koran."[76]

On the level of daily life, many young men and women consciously began to model their lives on the main characters of *What Is to Be Done?*[77] Fictitious marriages, although a phenomenon that existed prior to the appearance of the novel, blossomed under its influence. They were staged so that young women could escape an oppressive familial home or seek higher education. Likewise, many young couples consciously modeled their lifestyles on the novel, including the adoption of separate, inviolable rooms for each partner.[78] *What Is to Be Done?* was to remain particularly powerful for Russian women: even major figures of the early-twentieth century, such as Aleksandra Kollontai and Inessa Armand, continued to look upon the novel as a model of behavior.[79]

Following the actions of the novel's main character, Vera Pavlovna, many young Russians began to set up cooperative or communal ventures. Again, such phenomena had appeared before Chernyshevskii wrote his novel (the Grech Commune, for example), but after *What Is to Be Done?* communal ventures began to spring forth everywhere. According to Vera Zasulich, such enterprises sprang up like mushrooms after the appearance of the novel.[80] It was even reported that young people would sit around a table with a copy of *What Is to Be Done?* in front of them and plan a communal venture.[81] Perhaps the most famous of these communes, the Znamenskii Commune, founded by Vasilii Sleptsov, was inspired directly by *What Is to Be Done?* Most such ventures were not particularly successful, and others were utter failures.[82] But the image, seemingly offered by Chernyshevskii, continued to burn bright for generations, influencing many.

Other young Russians took up direct revolutionary activity under the novel's influence. The most flamboyant was one Nikolai Ishutin, who consciously modeled his behavior on the character Rakhmetov. Ishutin is said to have recognized only three great men in history: Jesus Christ, Saint Paul, and Nikolai Chernyshevskii. In a gesture that undoubtedly imitates Chernyshevskii's Rakhmetov, Ishutin obtained a job on a Volga River steamboat, using it as a base for his radical activities.[83] More significant was the group of young Russians who attempted to assassinate Tsar Alexander II in 1866. Members of this group, often referred to as the Karakazovites, had all read the novel and claimed that they had turned to terrorism under its influence.[84] They even chose April 4, 1866, as the date for their attempt to coincide with what many thought was an implicit call to revolution in *What Is to Be Done?*[85] Finally, much of the "to the people" movement of the 1870s owes its inspiration directly to *What Is to Be Done?*[86]

Despite the overwhelmingly positive reaction to the novel by the Russian youth, the Russian press took a different view. Numerous hostile evaluations of the novel appeared in which Chernyshevskii was accused of immorality.[87] Among the charges leveled at Chernyshevskii by his critics was that he was destroying the morals of Russian society by advocating free love and simultaneously preaching the destruction of the family.[88] Conservative contemporaries were appalled at Lopukhov's fake suicide, Vera Pavlovna's remarriage to her husband's best friend, and the acceptance of prostitutes into Vera Pavlovna's co-op. Fedor Tolstoi, writing in *Severnaia pchela,* accused Chernyshevskii of recommending "every comfort and seduction for shopgirls and streetwalkers, removing all obstacles for them, and giving them the right to take lovers into their rooms."[89] Likewise, Askochenskii suggested assigning Chernyshevskii's characters to hard labor to rid them of their silly emancipatory notions.[90] The conservative N. Solov'ev claimed that Chernyshevskii preached a type of free love that hardly differed from prostitution.[91] Przhetslavskii, in his second report on the novel, provided a most hostile view: "In general I must say that in the most recent literatures, even in the French, I have not happened to read anything so naively immoral as the novel under discussion. . . . Sheer debauchery, the communalism of women or men, is preached in place of the Christian idea of marriage . . ."[92] Przhetslavskii concluded his report by labeling the novel as both "harmful and dangerous in the highest degree." Finally, Professor Tsitovich in his *Chto delali v romane "Chto delat'?"* lists the laws of the Russian empire that the characters of the novel break, accusing them of abduction, bigamy, pimping, and fornication.[93] Tsitovich concludes his discussion by arguing that the novel is extremely dangerous and warns his male readers to keep their daughters and sisters from reading it.[94]

The reaction from Russia's literary community was also generally hostile, but its attack centered more on artistic rather than moral grounds. Turgenev, for example, expressed a very negative opinion of *What Is to Be Done?* His first reference to the novel comes in a letter to A. A. Fet in April 1863. Turgenev, with obvious irony, calls the first parts of the novel "charming." Later, he comments: ". . . but, I must confess, I am swallowing this style with the greatest difficulty."[95] Turgenev saved his strongest comments until he had completed the novel:

"[B]ut Chernyshevskii, if you please, I barely got through. His manner arouses physical disgust in me, like wormseed. If this—I do not even say artistry or beauty—but if this is intellect, . . . then the only thing left for our brother to do is to crawl somewhere under a bench. I had never met an author whose figures stank: Chernyshevskii has presented me this author. But we won't talk about this subject any more: I will only remark that

Chernyshevskii unwittingly appears to me a naked and toothless old man who lisps like an infant."[96]

Other Russian writers also had a negative opinion of *What Is to Be Done?* although most of them seemed to keep silent. In his letters and diaries, Tolstoi, for example, had very little to say about the novel, but it does seem clear that Tolstoi responded on a literary level when he wrote his "Infected Family."[97] Likewise, in a much later work ("The Living Corpse"), Tolstoi seems to have vented his feelings about Chernyshevskii's novel when he has a character label it "boring" and when he uses the fake suicide as the main motivation for the play's intrigue.[98]

Chernyshevskii's radical colleague M. E. Saltykov-Shchedrin surprised and angered many by his unenthusiastic reception of *What Is to Be Done?* In January 1864 in his series "Nasha obshchestvennaia zhizn'" Saltykov-Shchedrin wrote, "'with time' the dear nihilists will cut through human corpses with an impassive hand and at the same time take up dancing and singing."[99] Many on the left, especially those grouped around the journal *Russkoe slovo,* considered these words a mockery of Chernyshevskii's novel and responded heatedly.[100] In March 1864 Saltykov-Shchedrin responded to these attacks: "Last year the novel *What Is to Be Done?* appeared—a serious novel which developed the idea of the necessity of new, vital foundations and even pointed to these foundations. The author of this novel, without a doubt, fully mastered his idea. But because he passionately related to it, because he imagined it alive and incarnated, he could not escape a certain arbitrary regulation of details, especially those details, for whose prediction and depiction reality does not yet present enough data. For any rational person this fact is quite clear, and any reasonable person reading the above-mentioned novel will know how to distinguish its living and rational idea from the invented details which only spoil the matter."[101] As might be expected those words did not mollify Chernyshevskii's supporters but only increased their displeasure.[102] The accusations that Saltykov-Shchedrin had attacked or betrayed Chernyshevskii continued.[103] Pisarev, for example, was incensed that Saltykov-Shchedrin would not support *What Is to Be Done?*[104] Moreover, the scandal began to spread when members of the circle around the journal *Epokha* accused Saltykov-Shchedrin of hostility to Chernyshevskii.[105]

Saltykov tried to defend himself from the charges in an unpublished article of December 1864. In it he states that he indeed shares a different opinion from Chernyshevskii, but asks how it follows that his attitude toward the novel is hostile.[106] His remarks, however, seem rather disingenuous. It seems clear that he is tempering his remarks out of respect for the great radical figure and out of the need to present a united front. But in a private letter to E. I. Utin in 1881, Saltykov-Shchedrin leaves no doubt that he cared little for *What Is to Be Done?* precisely because he perceived it as an attempt to predict and regulate the details of the future.[107]

Aleksandr Herzen, an eminent figure among Russian progressives, remained publicly silent regarding *What Is to Be Done?* Herzen apparently did not read the novel until 1867.[108] In a letter to N. Ogarev (July 29, 1867), Herzen recounts his first, very negative reactions to the novel: "I am reading Chernyshevskii's novel. Good Lord, how basely it is written, how much affectation . . . , what style! What a worthless generation whose aesthetics are satisfied by this. . . . The ideas are beautiful, even the situations—and all this is poured from a seminarian-Petersburg-bourgeois urinal à la Niederhuber."[109] In later letters Herzen continues to argue that there are good ideas in *What Is to Be Done?* but that it fails artistically.[110] Despite his oft-stated reservations about the artistic qualities of the novel, Herzen refrained from public statements. He did intend to write an article on the novel but stopped in order "not to irritate its flock."[111] Herzen, whose prestige among the left in Russia had already declined at this point, apparently decided not to alienate Chernyshevskii's numerous followers. In addition, Herzen felt responsible to some degree for Chernyshevskii's arrest and this undoubtedly contributed to his decision to mute his criticism.

The impact of *What Is to Be Done?* lasted well beyond the 1860s and 1870s and even spread beyond the borders of Russia. Of the many revolutionary groups of the late-nineteenth and early-twentieth centuries, almost all revered Chernyshevskii as a forefather and sang the praises of *What Is to Be Done?* Among them were the anarchists, both Russian and Western. *What Is to Be Done?* was the favored reading matter of the anarchist and socialist leaders involved in the McCormick Reaper Strike and the Haymarket Riot in Chicago in May 1886. In addition, Emma Goldman notes in her autobiography[112] that she intended to establish a sewing co-op on the model found in *What Is to Be Done?* upon her arrival in America, and she soon fulfilled her intention in New York. Moreover, her close companion, Alexander Berkman, used the name Rakhmetov as an alias when on his way to assassinate the steel magnate Henry Clay Frick. Finally, the American anarchist Benjamin Tucker was one of the first translators of *What Is to Be Done?* into English.[113] In general, the anarchists held the novel in very high esteem. Perhaps Prince Petr Kropotkin best summed up the anarchist attitude to *What Is to Be Done?*: "No novel of Turgueneff and no writings of Tolstoy or any other writer have ever had such a wide and deep influence upon Russian Society as this novel had. It became the watchword of Young Russia, and the influence of the ideas it propagated has never ceased to be apparent since."[114]

The best known of the novel's worshipers were the Russian Social Democrats (SDs), especially the Bolsheviks. The Bolshevik founding fathers so revered Chernyshevskii and claimed him as their own that a straight line is often drawn from Chernyshevskii to Stalinist society.[115] The Russian SDs were almost unanimous in their admiration for *What Is to Be Done?*[116] Even the least enthusiastic of them, G. V. Plekhanov, appreciated its importance in the revolutionary struggle: "[L]et them show us as least one of the most remarkable, truly artistic works of Russian literature which, in terms of its influence on the moral and intellectual development of the country, could compete with *What Is to Be Done?*. No one can indicate such a work, because there was not one, and, probably, will never be. Since the appearance of the printing press in Russia right up to our day, not one printed work has had such success in Russia as *What Is to Be Done?*."[117]

The most ardent advocate of both Chernyshevskii and his novel was Lenin: young Lenin even wrote an admiring letter to Chernyshevskii in 1888 (which was never answered) and always kept an inscribed picture of Chernyshevskii with him.[118] Regarding *What Is to Be Done?* Lenin was unreserved in his praise:

> Do you realize what you are saying . . . ? How could such a monstrous and absurd idea come into your mind—to describe as crude and untalented a work of Chernyshevsky, the greatest and most talented representative of socialism before Marx! . . . I declare that it is impermissible to call *What is to be Done?* crude and untalented. Hundreds of people became revolutionaries under its influence. Could this have happened if Chernyshevsky had been untalented and crude? My brother, for example, was captivated by him, and so was I. *He completely transformed my outlook.* When did you read *What is to be Done?*? It is no good reading it when one is still a greenhorn. Chernyshevsky's novel is too complex and full of ideas to be understood and appreciated at an early age. I myself started to read it when I was 14. I think this was a completely useless and superficial reading of the book. But, after the execution of my brother, I started to read it properly, as I knew it had been one of his favourite books. I spent not days but several weeks reading it. Only then did I understand its depth. This novel provides inspiration for a lifetime: untalented books don't have such influence.[119]

Because of Lenin's reverence for the novel, it inevitably became a part of the literary pantheon of the early Bolsheviks and of the regime that followed October 1917. Although the reverence for *What Is to Be Done?* quickly assumed an artificial, ritualistic character under the Soviet regime,[120] it does seem clear that for many generations, the enthusiasm was genuine and the novel's influence colossal.

In addition to its influence in Russia, for a time *What Is to Be Done?* was somewhat known and appreciated in the West in the latter part of the nineteenth century. Numerous translations of it appeared on the European continent throughout the period. Translations appeared in most of the major European languages (French: 1875, German: 1883) and even many of the minor ones.[121] Accompanying the translations were several reviews that appeared in Western newspapers. For example, Tucker's translation of 1884 occasioned many favorable comments in the *Boston Courier, New York World, Boston Saturday Evening Gazette, Boston Traveller,* and *Providence Star.*[122] Moreover, it seems probable that *What Is to Be Done?* managed to find a literary echo in the West in Mary Bradley Lane's *Mizora.*[123] Even many years after its appearance, an occasional Westerner discovered the power of the book. The Frenchman E. Le Provost, for example, wrote to Tolstoi in 1903 about *What Is to Be Done?* singing its praises and asking for more information: "I have a book which I bought around 1892 in New York in a used bookstore and to me this book is a masterpiece. I dare to hope that you are of the same opinion about it, if you know it. . . . This book is a manifestation of strength and greatness of spirit, a bold experiment in which feeling and true art are united in harmony. I cannot express to you the rapture which this book calls forth in me. However, that doesn't keep me from seeking an objective evaluation of the writer and his work."[124] Despite such promising beginnings, *What Is to Be Done?* never succeeded in capturing the attention of the general reading public of the West. It was basically forgotten in the twentieth century and remains unknown to nonspecialists.

LITERARY AND CRITICAL RESPONSES

What Is to Be Done? engendered many responses, both literary and critical. Although elements of a response can easily be discerned in the literary works of several Russian writers, the most impressive comes in the oeuvre of Dostoevskii. It has long been known that Dostoevskii began his *Notes from the Underground* as an article against Chernyshevskii's novel. That Dostoevskii rejected the very notion that human existence could ever be rationally organized and argued for the irrational, for caprice, has been well discussed by critics.[125] The primary evidence often cited to this effect is the incident between the underground man and the officer, which echoes Lopukhov's collision. Likewise, the Crystal Palace, which appears in Vera Pavlovna's fourth dream, figures heavily in Dostoevskii's work.[126] Throughout his artistic works, Dostoevskii continued to echo elements of *What Is to Be Done?* Those echoes might appear in the form of ideas, such as Luzhin's parroting of Lopukhov's utilitarianism (*Crime and Punishment*) and Stepan Verkhovenskii's reading of *What Is to Be Done?* in order to understand the younger generation (*The Devils*), or in plot references, such as Epanchina's reference to Vera Pavlovna's abandonment of her mother on Nevskii Prospekt (*The Idiot*).[127] Chernyshevskii's novel served as material for Dostoevskii throughout the remainder of his career.[128] One could even argue that Dostoevskii's creative genius owes much to the stimulus provided by Chernyshevskii. One should remember, however, that for whatever purpose Dostoevskii uses material from *What Is to Be Done?* he treats it as a serious work; he is not dismissive of it.

Nikolai Leskov's novel *Nekuda* (1864) has long been considered a response to *What Is to Be Done?* and a hostile one at that. While it seems clear that *What Is to Be Done?* is a point of reference for *Nekuda,* the hostility in it seems more directed at hangers-on of the so-called nihilist movement.[129] Moreover, when we read Leskov's critical review from the previous year, it becomes clear that Leskov not only did not attack Chernyshevskii but actually defended both him and his novel. Leskov does defend the novel in a rather strange manner. He begins by noting that Chernyshevskii's novel is written with disdain for artistry and that it is quite burdensome to read: "Chernyshevskii's novel from the point of view of art is lower than any criticism; it is simply laughable."[130] Having made those statements, however, Leskov begins to defend Chernyshevskii's novel on the grounds that Chernyshevskii himself is not a writer of fiction by trade, but a publicist. Moreover, he goes on to credit Chernyshevskii for drawing accurate pictures of the Russian youth. In his opinion, Chernyshevskii's characters are fully believable and he states that he likes them: they are good, decent, hardworking people. Finally, perhaps anticipating the numerous charges that would later be made against the novel, he claims that there is nothing utopian about it and stresses that Chernyshevskii is very different from the average nihilist in that he includes nothing revolutionary in it. Leskov's basic evaluation of *What Is to Be Done?* is that it is "bold" and "useful."[131]

Another contemporary, Nikolai Strakhov, had much harsher words for *What Is to Be Done?* Whereas Leskov began his review by an out-of-hand dismissal of the novel as art, Strakhov argues that *What Is to Be Done?* has a certain solidity (*prochnost'*) to it and predicts that the novel will remain a part of Russian literature.[132] Strakhov goes on to state that there are things in the novel one would never have expected: keenness of observation, faithfulness to reality, and even some deftness in the depiction.[133] After those kind words, however, Strakhov begins an unrelenting attack on the "tendency" of the novel.

Strakhov admits that the novel is written with enthusiasm and that its author is consistent. But the basic idea of the novel is repulsive to him. For Strakhov, the essence of *What Is to Be Done?* is that "It consists of the idea of *happiness,* of the notion of a *happy life.* The novel teaches how to be happy."[134] Strakhov discusses at length the various events of the novel and notes that the lives of the characters are far too easy, their lives far too happy: the entire novel is the story of how they avoid discomfort and unhappiness. Strakhov is distressed by the fact that not only does Chernyshevskii dispense with struggle and suffering as a part of human existence, but he encourages others to adopt this philosophy.[135] As a result, Strakhov finds the message in the novel frightening and rejects it: "I cannot tell you how the message chilled me the first time I read it! It seemed to me that anyone who is alive while reading it should be seized with dread and should answer without a moment's hesitation: I don't need your kind of happiness! For this inhuman coldness, for this terrible emptiness which you call happiness, for this infallibility and indestructible tranquility I would not give up at any price my present life which is hard and meager but nevertheless full and warm and pulsing."[136]

Chernyshevskii's radical colleague, Nikolai Shelgunov, also provided a rather harsh appraisal of *What Is to Be Done?* Shelgunov begins his study, "Russkie idealy, geroi i tipy," by comparing the characters of *What Is to Be Done?* with their literary predecessors: the Onegins, the Pechorins, the Rudins, and so forth. In contrast to previous literature, Chernyshevskii's novel deals with the question of forming new families, family life, and the like: "In this respect the novel *What Is to Be Done?* stands immeasurably higher than all preceding works which portray wives who deceive their husbands and hypocritically assure them of their love while a lover has already been found."[137] After this rather positive assessment, however, Shelgunov begins to take the characters of the novel to task for their many shortcomings. In particular, he finds Vera Pavlovna greatly lacking as a model of a modern, emancipated woman. He notes how she is constantly being saved by the male characters and how the male characters are always intellectually superior to her.[138] Shelgunov even traces this patriarchal attitude to the very narrator who treats Vera Pavlovna as if she is a child, using endearing diminutives to describe her and her surroundings. Likewise, Shelgunov is disturbed by Vera Pavlovna's love of comfort, which is hardly characteristic of an emancipated woman devoted to the cause.[139]

The gist of Shelgunov's displeasure with the novel is the fact that Chernyshevskii makes the same mistake as all novelists: he draws heroes, not simple mortals.[140] The fault, Shelgunov argues, lies in Chernyshevskii's failure to present Russian society with a true collective ideal. What is needed is not an individual, heroic ideal, but a collective one: "But if we place the question somewhat further, if we take the second step, then we don't need heroes for this second step, not guardian angels, nor individual titans capable of moving mountains, but simple people whose combined efforts achieve much greater, useful results than the actions of individual titans."[141] Such an ideal simply is not present in *What Is to Be Done?* Shelgunov argues. He does note that such an attempt is made in the depiction of Vera Pavlovna's sewing co-op, but the attempt bears all the traits of heroism. Shelgunov does excuse Chernyshevskii on the grounds that his depiction is consistent with the times in which the novel is set. But for Shelgunov, Chernyshevskii fails to provide a true positive ideal.[142]

Finally, Dmitrii Pisarev, the author of the infamous "Destruction of Aesthetics," wrote a critical analysis of *What Is to Be Done?* that appeared in *Russkoe slovo* in 1865.[143] Pisarev, who, it must be remembered, was writing from a cell in the same prison where Chernyshevskii wrote the novel, boldly attacks Chernyshevskii's detractors. Pisarev begins his discussion very much in the realm of ideology, not aesthetics: "That is why all those who are fed and warmed by routine were exasperated beyond description by Chernyshevsky's novel. They saw in it a mockery of art, disrespect for the public, immorality, cynicism, and perhaps even the germ of all crimes. And, of course, they were right: the novel mocks at their aesthetics, violates their morality, shows the falseness of their chastity, and does not hide its scorn for its judges. But all that is not even one-hundredth of its transgressions; the main thing is that it has been able to become the banner of the trend they hate, to point out to it its immediate aims and to muster all that is young and full of life around them and for them."[144]

In between bashing the philistines and giving extended summaries of the novel's content,[145] Pisarev analyzes what is new and striking in Chernyshevskii's novel. Pisarev is enraptured by *What Is to Be Done?* because he considers it to be the exact answer to the radicals' call for a new type of activity and a new type of literature as well. The gist of his argument is that Chernyshevskii had achieved a milestone in Russian literature in that he was the first to deal with the "new type" (that is, the *raznochinets*) from close up. Pisarev contrasts *What Is to Be Done?* with *Fathers and Sons*, for which he also has strong admiration. He concludes that the two were different in that Turgenev approached the new type from a distance and as an outsider, whereas Chernyshevskii approached them as a close acquaintance, if not an actual member.[146]

Whereas Shelgunov finds Chernyshevskii's characters lacking as positive models, Pisarev thoroughly approves of them. He notes that the "new people" are hardworking and rational. Pisarev approves of their ability to harmonize inclination and duty, self-interest and the interests of mankind.[147] In short, Pisarev sees the depiction of the new type as a pivotal event in Russian culture: "That was why many an honest heart reacted to it, many a fresh voice answered this call to activity sent out to our women. In this respect Chernyshevsky, the destroyer of aesthetics, turned out to be the only one among our men of literature whose fiction had an immediate influence on our society, not on the greater part of it, it is true, but on the better."[148]

In general, Pisarev approves of the way Chernyshevskii dealt with his characters, finding them all quite believable, if somewhat unusual. The importance of Chernyshevskii's novel, according to Pisarev, is that he is trying to change society by means of his art. The characters, though indeed good and positive, are actually quite ordinary. Thus, Chernyshevskii shows his reader that such behavior is attainable.[149] As a result, Pisarev fully approves of what he considers to be Chernyshevskii's didactic purpose in writing the novel: to show the reader that a radiant future in which people are happy and dignified is an achievable goal.

It is important to note that all four critics, as varied as their reactions and interpretations of the novel may be, are united in the assumption that *What Is to Be Done?* is an innovative literary text.[150] Even Strakhov and Shelgunov, despite their displeasure with certain aspects of the novel, view it as something new on the Russian literary scene.[151] Additionally, Dostoevskii's sustained literary response indicates that the novel offered Russian literature and culture something innovative and serious, something not so easily dismissed. It is with this in mind that we return to the particular problem that has vexed many. That is, many have assumed a priori that the novel is weak, if not laughable, in terms of artistry and then have proceeded to ask how such a bad novel could have been so popular and influential. Generally, the answer is that the novel succeeded in spite of itself: its didactic message and model(s) of behavior, in addition to Chernyshevskii's martyrdom, so appealed to generations of young revolutionaries anxious for a manifesto that its artistic inadequacies were ignored.[152] But is this answer enough? Is Lenin correct when he states that an untalented work could not have had that kind of influence? Is there perhaps some artistry in the novel after all? Do not the quite varied, often contradictory reactions by nineteenth-century observers suggest that *What Is to Be Done?* is a rich, even innovative literary text? It is to those and related questions that we now turn.

Chapter One

The Question of Art

THE POLEMICAL CONTEXT

During his rather brief tenure at *Sovremennik* Chernyshevskii wrote a number of works devoted to aesthetics and practical literary criticism. As a theoretician Chernyshevskii wrote several essays, the most famous of which is his master's dissertation, *The Aesthetic Relations of Art to Reality*, which is devoted to the discussion of traditional aesthetic concepts and a (re)definition of those concepts on a nonidealistic basis.[1] As a practical critic Chernyshevskii reviewed many of the literary works of his day, both major and minor, including the works of figures such as Turgenev, Tolstoi, and Dostoevskii. Finally, Chernyshevskii demonstrated his mettle as an intellectual historian in his *Essays on the Gogol Period of Russian Literature*, in which he outlines the changes over time in the basic views of Russian writers and Russian critics.[2] In this large corpus he outlined his basic views on the nature of art and its place in society. This body of work, in addition to its intrinsic value, is also important because it has had so much bearing on how *What Is to Be Done?* has been interpreted both by contemporaries and by twentieth-century scholars. My purpose here is not to provide a complete exposition of Chernyshevskii's aesthetics, but rather to challenge the many assumptions that have been made about them both by his contemporaries and by Western scholars. The perception of his aesthetics by contemporaries was well known to Chernyshevskii and played a major role in the writing of *What Is to Be Done?* Likewise, the perpetuation of those negative stereotypes by Western scholars has long hindered interpretation of the novel.

Contemporary reaction to Chernyshevskii's aesthetic views focused mainly on his master's dissertation. Among the young generation the dissertation was accepted as the herald of a new era.[3] When the dissertation appeared in print in 1855, however, the reaction of the older generation was almost uniformly negative. Numerous reviewers at the time belittled the work, with one calling it a "horrible theory."[4] Ivan Turgenev, in particular, was incensed by the work. In one letter he labels Chernyshevskii's work as a "rotten corpse, . . . [a] result of malicious stupidity," and in another he claims that "his book is false and harmful."[5] Turgenev expressed his and many of his contemporaries' basic view of Chernyshevskii's aesthetics thus: "It's scarcely disguised hostility to art."[6] Elsewhere, Turgenev, not without a tinge of snobbery, expressed his displeasure not only with Chernyshevskii but with the *raznochintsy* in general: "With their insolence they want to wipe from the face of the earth poetry, the fine arts, all aesthetic pleasures and introduce their own coarse seminarist principles. They are literary Robespierres."[7] The reaction by other so-called aesthetes (Fet, Grigorovich, and so forth) was similar. Chernyshevskii was seen as hostile to the very concept of art.

Many Western scholars in their treatments of Chernyshevskii's aesthetics generally rely on the stereotypes and formulations made by his contemporaries. Chernyshevskii is often viewed as totally uninterested in either aesthetics or art. Isaiah Berlin expresses the general view of Chernyshevskii when he refers to him as an "art hating and dogmatic schoolmaster" and claims that he had a total lack of aesthetic sense.[8] Abbott Gleason is even harsher in his assessment, arguing: "His asceticism seemed to convey not only a programmatic joylessness but the desire to deprive others of pleasure, to narrow life, to make it gray."[9] From this rather negative view, there is little distance to the view of Chernyshevskii as an art-hating ideologue who subsumed an important area of human existence (that is, the aesthetic) to the nebulous idea of "the cause." Chernyshevskii is seen as dealing with questions of art and aesthetics only in order to avoid the censorship; he had no interest in such questions in and of themselves.[10] Herbert Bowman expresses this attitude succinctly when he argues that aesthetic considerations were always a pretext for Chernyshevskii; he treated them as a vehicle for his ideology.[11] Although there has been some reevaluation of Chernyshevskii's writings on aesthetics in the last decade, the general view is still quite negative.[12]

There remains the problem, however, that about one-half of Chernyshevskii's output during his best years is in some way devoted to art or aesthetics. One can agree with Dennis Reinhartz, that "[i]t does not seem completely logical for a responsible man like Chernyshevsky to have devoted such a substantial portion of his time and energies to a field which held little or no fascination for him. . . . And to believe that nearly fifty percent of Chernyshevsky's most significant work was nothing more than an aegis for the remainder is unrealistic to the point of being ridiculous."[13] Chernyshevskii was indeed a radical and his writings have a political bent to them. But one can be genuinely interested in both radical politics and questions of art: the two are not mutually exclusive. Thus, Chernyshevskii's aesthetic writings should not be dismissed a priori as mere propaganda.

Part of the reason Chernyshevskii has alienated so many is his use of literary criticism as a cover to discuss the political, social, and economic problems of Russian society. His turning over of the literary criticism section of *Sovremennik* to Dobroliubov in 1857 is treated as proof of his disdain for this field.[14] As Victor Terras states: "Černyševskij had little inclination and no talent for literary criticism. His interests lay in the areas of political science, sociology, and economics. He became a part-time literary critic and one of Russia's most influential writers on aesthetic theory, mainly because he realized that in Russia literature constituted virtually the entire intellectual life of the nation."[15] It is true that Chernyshevskii would discuss politics and social issues apropos a literary work. Although at the time it was a rather clever technique for avoiding the restrictions of the censorship, many have chosen to condemn him for this necessity of circumstance. The most oft-cited work in this regard is his "The Russian at the *Rendez-vous.*" Ralph Matlaw, for example, argues: "But most of Chernyshevsky's articles can hardly be considered as literary criticism at all. His most famous article, 'The Russian at the *Rendez-vous,*' ostensibly a review of Turgenev's elegiac story *Asya,* becomes an attack on the indecisiveness and weakness of Russian liberalism."[16] In short, Chernyshevskii is accused of a sort of intellectual dishonesty.[17]

However, in this article Chernyshevskii never claims to be performing a purely form-oriented literary analysis. Although he does use Turgenev's story as an occasion to discuss Russian society, he makes it quite clear that he is interested in the story precisely because of its accurate reflection of a phenomenon in that society.[18] Moreover, examination of the very title of the article reveals that Chernyshevskii is being quite honest. Whereas his true literary criticism would usually contain the title(s) and author under review, this article mentions neither the work nor the author in its title. It is only in the subtitle that both are mentioned. And here, too, Chernyshevskii is quite honest. The subtitle says not "an analysis" or "a review," but "Reflections upon Reading Mr. Turgenev's Tale *Asya.*"[19]

Although it is true that Chernyshevskii would often discuss politics, economics, and so forth apropos a literary work, this does not mean that he was unable to perform genuine literary criticism.[20] For example, his review of Tolstoi's early work is a masterpiece that continues to be of use to this very day. Even Matlaw, who has little use for Chernyshevskii's criticism, is forced to concede that "Chernyshevsky had some keen insights into literature and into problems of language" and that he "grasped immediately two salient features of Tolstoy's art: his psychological finesse and his concern with fleeting states, that is, with change."[21] It was in this same review that Chernyshevskii coined the terms "interior monologue" and "the dialectic of the soul," which have remained staples of literary criticism to this day.[22] Chernyshevskii must have possessed some talent to produce a masterpiece like this.[23] Gleb Struve, in particular, stresses the great critical insights Chernyshevskii must have possessed to write this review: "This fine analysis of the peculiarities of Tolstoy's genius, made long before Tolstoy wrote any of his great masterpieces, does credit to Chernyshevsky as a critic."[24] David Rampton is even more bold in his appraisal when he argues, "I submit that anyone who could write like this about literature had at least some of the gifts of a first-rate literary critic."[25] Chernyshevskii was as astute a critic as any of his contemporaries. Recognition of this fact gives the student of Chernyshevskii's aesthetic works the proper perspective from which to evaluate them.

The crux of Chernyshevskii's aesthetics is an intense battle against German idealist philosophy and the aesthetic schools based upon it.[26] Whereas German idealism posited the existence of a transcendental reality superior to the material one, Chernyshevskii denies its very existence. Whereas German idealism defined man as a being with a dual nature, a mortal body and an immortal soul, Chernyshevskii argued that man possessed only a single nature. His basic view on this matter is most clearly expressed in his 1860 essay, "The Anthropological Principle in Philosophy": "What is this 'anthropological principle in the moral sciences'? The reader has seen what this principle is from the very character of the essays. It is that a man must be regarded as a single being having only one nature; that a human life must not be cut into two halves, each belonging to a different nature; that every aspect of a man's activity must be regarded as the activity of his whole organism, from head to foot inclusively, or if it is the special function of some particular organ of the human organism we are dealing with, that organ must be regarded in its natural connection with the entire organism."[27] Chernyshevskii clearly considers dispensing with the concept of the duality of human nature the key to good philosophy. He dismisses previous philosophical thought precisely for this reason: "The same thing must be said about all the old theories of the moral sciences. Their neglect of the anthropological principle deprives them of all merit."[28]

It is this polemical context that forms the backdrop of all of Chernyshevskii's aesthetic writings.[29] For example, he begins *The Aesthetic Relations of Art to Reality* with some very clear statements of principle; namely that he intends to bring the discipline of aesthetics into line with a modern worldview: "Respect for real life, distrust of a priori hypotheses, even though they tickle one's fancy, such is the character of the trend that now predominates in science. The author is of the opinion that our aesthetic convictions, if it is still worth our while to discuss aesthetics, should also be brought into line with this."[30]

After throwing down the gauntlet, Chernyshevskii undertakes a systematic analysis of the basic conceptions of idealist aesthetics.[31] Rejecting the notion of any transcendental reality, Chernyshevskii rejects the idealist definitions of beauty, the sublime, the tragic, and so forth, and attempts to redefine those concepts on a nonidealistic basis. The idealist notion that the material world is inherently flawed and that therefore man's true quest is a search for perfection, for an ever higher realization of the Absolute, galled Chernyshevskii. Not surprisingly, he resented the notion that nature, by definition, according to the idealists, is imperfect and lacking in beauty and, moreover, that it must be improved.[32] Against the idealist notion of an inherently flawed material reality, Chernyshevskii argues that "beauty is life" and that the only beauty that exists is that found in material reality.[33] Further galling to Chernyshevskii, idealist aesthetics gave a special role to art and the artist in that they were somehow in touch with transcendental reality and by means of this could create beauty superior to that found in nature. Chernyshevskii is most adamant that art is not in touch with any transcendental reality and therefore higher than material, socially acknowledged reality. It is in this context that toward the end of his dissertation Chernyshevskii makes his infamous statement, "Art, too, must not claim to stand higher than reality."[34] Although this phrase is often interpreted as degradation of and hostility to art, Chernyshevskii is saying little more than that art is a part of material reality. Or, to be precise, that art is wholly a subset of reality; it does not exist outside of it.[35] In expressing those opinions Chernyshevskii's common-sense approach is very much in the mainstream of Russian aesthetic thought.[36]

Despite this fact, many misconceptions about Chernyshevskii's aesthetics appeared almost immediately among contemporaries and continue to this day. Among Western scholars, for example, it is sometimes claimed that Chernyshevskii did not even recognize the aesthetic as a legitimate part of human existence.[37] Chernyshevskii's writings, however, do not support such an interpretation. Rather, he openly acknowledges the importance of the aesthetic in human existence when he writes, "Only those who lack aesthetic sense can fail to admire Horace, Virgil and Ovid."[38] Moreover, Chernyshevskii labels the aesthetic sense both a "healthy sense" and a "true requirement."[39] In his own review of *Aesthetic Relations,* Chernyshevskii is even more explicit in defending the role of the aesthetic in human existence: "A man is not a snail; he cannot live exclusively for the purpose of filling his stomach. Intellectual and moral life (which develops properly when the body is healthy, that is, when the material side of a man's life is satisfactory)—such is the life that truly befits man and is most attractive for him."[40] It simply is not possible to argue that he ignored or degraded this area of human existence. Rather, Chernyshevskii viewed the aesthetic sense, and consequently art, as an essential component of human existence.

In a similar vein, Chernyshevskii is often viewed as hostile to the very discipline of aesthetics. In this regard, he is often linked to Dmitrii Pisarev, who provocatively entitled one of his essays, "The Destruction of Aesthetics."[41] For example, René Wellek states, "In Chernyshevskii aesthetics has reached its nadir: or rather it has been asked to commit suicide."[42] However, within the actual text of *The Aesthetic Relations of Art to Reality*

Chernyshevskii indicates at several points that he respects aesthetics as a discipline. In the introductory portion of the essay, he states: "We all recognize the high importance of the history of art, especially of the history of poetry; that being the case, the questions: what is art? what is poetry? cannot but be of high importance."[43] It is true that Chernyshevskii takes a somewhat hostile stance to traditional aesthetics. But he does not reject aesthetics as a discipline; rather, he seeks to define it on a new basis. In contrast to the idealist definition of aesthetics as "the science of the beautiful," Chernyshevskii seeks to redefine it as "the science of art."[44] In his review of Aristotle's *Poetics* he further defines aesthetics as "a system of general principles of art in general and of poetry in particular."[45] Moreover, while battling against the idealist definition of aesthetics, Chernyshevskii actually defends the discipline from those that would dispose of it.[46] Chernyshevskii even goes so far as to defend older aesthetic schools as having contributed to the sum of human knowledge; he is far from a nihilist.[47] In short, as Frederick Copleston argues: "It is a mistake to think that Chernyshevskii aimed at the abolition of aesthetic theory. He had one of his own. What he attacked was not aesthetics as such but idealist aesthetics."[48]

A long-standing interpretation of Chernyshevskii is that he despised artistic form in favor of content. Terras, for example, concludes that Chernyshevskii considered form merely an assemblage of mechanical details of execution and a decidedly secondary criterion of artistic merit.[49] Likewise, Pereira argues that Chernyshevskii was exclusively concerned with content and had no interest in art forms per se.[50] However, in his dissertation, the very document so often used to argue such a view, Chernyshevskii clearly defends form as an important component of art: "Beauty of form . . . is indeed an essential quality of every work of art."[51] Chernyshevskii does make statements against the idealist definition of beauty of form as the sole component of art. But his objections are not to the beauty of form itself, but merely to the idealist concentration upon it. As he states, "But this formal beauty, or unity of the idea and the image, of content and form, is not the special feature that distinguishes art from all other branches of human activity." In other words, while not disparaging beauty of form, Chernyshevskii argues that there must be something else that distinguishes art as art.[52]

Although Chernyshevskii does not devote an extraordinary amount of attention to the problem of form in his dissertation, he shows himself to be very much interested in such questions elsewhere.[53] In an 1855 article on Pushkin, for example, Chernyshevskii turns to questions of meter and rhythm, arguing for a change of metrical stresses to the natural accentuation of the language.[54] Elsewhere, in a work that shows a great deal of concern with form Chernyshevskii turns his attention to the question of whether Homer should be translated into hexameters.[55] Commenting on the content of these essays, Wellek, who has little use for Chernyshevskii's aesthetics, is forced to concede that they show "serious study of technical matters."[56] Chernyshevskii, as much as any of his contemporaries, was quite interested in questions of artistic form.[57]

An oft-repeated interpretation of Chernyshevskii's aesthetics is that it amounts to little more than an imitation theory. Bowman, for example, argues that Chernyshevskii saw the artist as a photographer and the work of art as essentially a photograph.[58] Chernyshevskii, however, goes to great lengths to distinguish his thesis, that "the first purpose of art is to reproduce nature and life,"[59] from the school of art that advocates lifeless copying: "we, nevertheless, think that the pseudo-classical 'imitation of nature theory' that prevailed in the seventeenth and eighteenth centuries demanded from art something different from the formal principle implied by the definition: 'art is the reproduction of reality.'"[60] As part of his explanation, Chernyshevskii carefully distinguishes between his word "reproduction" and imitation: "Our definition of the formal principle of art is similar to the view that prevailed in the Greek world: it is found in the works of Plato and Aristotle, and in all probability was expressed by Democritus. Their mimhsi§ corresponds to our term 'reproduction.' Later, this word was interpreted as 'imitation' (Nachahmung), but this translation is not exact, for it restricts the scope of the concept and suggests the idea of imitation of external form but not the conveying of the inherent content. The pseudo-classical theory did, indeed, interpret art as the imitation of reality with the object of deceiving the senses, but this was an abuse that belonged only to the epochs of corrupted taste."[61] Lest the reader misunderstand his point, Chernyshevskii explicitly states that "the more perfectly a useless imitation bears external resemblance to the original the more disgust it rouses."[62] Chernyshevskii also discusses this issue in his review of Aristotle's *Poetics*, repeating that by the term "reproduction" he means not "imitation" but the Greek concept of "mimesis." He further states explicitly that "it is wrong to think that by presenting the reproduction of reality as the supreme principle of art we compel it 'to make crude and vulgar copies and banish idealization from art.'"[63]

Throughout his aesthetic writings Chernyshevskii argues against imitation and defends the right of an author to idealize.[64] In the review of Tolstoi's work, he clearly states that there is much that is not relevant in a work of art; there is no need to copy all of reality. Likewise, in reviewing Avdeev's work, Chernyshevskii openly defends the artist's right to idealization (2:218). And in direct contradiction to the supposition that he advocated exact copying of reality, Chernyshevskii declares, "The main thing in poetic talent is so-called creative fantasy" (12:682).[65] Moreover, in the variants of the foreword to his unfinished novel, *Povesti v povesti,* Chernyshevskii stresses that novels are not copies but fiction: "Above all, my friends, you must find out who you are. You are people who understand that a novel must be read as a novel; that a novel is a creation of fantasy, that the characters acting in it are invented characters" (12:126).[66] In contrast to the assertion that he forgot that the work of art is a work of imagination,[67] Chernyshevskii repeatedly stresses that he does not overlook the importance of the imagination: "The first and general purpose of all works of art, we have said, is to reproduce phenomena of real life that are of interest to man. By real life we, of course, mean not only man's relation to the objects and beings of the objective world, but also his inner life. Sometimes a man lives in a dream—in that case the dream has for him (to a certain degree and for a certain time) the significance of something objective. Still more often a man lives in the world of his emotions. These states, if they become interesting, are also reproduced by art. We mention this in order to show that our definition also takes in the imaginative content of art."[68] Thus, we see that, far from dismissing the human imagination, Chernyshevskii had a healthy respect for it and took it into account.[69] Chernyshevskii is opposed to escapism, but he does not deny the existence or the importance of the imagination.

Although statements that art is inferior to reality do occur in Chernyshevskii's dissertation, Chernyshevskii never says anything that is hostile to art per se.[70] Well aware of the general opinion of his type of aesthetics, he anticipates that his discussion will be seen as inimical to art and tries to answer it: "But does not what the author says degrade art? Yes, if showing that art stands *lower* than real life in the artistic perfection of its works means degrading art. But protesting against panegyrics does not mean disparagement."[71] Moreover, in his own review he tries to answer even more clearly this charge, by openly stating his respect for art: "As it is, notwithstanding the fact that Mr. Chernyshevsky's whole essay breathes respect for art because of its great importance for life, some people may refuse to notice this sentiment because a few pages of the essay are not especially devoted to it."[72] In short, Chernyshevskii's theoretical statements on art consistently defend it as an essential part of human existence; Chernyshevskii was not a hater of art.

Not only is Chernyshevskii often seen as degrading art in theoretical terms, he is often viewed as severely restricting the freedom of art and the artist by attempting to dictate the content of art.[73] However, the texts do not support such a harsh view. In fact, Chernyshevskii's aesthetic writings are one long crusade for the freedom of both art and the artist. For example, in his dissertation Chernyshevskii quite explicitly defends the freedom of the artist when he says, "'Write about what you want to write about' is a rule that the poet rarely dares to follow. Love, appropriately or inappropriately,—this is the first harm that is inflicted on art by the conception that 'the content of art is beauty.'"[74] Far from subordinating or denigrating art, Chernyshevskii fights hard to free it from the bonds of previous aesthetic norms. For example, regarding the theme of love, he states: "We do not by any means think that the poet ought to be prohibited from describing love; but aesthetics must demand that the poet should describe love only when he actually wants to do so. Why put love in the forefront when, properly speaking, not love, but some other aspects of life are dealt with."[75] An essential part of Chernyshevskii's polemic with idealist aesthetics is that it has severely restricted the realm of art: "Usually it is said that the content of art is beauty; but this restricts the sphere of art too much."[76] Moreover, he goes into some detail about how this definition is harmful to art:

> [O]ne of the conditions of beauty is that all the details must develop out of the plot: so we are given such profoundly thought-out plans of action of the personages in novels and plays as persons in real life scarcely ever draw up; and if one of the personages takes an instinctive, thoughtless step, the author deems it necessary to justify it on the grounds of the essence of the personage's character, and the critics are displeased with the fact that "no motive is given for the action," as if an action is always prompted by individual character and not by circumstances and by the general qualities of the human heart. . . .
>
> The consequence of this is the monotony of poetical works: the personages are all of the same pattern, events develop according to known recipes, it is evident from the first pages what will happen further on, and not only what will happen, but how it will happen.[77]

In contrast to the restrictions imposed by idealist aesthetics, Chernyshevskii advocates expanding the sphere of art: "The simplest way to solve this riddle would be to say that the sphere of art is not limited only to beauty and its so-called elements, but embraces everything in reality (in nature and in life) that is of interest to man not as a scholar, but as an ordinary man; that which is of common interest—such is the content of art."[78] Thus, Chernyshevskii in no way restricts the sphere of art in his dissertation. Rather, he defends it from the restraints imposed upon it by idealist aesthetics.[79]

In his other writings Chernyshevskii consistently defends the sphere of art from the demands of certain aesthetic schools. He insists that art and the artist must be autonomous from those who would dictate. For example, in his review of Tolstoi's early work, Chernyshevskii defends Tolstoi from those who attacked his *Childhood* and *Boyhood,* because those works do not follow a prescribed set of literary conventions:

> But it is worth noting that people who talk a great deal about artistry are the ones who understand least what its conditions are. We read an article somewhere that expressed surprise at the fact that the foreground of *Childhood* and *Boyhood* lacked a beautiful girl of eighteen or twenty who would fall in love passionately with some sort of handsome youth—an astounding conception of artistry! The author clearly wanted to depict childhood and boyhood, not ardent passion; and can you really fail to feel that if he had introduced these figures and that inspiration into it, the children on whom he wanted you to turn your attention would have been crowded out; their nice feelings

> would have ceased to interest you once passionate love appeared in the story—in short, can you really fail to feel that the unity of the story would have been destroyed, that the conditions of art would have been violated? The author could not introduce into his story of children's lives anything that would make you forget the children and turn away from them, precisely because he had to observe the laws of art.[80]

Here we see that, as in his dissertation, Chernyshevskii continues to battle with a stale set of literary conventions and their resulting monotony. He clearly defends the right of the artist to do as he pleases.

Likewise, in an 1857 review of Shcherbina's poetry, Chernyshevskii again denounces the act of demanding that an artist create according to the dictates of a particular aesthetic school:

> Mr. Shcherbina, who even today occupies an honorable place among poets, should stand much higher when he decides to give space to his vivacious inclinations, having completely rejected the coercion of his talent for the sake of theoretical biases. He began with poems in the classical style,—this style is the least capable of arousing the lively sympathy of the contemporary world. But, unfortunately, many so-called connoisseurs of art, who understand art as artificiality,—greatly value the classical style partly because it is difficult, partly because it is most often artificial. In spite of the unattractiveness of the style dominating in Mr. Shcherbina's first poems, they were accepted with loud approval because they spontaneously arose from the fantasy of the poet. . . . Lovers and connoisseurs of artificiality interpreted Mr. Shcherbina's success thus: he enjoys success not because he is a man with talent who does not coerce his talent, but because he writes in the classical style which is more exquisite than all other styles. So let him continue to write in the classical style eternally, no matter what the cost. (4:542–43)

In contrast to letting one aesthetic school dominate art, Chernyshevskii defends the right and the necessity of the artist to create as his heart tells him: "[T]he poet, for the most part, must be free. His lips should speak about that which his heart is overfilled. . . . Let him [Shcherbina] write classical poems only when his talent turns to the classical world,—at a different time, in minutes of other moods, let his pen forget about antiquity, as his heart forgets, let him give his thought to take form freely in images, which are born by its essence, not by forcibly squeezing it into frameworks alien to it" (4:543).[81] Lest the reader misinterpret his defense of artistic autonomy, Chernyshevskii ends the review by openly proclaiming: "Autonomy is the supreme law of art. If he will observe this supreme law of poetry,—'preserve the freedom of your talent, poet,'—what he will write? . . . who has the right to demand that the poet coerce his talent? One can only demand that he develop himself as a person. . . . Let him guard the freedom of his talent from any coercion; let him with all his fantasy give himself to that which overfills his soul; the lips of the poet must speak from an abundance of the heart" (4:543–44). With such public statements as this, can there really be any doubt that Chernyshevskii was an avid defender of artistic freedom against the strictures of aesthetic theory?[82] Throughout his aesthetic works Chernyshevskii consistently defends art from the then-prevailing aesthetic norms and seeks to expand its boundaries.[83] Or to phrase it differently, Chernyshevskii attacked idealist aesthetics for wanting to mummify art (and reality) and for declaring an immutable absolute standard to be imposed upon everyone eternally.[84] As Lunacharskii pointed out long ago, "This is not what Chernyshevsky wants. He wants life to pulsate—only then is it beautiful. He wants it to be constantly altering."[85]

In conjunction with the claim that Chernyshevskii attempted to dictate to art its proper role, he is often viewed as demanding that art must serve a social cause, a certain tendency. That is, many have interpreted his aesthetics as insisting that art must be propaganda, that it be blatantly didactic.[86] Again, there is very little in the actual texts to support such a view. Chernyshevskii does say that the poet, as a human being, cannot help but be subjective:

> But, being interested in the phenomena of life, man cannot but, consciously or unconsciously, pronounce judgment on them. The poet, or artist, being unable to cease to be a man, cannot, even if he wanted to, refrain from pronouncing judgment on the phenomena he depicts. This judgment is expressed in his work—this is another purpose of art, which places it among the moral activities of man. . . . But if a man, whose mental activity is powerfully stimulated by the problems that are roused in his mind by his observation of life, is gifted with artistic talent, he will, in his works, consciously or unconsciously, express the striving to pronounce judgment on the phenomena that interest him (and his contemporaries, for a man who thinks cannot ponder over insignificant problems that interest nobody but himself).[87]

Moreover, Chernyshevskii argues elsewhere that literature is inherently subjective, explicitly denying any notion of objectivity: "Literature cannot but be the servant of one or another tendency of ideas—this is a purpose which it has not the capacity to reject, if it wished to reject it. . . . The words 'art must be independent of life' always served merely to conceal the struggle against trends in literature disliked by those people, with the aim of making it the servant of another trend which was more to the taste of those people."[88] It is important to remember that Chernyshevskii is being *descriptive*, not prescriptive, here. That is, the artist, being a human being, is subjective by his very nature. It is true that Chernyshevskii views art as inherently serving one group or another.[89] Art, like science, is far from neutral but has a long history of being employed by varying social factions.[90] But Chernyshevskii is not saying what should be, merely what is. And nowhere does Chernyshevskii advocate open propagandizing in art.[91]

On the contrary, Chernyshevskii defends art from those who would insist that it serve a social cause, that it be blatantly didactic. For example, in his review of Tolstoi's early fiction Chernyshevskii reacts to a criticism leveled at the young Tolstoi:

> [I]n the same article we found something in the nature of a hint that Count Tolstoy erred in failing to present a picture of social life in *Childhood* and *Boyhood.* Isn't there a lot he has left out in these tales? They contain neither war scenes nor depictions of the Italian countryside nor historical reminiscences. In general a great deal that might have been introduced, but would have been out of place and should not have been related, is missing. After all, the author wants to transport you into the life of a child, and what does a child understand of social questions, what conceptions does he have of social life? That entire element is as foreign to the life of a child as military life, and the conditions of art would have been violated just as much if military or historical life had been described. We want literary works to describe social life as much as anyone does. But one must still understand that not every poetic idea permits social questions to be introduced into the work. One must not forget that the first rule of art is the unity of the work, and that consequently, in depicting *Childhood,* it is precisely childhood that one must describe, not something else, not social questions, nor military scenes, nor Peter the Great nor Faust, nor Indiana nor Rudin, but the child with his feelings and his concepts. And people who express such narrow demands talk about the freedom of creative art! . . . One must understand that a poetic idea is destroyed when elements foreign to a work are introduced into it.[92]

Here then is an explicit denial that social questions are the sole content of art. Chernyshevskii does express a personal preference for such art, but he clearly states that social questions are not always relevant and defends Tolstoi from the demand that art must deal with social questions. As in his dissertation, Chernyshevskii consistently seeks to defend the autonomy of art from those who would restrict its freedom: he in no way attempts to restrict it himself.

Likewise, in a private letter of 1856 to Nekrasov, Chernyshevskii states his own personal liking for nonpolitical art. In contrast to those who have argued that Chernyshevskii excused an untalented writer provided his ideology was good, Chernyshevskii states, "a good tendency cannot make up for a weak talent. I know this as well as anyone."[93] He goes on to defend nonpolitical poetry and to say that he prefers it:

> But I myself know from experience that convictions are not everything in life; the heart has its needs, too, and the life of the heart means for each of us real grief or real joy . . . and I know that the poetry of the heart has its rights just as the poetry of the mind, and I find the first more attractive than the second. . . .

> If I have been frank about myself, it is to let you know that I [personally] by no means regard poetry merely from a political standpoint. On the contrary, politics forces its way into my heart—a heart which does not live by politics at all, or at least which has no desire to live by politics.[94]

Such statements are not at all isolated incidents. Seven years later in his preface to *Povesti v povesti,* Chernyshevskii states: "In our literature we all are occupied with social questions. This is wonderful. But there is also a necessity for a rest from serious thoughts, a necessity to forget, if only for an hour, that we are citizens, to dream the light, bright fancies of pure poetry, which is foreign to any social service" (12:133). What emerges from Chernyshevskii's writings is that art, by its very nature as a product of human beings, is not neutral or objective, but extremely subjective. Chernyshevskii merely wishes us to own up to this fact. But while stating the obvious, Chernyshevskii never demands that art's sole function be to serve a social cause, or more specifically, as is often charged, he never demands that art must serve *his* social cause.[95] Throughout his writings Chernyshevskii shows a clear awareness that the autonomy of art must be respected or art is totally degraded.

As part of Chernyshevskii's supposed dictate to art, it is often argued that he espoused a utilitarian aesthetics. Victor Terras, for example, describes Chernyshevskii's aesthetics as "frank and thorough utilitarianism."[96] Again, evidence for such an interpretation is strikingly absent. It is true that Chernyshevskii says such things as "A useless thing has no right to respect."[97] In addition, he does spend time demonstrating how art can be and is "useful." This is not, however, utilitarianism. Rather, it is an attempt to keep art from being an abstraction, and, more important, an abstraction with power over human beings.[98] Chernyshevskii is more explicit on this point in his review of Aristotle's *Poetics:*

> Plato protests against art because it is useless to man. We shall not refute this horrible reproach with the obsolete idea that "art must exist only for art's sake," that "to make art serve human needs means degrading it," and so forth. This idea had some meaning when it was necessary to show that the poet must not write magnificent odes, must not distort reality for the sake of various arbitrary and sentimental maxims. . . . At the present time it is certainly useless; art has succeeded in upholding its independence and must now think of how to utilize it. The idea of "art for art's sake" is as strange in our times as "wealth for wealth's sake," "science for science's sake," and so forth. All human activity must serve mankind if it is not to remain a useless and idle occupation. Wealth exists in order that man may benefit by it; science exists in order to be man's guide; art, too, must serve some useful purpose and not fruitless pleasure.[99]

Elsewhere, lest the reader mistake his statements about art's usefulness as utilitarianism, Chernyshevskii's provides the following passage:

> [A]lthough there is a difference between aesthetic pleasure and material interest, or the practical view of an object, they do not contradict each other. It will be sufficient to point to the evidence of experience that a real object may seem beautiful without arousing material interest: what selfish thoughts are roused in our minds when we admire the stars, the sea, or a forest (when I look at a real forest, must I necessarily think of whether the trees would be suitable for timber for building a house, or for firewood to heat it?); what selfish thoughts are roused in our minds when we hear the rustle of leaves, or the song of the nightingale. We often love a person without any selfish motives, without in the least thinking of ourselves; all the more likely are we to find aesthetic pleasure in him without it rousing any material (stoffartig) reflections about our relation to him.[100]

A more striking denial of utilitarianism, crude or otherwise, is not to be found. Moreover, the very motivation behind Chernyshevskii's insistence on the usefulness of art is not to degrade it, but rather to stress its prominent place in human existence, to save it from being marginalized as an escapist pastime.[101] Chernyshevskii makes precisely this point in his review of *Aesthetic Relations:* "This conclusion [that is, art's usefulness], in our opinion, is insufficiently developed. It still leaves for many people grounds for assuming that the significance of art is actually belittled by the rejection of fulsome praise of the absolute merit of its works, and by the substitution of the needs of man as its origin and aims for immeasurably lofty transcendental origin and aims. On the contrary, this is precisely what enhances the real significance of art, for this explanation gives it an unchallengeable and honourable place among the activities that benefit man; and to be of benefit to man means having the right to the highest respect of man."[102] Thus, far from the hater of and dictator to art he has been made out to be, both by hostile contemporaries and by twentieth-century Western scholars, Chernyshevskii held art in high esteem considering it one of the basic elements of human existence and vigorously defended its autonomy.

THE PLAN OF *WHAT IS TO BE DONE?*

I have devoted so much space to a discussion of misconceptions about Chernyshevskii's aesthetic views because they are directly relevant to his writing of the novel and to interpretation of it. Basing their arguments on an interpretation of Chernyshevskii's basic aesthetic views as hostile or degrading to art, many scholars have taken an overly negative approach to the novel. For example, some observers insist on interpreting Chernyshevskii's aesthetics as reducing art to a mere imitation of reality and then dismiss his novel as failing to live up to his own standards.[103] Proceeding from the view that Chernyshevskii was interested in aesthetic questions only as a cover for expounding his radical political views, Chernyshevskii is often seen as writing the novel merely as a cloak for the same views. The basic attitude toward *What Is to Be Done?* both by hostile contemporaries and twentieth-century scholars is best exemplified by Afanasii Fet. Fet argued that normally when one approaches a real work of art, such as those by Goethe, the observer must be careful. However, "[d]uring an analysis of the novel *What Is to Be Done?* such difficulties do not exist. *Sovremennik* and K° long ago taught us their view of literature. We know of their contempt for art for art's sake. Thus the novel is a matter of content, not art, of which, according to the author's words, 'there is not even a hint here.' And truly, there is no sign of any skill."[104] In addition, beginning with N. Leskov, many have argued that Chernyshevskii wrote the novel only because he was not allowed to write and publish his traditional publicistic articles in prison.[105] This notion was later repeated by Plekhanov when he argued that the love story of *What Is to Be Done?* is merely a cover for the author's ideology.[106] This thesis has generally been repeated by most twentieth-century scholars, both Soviet and Western.[107] Thus, in Western and in much of Soviet scholarship *What Is to Be Done?* has come to be viewed as a mere transparent, political treatise rather than a literary work. Even among the few who see a literary motive behind the novel, the negative perception of Chernyshevskii's aesthetics influences their interpretation. For example, Moser, seeing in Chernyshevskii's aesthetics hostility to art, argues that Chernyshevskii wrote *What Is to Be Done?* to degrade art, to show its utter artificiality.[108]

If, as we have seen, Chernyshevskii was not hostile to art, this alone should give us pause to reconsider the motives behind the writing of *What Is to Be Done?* Moreover, there is the important evidence of Chernyshevskii's attempts at creative writing at a very early age. There are still extant manuscripts of his attempts at literature, written while he attended the university in Saint Petersburg. Although those youthful attempts were for the most part unsuccessful, they do demonstrate that Chernyshevskii's turn to literature was not so sudden or unmotivated as it has been made to seem.[109] N. Naumova, for example, argues that in many ways those youthful works are similar to *What Is to Be Done?* They deal with the same milieu, the same themes. She argues that they are an early sketch for *What Is to Be Done?* and are proof that the novel did not suddenly spring up in 1862: Chernyshevskii had had this on his mind for a long time.[110] Moreover, throughout the remainder of his life, Chernyshevskii wrote numerous stories and novels, for many of which we still have the texts.[111] And in 1883 Chernyshevskii expressed regret that when he was younger he had not noticed his true calling: to write tales, novels, and fairy tales (15:390). Such do not sound like the words of a man who had no interest in and no use for creative literature.[112]

The evidence most often used to argue that Chernyshevskii turned to fiction out of ulterior motives is a passage that occurs in the foreword to *What Is to Be Done?* Here is what Chernyshevskii's narrator says:

> I'll tell you what sort of writer I am.
>
> I possess not one bit of artistic talent. I even lack full command of the language. But that doesn't mean a thing; read on, dearest public, it will be well worth your while. Truth is a good thing; it compensates for the inadequacies of any writer who serves its cause. Therefore, I shall inform you of the following: if I hadn't warned you, you might well have thought that this tale was being told artistically and that its author possessed great poetic talent. But now that I've warned you that I have no talent whatever, you know that any merit to be found in my tale is due entirely to its truthfulness. (48)[113]

Many observers have tended to equate the biographical author with the narrator of the novel. It is generally assumed, without the slightest reservation, that the views expressed by the narrator in this passage (and throughout *What Is to Be Done?*) are Chernyshevskii's own views.[114] Thus, most have simply taken this passage literally and assumed that Chernyshevskii himself is apologizing for his lack of ability as a writer while promising to compensate with good ideology. Abbott Gleason, for example, argues that this passage demonstrates that Chernyshevskii is going to give the reader truth, not poetry.[115] Likewise, G. Žekulin argues that this passage demonstrates that Chernyshevskii is far more concerned with truth than with art.[116] It is a given in the scholarship that Chernyshevskii himself realized he had no literary talent and is using the novel form only to get his message across.[117] Taking their cue from the author's supposed confession, most Western scholars have been dismissive of *What Is to Be Done?* as a work of art.

All is not so clear, however, regarding this passage. As the foreword develops, the narrator intentionally scandalizes his public by addressing it directly and letting loose his spite. He attacks the general public for its low level of sophistication, calling it "undiscriminating and slow-witted" (47).[118] However, recognizing the situation as it is, the narrator promises to keep things at the general public's level, stating that the public will "know the outcome of every situation at least twenty pages in advance" (47–48).[119] It is at this point that the actual reader, not the reader whom the narrator addresses, starts to get suspicious.[120] Indeed, with an author like Chernyshevskii, who was famous for his mastery of Aesopian language, this promise by the narrator is strangely out of character. For the careful reader the promises of clarity by Chernyshevskii's narrator should seem very suspicious, an obvious case of protesting far too much. Moreover, the narrator makes direct reference to the public's inability "at deciphering unstated meanings" (48).[121] This seems a clear signal to the reader that what follows is not clarity but something that will require decoding. As Morson has argued: "Chernyshevsky's reference to 'guessing what has been left unsaid' implicitly points to something *he* has left unsaid, but expects to be widely understood: namely, that this very work, which was written through a censor, . . . contains meanings beyond its apparent meanings."[122] There is no doubt a large grain of truth to the common conclusion that Chernyshevskii introduces these passages to belittle conventional literature and to attack the views of his ideological opponents, the aesthetes. However, this can hardly be the whole story; something else is at work. The narrator's continual insistence that everything is crystal clear, that all has been explained, should serve as a clue that this is, in fact, far from the case. Those passages, rather than explaining anything, only mislead. In short, the narrator's direct addresses to the reader must be approached with great caution.

Let us return for a moment to the notion of Chernyshevskii's actual writing of *What Is to Be Done?* Before us is a man in prison, well aware that he is being very closely watched. Obviously, when writing this novel, Chernyshevskii knew that it had to be put together in a careful manner. In his discussion of Dostoevskii's *Diary of a Writer,* Morson notes that during this period in Russian culture the censor had long been an implied, conventional reader for authors.[123] This is an important consideration when interpreting Chernyshevskii's novel, but perhaps such recognition should be extended even further. In Chernyshevskii's particular situation the presence of the censor was far more than a literary fact, it was in a very real sense a matter of life and death. He certainly knew that anything he wrote must appear absolutely harmless.

Thus, the narrator's statements, far from being straightforward proclamations, are clearly meant to mislead the government authorities. The narrator's continual emphasis that everything is clear was obviously meant to persuade the authorities that such was the case. Moreover, when the plot turned out as predicted by both the narrator and the "perspicacious reader," it demonstrated that the novel was transparent, safe. On the surface the novel seems purely to follow and play with the conventions of traditional literature (that is, the love intrigue), with the supposed author occasionally making a few digressions in which to harangue his opponents. Such a construction may have lured the authorities into thinking that *What Is to Be Done?* was little more than a traditional novel with some petty bickering by the author. As such, they would have judged it safe, harmless, and let it pass.[124] Such a straightforward promise may have helped to disarm the authorities, who, no doubt, were expecting Chernyshevskii to fail as a writer of fiction.

It is the desire to fool the censor that provided an important creative impulse for Chernyshevskii. As we have already seen, the fact that the novel was written in installments, along with Chernyshevskii's note promising a continuation of the novel, were most likely part of the attempt to fool the censor. In a similar vein, Emily Klenin's recent work reveals that the obvious references to George Sand's *Jacques* that occur in *What Is to Be Done?* are a false outer layer designed to fool the censor while hiding a true inner layer for the reading public. According to Klenin, *Jacques* was already well established in Russian culture and allusions to it were likely to have been readily identified. As she argues, the obviousness of the allusions to *Jacques* may have promoted the novel's approval by the censor: the light-hearted reminiscences of *Jacques* might have seemed to promise a negative response to George Sand, and as such, disarmed a careless representative of the authorities.[125]

One can see that Chernyshevskii actually plays with the fact that the censor will undoubtedly seek hidden meanings in the text of the novel. He places several taunts to this effect throughout the text: the narrator's reference to unstated meanings (48), Lopukhov's use of the term *allegory* (106), and Vera Pavlovna's reference to speaking in obscure phrases (*temnymi slovami;* 265). In short, Chernyshevskii felt it necessary to give the censor a bone to fool him all the more. For example, the way in which Lopukhov's fake suicide is presented in the novel gives the impression that it is meant to be a closely guarded secret. Neither the narrator nor any of the characters ever states that Lopukhov has faked suicide; it is something that must be deciphered. However, the manner of presentation is far too obvious and Chernyshevskii deliberately leads the reader to the answer. In particular, in the infamous foreword, the male reader breaks in with the statement "I know for a fact that the gentleman who committed suicide did not really commit suicide" (47).[126] Although the narrator immediately cuts off the male reader and begins to abuse him, the cat is, of course, out of the bag. Chernyshevskii does keep up the pretense throughout the novel that Lopukhov's fake suicide is something that cannot openly be stated: in particular, the reader is not presented with the contents of the note Rakhmetov brings to Vera Pavlovna. But Chernyshevskii can hardly have expected to fool anybody with this. And, indeed, he did not, least of all the Tsarist authorities: "For the reader, although he is not informed of the content of the note, it becomes clear that Lopukhov did not kill himself, that he really only 'left the stage' and made arrangements to remain eternally behind the scene so that his pseudo-widow could marry her beloved."[127] On the surface, Chernyshevskii seems to have failed to fool anybody. But this is clearly intentional on his part: by letting the authorities decipher this key, which is clearly tied to the core conflict of the plot, he disarms them from looking for others.

Finally, Chernyshevskii seems to have deliberately intended for his reader, especially the censor, to interpret his novel as a mere response to Turgenev's *Fathers and Sons.* Such a move was certainly one to be expected. Chernyshevskii and most radicals looked upon Turgenev's novel as an attack on the younger generation in general and on the recently deceased Dobroliubov in particular.[128] Moreover, Chernyshevskii thought little of the portraits of the younger generation in the novel and it seems reasonable to expect some kind of response (10:185). Most observers, expecting the obvious, have concluded that *What Is to Be Done?* is a direct counterblow to Turgenev's novel. Evidence for this view can be found in Chernyshevskii's borrowing of the surname Kirsanov for one of his characters. Likewise, Lopukhov's name comes from the burdock (*lopukh*) that grows on Bazarov's grave.[129] Other elements can be adduced that point to Turgenev and his works: the narrator's reference to Lopukhov and Kirsanov cutting up an enormous quantity of frogs; the chapter title "First Love and Legal Marriage," which recalls the title of Turgenev's short story; and Rakhmetov's falling in love with one of his father's mistresses, which recalls the story's plot. However, none of these facts in any way constitutes a direct polemic, nor do they in any way enlighten matters.[130] Indeed, they seem more designed to mislead, to mystify. And here we come to their artistic purpose: these references to Turgenev's works exist to deceive the reader, or a particular reader, into dismissing the novel as a mere retort to that author. Chernyshevskii seems to have succeeded remarkably well, for O. A. Przhetslavskii in one of his secret reports drew precisely the desired conclusion: "From that which has appeared in print up to this point one can already guess the main idea of the novel. Apparently, it is written as an answer to the famous work *Fathers and Sons* and forms a counterweight (*contropoids*) [*sic*] to the characterization of nihilism, embodied by Turgenev in the form of Bazarov. *What Is to Be Done?* is an apology of nihilism, an exposition of its true doctrine, with its good sides. Mr. Chernyshevskii's *Lopukhov* in his main features is just like Bazarov, supplemented and ennobled by motivations of higher humanity, which, according to the opinion of the author, is the distinguishing feature of *the new people* (they are nihilists, as one should infer)."[131] This passage clearly shows that the tsarist authorities were indeed somewhat disarmed by the references to Turgenev. Likewise, Chernyshevskii's contemporaries also interpreted *What Is to Be Done?* in large part as a retort to Turgenev. An anonymous contemporary proclaimed in the pages of *Otechestvennye zapiski* in 1863 that *What Is to Be Done?* was actually little else: "Mr. Chernyshevskii's novel is written against *Fathers and Sons.* Everywhere you sense an answer to someone else's words, and not something independent. This is not a novel but a polemical article like the articles of Misters Antonovich and Pisarev."[132]

On many different levels, Chernyshevskii was doing all he could to fool the censor into thinking that *What Is to Be Done?* was a harmless novel, something that merely responded to previous literary texts. Based on the evidence of contemporary reactions, he was quite successful in his intentions. However, this fact explains only individual elements of the novel, not the design of the novel as a whole. Perhaps, there is something more that has not been adequately explored.

Writing in the 1960s Francis Randall observed that Chernyshevskii had some fun in tying his plot together with deliberate clumsiness.[133] Other scholars have also come close to the observation that much of the inartistic nature of *What Is to Be Done?* seems deliberately cultivated. Vail' and Genis, for example, argue that, although at first glance the novel produces an impression of clumsiness, it is not an amorphous heap of pages but has its own style.[134] Likewise, Irina Paperno in her study states that Chernyshevskii in large part relies on the anti-aesthetic.[135] Having made such interesting observations, however, these scholars do not pursue them further. Rather, they conclude that *What Is to Be Done?* fails as a work of art. What is often forgotten, however, is that it is Chernyshevskii himself who makes artistry the question of *What Is to Be Done?* It is he who introduces it in the foreword and constructs much of the meta-narrative in the novel around it, never letting the reader forget the question.[136] With this in mind, we must ask if there is not a larger game being played. It is Iu. K. Rudenko who asserts that Chernyshevskii deliberately cultivates the inartistic appearance of *What Is to Be Done?* not due to lack of talent, but precisely as a new form of art. As Rudenko states: "This clear demarcation of the entire mass of real readers of the novel into two large groups, each of which understands the sense of the work in its own way and certainly in a distorted manner, is premeditated on the part of the novelist and consequently is transformed by him into a principle organizing the artistic structure of the work as a whole."[137] In effect, Chernyshevskii intentionally invites an unsophisticated reading of his novel to lure his reader, especially the censor, into thinking the novel was an artistic failure.

In terms of *What Is to Be Done?* appearing as a weak, inartistic work, several devices come into play early in the novel. For example, Rudenko notes that the very beginning of the novel imitates and parodies the contemporary adventure narrative. The adventure narrative was considered a low genre of the time, and beginning the novel in that way seems to promise a work that itself is built on a low level. As Rudenko argues, a reader raised on traditional aesthetics must perceive the beginning as evidence of the writer's lack of talent and his bad taste.[138] Likewise, the use of the love triangle seems to promise a lack of talent on the author's part, and certainly a lack of originality. This motif was so commonly used in literature of the early-nineteenth century that Chernyshevskii must have known that it was clichéd. Chernyshevskii calls attention to this fact by means of the narrator's conversations with the so-called perspicacious reader. They expose the very banality of the situation that forms the novel's core: the love triangle. Throughout those conversations the perspicacious reader continually guesses the outcome of the novel's situations, which underlines their utter banality (that is, even an idiot like the perspicacious reader can guess them).[139] And, as Emily Klenin points out with regard to the Sand variant, Chernyshevskii certainly could not "have hoped to excite much interest by promising his readers *Jacques* with a Russian face." Several Russian writers had long preceded him in that regard.[140] Finally, the theme of a young girl marrying to escape an oppressive household was by no means a new one by the time Chernyshevskii wrote *What Is to Be Done?* Pomialovskii's work, *Molotov*, was still fresh in everyone's mind, and Chernyshevskii was certainly aware of that fact.[141] In the rough draft Chernyshevskii originally included the names of Pomialovskii's works, making the connection unavoidable (LP 356). Finally, Chernyshevskii inserts into the text of *What Is to Be Done?* a tale of a virtuous prostitute, Kriukova, who conveniently dies of the stereotypical disease of nineteenth-century literature: consumption. This dull, insipid tale is so clichéd that a hostile reader cannot help but conclude that Chernyshevskii is utterly untalented as a writer. Thus, it seems quite evident that Chernyshevskii was purposely constructing his work to reflect previous literary texts, all with the intention of appearing unoriginal, thus untalented.

Considerably aiding Chernyshevskii's cause in this matter were the negative perceptions of him held by many contemporaries, of which he was well aware. At the most basic level, Chernyshevskii was also aware of the distorted image of the seminarian: for educated Russian society, the term *seminarian* was synonymous with a deprecation of art.[142] Likewise, Chernyshevskii was aware of the fun made at his expense as a "stinking" seminarian and the hostility toward his aesthetic views as expressed in *The Aesthetic Relations of Art to Reality*.[143] Chernyshevskii gives evidence of his awareness of his public image in a letter to Nekrasov of 1856, after the scandal of "A School for Hospitality" and the publication of *Aesthetic Relations*.[144] Here Chernyshevskii states: "[B]esides, I am not an exclusive supporter of tendencies—it only seems thus because I am a person of extreme opinions and I sometimes find it necessary to defend them against people who have absolutely no way of thinking" (14:322). Chernyshevskii must have been well aware of his overwhelming negative image as an art-hating seminarian if he felt the need to explain himself to such a close colleague as Nekrasov. Likewise, in the projected foreword to his novel *Povesti v povesti*, Chernyshevskii demonstrates an awareness of the enmity he had earned: "As a publicist I am an object of sympathy and antipathy" (12:133). But perhaps the most persuasive evidence is an 1875 letter Chernyshevskii wrote while in exile. In this letter Chernyshevskii, out of the desperation to appear in print, offers to write poetry in English under a pseudonym: "It cannot be pleasant for anyone to have anything to do with Chernyshevsky. But you will have nothing whatever to do with him. You will only have to deal with Mr. Denzil Elliot. . . . The Russian public is well aware that Chernyshevsky has never published a single verse. . . . Denzil Elliot, who is fond of writing verses, a weakness to which Chernyshevsky, *as every educated person in Russia knows*, was never subject" (emphasis mine).[145] In short, Chernyshevskii was well aware of his negative public image as a "seminarian writer" and utilized it as an effective way to outsmart the vigilant authorities.[146]

In this same vein, Chernyshevskii goes to great pains not only to invite a reading of the novel as weak and untalented, but also to give it the appearance of being blatantly didactic. As Rudenko argues, didacticism functions as a key artistic principle in *What Is to Be Done?* and misunderstanding that fact causes one to deny any artistic value to the novel.[147] For example, in the second minichapter, Vera Pavlovna is singing a French song, a well-known anthem of the French Revolution, when news is brought to her of Lopukhov's suicide (LP 11). Although the words of the French song are incorporated into the text, a prose "translation" is also provided. In addition, the content of the song is somewhat distorted, giving it an even more ideological character. Placing and distorting such a well-known song so early in the novel cannot have gone unnoticed by Chernyshevskii's readers, particularly those who were well educated. By doing this Chernyshevskii gives the impression that he has lost all artistic tact and that he is blatantly introducing socialist doctrines into his text.[148] Likewise, throughout the novel, Chernyshevskii places long monologues or dialogues in the mouths of his characters that are notable for their intellectual content. Considerable space is given to Lopukhov's exposition of his utilitarian ethics. On a superficial level, the novel has the appearance of a heavy-handed, didactic novel.

The ultimate in "inartistry" and didacticism, however, comes in the infamous foreword to the novel. In the passage quoted earlier the narrator openly proclaims his lack of talent and the fact that he is going to give the reader truth. Indeed, the narrator posits that truth is far more important than artistry. Here Chernyshevskii intentionally irritates those readers opposed to didacticism by claiming that an author must teach.[149] This does much to set the tone, and most readers, especially twentieth-century literary scholars, have accepted it without question. Adding to this impression, Chernyshevskii creates a parody of naked didacticism by his use of an obvious hagiographical literary device. As Julia Alissandratos has noted, the promises of truth (and the denial of talent) in Chernyshevskii's foreword are very similar to passages found in medieval Russian hagiography. Alissandratos compares this passage with a similar one that occurs in the *Life of Saint Stephen of Perm* by Epifanii the Wise. In her words, "both examples may be viewed as realizations of the hagiographical commonplace of feigned ignorance, which can take the more specific form of the motif of the denial of literary talent."[150] Alissandratos concludes, however, that "Chernyshevsky's work resembles medieval Russian literature in its heavy-handed didacticism and sense of messianic vision. For Chernyshevsky and the medieval writer, literature was not an end in itself, but the means to an end."[151] What she misses is the fact that this similarity to medieval Russian literature with all its didacticism is a deliberately cultivated one; it is a false layer placed upon the work to fool a certain group of readers. Chernyshevskii's seminarian origins were quite well known to his contemporaries, and this use of a hagiographical device played quite well into their biases: indeed, what else besides blatant didacticism was to be expected of a seminarian?

There can be little doubt that Chernyshevskii developed many of the devices he uses in order to deceive the censor. But is the presence of the censor the only motivating factor in the design of the novel, or is there yet another level?[152] Although many of the techniques discussed previously do function as cloaking devices, they also parody and subvert both trite devices and serious literary works of the mid-1800s. The adventuristic beginning of the novel, for example, is partially intended to parody the genre. Likewise, Chernyshevskii uses the motif of the love triangle, in large part, to respond to its previous usage by Russian writers.[153] But there seems to be an even deeper polemic going on by means of the cultivation of the appearance of inartistry and didacticism in the novel. We have already discussed Chernyshevskii's battle against idealist aesthetics and its assertion that beauty is the sole content of art. Chernyshevskii continues this battle within the text of *What Is to Be Done?* He quite consciously constructs the novel around the question of artistry precisely to battle such a restricted definition of art. Whereas Chernyshevskii's opponents insisted on the beauty of form, Chernyshevskii deliberately invites the reader to view his form as inartistic. For example, in addition to the seemingly overt didacticism and admissions to a lack of any artistic talent whatsoever, this apparent inartistic form takes a concrete existence in the absence of nature descriptions in *What Is to Be Done?* This fact has been noticed in the criticism, but usually it is cited as further evidence of Chernyshevskii's lack of talent.[154] However, when we remember that much of the poetic theory and practice of Chernyshevskii's opponents, such as Turgenev and Fet, consisted in the depiction of beautiful scenes of nature, we begin to see not a lack of talent, but a conscious polemic on Chernyshevskii's part. Furthermore, Chernyshevskii sets his novel in the urban eyesore of Saint Petersburg instead of the aesthetic countryside. In short, he deliberately makes his work void of the beauty so prized by his opponents. Thus, any reader schooled in conventional aesthetics must conclude that *What Is to Be Done?* is lacking in beauty, and thus lacking in artistry.

Chernyshevskii continues his polemic with traditional aesthetics by drawing on the general negative view of his own aesthetics. That is, he attempts to force his hostile readers into interpreting his novel from the point of view of crude realism, giving the impression that he merely copied from reality. Thus, he would again seem to confirm the view that he was devoid of true creative talent. Within the novel itself, this impression is created by several devices. First, in the foreword, the narrator tries to persuade the reader that he is the actual author, stating that this is his first novel (47).[155] In the rough draft of the novel, the connection is even more apparent in that the narrator has Chernyshevskii's first name and his age.[156] Moreover, the narrator asserts that he is personally acquainted with the heroes. This fact was interpreted so literally that most contemporaries traced the central love conflict to the real love triangle of Obrucheva, Bokov, and Sechenov. So entrenched did this legend become that works later published about the members of this triangle were entitled *The Heroes of "What Is to Be Done?"* (*Geroi 'Chto delat'?'*) or *The Heroine of the Novel "What Is to Be Done?" in Her Letters* (*Geroinia romana 'Chto delat'? v ee pis'makh*).[157]

Chernyshevskii's intentional allusions to copying reality seem designed to make a joke at his ideological opponents' expense. Fully aware of the general interpretation of his aesthetics, Chernyshevskii deliberately provokes the hostile reader into reducing the novel as mere imitation. In the rough draft, the bait was even stronger: "If I were writing a novel, I would have finished it with this. But I have no pretensions to writing a novel,—for that talent would be necessary which I do not have,—I am simply relating the life of one of my good acquaintances and of the people close to her, which it seems to me is not without interest, and perhaps is even of use to the public. Thus, I must add a few more pages" (LP 712–13).[158] Here Chernyshevskii combines several of the key motifs intended to cause a negative reading of the novel. Confession to a lack of talent is directly associated with mere copying of reality and both motifs are then linked to that of didacticism. Chernyshevskii's enemies, the so-called aesthetes, could not have helped but react negatively to such passages. Indeed, the bait is too obvious here and may be the reason Chernyshevskii removed this passage from the published version.[159]

Lest the reader think I give too much credit to Chernyshevskii on this point, it must be noted that Chernyshevskii refers to the device in the variants to the foreword of his novel *Povesti v povesti.* In that work, Chernyshevskii is at his most caustic, for example, when he writes: "These are not copies of my acquaintances. But dear friends of the author, not you alone will read my novel. The others, 'those not knowing how to read' as they are called in the novel, all search: from whom did the author copy this character? Did he depict himself, his cousin, or his friend?" (12:680).[160] In the foreword Chernyshevskii further belittles the crude aesthetic sensibilities of some of his readers: "What do I see and find natural? The fact that if I translated Shakespeare, some people would begin to search for and to argue who I am there: Iago or Macbeth, or even Lady Macbeth herself. If I were to translate the Edda, they would begin to search for and to argue who I am there: Surtr or Loki, Fenrir or Hel" (12:134). In short, Chernyshevskii plays upon the rather crude definition of realism attributed to him by his enemies to mock them, to expose their own lack of aesthetic sensibility.

That Chernyshevskii expected a hostile reaction to his novel is hardly in doubt. For example, in a variant of his foreword to *Povesti v povesti,* written shortly after the completion of *What Is to Be Done?* Chernyshevskii openly refers to it: "Those who are of the second opinion are my friends. This publicist took it into his head to write novels. Here again the previous difference of opinions has appeared. Some found that whatever might be there was all the same. I don't even know of the filth which was printed regarding my novel *What Is to Be Done?* I have not read a single one of these articles, incidentally, because I am not a lover of reading the works of idiots" (12:681).[161] Likewise, in the actual foreword he states: "The attitude of the people who show me the honor of their hatred for me as a publicist awakens in them the irresistible necessity for them to search in my poetic works for material for the satisfaction of the hostility which they are completely well-justified in nourishing for me as a publicist" (12:134). Moreover, Chernyshevskii uses a device similar to that in *What Is to Be Done?* That is, he purposely invites this hostile reaction, provoking his enemies with the reminder that he is a seminarian and a publicist: "And so, Efiop is I, retired titular councilor N. Chernyshevskii, a seminarian, a man who has studied a lot, even more who has thought about very serious subjects, incidentally about the human heart and about love and about poetry, a publicist very severe and extraordinarily coarse" (12:134).

That Chernyshevskii's opponents took the bait provided in *What Is to Be Done?* and interpreted the novel as an utter artistic failure is only too well known. Afanasii Fet, for example, obviously taking the narrator's admission of a lack of talent literally, interpreted the novel as a colossal failure: "Our total agreement with the author on this point grew with every new page and reached a zenith in the last line of the novel. The poverty of imagination, the positive absence of creativity, the incessant repetition, the premeditated affectation of the worst sort in terms of the form and that totally helpless clumsiness of language, make the reading of the novel a difficult, almost unbearable, task."[162] The Russian press was filled with similar hostile attacks on the novel, labeling it inartistic as well as immoral.[163] F. M. Tolstoi, for example, described the novel as "one of the ugliest works of Russian literature."[164] P. Kapnist also denounced the novel because of "the poverty of its practical ideal and the absence of any artistic merits."[165] That Chernyshevskii succeeded in his design is only too evident. As Rudenko succinctly describes it, when Chernyshevskii's enemies vociferously attacked the novel, they merely succeeded in fulfilling his will.[166] Few writers have ever been so successful at manipulating their readers.[167]

Let us turn once again to the notion of Chernyshevskii's supposed confession. As quoted previously, his narrator does openly proclaim his lack of talent in the foreword. However, in a passage that immediately follows, the narrator also claims that he has a great amount of talent: "When I say that I have not one bit of artistic talent and that my tale is a very weak piece of work, you should by no means conclude that I'm any worse than those authors whom you consider to be great, or that my novel is any poorer than theirs. That's not at all what I mean. I mean that my tale suffers from imperfections when it's compared with the works of genuinely gifted writers.[168] As far as the worth of its execution is concerned, you can confidently place my tale side by side with the most famous works of your well-known authors. Perhaps you'd not do wrong to place it even higher than theirs! It certainly contains more artistry—rest assured on that point" (48).[169] Here, in direct negation of what he has said before, the narrator proclaims his talent and claims that he is among the very best writers. The narrator has both denied and proclaimed his talent: which is the true statement?[170]

In his letters Chernyshevskii also seems to belittle his own poetic talent. For example, in letters of 1883 Chernyshevskii says, "My language in them is somewhat awkward" (15:390) or "I am a very bad stylist" (15:392). However, in these same letters Chernyshevskii also states, "But my prose is good poetry" (15:390). Likewise, in other letters Chernyshevskii states that he is quite capable of writing works with high literary merit (14:615, 616). This would seem an irresolvable contradiction if Chernyshevskii did not go on to explain what he means when he says that he is a bad stylist. He argues that his language is that of Gogol': "[M]y very language has always been awkward. It is not the language of Pushkin or Lermontov, but the language of Gogol': awkward expressions, inexactitude in the usage of words, . . . in short, bad language" (15:392). Chernyshevskii is quite consciously placing himself in the tradition of Gogol', whose style introduced much that had previously been considered vulgar and awkward. Far from viewing himself as a bad writer, Chernyshevskii sees himself as a talented innovator expanding the boundaries of art. As V. V. Shcheulin argues, Chernyshevskii's words acquire a very specific sense: he is a bad stylist only from the point of view of the puritans of Russian literature.[171] When Chernyshevskii confesses to his lack of talent, he means a lack of talent only from a certain viewpoint: that of conventional idealist aesthetics. Thus, we see that the passages in *What Is to Be Done?* by no means form a true confession to a lack a talent but rather a signal to the attentive reader that the novel cannot be judged by conventional aesthetics.

In designing *What Is to Be Done?* Chernyshevskii consciously manipulates those readers who subscribe to conventional aesthetics to reject the work as an artistic failure. An example of this process at work can be found in the analysis by G. Žekulin. Žekulin approaches *What Is to Be Done?* from a specific set of aesthetic criteria that are in many ways similar to those held by Chernyshevskii's opponents and that he criticized in his essays. The first criticism Žekulin provides is that the novel is far too long, that it contains too much extraneous material. In effect, he is disturbed by the generic impurity of the work.[172] But his main criticism of the novel is that it lacks tension, which he calls a "prerequisite of art."[173] Žekulin particularly criticizes the section where Vera Pavlovna is in conflict with her family: "This conflict could provide enough tension for a full novel of its own. But Chernyshevsky destroys it when the reader begins to be involved by introducing Lopukhov and thus the inevitability of Vera Pavlovna's liberation from this hell. After 53 pages this conflict is resolved, if not yet by the march of events in the novel, then by the writer's attitude to the conflict."[174] What Žekulin is reacting to is the interruption of the novel by the narrator at the end of chapter 1. Whereas a conventional novel would leave off at the moment of tension to excite the reader, Chernyshevskii's narrator breaks in and says: "If I wanted to create powerful confrontations, I would provide a thunderous resolution for this predicament. In fact, it wasn't like that at all. If I wanted to entice you with uncertainty, I wouldn't be telling you now that nothing of the sort took place. But since I'm writing without setting any traps, I'll say in advance that there will be no thunderous confrontation; this predicament will be resolved without storm, thunder, or lightning" (87).[175] That Chernyshevskii is playing with and subverting the form of conventional novels is quite evident. Žekulin is aware of this fact and grants Chernyshevskii a modicum of talent.[176] He even grants that Chernyshevskii was an accomplished craftsman in the way he manipulates form.[177] But so restricted is he in his particular aesthetics that he concludes that, although Chernyshevskii could have written a good novel if he wanted to, *What Is to Be Done?* fails as a work of art.[178] Žekulin is so convinced that tension is an inherent part of art that in spite of the deliberate attempts of Chernyshevskii to subvert that norm, he concludes that Chernyshevskii fails as an artist.

Earlier in this century the warning was sounded about the dangers of one particular school of aesthetics coming to dominate literary criticism, that such a fact would inevitably endanger the discipline's ability to interpret the wide variety of art.[179] A somewhat similar warning is sounded by Wasiolek in his attempt to protect Tolstoi's *The Death of Ivan Ilych* from those who approach the work from a set of aesthetic criteria hostile to the author's basic method. As he argues, authorial intrusion is part of Tolstoi's narrative stance; if the novel is approached with a prejudice against such a strategy, naturally only an unfavorable judgment of the work is possible. Wasiolek further warns: "I suppose every age, and ours no less, is ever in danger of elevating to universal law what may be the preferences of the day."[180] As I discussed in the earlier part of this chapter, Chernyshevskii began fighting such battles over a century ago. In his dissertation he rejects the notion that artists must create according to set aesthetic criteria and in his review of Tolstoi, he rejects the notion that works of literature should be judged by stale criteria hostile to the author's artistic method. In short, he defends the autonomy of the artist to create as he pleases and appeals to the critic to change his conception of art as the nature of art changes, not to adhere to a rigid set of prescribed rules for it. I believe a similar motivation is at work in Chernyshevskii's writing of *What Is to Be Done?* That is, Chernyshevskii is attempting to make a great statement on the nature of art. Whereas others have seen this statement as hostility to art,[181] I think Chernyshevskii baits and forces his readers into a misreading of the novel, intentionally flouting traditional aesthetic principles, to demonstrate that art should be free: creating and interpreting art by a prescribed set of immutable aesthetic criteria inherently diminishes and impoverishes it.

Unfortunately, most observers, biased against the novel even before reading it, have been either unwilling or unable to avoid Chernyshevskii's snare. As a result, much of Western literary criticism on the novel has been trapped in an incessant repetition of the judgments made by Chernyshevskii's hostile contemporaries. For a more accurate understanding of the novel, however, we should not be lured by the narrator into the trap of making a lazy, unsophisticated reading. Chernyshevskii, while clearly setting traps for certain groups of readers, did not intend for all readers to approach the novel in so crude a manner. It is incumbent upon the modern reader not to lapse into stale slogans and stereotypes, but to delve deeper. Thus, we now turn in detail to a text that is not a transparent, political treatise, but a complex work of literature with the irony, ambiguity, multiple layers of meaning, and even multiple interpretations that this implies.

Chapter Two

What Is to Be Done? as Literature

STRUCTURE AND COMPOSITION

Despite its negative reputation as an ideological treatise, *What Is to Be Done?* is generally devoid of what might be called blatant didacticism. Much of the novel is devoted to a love intrigue that runs throughout the book. And, far from being a mass of incoherent, disorganized material, there is a clear underlying structure to *What Is to Be Done?* As Iu. K. Rudenko convincingly demonstrates, it is built on a cyclical principle. The subtitle (*From the Tales about New People*), he argues, is very important in this respect: it indicates that *What Is to Be Done?* is a series of episodes, not pretending to be complete. However the novel is not at all like a collection (*sbornik*) of tales; the action does not disintegrate into fragments isolated from one another. Rather, each chapter contains one or more elements in the unbroken progression of the action of the novel: that is, the love intrigue.[1]

As a result of this cyclical construction, each chapter of *What Is to Be Done?* has its own ministructure, its own *zaviazka* (literally, "tying of the knot") and *razviazka* (outcome, denouement). As G. Verkhovskii pointed out long ago, the novel moves in gradations, with the *razviazka* of one story leading to the *zaviazka* of the next. He argues that each chapter-stage has a definite compositional closure and independence.[2] N. Naumova concurs with this evaluation, stating that the novel is constructed as if there is a series of closed *siuzhety* (intrigues, plots) in it following one after the other. She further argues that throughout the novel, there is a deceptive sensation of an ending, only to have a new *siuzhet* appear. Chernyshevskii's play with his reader in this regard is most evident in chapter 5.[3] That chapter contains the word *razviazka* in its title, but a series of new characters are introduced, prompting the reader to ask what kind of *razviazka* it is.[4] Although the novel has a clear cyclical structure, it is a closed, finished work. The series of episodes cannot be extended indefinitely; at the end of the novel the main characters have achieved some definitive stage in their development (the winter picnic scene) and chapter 6, consisting of a mere one page, breaks the string of each chapter containing a fully developed, independent *siuzhet.* Both thematically and structurally, closure is achieved and the novel is over.[5]

Although it is easy to establish that *What Is to Be Done?* is a single, unified work, the question of its genre is far more difficult. Scholars have been unable to find an adequate label for it, with some questioning whether the term *novel* is even appropriate.[6] It is clear that Chernyshevskii himself considered it a novel; at least he referred to it as such (12:681). Most scholars do accept that *What Is to Be Done?* is a novel, with most of the discussion centering around which type of novel it is. Numerous labels have been proposed: socialist, sociophilosophical, sociopolitical, philosophical-revolutionary, historical-political, utopian, intellectual, and so forth. None of those labels, however, is satisfactory in that they all refer to only one aspect of the novel, not the novel as a whole.[7] Strongly connected to this problem is the question of who is the hero of the novel. Basing themselves primarily on the supposed content of the novel, many scholars, especially Soviet, have concluded that Rakhmetov is the hero.[8] Other scholars have pointed out that he plays a very minor role in the plot and have suggested other alternatives, such as Lopukhov.[9] However, if *What Is to Be Done?* is approached purely from a standpoint of structure, not ideological content, Vera Pavlovna is clearly the organizing pole.[10] She is the one character who appears consistently throughout the novel, with her story being the focus of its account.[11] Any interpretation of the genre of the novel must take this fact into account.

A more fruitful approach is to use the series of designations created by German scholars: *Erziehungsroman* (novel of education) and *Bildungsroman* (novel of formation). The *Erziehungsroman* may be thought of as a how-to novel with the implied instruction to the reader to imitate what he or she has read, whereas the *Bildungsroman* seeks to present the formation of a particular individual without necessarily holding him or her up as an ideal for emulation. One of those designations captures the essence of *What Is to Be Done?* quite well, but it is essential to be clear about which one we choose. As Russell Valentino states, "this distinction, like any distinction of genre, is no quibble over classification but a matter of interpretive stance."[12]

The genre of *What Is to Be Done?* is that of the *Bildungsroman.*[13] Throughout the novel there is the continuous presence of one major character, Vera Pavlovna, who is shown in various stages of development.[14] She is first presented to the reader as a naive sixteen-year-old girl, whereas the reader's last glimpse of her is as a budding political radical in the winter picnic scene.[15] The cyclical structure of *What Is to Be Done?* is very much a part of Vera Pavlovna's development. Chapter 1, for example, corresponds to her home life with her oppressive mother. Chapter 2 corresponds to her meeting a "new person" and her release from the parental home, and so on. Vera Pavlovna is exposed to the tendencies of the time and clearly goes through some kind of development in each of chapters 1 through 5: she is not the same person at the end of each chapter that she was at the beginning. It is this element of the *Bildungsroman,* the story of Vera Pavlovna's development into a mature individual, that provides a unifying principle for *What Is to Be Done?* Vera Pavlovna is the main character of the novel and, no matter how far the action or the narrator may stray, everything eventually returns to her. For example, chapter 5, with its title of "New Characters and the Conclusion," seems to be one long digression from the main story. However, it culminates in Lopukhov's visit to Vera Pavlovna and the two couples' settling down next door to each other. Even in the final scene of chapter 5, in which a host of new characters is introduced, Vera Pavlovna (and the other major characters) are present. It is in that scene (the winter picnic) that Vera Pavlovna and her company achieve a definitive stage in their intellectual and radical development.[16] Despite the fact that the story may introduce and desert various characters, the reader is never in doubt that it is indeed a single, whole work.

A distinguishing feature of *What Is to Be Done?* is the individualization of the language of the characters. This gives the characters a tangible quality and clearly helps to distinguish one from another. Chernyshevskii has not, however, been credited with that accomplishment. A. Skaftymov, for example, provides a very harsh analysis of Chernyshevskii in this regard, arguing, "Chernyshevskii's dialogues do not have the live sound of unforced conversation; the speeches do not have any individual manner of reciprocal questions and responses."[17] Skaftymov views only the speech of Mar'ia Aleksevna as successfully individualized. His view is not quite accurate and also ignores that Chernyshevskii used stylization of language not only in his fiction but also in his publicistic work.[18]

Skaftymov is correct to some degree: the most successful example of individualization is in the character of Mar'ia Aleksevna, Vera Pavlovna's mother. Mar'ia Aleksevna is from the petit bourgeois strata and has had a very rough life, all of which is quite evident in her vulgar language and behavior. She constantly uses terms of abuse or uses certain words in an abusive manner. For example, she refers to Vera Pavlovna as a Gypsy and a scarecrow (*chuchelo*) or uses such words as mug (*rozha*) instead of face (53; LP 17). Her use of such expressions as "If you don't touch shit, it doesn't stink!" (57) leaves little doubt in the reader's mind that Mar'ia Aleksevna is a very crude and vulgar woman.[19] Mar'ia Aleksevna is also successfully characterized by the discrepancy between her words and her actions. For example, no extra words are needed when she unexpectedly knocks Vera Pavlovna on the head for not crossing herself in front of a church. That knock on the head is accompanied by her statement "Can't you see that all good people cross themselves?" (53).[20] The contrast between Mar'ia Aleksevna's insistence on decency and her own lack of it are very evident and instantly communicates to the reader exactly what type of person Mar'ia Aleksevna is. The reader is presented with the clear image of a petit bourgeois, domineering matriarch who is willing to go to any length for financial and social gain.

Despite Skaftymov's assertion that only Mar'ia Aleksevna's speech is individualized, successful stylization can also be found in the speech of Kirsanov and Lopukhov. Both speak in a relatively elevated style permeated with the scientific terms and analogies that befit university medical students. Their materialistic and utilitarian jargon reaches its apogee in the subsection entitled "A Theoretical Conversation," where both men engage in a verbal duel filled with all sorts of scientific and philosophical terms (252–58). Furthermore, Kirsanov's and Lopukhov's language differs greatly from that of Vera Pavlovna. The contrast is most striking, for example, in the conversations between Vera Pavlovna and Lopukhov during which he explains his ethical theory. Lopukhov uses elevated terms and speaks in the manner of cold, rational analysis, using many naturalistic analogies: "Yes, they are telling the truth. What we call sublime emotion or ideal aspiration—all that, in the general course of life, is completely insignificant in comparison with each person's pursuit of his own advantage. And in essence these things constitute the same pursuit of advantage" (115).[21] Lopukhov then explains further by use of his own situation, elaborating at length that he chose to become a doctor to get "a big hunk a bread."[22] This contrasts starkly with Vera Pavlovna's far more emotional view and her tendency to reduce things to the simplest language possible. In contrast to Lopukhov's long-winded statements, she penetrates to the heart of the matter in clear, precise language: "All actions, as far as I can see, can be explained by advantage. But isn't that theory rather cold?" (115).[23]

The successful individualization of the characters' speech allows Chernyshevskii to mix discourses for striking narrative effect. Chernyshevskii clearly manipulates his linguistic material, with the intrusion of the word of the other (*chuzhoe slovo*), as described by Bakhtin, appearing throughout the text of *What Is to Be Done?*[24] For example, in chapter 1, when Vera Pavlovna has locked herself behind her door, her mother says: "Что ты сделала, Верка проклятая?" (What on earth have you done, damn you, Verka?). The narrator immediately seizes upon the word *prokliataia* and also the rude diminutive Verka[25] and uses it for his own humorous purpose:

> —но *проклятой Верки* уже не было в зале; мать бросилась к ней в комнату, но дверь верочкиной комнаты была заперта; мать надвинула всем корпусом на дверь, чтобы выломать ее, но дверь не подавалась, а *проклятая Верка* сказала (LP 28; emphasis mine)
>
> But the accursed Verka was no longer in the drawing room. Her mother followed her to the bedroom, but her door was locked. Mar'ia Aleksevna hurled all her weight against the door to break it down, but the door didn't budge, and the accursed Verka replied. (66)

This intrusion of the *chuzhoe slovo* is also evident in the course of the third-person narration, without the direct quotation of the character's speech. That is, the narrator anticipates the discourse of his characters and appropriates from their vocabulary as he sees fits. In this same scene, the narrator relates Mar'ia Aleksevna's thoughts on the situation, using her language:

> Needless to say, Mar'ia Aleksevna did not exactly take these words to heart, but her exhausted nerves needed a rest; it also occurred to her that it might even be better to enter into negotiations with her daughter, since the wench [*merzavka*] was getting completely out of hand. Without Vera's agreement, nothing could be done: there was no way of marrying her off to that fool Mishka unless she was willing. And Mar'ia Aleksevna still had no idea what Verka said to him—after all, they did hold hands. What did it all mean? (66)[26]

This paragraph is indirect narrated speech. No conversation is recounted by the narrator; rather, he relates the situation using Mar'ia Aleksevna's language and attitudes. The abusive word *merzavka* is obviously not the narrator's but Mar'ia Aleksevna's. Likewise, the narrator, when describing Mar'ia Aleksevna's rage after her plans have been foiled, recounts her plans for revenge in the third person; no quoted speech is given (163). However, the plans are related from her point of view and the discourse is saturated with her speech. The use of the word *razboinik* (LP 109, 111) is a clear marker that the narrator has appropriated Mar'ia Aleksevna's discourse to relate the events, all for humorous effect.[27]

The mixture of discourses is used quite often by the narrator and sometimes with the direct intention of disorienting the reader. For example, in another passage recounting Mar'ia Aleksevna's thoughts, the narrator begins by using his own discourse; that is, he narrates her thoughts in his language:

> Марья Алексевна решительно не знала, что и думать о *Верочке*. Дочь и говорила, и как будто бы поступала решительно против ее намерений. Но выходило то, что дочь победила все трудности, с которыми не могла сладить Марья Алексевна. Если судить по ходу дела, то оказывалось: *Верочка* хочет того же, чего и она, Марья Алексевна, только, как ученая и тонкая штука, обрабатывает свою материю другим манером (LP 44; emphasis mine)

> Mar'ia Aleksevna had absolutely no idea what to think about Verochka. In both word and deed her daughter appeared to be contradicting her wishes. But now it turned out that her daughter had overcome all obstacles that had stymied Mar'ia Aleksevna. To judge by the progress of this affair, it seemed that Verochka was hoping for the same outcome as she, Mar'ia Aleksevna; however, being the learned and refined person she was, her daughter was manipulating the material in a different way. (85)

The use of the affectionate diminutive Verochka denotes that this is the narrator's speech. But midway through this paragraph, the narrator, without any warning whatsoever, switches over to Mar'ia Aleksevna's language. The use of words such as *zver'* (wild beast) and the rude diminutive Verka are clear signs to this effect:

> ... А между тем как же быть, если он и ошибочен, если дочь действительно не хочет идти за Сторешникова? Она такой *зверь*, что неизвестно, как ее укротить. По всей вероятности, негодная *Верка* не хочет выходить замуж,—это даже несомненно,—здравый смысл был слишком силен в Марье Алексевне, чтобы обольститься хитрыми ее же собственными раздумьями о *Верочке* как о тонкой интригантке (LP 44–45; emphasis mine)

> What if her conclusions were wrong? If her daughter had no real intention of marrying Storeshnikov? She was such a wild beast—Mar'ia Aleksevna had no idea how to tame her. In all likelihood that worthless Verka didn't want to get married—that was beyond doubt. Mar'ia Aleksevna had too much common sense to be deluded by her own cunning conclusion that Verochka was a skillful schemer. (85)

If this were not enough, the narrator mixes the two discourses (that is, Verka and Verochka) within the same sentence, which is both disorienting and amusing. Moreover, after several sentences in which the rude diminutive Verka appears, the narrator switches back to his own language for the rest of the section, which is signaled by the presence of the affectionate diminutive Verochka:

> Но соблазнительна была для нее мысль, осуждаемая ее здравым смыслом, что *Верка* ведет дело к свадьбе. Все, кроме слов и поступков *Верочки,* подтверждало эту мысль: жених был шелковый. Мать жениха боролась недели три, но сын побивал ее домом, и она стала смиряться. Выразила желание познакомиться с *Верочкой,—Верочка* не отправилась к ней (LP 45; emphasis mine)

> Nevertheless, the conclusion that Verka was moving toward a match, although in complete opposition to her own good common sense, was still very tempting. Everything, except for Verochka's words and actions, confirmed this interpretation. The suitor behaved as smooth as silk. His mother protested for three weeks or so, but the son kept returning to the question of the house, and his mother began to yield. She expressed a desire to make Verochka's acquaintance, but Verochka would not go to see her. (85–86)

As the preceding examples demonstrate, *What Is to Be Done?* is a rich verbal text that mixes various discourses. Chernyshevskii clearly devotes some effort to manipulating his linguistic material. As a result, *What Is to Be Done?* is not a careless, transparent text, but a rich, literary one.

As the examples show, *What Is to Be Done?* is an entertaining, funny novel.[28] Chernyshevskii fills the text with numerous puns and situations of misunderstanding that are quite humorous. Much of Chernyshevskii's humor might be described as intellectual in nature, requiring a considerable amount of background knowledge to be appreciated. One must be familiar with the ideological controversies that raged through Russian culture during the nineteenth century. But all humor is heavily dependent upon the perceiver's knowledge of the cultural code. The fact that the perceiver fails to appreciate the humor does not at all mean that the object is not funny, but only that he does not have sufficient understanding and knowledge to appreciate it. Moreover, not all of Chernyshevskii's humor is so specialized. There is much that is universal in nature and translates well into any language and culture.

The humorous, flippant tone of the novel is set immediately in the very first minichapter. When describing the adventures of the unnamed gentleman (that is, Lopukhov) the narrator applies a flippant, nonserious tone to what is indeed a serious situation. This becomes most evident when the crowd that has gathered around the Liteinyi Bridge is divided into the conservatives and the progressives by the narrator (40–41). The division of the usual crowd that gathers after some sort of accident along lines normally reserved for political groups is a rather amusing device that serves to keep the reader from taking the events too seriously. Such humorous lowering of generally elevated terms and concepts also occurs in the scene when poor Pavel Konstantinovich returns home from work after Vera Pavlovna abandons Mar'ia Aleksevna on Nevskii Prospekt. The unfortunate Pavel Konstantinovich "caught it too, both 'ideally' and 'materially'" (161).[29] Likewise, in relating Mar'ia Aleksevna's plans for revenge against Lopukhov, the narrator calls them poetry (*poeziia;* 163). This device, this use of elevated terms in situations in which they are not at all appropriate, is one that Chernyshevskii uses throughout the novel for humorous effect.

Chernyshevskii also uses situations of misunderstanding to create humorous effects that can be universally appreciated. When Vera Pavlovna and Lopukhov first set up house together, their landlords find their behavior completely incomprehensible. They cannot at all understand why a newlywed couple would have not only separate beds, but even separate rooms. They conclude that Vera Pavlovna and Lopukhov must belong to some sort of strange religious sect (170–71). Nothing could be further from the truth, and for the reader in the know, the misunderstanding is quite humorous.

Perhaps the most amusing situation in the novel, however, comes when Mar'ia Aleksevna misunderstands the books that Lopukhov brings for Vera Pavlovna to read:

> Once when Verochka had gone to visit a friend, Mikhail Ivanych[30] was paying a call on Mar'ia Aleksevna. Mar'ia Aleksevna picked up some of these books and brought them in to show him.
>
> "Have a look, Mikhail Ivanych. I've almost figured out the title of this French book all by myself: *Gostinaia,* that must mean it's a manual on social etiquette, but I can't make out the German one."
>
> "No, Mar'ia Aleksevna, it's not *Gostinaia,* it's *Destinée,* that means destiny."

"What kind of destiny? Is that the title of a novel, a fortune-telling guide, or a book on dream interpretation?"

"Well, Mar'ia Aleksevna, let's have a look and find out." Mikhail Ivanych flipped through a few pages. "Most of it deals with series, Mar'ia Aleksevna. It's a scholarly book."

"Series? That's good—that means how to conduct monetary transactions."

"Yes, that's what it's all about, Mar'ia Aleksevna." (112)[31]

This passage is highly dependent upon the reader's knowledge of the actual book under discussion: Considérant's *La destinée sociale.* For the reader in the know, this scene is quite amusing. In her ignorance Mar'ia Aleksevna tries to pronounce the French title as if it were Russian, thus reading the French word *destinée* as the Russian *gostinaia.* Furthering the misunderstanding is the word "series" (*seriia* in Russian). Whereas Considérant used the term to denote a form of cooperatively organized labor, Mar'ia Aleksevna and Storeshnikov interpret it as a financial term.[32] This leads her to conclude that Lopukhov is a moneygrubbing soul just like she is.

The passage continues with an even more egregious mistake:

"Well, and what about the German book?"

Mikhail Ivanych read the title slowly: "*On Religion,* by Ludwig, that is, by Louis XIV, Mar'ia Aleksevna. It's a book by Louis XIV. He was king of France, Mar'ia Aleksevna, the father of the king whose place is now occupied by Napoleon."

"That means it's a book on religious matters?"

"Yes indeed, Mar'ia Aleksevna."

"That's good, Mikhail Ivanych. Although I know that Dmitrii Sergevich is a respectable young man, nevertheless you have to keep your eye on each and every young man. . . . But here's what I'm wondering, Mikhail Ivanych: what religion was the king of France?"

"Catholic, naturally."

"And in his book, is he trying to convert others to the papist religion?"

"I think not, Mar'ia Aleksevna. If a Catholic archbishop had written it, then undoubtedly he'd be trying to convert others to the papist religion. But a king wouldn't concern himself with such matters. As a wise ruler and politician, he simply wishes to instill piety." (112–13)[33]

Again, for the reader who knows that the book under discussion is Ludwig Feuerbach's *Lectures on the Essence of Religion,* this passage is quite amusing. Mar'ia Aleksevna's mistaking Feuerbach's book for one that teaches traditional religious values is particularly entertaining. Storeshnikov's mistaking Ludwig for Louis XIV of France provides additional humor that makes this scene priceless.[34] Finally, Chernyshevskii uses this scene as a pretext for another humorous aside later in the novel: "Mertsalov was at home alone reading some recent work, either by Louis XIV or by someone else of the same dynasty" (156).[35]

The narrator himself and his numerous interjections also provide much humor in the novel. In this regard Chernyshevskii follows in the tradition of Gogol. For example, although Chernyshevskii's narrator is supposedly omniscient, he feigns ignorance on many occasions.[36] The narrator's first intrusion into the main narrative, excluding the foreword, is simply to say that he does not know something (50). Such "ignorance" on the part of the narrator reaches its peak in chapter 5: "The patient showed no signs of any known illness, yet her strength was failing rapidly. Some disease had to be found. The attending physician finally came up with *atrophia nervorum*, "the suspension of nervous nutrition." *I don't know* whether such a disease exists in the whole world or not, but if it does, I'm sure it must be incurable" (390; emphasis mine).[37] This device, while providing some humor to the text, also serves to further the illusion that the narrator is indeed a person familiar with and close to the characters and thus bound by normal human limitations.

In contrast, the narrator also displays his omniscience on occasion, creating a humorous effect. When any of the negative characters lie or exaggerate, the narrator corrects them. In chapter 1, section 8, Anna Petrovna attempts to buy the Rozal'skiis' compliance by giving them several valuable items. As she hands the items over to Pavel Konstantinovich, she stresses how little they have been used and how expensive they are. The narrator, however, knows better and immediately corrects this in parentheses for the reader's benefit.

> "This is a gift for your wife. It cost me a hundred fifty rubles" (actually only eighty-five) "and I've worn it only twice" (actually more than twenty times). "And here's a present for your daughter." Anna Petrovna gave the manager a very small lady's watch. "I paid three hundred rubles for it" (actually only one hundred twenty). (82)[38]

Such interference by the narrator, however, should not be interpreted as an absolute commitment to the truth by the author.[39] Not long after this passage, for example, the narrator affirms what he and the reader know to be impossible with regard to a statement by the Lopukhovs' first landlady:

> It was truly amazing that Petrovna had seen two stars on Serge, who didn't have any at all, and, if he did, he probably wouldn't have worn them while escorting Julie. But that she actually saw two stars and was neither mistaken nor bragging, it's not she who so testified, but I who vouch for it. She did see them. You and I know very well that he had no stars; however, from Petrovna's point of view, it was impossible not to see two stars on someone with that appearance. And so she saw them. I'm not joking when I say that she really did. (177)[40]

Likewise, shortly before this passage, Chernyshevskii engages in an obvious joke when his narrator states: "Julie's elegant carriage . . . produced a staggering impression on the inhabitants of the Fifth Line between Middle and Small Prospekts, where nothing comparable had been seen at least since the time of Peter the Great, if not earlier" (176).[41] As William Wagner notes, no street could have existed at this spot before the founding of Saint Petersburg by Peter the Great. Chernyshevskii is obviously engaging in humor with these insertions by the narrator, and any attempt to draw philosophical or ethical conclusions based on such passages should best be resisted.

Humor is also abundant in the narrative digressions from the plot proper, particularly in the narrator's conversations with the perspicacious reader. Throughout these digressions the narrator is openly abusive. The fact that a purported author would be so abusive to his own reader is in itself a rather humorous construction. One example is when the narrator has had enough of the perspicacious reader and stuffs a napkin in his mouth:

> "Oh, I know. . . ."
> What's that? A familiar voice. . . . I turn around to look. . . . Sure enough! It's he, the perspicacious reader, recently banished in disgrace for his total ignorance of the ABC's of art. Here he is again, once more with his old perspicacity, claiming that he knows something!
> "Oh, I know who wrote that. . . ."
> I hastily seize the first convenient object that comes to hand which will suit my purpose—it's a napkin, because having transcribed the letter written by the former medical student, I've just sat down to lunch. So I seize a napkin and stuff it in his mouth. "Well, what if you do! Is that any reason to shout it from the rooftops?" (323)[42]

The scene, although a bit slapstick, is humorous precisely for that reason. Chernyshevskii oversteps the bounds of good taste and introduces a low, almost vaudevillian element. In addition, the scene is a sort of catharsis for the reader. That is, Chernyshevskii smashes normal social mores, if not legal boundaries, with this literary act upon the perspicacious reader, providing the reader with a humorously satisfying, vicarious revenge.

Finally, humor is also present at the level of language; that is, Chernyshevskii often uses puns for humorous effect. For example, when Mar'ia Aleksevna invites Lopukhov to Vera Pavlovna's birthday celebration, Lopukhov immediately assumes that he has been invited due to the lack of dance partners: "Понятно, в кавалерах недостаток, по обычаю всех таких вечеров." (Clearly there was a shortage of men, as is usual at such parties) (LP 54; 97). The word used for dance partner is *kavaler*, which has the additional meaning of "suitor." In the scene depicting Vera Pavlovna's birthday party, the narrator plays with these various meanings by referring to the young women's dance partners as suitors (*zhenikhi*):

> Осматривая собравшихся гостей, Лопухов увидел, что в кавалерах нет недостатка: при каждой из девиц находился молодой человек, кандидат в

женихи или и вовсе жених. Стало быть, Лопухова пригласили не в качестве кавалера; зачем же? (LP 54)

In surveying the assembled guests, Lopukhov noted that there was no shortage of men. Each young woman was paired with a young man, either a potential or an actual suitor. Consequently, Lopukhov had not been invited as a dancing partner. So what was it, then? (97)

The pun is made all the more effective by further plot developments: Lopukhov does indeed become Vera Pavlovna's suitor because of this very invitation. It is here that he has his first real conversation with her as her dance partner, which leads to his becoming her suitor and later her husband.

CHERNYSHEVSKII AND PREVIOUS LITERARY TRADITION

What Is to Be Done? was not written in a vacuum, but operates within the existing literary tradition, both Western and Russian. At the most basic level this is obvious in the direct references to preexisting literature given within the text of the novel. There are direct quotations from the poetry of Goethe, Walter Scott, Kol'tsov, and others, which make up a very large portion of the winter picnic scene in chapter 5. Throughout the novel the names of numerous authors and literary works are cited, ranging from medieval authors (Saxo Grammaticus and Boccaccio) to the nineteenth-century Thackeray and Sand. The constant appearance of direct references to other literature, whatever their purpose may be in their immediate context, does much to remind the reader that *What Is to Be Done?* is a literary work self-consciously operating in an established tradition.

Among the Western literary works relevant to a discussion of *What Is to Be Done?* George Sand's *Jacques* is the most discussed in scholarship on Chernyshevskii.[43] Observers have long noticed that Sand's novel, in which the older husband commits suicide to leave his young wife free to marry her lover, must be a pretext for Chernyshevskii's novel. Chernyshevskii had read the novel and, as a youth, had been particularly enthralled by Sand. He retained an appreciation for Sand throughout his life. Thus, there can be little doubt that *Jacques* is an important precursor of *What Is to Be Done?* However, as Emily Klenin cautions us, between Sand's novel and Chernyshevskii's there was a long tradition of Sand's reception in Russia that must be accounted for. Klenin stresses that Chernyshevskii is reacting not merely to *Jacques* itself but to *Jacques* through the prism of its Russian reception and response in such works as Druzhinin's *Polinka Saks*, Avdeev's *Podvodnyi kamen'*, and Herzen's *Who Is to Blame?* She correctly cautions against viewing *What Is to Be Done?* as a mere transposition of *Jacques* to Russian soil and argues that the references to *Jacques* contained in *What Is to Be*

Done? are a false, outer layer designed to mislead. Finally, there are other Sandian novels, Klenin argues, that are more relevant for the study of *What Is to Be Done?* such as *La Comtesse de Rudolstadt.*[44]

Chernyshevskii was also well read in English literature and utilizes many of the narrative devices of English writers, particularly those of Sterne, Thackeray, and Dickens.[45] For example, Brodskii and Sidorov argue that Chernyshevskii borrows the technique of "laying bare the device" from Sterne's fiction.[46] Likewise, Iurii Steklov suggested that Dickens's novel *Our Mutual Friend* was a direct model of *What Is to Be Done?* because it has the same artistic formation, dialogue, and psychological analysis.[47] Perhaps most relevant, however, is Thackeray's novel *Vanity Fair*, echoes of which abound in *What Is to Be Done?* Rudenko argues that *What Is to Be Done?* directly orients itself on *Vanity Fair,* which is most evident in the former novel's parodic foreword.[48] In addition, Chernyshevskii utilizes a formal composition similar to *Vanity Fair* in his novel, where there is nothing of the traditional hero in the main characters and there is even argument over who is the main character.[49] Likewise, similar to Thackeray, Chernyshevskii displaces from the center what should be the high point in a traditional novel (Lopukhov's fake suicide) and instead gives the reader the purely episodic figure of Rakhmetov, who plays almost no role in the novel's plot. *Vanity Fair* also seems to be the main prototype for the kind of framed narrative found in *What Is to Be Done?*[50]

Chernyshevskii's motivation for using the models provided by English literature has sometimes been interpreted as nonliterary. Reinhartz, for example, argues that Chernyshevskii uses the English Victorian model because it lends itself so easily to didacticism.[51] In other words, Chernyshevskii chose a form appropriate to an author who is by temperament a social activist, not a writer of fiction. In his analysis, Rudenko is more detailed but comes to an essentially similar conclusion.[52] For this interpretation to be valid, however, one would expect a large amount of blatant didacticism in the novel. Yet there is remarkably little.[53] Moreover, much of the space taken up by the devices derived from the English writers is devoted not to social commentary but to meta-narrative, to the discussion of the nature of literature. In effect, Chernyshevskii uses the models provided by his English predecessors as a frame of reference for a very literary discussion.[54]

The Russian literary tradition, no less than the Western one, also functions as an important predecessor for *What Is to Be Done?* In creating a novel that employs and yet breaks with literary convention, Chernyshevskii follows an established Russian tradition. *What Is to Be Done?* is an idiosyncratic novel, but it is far from the first such novel in Russian literature. Pushkin's *Eugene Onegin,* Lermontov's *Hero of Our Time,* and Gogol's *Dead Souls* had long preceded Chernyshevskii in this regard. Chernyshevskii does utilize specific narrative devices from each of those novels, but the main feature he takes from those writers is the very concept of the idiosyncratic novel. Chernyshevskii constructs his novel in such a deliberate and self-conscious manner that only crude and ridiculous imitations can result from any attempt to follow the model. As Pushkin's novel in verse remains a unique phenomenon in Russian literature, so too does *What Is to Be Done?*[55]

Like any other Russian writer of the period, Chernyshevskii was engaged in a dialogue, if not a polemic, with his contemporaries. A simple comparison of the titles of Herzen's *Who Is to Blame?* and Chernyshevskii's novel demonstrates this fact. Moreover, Chernyshevskii makes his own contribution to the theme of the love triangle as developed by Herzen and Druzhinin. However, the question of Chernyshevskii's polemic with Turgenev has been the best discussed in the criticism. Briefly stated, most scholars have tended to interpret *What Is to Be Done?* as largely, if not entirely, intended as an ideological retort to Turgenev's *Fathers and Sons.* Chernyshevskii found the depiction of the nihilists inadequate and slanderous, it is assumed, so he wrote his own novel to combat Turgenev's lie and to provide a positive portrait of the younger generation.[56]

As we have seen, there is serious doubt about this interpretation. It is true that numerous elements, such as Kirsanov's name and the reference to cutting up frogs, in *What Is to Be Done?* point to Turgenev's *Fathers and Sons.*[57] However, that novel is not singled out. The very title of Chernyshevskii's novel seems more to be oriented at an earlier Turgenev novel, *On the Eve,* particularly Elena's question "What is there to do in Russia?"[58] Other elements, such as the subtitle *First Love and Legal Marriage,* indicate that Turgenev's work as a whole is involved. But those individual elements, present though they are, do not constitute the essence of Chernyshevskii's novel. To a large degree they are mere decoration. Turgenev's *Fathers and Sons* is very much relevant when reading *What Is to Be Done?* but the latter novel is not constructed around a polemic with it.[59] Not only are the plot situations far different, but Chernyshevskii is also engaged in many polemics at once, not just with Turgenev.

Chernyshevskii engaged in a polemic with two other giants of the nineteenth century: Dostoevskii and Tolstoi. The polemic with Tolstoi, however, has often been missed by observers and has led to some extremely harsh evaluations of *What Is to Be Done?* For example, it is sometimes argued that Chernyshevskii was essentially indifferent to the family, or was even antifamily. Much has been made of the lack of children in the novel. E. H. Carr, for example, berates Chernyshevskii for not having more children in the novel.[60] Likewise, Kathryn Feuer argues that Chernyshevskii pushes children to the side in *What Is to Be Done?*[61] The interpretation that sees Chernyshevskii as somehow opposed to or as grossly negligent in ignoring children is an old one. Chernyshevskii's contemporaries, Afanasii Fet and Vasilii Botkin, stated about the novel that "children are not assumed."[62]

N. Solov'ev claimed that because Chernyshevskii's theory did not presuppose children, it preaches debauchery.[63] In short, Chernyshevskii's opponents have long used the lack of children in the novel as proof that it is a sermon for debauchery, for the lack of need for marriage, family, and, of course, children.[64] Is there a paradox here, as Feuer argues, in that Chernyshevskii, who was himself a notably devoted parent, could be so dismissive of children in his "theory"?[65] Or is there a more literary explanation to the lack of children in the novel?

The answer to the question lies in Chernyshevskii's views on the women's question. By means of *What Is to Be Done?* he polemicizes with preceding Russian literature and the conservative stance it had taken regarding women. Chernyshevskii's predecessors had generally taken the position that biology is destiny and viewed women only in terms of the traditional roles of wife and mother, which were the posited goals for all women. Joe Andrew has demonstrated quite well how *What Is to Be Done?* sets out to subvert many of the traditional roles and stereotypes allotted to women, as well as their traditional plots. He argues that *What Is to Be Done?* polemicizes with the conservative stance taken by Turgenev in his fiction, particularly *On the Eve.*[66] Andrew's arguments have merit but do not exhaust the possible sources of Chernyshevskii's displeasure with his predecessors. Tolstoi's *Family Happiness* (1859) is perhaps the text that Chernyshevskii had in mind more than any other.

That *What Is to Be Done?* directly recalls *Family Happiness* is revealed in the similarity in abstract conversations that take place in both works. In *Family Happiness,* when Sergei Mikhailich approaches the subject of his love for Mar'ia Aleksandrovna, he resorts to an abstract formulation in which to protect himself: "Just imagine the existence of a man—let us call him A—who has left youth far behind, and of a woman whom we may call be B, who is young and happy and has seen nothing as yet of life or the world. . . . But he forgot that B was so young, that life was still all a May-game to her."[67] Sergei Mikhailich continues the use of this abstract formulation in his conversation with Mar'ia Aleksandrovna. In the "Theoretical Conversation" Lopukhov resorts to a similar formulation, referring to the participants in the abstract, thus veiling the true nature of his discussion with Kirsanov. He even resorts to the terminology of A and B to get a point across (356). And, in what may be a direct thrust at Tolstoi, Chernyshevskii subverts Tolstoi's situation by having Lopukhov use that formulation as part of his attempt to suggest a ménage à trois, something absolutely abhorrent to Tolstoi's militant moralism.

The real ire caused by *Family Happiness* can be found in its story of the heroine's development. As she matures, Mar'ia Aleksandrovna recognizes the falseness of the other options available to women. By the end of the work she willingly embraces the traditional role of faithful wife and mother: "That day ended the romance of our marriage; the old feeling became a precious irrecoverable remembrance; but a new feeling of love for my children and the father of my children laid the foundation of a new life and a quite different happiness; and that life and happiness have lasted to the present time."[68] That Tolstoi intended to convey the message that a woman's happiness lies only in the role of wife and mother is hardly in doubt. That Chernyshevskii found such a message repugnant is also hardly in doubt. It is this context that explains the lack of emphasis on children in Chernyshevskii's novel. Chernyshevskii was engaged in an intense polemic with traditional stereotypes regarding women; one can hardly expect him to have repeated the very stereotype he found so repugnant. Thus, there are no odes to motherhood in *What Is to Be Done?* However, it should be stressed that motherhood is not forgotten in the novel. After three years of marriage to Kirsanov, Vera Pavlovna does have a child, Mitya (350). Likewise, by the end of the novel, Katerina Polozova has a child from her marriage to Lopukhov (431). Although mentioned, motherhood is simply not dwelled upon in detail and is not offered as the end-all of a woman's existence. The polemical thrust of this fact becomes clear in the reference to Katerina Polozova's son. The reader learns of the existence of this child only when Polozova states, "I feel much better about my son" (431). After this statement the narrator inserts the sarcastic parenthetical statement "Obviously she has a son," obviously directed at conventional literary expectations. Thus, Chernyshevskii's novel must not be taken as having a bias against children or even the family unit. Chernyshevskii seeks not to abolish but to preserve marriage and family, albeit on a new, nonpatriarchal basis.[69] In what might be interpreted as a strain of conservatism, it is no accident that both Vera Pavlovna's son and Polozova's are born in wedlock, reaffirming the family structure.[70] What separates the families of the new people from those of the old is that the new families are founded on love, freedom of choice, and the independence of each participant, and thus, at least implicitly, are happier.

It is commonly accepted that Dostoevskii's *Notes from the Underground* was written as a direct response to *What Is to Be Done?* However, the literary exchange between the two writers had begun earlier. For example, in *What Is to Be Done?* there are direct references to an earlier work by Dostoevskii, *Uncle's Dream.* In Dostoevskii's work there is a predecessor of Chernyshevskii's Mar'ia Alekseevna, one Mar'ia Aleksandrovna. In both stories the respective Mar'ias are less than savory characters and both have weak, ineffectual husbands. A most striking similarity is that both female tyrants are described as poets.[71] Regarding his Mar'ia, however, Dostoevskii's narrator says: "I may as well confess in advance to a slight weakness for Mar'ia Aleksandrovna. I had intended to write something in the manner of a eulogy to that magnificent lady and to represent the whole business in the form of a playful letter to a friend. . . . But since I have no such friend and suffer, what is more, from a certain congenital literary shyness, my composition has remained in my desk drawer."[72] Whereas Dostoevskii's narrator quite consciously fails to provide the eulogy (*pokhval'noe slovo*) for his negative character, Chernyshevskii's narrator does precisely that, devoting three pages (167–69) to explaining, though not forgiving, Mar'ia Alekseevna's behavior.[73] It is possible that this obvious response to his literary work, as much as any ideological disagreements he may have had, provoked Dostoevskii to action in *Notes from the Underground.*

In constructing *What Is to Be Done?* Chernyshevskii quite consciously subverts many of the plot devices and themes of his literary predecessors. This subversion begins at the level of genre. *What Is to Be Done?* displays a remarkable lack of concern for generic purity, which may owe something to Lermontov's *Hero of Our Time.* As U. A. Gural'nik states, "no Russian writer cared so little about the generic purity of his works as Chernyshevskii."[74] Within the text of *What Is to Be Done?* Chernyshevskii inserts elements of the contemporary adventure (*avantiurnyi*) novel, personal letters, diaries, a conventional love story, a tale of a virtuous prostitute, a modern-day saint's life, and other elements of medieval literature. Likewise, vastly different stylistic elements are combined in the novel, from scientific discourse to obvious biblical imagery; from detailed, somewhat dry description of Vera Pavlovna's sewing co-op to the dithyrambic discourse of her dreams. This results in a work that is anything but a model of stylistic purity and gives proof to Bakhtin's notion of the novel as a combinatory genre.[75] Thus, at first glance *What Is to Be Done?* seems to be a mass of different, often irreconcilable materials.[76] However, the mixture of varying, even incompatible elements is done in a highly conscious manner with the intention of subverting canonical forms of literature and training a new, more sophisticated type of reader. N. Naumova sums up Chernyshevskii's stance in *What Is to Be Done?* quite well when she argues: "*What Is to Be Done?* has a martial, polemical character not only in its content but in its artistic structure which itself is deeply rich in content. It is not merely an innovative work. It is written as if to rupture the fixed novelistic forms from within. . . . This work is a new type both in form and content."[77] As an example of this rupture Naumova cites the love *siuzhet.* For any other novelist Vera's finding full love would be the end of the novel, but for Chernyshevskii it is merely a point of departure, the beginning of a new cycle of development.[78]

Chernyshevskii begins the novel in medias res. In the first two mini-chapters the reader is presented with the mystery of the man who has seemingly committed suicide and his action's consequences. The action is presented in a mysterious manner, with the gentleman concerned remaining unnamed. At the most superficial level this functions to attract the reader's attention. Such a beginning is a *zaviazka* taken from the contemporary adventure novel and is purely parodic. Chernyshevskii does not seek to imitate the adventure novel but uses certain elements of it to stress its stereotypicality.[79] Lest the reader miss the point, the narrator lays bare the device in the so-called foreword: "I employed the conventional ruse of a novelist: I began my tale with some striking scenes taken from the middle or the end, and I shrouded them with mystery. . . . Since this is only my first novel, you haven't yet formed an opinion of my literary talents. . . . My name could not have attracted you. So I was obliged to bait my hook with striking scenes. Don't condemn me for it: you deserve all the blame. It's your own simpleminded naïveté that compelled me to stoop to such vulgarity"(47).[80] In an attempt to play with the conventions of the literature of his day, Chernyshevskii, following Sterne and Pushkin, purposely introduces the foreword well after the action has begun.[81] By beginning the novel in such a manner, Chernyshevskii immediately signals to the reader that a polemic with traditional, conventional literature has begun.

In addition to exposing the triteness of certain plots, Chernyshevskii subverts the traditional situations with an eye to saying something new. For example, in *What Is to Be Done?* the story of a young girl (Vera Pavlovna) being forced into marriage against her will, but saved by marriage to a man of her own choosing (Lopukhov), occupies much of the first two chapters. Such a theme was hardly new in Russian literature and was quite clichéd by Chernyshevskii's time.[82] Pomialovskii's *Molotov* was still fresh in the minds of the Russian reading public. In a typical story a pair of lovers go through many obstacles and trials but eventually overcome them and are married, after which the work traditionally ends. Chernyshevskii, however, does not simply repeat this traditional structure but alters it. In contrast to the numerous, extended difficulties of the typical plot, Chernyshevskii has the conflict resolved comparatively easily and, more important, early in the novel, adding considerable space to the couple's relationship after the marriage.[83] Thus, what had previously been a conflict, strong enough to form the basis of an entire literary work, by no means constitutes the essence of *What Is to Be Done?* but is merely one among its many elements.[84]

After that trite plot has been exhausted and dismissed, Chernyshevskii incorporates another, namely the rather banal plot of the love triangle. He polemicizes with the traditional literary depiction of love triangles, in both Western and Russian literature, as something inherently tragic, harmful.[85] The models that Chernyshevskii may have had most in mind are George Sand's *Jacques* and Herzen's *Who Is to Blame?* In Sand's *Jacques,* for example, the hero of the title realizes that his younger wife is in love with another and commits suicide to free her, staging it as an accident to spare her the guilt.[86] In this case, the love triangle has led to particularly disastrous consequences. Likewise, by the end of Herzen's novel, all three participants in the love triangle are ruined beyond repair: Beltov has left the town where he intended to be useful, Dmitrii Iakovlevich has sunk into drunkenness, and Liubov' Aleksandrovna is in a state of decline.[87] Despite whatever cultural, ideological, or poetic differences that existed among authors, works treating the love triangle, especially Russian literary works, consistently finished with a tragic ending for all.[88]

That Chernyshevskii would find such a repetitive pattern annoying should not be surprising. As we have seen, he had denounced monotony in literary production and argued for an expansion of the boundaries of art, and, correspondingly, some variety. Likewise, Chernyshevskii also showed himself to be an ardent foe of the traditional concept of the tragic. While opposed to the concept of the tragic because of its roots in idealist philosophy, Chernyshevskii was also displeased with it because it gave rise to monotony in art.[89] As Mathewson states, for Chernyshevskii "tragic 'rules' are harmful because they offer only a single mold into which a countless number of human situations must be forced."[90] Thus, Chernyshevskii has two things in mind when taking on the traditional plot of the love triangle: to provide some variety and to put an end to tragic endings.

In *What Is to Be Done?* the reader is presented with what seems to be a very traditional plot situation. A young woman has fallen in love with someone other than her husband with no happy solution apparent. The situation seems wrought with the potential for tragedy. The penetrating analysis of the situation provided by Lopukhov in his deliberations and by Vera Pavlovna's third dream seem to lead the reader to the inevitable, unhappy climax, and the reader knows from the beginning of the novel that some amount of unhappiness is forthcoming: a weeping Vera Pavlovna is given to the reader in the second minichapter at the beginning of the novel. Yet, the climax that has been building for so long is almost ignored in the middle of the novel, where it belongs. The events on the Liteinyi Bridge are referred to only obliquely. Moreover, despite some initial unhappiness by Vera Pavlovna, after reading the note provided by Rakhmetov, she is quite relieved and immediately begins her happy life with Kirsanov. By all accounts, the participants of the love triangle recover rather quickly from the experience and find greater happiness than they have ever known. In a final gesture that flaunts the traditional plotline, when Lopukhov returns to Russia and subsequently remarries, the two couples settle down next to each other in complete amicability. No residue of pain lingers from the love triangle. As Emily Klenin correctly argues, Chernyshevskii has stood the tradition on its head.[91] Moreover, in creating this new plotline for the love triangle, Chernyshevskii is careful to construct the novel on what George Lukács calls polemical self-irony. That is, what seems to be a conflict or a catastrophe (Lopukhov's "suicide," for example), turns out to be a comedy.[92]

In contrast to his literary predecessors, Chernyshevskii does not construct *What Is to Be Done?* entirely around the conflict of the love triangle.

Rather it is introduced, developed, and solved in a mere chapter, albeit the longest one. The sufferings and trauma of the protagonists, though referred to, are not given too much space, nor are they extended into a great conflict.[93] Finally, in contrast to conventional literature, *What Is to Be Done?* does not conclude with resolution (or nonresolution) of the love triangle, but continues with two more full chapters devoted to the further development of the protagonists.

Chernyshevskii does not attempt to deny that there are unfortunate events in human existence—tragedy, so to speak. But although such unfortunate phenomena such as love triangles do occur, they need not be life-threatening, they need not be destructive.[94] Chernyshevskii attempts to show his reader that people can and do recover from unfortunate situations: not everyone commits suicide, lapses into drunkenness, or dies a consumptive death. Chernyshevskii also attempts to show that if a person is in a bad match, it is correctable. In short, for Chernyshevskii, tragedy is not inherent in human life, nor in human art.[95] Rather, the emphasis on the tragic nature of the love triangle is due solely to stale patterns that have entrenched themselves in literary production. Chernyshevskii opposes, both in theory and in poetic practice, this distortion of human life according to a rigid, preconceived pattern and argues for the liberation of both human life and human art from the shackles imposed upon it.[96] That Chernyshevskii touched upon something important is revealed by the critical reaction to this issue. Among his contemporaries, Nikolai Strakhov criticized the novel precisely for its handling of the love triangle, arguing that it is solved too easily.[97] Among twentieth-century scholars, G. Žekulin finds Chernyshevskii's treatment of the love plot lacking because he does not adequately develop the traditional conflict inherent in such a situation.[98] Both Strakhov and Žekulin view *What Is to Be Done?* as somehow devoid of narrative interest because the love conflict is solved too easily and, implicitly, does not end tragically, ignoring the fact that a character who is driven to fake a suicide is evidence of anything but ease. Moreover, the plot does provide narrative interest, particularly in its novel handling of a traditional situation. In short, both critics criticize the novel from the very point of view against which Chernyshevskii directed his polemical thrust. Their irritation with *What Is to Be Done?* on this ground serves only to reveal that Chernyshevskii indeed created something new that broke with the traditional boundaries of literary production.

Finally, Chernyshevskii also inserts smaller parodies of conventional literature into the text of *What Is to Be Done?* A prime example is the brief story told by Nastas'ia Kriukova (chapter 3, section 14). Kriukova, a reformed prostitute, relates to Vera Pavlovna (and the reader) the story of her relationship with Kirsanov. At first glance this tale is flat, dry, and boring. It hardly stirs great feelings in the reader because of the utter banality of the situation. That, however, is precisely the point. The tale of the reformed fallen woman, and, especially, the tale of the heroine dying of consumption were already clichéd in Chernyshevskii's time. The narrator alludes to such banality when he comments on Kriukova's situation, stating that "her end was fast approaching" (228).[99] The narrator uses the term *razviazka* (LP 163–64), which, although not exclusively a literary term, has the literary "denouement" as its primary meaning.[100] Moreover, the triteness of the tale's plot is furthered by the narrator's calling attention to the device of deus ex machina; that is, to the accidental circumstance of Kirsanov's and Kriukova's reunion (228). By inserting this small tale within the novel, Chernyshevskii shows the banality of such a plot but does not give it too much space, which would destroy his own work.

DIGRESSIONS, NARRATOR, AND READER

Any plot summary of *What Is to Be Done?* necessarily overlooks one of the most important aspects of the novel: the narrative digressions from the love *siuzhet,* which are almost as prevalent as the actual story. The stylized images presented in the digressions are so forceful that they almost form a second story on their own.[101] However, the narrative digressions do not at all hinder the reader's perception of the novel. Rather, in all the disparate material that makes up *What Is to Be Done?* the narrator's overt presence in the digressions is a unifying principle that provides a consistent point of view to draw the work together as a whole.[102]

On occasion the digressions become so far removed that they seem to escape the narrator's control. Chernyshevskii inserts such digressions into the novel to lay bare the device.[103] For example, in chapter 2, section 7, the narrator engages in what seems to be a long, serious discussion in which he mentions Napoleon, Metternich, and others. Moreover, the narrator seems to engage in some very serious discussion of the process of world history and the importance of deception in it. He even makes the high-sounding statement that "that's the whole secret of world history" (110).[104] However, the narrator immediately undercuts this when he says "But there's really no need to delve into world history here. We're telling a tale, so let's get on with it" (110).[105] This last statement both undercuts the import of the discussion of world history and lays bare the device of the narrative digression. This technique continues to be used throughout the novel, for example, when Chernyshevskii inserts the word *digression* into one of the subtitles: "A Digression on Bluestockings." And, the narrator again calls attention to the device when he states, "This conversation about bluestockings has been very useful for the perspicacious reader (who is one himself), but it's taken me away from my account of how Vera Pavlovna spends her days now" (352–53).[106]

An important component of *What Is to Be Done?* is the overt presence of the narrator throughout the text. It is in the foreword that the narrator first introduces himself as the purported author, breaking the string of pure third-person narration.[107] He introduces himself by means of a conversation with his readers—a friendly female reader and a hostile male one:

> "The subject of this work is love, the main character is a woman; that's fine, even if the work itself is not that good," says the female reader.
>
> "That's true," I reply. (47)[108]

The narrator continues his conversation with his public, referring to himself as the actual author of the novel: "Since this is only my first novel, you haven't yet formed an opinion of my literary talents. . . . My name could not have attracted you" (47).[109]

The narrator does not limit such self-referential statements only in the foreword, but goes on at length, continually referring to himself as "I." This sets the stage for an overt presence throughout the remainder of the novel. The narrator continually refers to himself and his thoughts, feelings, and experiences, and engages in long digressions that have very little to do with the story at hand. In many cases these do nothing to further the plot but serve as a device to slow the tempo of the text. For example, the narrator recounts the experience of a fire he saw as a boy: "I remember how frightened I was when, as a twelve-year-old child who'd never seen a fire, I was suddenly awakened by the very loud noise of a general fire alarm. . . . I shook feverishly. . . . From that time on I knew that if one is afraid of a large fire, then one must run toward it and work very hard; one will no longer be afraid" (348).[110] Although Chernyshevskii's narrator attempts to lure the reader into identifying him as the actual author, it can never be forgotten that the image of the author in *What Is to Be Done?* is very much a literary construct and cannot be identified with the actual biographical author.[111]

In conjunction with the continual references to himself, the narrator claims to be very close to the characters, whom he says he knows personally. On one occasion the narrator addresses Vera Pavlovna as a close, dear friend, using the affectionate diminutive Verochka. In this instance he acts as if she can hear him and as if the two are in dialogue with each other (103–5). On another occasion, he claims to have her permission to relate her story (89). In commenting on Vera Pavlovna's decision to study medicine, the narrator claims that she is one of the first women that he knew of to do this (348). Likewise, in his account of Rakhmetov's history, the narrator relates an incident in which he made Rakhmetov's personal acquaintance (284–87).[112] Thus, although he never directly participates in the action of the plot, the narrator is a constant presence that establishes an atmosphere of close intimacy. N. A. Verderevskaia describes this device quite well, stating that it is a rare event when "the author is present in the work not as a storyteller-narrator, but as a personality, who knows the heroes intimately and stands between them and the reader. Not taking part in the action, but standing as if off to the side (the narration is from the third not the first person), the author keeps for himself the right to commentary, confidential conversation with the reader, and evaluation of the events and the heroes."[113] This device, moreover, creates the illusion that the characters of the novel are indeed real, living human beings whom he is describing, making the events of the novel all the more believable.

In constructing such a narrator, Chernyshevskii is, of course, drawing upon the model established by Pushkin in *Eugene Onegin.*[114] In so doing, Chernyshevskii borrows several of the key characteristics of Pushkin's work: the narrator claims to know the characters personally and engages in long digressions from the main narration in which he directly addresses the reading public. In many respects Chernyshevskii's novel is quite different from Pushkin's novel in verse. The digressions in *Eugene Onegin* are lyric, whereas Chernyshevskii's are publicistic.[115] However, the overlap between the two cannot be ignored.

Finally, the reader quickly learns that the narrator is not to be trusted entirely. In keeping with the principle that things are not always what they seem in the novel, Chernyshevskii's narrator often states quite the opposite of the actual state of affairs. For example, in his discussion of Lopukhov and Kirsanov, the narrator states that they are basically the same: "When I spoke of Lopukhov, it was difficult to distinguish him from his closest friend, and I was unable to say anything about him which could not also be said about Kirsanov. All that the perspicacious reader can really discover from the following list of Kirsanov's characteristics will be a repetition of the description of Lopukhov" (208).[116] However, in the description that follows he continually enumerates the differences that exist between them, thus belying his previous statement. For example, the narrator asks the question, "What sort of man was Lopukhov?"[117] and proceeds to answer it. After providing a small discussion of Lopukhov's education, the narrator turns to Kirsanov. In spite of his statement that the two can barely be distinguished from one another, he begins his description of Kirsanov's education with the phrase "It was different with Kirsanov" (209).[118] Lest the reader miss the point, Chernyshevskii's narrator openly plays with the fact that he cannot be trusted. For example, the narrator responds to the perspicacious reader's charge of immorality thus: "'Much more immoral,' I reply. And no one knows whether I'm telling the truth or making fun of the perspicacious reader" (329).[119] This statement demonstrates that the narrator is aware (as is the author, of course) that he has been speaking in double-talk throughout much of the novel, thus alerting the reader that caution must be taken in accepting any statement as literal.

In addition to the stylized image of the author, Chernyshevskii introduces that of the reader (or readers).[120] It is first introduced in the foreword, where two distinct images of the reader emerge: there is the friendly female reader versus the hostile male one.[121] The female reader is far more kindly disposed to the narrator and vice versa. There is no hostility at all between the two and as a result, little space is actually devoted to the image of the female reader. However, the relationship between the image of the male reader and the narrator is adversarial and thus given far more attention. After the narrator notes that the female reader is correct in her estimation of the novel, the narrator immediately adopts a hostile stance toward the male one: "The male reader does not confine himself to such easy conclusions, since from birth man's intellectual capability is greater than woman's and also much better developed. . . . the male reader says: 'I know for a fact that the gentleman who committed suicide did not really commit suicide.' Seizing upon the phrase 'know for a fact,' I reply, 'You don't know it for a fact, because you haven't been told it yet. Why, you know nothing at all by yourself! You don't even know that in the way I started this work, I insulted you and humiliated you. You didn't know that, did you? Well, now you do!'" (47).[122]

The stylized image of the reader as introduced in the foreword remains a constant presence throughout the text of *What Is to Be Done?* Chernyshevskii's narrator continually addresses the reader and even engages in conversations with him. Considerable space within the novel is given to these addresses and, as a result, the image diverges into distinct types of readers. In all, three different, identifiable types of readers are discernible: the friendly reader, the neutral reader, and the hostile reader.[123]

The friendly reader receives the smallest amount of attention in the novel. Basically, the image of the friendly reader is the continuation of that of the female reader as introduced in the foreword. It is assumed that such a reader already understands what he or she needs to know, so that there is little need for the narrator to devote much attention to him or her. Indeed the narrator says as much:

> Yet there is among you, dear readers, a particular group of people—by now a fairly sizable group—which I respect. I speak arrogantly to the vast majority of readers, but to them alone, and up to this point I've been speaking only to them. But with the particular group I just mentioned, I would have spoken humbly, even timidly. There is no need to offer them any explanation. I value their opinion, but I know in advance that they're on my side. Good, strong, honest, capable people—you have only just begun to appear among us; already there's a fair number of you and it's growing all the time. If you were my entire audience, there'd be no need for me to write. If you did not yet exist, it would be impossible for me to write. But you're not yet my entire

audience, although some of you are numbered among my readers. Therefore, it's still necessary and already possible for me to write. (48–49)[124]

After this direct address, the friendly reader is given little space within the bounds of the novel. Because this reader and the narrator are like-minded people, there is no real need for the narrator to address him or her. However, the image of the friendly reader never quite goes away. From time to time the narrator refers to this reader, if only to say that there is no need to say anything to this reader: "My female reader and the common reader who doesn't go on at length about art already know the answer" (294).[125]

As can be seen from this last quotation, *What Is to Be Done?* contains a stylized image of the reader that can be best termed the neutral reader. In effect, this reader is the stylized image of the general reading public.[126] Despite the narrator's low opinion of the neutral reader's literary sophistication, the narrator is not hostile to him. Rather, the narrator treats this reader precisely as neutral and does his best to win him over to his side. It is this reader for whom the novel, the narrator claims, is written, to educate him and raise him to a higher level (48–49). Overt hostility is reserved for the third stylized image.

By far, the most prominent image of the reader is the third type: the hostile reader. The narrator is hostile to this reader from the very beginning, making no attempts to conceal his contempt. This technique was first developed by Chernyshevskii in his publicistic articles. There he creates a personification of his ideological opponents, with whom he argues.[127] This image, like so much else in the novel, is introduced in the foreword. This sets the tone for the rest of the novel, in which an adversarial relationship develops between the stylized images of the narrator and the so-called perspicacious reader.[128]

The perspicacious (*pronitsatel'nyi*) reader, as he is labeled by the narrator, is the stylized image of Chernyshevskii's ideological enemies. He is a philistine who embodies the views of Chernyshevskii's favorite whipping boy, the self-appointed defenders of art known as the aesthetes.[129] Throughout the novel, the narrator continually addresses the perspicacious reader in a most insulting manner and does his best to expose him.[130] Unlike the common or neutral reader, the perspicacious reader is treated as the self-appointed guardian of philistine tastes and aesthetic views. As such, the narrator never tries to educate or to win over the perspicacious reader, but rather to expose him to the general public for the intellectual fraud that he is. For example, the narrator says to the perspicacious reader, "It's not so hard to guess if you've even the least notion of art, about which you so love to blather" (294).[131] This hostility is taken to the extreme when the narrator relates the fact that he takes physical action against the perspicacious reader (323).

In his numerous digressions, including his conversations with the perspicacious reader, the narrator devotes considerable space, in some cases entire subsections, to the question of how and why the novel is being written and to the question of art in general.[132] In this respect Chernyshevskii clearly follows in the tradition of Gogol', whose novel *Dead Souls* both takes a polemic stance to conventional novels and self-consciously discusses that fact.[133] The numerous digressions in *What Is to Be Done?* are present in large part to make the reader a witness to how the novel is being created before his very eyes, as if in his presence.[134] The novel could easily be described as a masterpiece in the genre of the meta-novel. As Gary Saul Morson has described the novel, *What Is to Be Done?* consists of a constant alternation between narrative and meta-narrative, with the meta-narrative interrupting the narrative at key points.[135]

As part of this meta-narrative the narrator engages in statements directed at the aesthetic principles of the perspicacious reader and the aesthetes whom he represents. The narrator makes numerous one-liners in which he criticizes, with evident irony, his characters for some perceived failing. When describing Vera Pavlovna's singing, the narrator says, "Perhaps there was even a little too much feeling; it was a bit too unaesthetic" (66).[136] Likewise, the narrator, in describing Vera Pavlovna after her third year of marriage to Kirsanov, states that she still has many "unpoetic, unrefined, and unseemly habits" (349).[137] In addition to those one-liners, the narrator explicitly names the aesthetes as the target of his attacks. For example, he belittles the aesthetes by suggesting that they can relate to a young woman only in terms of how good she looks (125–26). Moreover, a favorite tactic of the narrator is to note that the way he has described his characters does not live up to contemporary aesthetic principles. When commenting on Katerina Polozova's and Beaumont's conversations, the narrator asks what sort of people they are and says that he is ashamed of himself, asking, "Can it be that my fate as a novelist consists in compromising all my heroes and heroines in the eyes of well-bred people?" (421).[138] Such statements occur throughout the text, never letting the reader forget that a polemic with the prevailing aesthetic norms forms an integral part of the text.

A large component of Chernyshevskii's meta-narrative polemic is built upon irony. Throughout the novel, Chernyshevskii's narrator seems to agree with the opinions of his opponents or of an inexperienced reader: "Most of the time Chernyshevskii at first affirms with deceptive seriousness exactly that which might first of all come into the inexperienced reader's head. But then he laughs at the fact that the latter swallowed the bait, and, as if laying bare the device, he explains the truth."[139] Likewise, Skaftymov notes that Chernyshevskii's favorite method is to seemingly agree with his opponent: "Chernyshevskii, just like Thackeray, pretends to speak against himself, taking the side of his opponent. But his approval is flagellation. His seeming patronage breathes with extraordinary contempt."[140] This fact is evident from the outset in the narrator's address to the general public in the foreword. For example, in the infamous "not one bit of talent" passage, the narrator seemingly agrees with future critics of the novel that he lacks any artistic talent (48). However, shortly after this seeming agreement with his opponent's views, the narrator states that he has talent, far more than those writers the public considers talented. The narrator has seemingly agreed with his enemies only to expose them later as frauds.[141]

The meta-narrative aspect of the novel first appears in the infamous foreword. There the narrator openly addresses the reading public, commenting on its low level of literary sophistication.[142] In so doing, the narrator makes explicit comments on how the novel will be written.[143] For example, the narrator confesses to his public that he "employed the conventional ruse of a novelist"[144] by beginning the novel with some "striking scenes taken from the middle or the end" (47).[145] Moreover, the narrator makes an explicit statement about how he will continue with the novel: "But now that you've fallen into my hands, I can continue the story as I see fit without further tricks. No mysteries lie ahead: you will always know the outcome of every situation at least twenty pages in advance. And to begin with, I shall even tell you the outcome of the entire novel: it will end happily, amidst wine and song. There will be neither striking scenes nor embellishments" (47–48).[146] Such commentary about how the novel will be written and why the narrator makes the choices he does appears throughout the text. The reader is never allowed to forget that this novel is a verbal artifice that is dependent upon the mood of its creator. For example, in discussing the outcome of Vera Pavlovna's unbearable situation in her family's household, the narrator says: "If I wanted to create powerful confrontations, I would provide a thunderous resolution for this predicament. In fact, it wasn't like that at all. If I wanted to entice you with uncertainty, I wouldn't be telling you now that nothing of the sort took place. But since I'm writing without setting any traps, I'll say in advance that there will be no thunderous confrontation; this predicament will be resolved without storm, thunder, or lightning" (87).[147] Paradoxically, however, many of the narrator's meta-narrative addresses have precisely the opposite effect. Although seemingly calling attention to the verbal artifice, such passages convey an impression that the main characters are indeed real people, not fictional ones. For example, in discussing the relationship between Mar'ia Aleksevna and Lopukhov, the narrator says: "Mar'ia Aleksevna's relations with Lopukhov verge on farce and show her in a comic guise. Both of these outcomes are decidedly unintended. If I had wanted to concern myself with what we usually call artistic merit, I would have concealed Mar'ia Aleksevna's relations with Lopukhov, the account of which lends an air of vaudeville to this part of the novel. It would have been very easy to conceal them" (119).[148] The references to vaudeville and the fact that this is a novel directly draw the reader's attention to the verbal artifice. However, at the same time, the narrator claims that Mar'ia Aleksevna has been put in a ridiculous position against his will. Commenting on this fact, he says: "But I'm recounting this affair the way it happened, rather than the way needed to establish my artistic reputation. As a novelist I very much regret that I wrote several pages in which I stooped to the level of vaudeville" (119).[149] In effect, the narrator is stating that he is relating real events over which he has no control. Thus, despite the references to the verbal artifice, this, in effect, is an assertion that reality is being dealt with, not a mere verbal artifice. The net result of this passage (and those like it) is actually to give the reader an even stronger impression that the characters are real, living human beings.

This paradox is quite similar to, if not borrowed from, Pushkin's *Eugene Onegin.* In *Eugene Onegin* the narrator claims to know the characters personally, giving the impression that they are real, living human beings and simultaneously calling attention to the verbal artifice of the work.[150] Chernyshevskii uses this dichotomy throughout *What Is to Be Done?* His narrator claims to know the characters personally and insists he is relating what really happened. Yet in the numerous meta-narrative addresses to the reader, the narrator consistently calls attention to the verbal artifice, never letting the reader forget that this is not reality.[151] It is the constant alternation of the illusion of reality followed by the smashing of that illusion that forms one of the organizing principles of *What Is to Be Done?*

THE QUESTION OF ARTISTIC DETACHMENT

The question of the relationship of the author to the main characters is one that has not been adequately explored. Generally, not only is it assumed that the narrator is actually Chernyshevskii, but that, moreover, the novel is one long paean of praise to the main characters and that they are mere mouthpieces for Chernyshevskii's views.[152] There is little doubt that part of Chernyshevskii's purpose in writing *What Is to Be Done?* was to give a positive portrayal of the younger generation, the so-called new people. Chernyshevskii did think highly of this group, respecting its energy and courage. However, Chernyshevskii did not worship this generation and never gave it a blanket endorsement.[153] The same may be said of *What Is to Be Done?* It is clear that the narrator, and also the actual author, sympathize with the three main characters. However, none of the characters is Chernyshevskii himself; rather, they appear as the bearers of an autonomous consciousness, and Chernyshevskii's narrator carefully guards against too close an identification with the characters.

The narrator adopts a slightly superior, condescending attitude toward the three main characters, Vera Pavlovna, Lopukhov, and Kirsanov.[154] He laughs at and mocks them on occasion, and also disagrees with them when he sees fit. The narrator displays a very patronizing attitude toward Lopukhov's and Kirsanov's materialism and utilitarianism, which he tolerates at best.[155] For example, the narrator flippantly refers to Lopukhov's and Kirsanov's devotion to science, especially their obsession with cutting up frogs:

> And so, in the name of their beloved science (they delight in abusing medicine, even though they devote all their efforts to it), they reject wealth, even prosperity, and, you see, they sit in hospitals making interesting scientific observations. They dissect frogs, cut open hundreds of corpses a year, and at the first opportunity they outfit themselves with a chemical laboratory. (92)[156]

> Now they were both working on their doctoral dissertations, using up an enormous quantity of frogs. (93)[157]

Though obviously having some fun at his character's expense, the narrator's tone is not hostile. Yet this is not at all a straightforward ode to the glories of science. The narrator's use of humor prohibits the reader from interpreting the passage as a call to arms. Quite to the contrary, the passage reflects the rather subtle criticism by Chernyshevskii of the younger generation's narrow obsession with science, physiology in particular.

The fact that the narrator esteems and values Lopukhov and Kirsanov is never in question. He makes many statements in which he obviously approves of their decency, honesty, steadfastness, and so forth. There seems to be no reason to distrust the narrator when he says: "Because I don't belong to this type, I can express my unabashed admiration for it. Unfortunately, I'm not praising myself when I say that these people are truly splendid" (211–12).[158] However, the narrator is aware of Lopukhov's shortcomings and even laughs at them. For example, the narrator is careful to note that Lopukhov is a rather dry, cold person: "In addition to his friends and two or three professors who'd recognized in him the makings of a good scientist, he met only the families of those young people he tutored. But he only 'met' the families: he avoided any intimacy like the plague and treated all the members of the family coldly, except for his young pupils (93–94).[159] The narrator's gentle mockery of the younger generation, the male characters in particular, reaches its apogee in the narrator's comments on the men's tendency to learned discourse. In siding with the female characters' pursuit of enjoyment over the male characters' propensity to learned discourse,[160] the narrator clearly indicates that not all is praiseworthy in the new people.

Most observers have concluded that the views of the characters must necessarily reflect Chernyshevskii's own views.[161] It is simply assumed the main characters are merely Chernyshevskii's mouthpieces. For example, Marcia Morris argues that *What Is to Be Done?* "can thus be said to be an extreme example of the novel which reflects only its author's own views."[162]

Analyzing the novel in this manner, most scholars have generally assumed that Chernyshevskii is preaching materialism, utilitarianism, utopian socialism, even positivism by this novel. Yet, as Franco Venturi noted, such views do not at all match those that Chernyshevskii held at the time he wrote the novel.[163] Could the identification of the characters' views as Chernyshevskii's own be false?

To help solve this problem, it must be remembered that Chernyshevskii has also been credited as an important precursor of the concept of the polyphonic novel. In his *Problems of Dostoevsky's Poetics,* Mikhail Bakhtin discusses Chernyshevskii and his plans for an "objective" novel. Bakhtin uses one of the variants of the foreword to Chernyshevskii's unfinished novel, *Povesti v povesti.* There Chernyshevskii discusses his intention to write a novel in which the author's actual views would be hidden and the characters would speak for themselves:

> To write a novel without love—without a single female character—is a very difficult thing. But I felt the need to try my strength at a task even more difficult: to write a purely objective novel, in which there would be no trace not only of my personal attitudes, but also of my personal sympathies. In Russian literature there is not a single such novel. *Onegin* and *A Hero of Our Time* are unabashedly subjective things. *Dead Souls* contains no portrait of the author nor portraits of his acquaintances, but the personal sympathies of the author have certainly been incorporated; they are in fact the source of that strong impression the novel produces. It seems that for me, a man of strong and fixed convictions, the most difficult thing would be to write as Shakespeare wrote: he portrays people and life without saying what he himself thinks on the questions that are resolved by his characters in a way appropriate for each. Othello says "yes," Iago says "no," Shakespeare says nothing, he has no desire to state his love or lack of love for a "yes" or a "no." It is understood that I am speaking of the manner, and not of the strength, of the talent. . . . Try to discover whom I sympathize with and whom I don't. . . . You won't find out. . . . In *The Pearl of Creation* each poetic position is examined from all four sides—try to discover which opinion I sympathize with, which I do not. Try to discover how one point of view passes over into another completely incompatible with it. This is the true meaning of the title "The Pearl of Creation"—here, as in mother-of-pearl, are all the shades of colors in the rainbow. But as in mother-of-pearl all these shades slide by one another, and play against a background of snowy whiteness. It is thus to my novel that the lines of verse in the epigraph refer:
>
> Wie Schnee, so weiss,
> Und Kalt, wie Eis,
>
> The second line refers to me.
>
> There is "whiteness, like the whiteness of snow" in my novel, "but coldness, like the coldness of ice" in its author . . . to be cold, like ice, this was difficult for me, for a person who loves ardently what he loves. But I succeeded. Thus

> I see that I have the necessary power of artistic creativity to become a novelist. . . . My characters are very diverse in the expressions their faces must assume. . . . Think of each what you will: each says for himself: "The full right is on my side"—you be the judge of these conflicting claims. I do not judge. These characters praise one another, condemn one another—all that is none of my business.[164]

As can be seen quite clearly from this passage, Chernyshevskii was indeed quite capable of artistic detachment and, at least conceptually, was far ahead of most of his contemporaries.[165] As Bakhtin argues, Chernyshevskii is clearly groping toward a new structural form.[166] It is significant that this foreword was written shortly after Chernyshevskii finished writing *What Is to Be Done?*[167] Thus, unless one is willing to argue that he had a complete change of character overnight, it must be allowed that Chernyshevskii was quite capable of such a concept while he was writing *What Is to Be Done?*[168]

A close reading of *What Is to Be Done?* reveals much evidence that argues against a direct identification of the main characters' views with those of the narrator or of Chernyshevskii himself. For example, the narrator is quite careful to distance himself from the views expressed by Kirsanov. Although the narrator describes in detail Kirsanov's utilitarian deliberations regarding his love for Vera Pavlovna, he is always careful to stress that such utilitarian views are Kirsanov's, not his own, labeling them "Kirsanov's theory." Moreover, the narrator displays a somewhat mocking attitude toward Kirsanov's utilitarianism when he comments on Kirsanov's situation, saying "Besides, according to Kirsanov's theory, it shouldn't be painful, but even pleasant" (235).[169] Likewise, the narrator maintains his distance by his treatment of the vocabulary of his main characters. Key words from Lopukhov's vocabulary, such as "sacrifice [*zhertva*]" (155; LP 102),[170] or from Vera Pavlovna's, such as "cellar [*podval*]" (154; LP 102), are enclosed in quotations marks (*kavychki*) by the narrator, indicating that they are not his words but those of his characters.[171] The narrator consistently relates in this manner (at least on first usage) to the key vocabulary of the main characters. Chernyshevskii does this precisely so that there will not be too close an identification between his narrator and his main characters.[172]

Finally, the narrator stresses that he is of a different generation from the three main characters: "This type arose quite recently. It didn't exist yet during my time, though I'm not very old, perhaps not old at all. I myself couldn't develop in that way, since I grew up in a different era" (211).[173] This statement implies that they are the products of different eras and thus hold different worldviews to some degree. In addition, the narrator openly states that there is much that he does not approve of regarding the main characters: "There's much that I don't condone here. In fact, to tell you the truth, I don't condone any of it" (328).[174] This passage, it is true, does come in the context of the polemic with the perspicacious reader and therefore cannot be trusted totally. However, combined with other evidence in the novel, it is evident that there is a grain of truth in this statement. Thus, there cannot be a straightforward identification of the views of the narrator and those of the characters. Differences do indeed exist. When the characters express opinions on certain topics they are expressing their own views, not those of the narrator, nor those of the even more distant author.[175]

Not only does Chernyshevskii distance himself from his characters, but he clearly differentiates between his characters. That is, his characters are not identical in terms of their worldviews and opinions, but each is treated as an autonomous consciousness. His narrator states this much: "But just as Europeans among the Chinese seem to have one and the same face and one way of acting only in Chinese eyes, in fact there are incomparably more variations among Europeans than among the Chinese. So, too, in this new, apparently single type, the diversity of personalities develops into numerous varieties that differ from one another among themselves. There are all kinds: sybarites and ascetics, stern people and tender, and others, and others besides" (212).[176] In addition to these stated differences among the new people, throughout the novel the new people are engaged in a constant dialogue with another, often taking antithetical points of view. It is left to the reader to sift through this dialogic activity; there is no monologic statement by the author.

Besides placing markers designed to distance himself from his main characters, Chernyshevskii relies on certain techniques designed to let them speak in their own voice, to express their own autonomous consciousness. In addition to coining the term *interior monologue,* Chernyshevskii uses the technique in *What Is to Be Done?*[177] For example, in chapter 2, section 16, things are turned over entirely to Vera Pavlovna's interior monologue, in which she analyzes her situation and contemplates suicide:

> When you do throw yourself out a window, how fast you travel! It's as if you're flying instead of falling. It must be very nice. But then you hit the sidewalk—how hard it is! Is it painful? No, I doubt there's time enough to feel the pain. Still it's very hard. But that's for one brief moment; on the other hand, before that moment, there's the air—soft as a featherbed—and it parts so easily and gently. . . . Yes, that's lovely. . . .
>
> And then what? Everyone will stare—the skull's split open, the face is smashed, bloodied, and muddied. . . . No, if only you could spread some clean sand on the spot beforehand—but even the sand here is dirty. . . . No, I mean some of the cleanest, whitest sand: now that would be nice! Then your face wouldn't be so smashed. It would stay clean and wouldn't frighten anyone. (139)[178]

In this interior monologue Vera Pavlovna's thoughts spontaneously shift: the unbearable nature of her situation sparks thoughts of throwing herself out of the window, which in turn sparks thoughts of the beauty of free-falling, and so on.[179] There is no narrative intrusion here; rather the reader is left alone to view Vera Pavlovna's thought process, in which she jumps from thought to thought. This section provides a look into Vera Pavlovna's psychology and faithfully reflects what one would expect from a young girl in her situation.[180] Moreover, there is very little ideology present in this passage. Indeed, from the point of view of writing a propaganda novel, this passage is entirely superfluous. Its very existence casts considerable doubt that such is Chernyshevskii's intent.

As we have seen, *What Is to Be Done?* is a rich, literary text. The novel operates within an established literary tradition and is engaged in a dialogue with that tradition. It employs complicated narrative devices that add several layers of meaning to the text and require careful reading to decipher. Any attempt at interpreting the novel must account for that fact. This is not to argue that *What Is to Be Done?* is not political; it is very much so. But to ascertain its content, a more sophisticated approach to its form is required; it is not simply a transparent political tract disguised in the fictional form. By treating the novel as a simplistic how-to manual, for example, we would be forced to the ridiculous conclusion that Chernyshevskii preached for all husbands to feign suicide to free their wives to marry their lovers.[181] But when we recognize the novel's connection with the previous literary tradition, we realize that the novel's plot is not Chernyshevskii's prescriptive message to the world, but his contribution to the literary motif of the love triangle. With the need for a more sophisticated treatment in mind—that is, that *What Is to Be Done?* is indeed a literary work—I will now turn to the favorite theme of scholars regarding the novel: its ideational content.

Chapter Three

Ideational Content

THE WOMEN'S QUESTION

Chernyshevskii was a major figure in the development of the women's question in nineteenth-century Russia.[1] He developed his views on the women's question largely under the influence of Western figures such as George Sand. Chernyshevskii expressed his basic views early in his youth, when he stated the necessity to change relations between men and women: "In my opinion a woman occupies an unworthy place in the family. Any inequality disturbs me. A woman should be equal to a man. But when the stick has been bent in one direction for so long, one must bend it back the other way in order to straighten it out. Now, women are lower than men. Every decent man is obliged, in my opinion, to place his wife higher than himself—this temporary superiority is necessary for future equality" (1:444). Chernyshevskii lived by his convictions and structured his own marital life accordingly.[2] In his publicistic work Chernyshevskii did not often openly address the women's question, although he did produce one work, a review of "Notes on Women," which appeared in *Sovremennik* in 1854.[3] In it, Chernyshevskii objects to a new trend in European science that viewed women as inherently inferior to men and tackles directly the question of whether women are inherently intellectually inferior.[4] Chernyshevskii stresses that this question is unfairly posed because women do not receive the same education or possess the same social standing as men (16:281). Chernyshevskii boldly proclaims that the role of upbringing (*vospitanie*) is huge and that the essential intellectual and moral differences between men and women are minor. He goes on to state that "[w]e know for certain only that in all areas of activity which are equally open to men and women by social opinion, women display no less intelligence, character, genius than men" (16:281–82). Moreover, Chernyshevskii even argues that in some respects, women are superior to men and are prevented from reaching their potential by external circumstances (16:282). In spite of the trend of nineteenth-century science and its emphasis on physiology, Chernyshevskii's makes a bold statement: "[W]e say only that this natural intellectual difference between the sexes is insignificant in comparison with the influence that upbringing, social traditions and demands, and the difference in familial and social situation render on the development of the features of the female mind and character. And to determine exactly the boundaries of this influence is difficult now" (16:283). Finally, Chernyshevskii argues, "Regarding the opinion alleging that woman differs from man not only in intelligence, but is even lower than man in intelligence, it has long been rejected as the boasting of barbaric [*grubyi*] times, when the merit of a person was measured by physical strength" (16:283).

In *What Is to Be Done?* Chernyshevskii created a work where, throughout, the women's question is a burning one.[5] Indeed, Francis B. Randall argues that *What Is to Be Done?* "is a novel about women's emancipation."[6] The novel was received by the Russian youth as a manual to proper relations between the sexes. For young Russian women the novel was a revelation: "According to an official report of the censorship, many women ran away from their parental or conjugal home under the influence of the novel. They moved to the big cities and often to countries in Western Europe in search of employment, personal freedom, and education."[7] Several Russian women who would later play major roles in radical movements counted *What Is to Be Done?* as a decisive influence in their radicalization and in many ways consciously patterned themselves on the behavior of its leading characters.[8] Although Chernyshevskii was not the first to take up the women's question in Russia, he expanded the parameters of the discussion by linking women's liberation to the goal of the liberation of humanity as a whole.[9] In many respects it was Chernyshevskii who gave the women's question the pronounced, radical tone it was to have for the rest of the century.[10]

Previous scholarship has devoted substantial discussion to the feminist content of *What Is to Be Done?* Most of those analyses have tended to concentrate on the unconventional living arrangements of Vera Pavlovna's marriages or on passages in the novel in which the characters, especially Kirsanov, state certain opinions regarding women and their situation in society. What should be noted, however, is that for all its seeming radicalism regarding the women's question, for all the daring its author shows at many points, *What Is to Be Done?* is in many respects a traditional Russian novel. That is, Chernyshevskii operates within the well-established literary tradition in which women are almost always superior to men. From Liza and Erast in Karamzin's "Poor Liza," to Tat'iana and Onegin in Pushkin's *Eugene Onegin,* to Natal'ia Alekseevna and Rudin in Turgenev's *Rudin,* before *What Is to Be Done?* Russian literature was filled with morally superior and strong heroines and their weak, unworthy male counterparts. In many respects, *What Is to Be Done?* repeats that dichotomy. In almost every conceivable instance in the novel, women are stronger and more active than men, no matter what the milieu.[11]

The dichotomy between women and men can be found among even the minor characters. When Lopukhov asks Mertsalov to perform the wedding ceremony for Vera Pavlovna and himself, Mertsalov is at first hesitant, fearing the trouble that Vera Pavlovna's family might cause. It is only under the admonition of his wife, Natal'ia Andrevna, that Mertsalov overcomes his doubts and performs the ceremony. Afterward, in a confession of his own weakness and recognition of his wife's strength, he states: "Now I'm very glad that Natasha gave me such strong encouragement" (159).[12]

The division between women and men is also evident among the three main characters. Vera Pavlovna is obviously both the narrator's and the author's favorite character. Whereas the narrator often mocks Kirsanov and Lopukhov, he is much kinder and gentler in his treatment of Vera Pavlovna. Although it has been argued that Vera Pavlovna is continually being saved by male characters, it does not change the fact that she is, in effect, superior to them.[13] Foremost among Vera Pavlovna's qualities is her vitality, her capacity to act. Her male counterparts, for all their positive qualities, tend to be rather passive and react rather than act.[14] Vera Pavlovna, on the other hand, waits for nothing, taking matters directly into her own hands. It is she who undertakes the practical activity of setting up the sewing cooperative. As Lopukhov notes, it is Vera Pavlovna who puts into practice what the male characters only theorize about: "We all talk a lot but do nothing. You began thinking about all this after we did, but you resolved to get down to work sooner" (173).[15]

Again, in creating female characters that are superior to their male counterparts Chernyshevskii does nothing new, but follows an established Russian tradition. However, within those parameters Chernyshevskii's fiction marks a major shift in how the relations between the sexes are depicted. Whereas many of Chernyshevskii's predecessors (and successors) often depicted Russian men and women as almost polar opposites, destined never to find a happy union, Chernyshevskii's male and female characters are not that far apart. Differences, even major differences, do exist between the sexes, but that does not prevent the characters from forming happy, complementary unions. That is, the majority of Russian fiction prior to Chernyshevskii presented models of women whose moral superiority or strength of will bordered upon perfection, an extremely idealized image of woman. Male characters, in contrast, were morally bankrupt, hopelessly weak, or otherwise lacking. The gap between the two extremes was simply unbridgeable and happy unions were a rare event. In Chernyshevskii's novel, however, the gap is bridgeable. In this way, Chernyshevskii is kinder to his male characters. Although clearly inferior to Vera Pavlovna in several respects, Lopukhov and Kirsanov are decent men, worthy of the love of a woman; they are far from the weak-willed and useless figures so prominent among their literary predecessors. On the other hand, Vera Pavlovna is no ideal embodiment of virtue, serving as a source of inspiration for the male characters.[16] Rather, she is depicted as an autonomous being in her own right. What Chernyshevskii has done is to remove his female character from the pedestal of his predecessors, to remove the burden of terrible perfection and place her closer to her male counterparts. As a result, happy unions are possible between the male and female characters. Although Vera Pavlovna and Lopukhov must separate due to a mismatch, both are worthy of love and find it by the end of the novel.[17] It is this manner of depicting the relations between women and men, as much as any speech by a character or the living arrangements presented, that forms the essence of Chernyshevskii's contribution to the women's question.

It should be noted that *What Is to Be Done?* differs greatly from its literary predecessors in that it deals with the relations between men and women after marriage.[18] That is, much of preceding Russian literature, while of course paying lip service to the ideal of marriage, actually dealt very little with the life of a woman once she had married. Once she had achieved what was considered the end-all of her existence, her story was over.[19] In *What Is to Be Done?* however, Vera Pavlovna marries quite early in the novel, yet she continues to be the organizing pole of the narrative and her subsequent development is presented in considerable detail. The reader is presented with Vera Pavlovna's activity in the co-op, her decision to become a doctor, and so forth, all of which occur *after* her marriage to Lopukhov. Most of Vera Pavlovna's development, her maturation, comes precisely after she has married. Moreover, Vera Pavlovna continues to develop until the very end of the novel, perhaps indicating that a final point has not yet been reached. As Joe Andrew argues, Chernyshevskii's polemic thrust here is that "her marriage is not at all the end of her personal development, but the beginning. In other words, women remain of narrative interest even after they cease to be sexually available."[20]

LOVE

In the scholarly literature on both Chernyshevskii and *What Is to Be Done?* it has often been maintained that Chernyshevskii ignored or denied the importance of love, sex, and family. Chernyshevskii's oft-cited statement "Forget about them, those erotic questions!" is treated as evidence that he dismissed this aspect of human existence.[21] This statement, however, was uttered by Chernyshevskii in a highly specific, polemical context and in no way indicates his position regarding love.[22] Once it has been established that Chernyshevskii gave primacy to human emotions and intuition over rationality and abstract theorizing, it should not be surprising to find that the quintessential human emotion, love, forms a major element in the novel.[23] It is love that forms by far the most important positive content of *What Is to Be Done?*[24] The various subversive and ideological aspects of the novel, important as they may be, take second place to this all-important topic.[25] More important, the question of love explains much of the ideological content of the text. That is, Chernyshevskii's views on the women's question are very much tied to the belief that as long as women are held in an unequal position, neither men nor women will truly be able to love.[26] It is by no means an exaggeration to argue that, in many respects, love is what *What Is to Be Done?* is all about.[27]

Chernyshevskii follows very much in the tradition of previous Russian literature by using love as a metaphor. That is, the characters' worthiness is, in large part, measured by their ability to find successful love. By the end of the novel, the three main characters plus Katerina Polozova have proved themselves worthy of and useful to society. Because those four characters have been successful in finding love and sustaining it, the new people as a type are presented to the reader as strong and useful, therefore positive, in stark contrast to their literary predecessor, the superfluous man.[28] As Kathryn Feuer succinctly states, "reading through the great nineteenth-century Russian novels one finds that the test by which society is measured is the test of successful love between men and women. And no one makes the test more crucial than does Chernyshevsky."[29] However, Chernyshevskii is also concerned with the meaning of love, in and of itself. Love functions in the novel not merely as a necessary given for the plot, but as a burning question that engages both the characters and the narrator. Much of the novel is devoted to defining this essentially indefinable concept, with several of the characters presenting their own definitions of what constitutes love. Each of those definitions differs slightly, if not entirely, from the others. The interplay and clash between definitions is heightened by the participation of the narrator, who reveals himself to be most interested in that question.

The question of love first arises for Vera Pavlovna in regard to her mother's plans to marry her off to Storeshnikov. Here Vera Pavlovna is presented with a point of view that reduces love from a sublime emotion to a mere bargaining chip. Vera Pavlovna is given an example of this viewpoint in practice by her mother, who views other people and their feelings only in terms of financial gain. Even before her attempt to marry off Vera Pavlovna, Mar'ia Aleksevna has demonstrated her willingness to use the feelings of others to her own benefit (53–54). She is far more concerned with providing for her own future than she is with her daughter's happiness. The fact that her daughter does not love Storeshnikov and his utter lack of character matter not to Mar'ia Aleksevna. For Mar'ia Aleksevna and her kind, love, whether familial or erotic, is merely an unhealthy phenomenon that is to be avoided in oneself but exploited for financial gain in others.

Mar'ia Aleksevna offers Vera Pavlovna a practical example of the degradation of love. It is Julie who offers her a theoretical justification for it.

Although Julie seems to want to help Vera Pavlovna and even condemns Mar'ia Aleksevna, she actually does little more than suggest to Vera Pavlovna that she adopt her mother's outlook.[30] Julie reveals that she holds the same worldview as Mar'ia Aleksevna, stating that "life consists of prose and calculation" (74).[31] She suggests that Vera Pavlovna marry Storeshnikov and make him her slave. In effect, she tells Vera Pavlovna to follow in her mother's footsteps and dominate her husband. The question of love does not figure in Julie's deliberations for she too, by her own admission, is a corrupted woman (75).

In her first experience with love Vera Pavlovna reveals herself to be quite inexperienced and naive. When Julie asks her if she has a lover, she is simply unable to respond to the question (70). The matter with Storeshnikov is Vera Pavlovna's first experience with the erotic world, and she is quite unequipped to deal with it: she has no positive models of behavior to follow. Only her own feelings, her intuition, combined with her fierce desire for independence protect her. It is at this point, because there is such a lack of a positive model for Vera Pavlovna, that the narrator inserts himself into the discussion. When Storeshnikov is upset over Vera Pavlovna's refusal, she states that she recognizes the sincerity of his love. The narrator responds immediately to her statement: "(Verochka! This isn't love at all! It's a mixture of tawdry vulgarity and filthy rubbish! That's not what love is! Not every man who finds it upsetting to have his offer refused actually *loves* the woman! That's not love at all. But Verochka still doesn't know all this and she's touched)" (84).[32] Here the narrator acts as if he is in an actual dialogue with Vera Pavlovna, as if she can hear and respond. She cannot, of course, but the reader is presented with the narrator's views on what constitutes or does not constitute love. Love is viewed as so important by the narrator that he will not allow its definition to be left only to the characters, whose understanding of the term may be inadequate.

Chernyshevskii allows the positive characters to argue their case forcefully, so forcefully in fact, that many have taken the characters' deliberations as the message of the novel. Be that as it may, no single character has a monopoly on the true definition of love, and each of the definitions provided by the characters is subject to narrative commentary. The best example can be found with regard to Lopukhov. During their first conversation, Vera Pavlovna and Lopukhov turn toward the question of her relationship to Storeshnikov and the question of what love is. Here, Lopukhov performs the function of removing her illusions regarding Storeshnikov's love. He asks Vera Pavlovna, "But does he look at you the same way?" When she is unable to answer, he repeats the narrator's comment and informs her, "That's not love, Vera Pavlovna" (102).[33] This short exchange, in effect, starts Vera Pavlovna on the quest to find out what love is. In response to the perceived question "If it's not love, what is it?" Lopukhov attempts to provide Vera Pavlovna with a general definition of the phenomenon. He leads her to the statement that she would sooner die than cause torment to another. Building up this exchange Lopukhov summarizes: "There. You said it yourself. Now *that's* love. But that love is simple affection, not passion. But what is love as passion? How is passion different from simple affection? In intensity. Thus, if love as simple affection in its weakest form (too weak when compared to passion) places you in such a relation to another person that you say, 'It's better to die than cause that person pain,' if simple affection says that, what will passion say, since it's a thousand times more intense? It will say: 'I'd sooner die, than . . . demand? ask? No, than even permit that person to do anything for me except what he himself would find pleasant. I'd sooner die than have him feel pressured or force himself.' Love is the kind of passion that would say that. If it isn't, then it's pure passion, and not love at all" (102).[34]

In this exchange, Lopukhov has presented only a very generalized definition of love. Though by no means incorrect, it is hardly exhaustive. In response, the narrator supplements the discussion with his own views on love, providing a negative manner of definition; that is, he states what love is not, rather than what it is. In what is presented as a conversation with Vera Pavlovna, the narrator states: "Love is considered to be a disquieting emotion. But you'll fall asleep tonight like a baby, and your sleep won't be troubled or disturbed by dreams, unless you dream of happy children's games, forfeits or catch, perhaps of dancing, also happy and carefree. This may appear strange to others, but you don't know that it's strange, while I know that it's not. Anxiety in love isn't real love; if there's any anxiety, then something isn't as it should be, for love itself is happy and carefree" (103).[35] The narrator does not directly respond to Lopukhov's definition of love here; that is, he does not confirm or deny Lopukhov's statements. Rather, he argues past them, providing a totally different perspective. Immediately the reader has been presented with two very different, although not necessarily antithetical, points of view that are vying for his attention. This process will continue throughout the novel, with more and more points of view on love being added. The situation is further complicated by the fact that as the main characters grow and develop, their own views on love change. What results is a medley of voices that somewhat bewilders the reader.

For example, in contrast to the generalized definition he gives regarding love, Lopukhov maintains a rather cold, utilitarian outlook. During the conversation in which he reveals his utilitarianism to Vera Pavlovna, he advises her to adopt such methodology to determine whether she should marry Storeshnikov or not. Lopukhov speaks not of love, but of advantage. Far from advising her to marry only out of love, Lopukhov advises her to analyze the situation dispassionately and even argues that if she marries out of calculation (rather than love) no one has the right to censure her (116–17). Although Lopukhov dominates the stage here by the exposition of his theory, his cold, dispassionate outlook is in conflict with the essential thrust of the novel, which emphasizes the importance of feeling and intuition over theory. Moreover, his statements here (that is, that she accept things as they are and make the best choice) come very close to the advice offered by Julie and the example offered by Mar'ia Aleksevna. Lopukhov's diatribe is not the message of the novel, but merely one of the many different points of view provided to the reader.

Despite his willingness to issue general statements on love, Lopukhov resists the application of the term to his own relationships. Though he has given an essentially nonsensual definition of human love when referring to Vera Pavlovna and Julie, both he and Kirsanov refuse to acknowledge that their friendship is based on the warmth of human feelings. When Vera Pavlovna explicitly labels their relationship love, both men resist the label:

> "Vera Pavlovna, why do you want to come between our two loving hearts?"
>
> "Precisely because they're so loving," said Verochka, shaking Kirsanov's hand. Smiling all the while, she wondered aloud, "Will I come to love him the same way you do? You love him very much, don't you?"
>
> "Me?" replied Kirsanov. "I love only myself, Vera Pavlovna."
>
> "You don't love him?"
>
> "We lived together and didn't argue. That's enough."
>
> "And he doesn't love you?"
>
> "Not that I've noticed. But let's ask him. Do you love me, Dmitrii?"
>
> "I have no particular dislike for you." (158)[36]

Although the male characters' reluctance to admit to the term *love* may be due to traditional male reserve, it is also clear that they are under the influence of their utilitarian ethics in defining their relationship. Their theory prevents them from any open expression of emotion; rather they express themselves in terms of the utilitarian pleasure-plain calculus: they remain friends because neither causes the other any discomfort.

The narrator's contribution to the discussion reaches its apogee in chapter 4 when he explicitly begins to differentiate the nature of erotic love among the new people from love as conceived by their literary predecessors during the Romantic period. The narrator begins by stating that in Romantic love, "often when lovers were united, the poetry of their love would quickly disappear." In other words, the Romantics confused love with mere passion or infatuation. He goes on to argue, however, that among the new people, it's not like that at all. According to the narrator: "After they unite their love, the longer they live together, the more they're illuminated and warmed by its poetry, until the end of the day, when their solicitude for their growing children will engulf all other concerns. Then this solicitude, much sweeter than personal enjoyment alone, takes precedence; but up to that time the personal enjoyment keeps growing. What people used to experience for only a few fleeting months contemporary people manage to preserve for many, many years" (353).[37] The narrator tells the reader that in contrast to Romantic love, true love grows stronger with time, it does not fade. What separates the new people from their Romantic predecessors is that they seek long-lasting love, not mere passion as a form of distraction from ennui. The new people also differ from their predecessors in that they are able to sustain love over time. It is this that makes them worthy, positive images. The narrator admonishes his reader to follow their example and to seek not Romantic passion but true love: "But what's experienced by very few is the fact that the fascination that love imparts need not be a momentary phenomenon in a person's life. This bright light of our life need not illuminate merely the period of search and aspiration which we can simply call courtship or wooing. No, this period should really be only "the dawning, gentle and beautiful in and of itself, but merely the harbinger of a day that shines with incomparably more light and warmth than the dawn. Its light and warmth will grow and grow, especially the warmth, and will keep on growing long past noon" (353).[38]

The narrator's contribution to the question of love reaches its peak when he purports to have the secret to true love. Here the narrator has greatly digressed from the plot to treat a question that has obvious significance for him. He presents himself as all-knowing and purports to reveal to the reader an important truth:

> Why is this so? It's a secret, but I suppose I can reveal it to you. It's a fine secret, easily applied and not difficult to use, but one must have both a pure heart and an honest soul, as well as a contemporary notion of the rights of man and respect for the freedom of the individual you live with. That's all. It's no more a secret than that. Regard your wife as you did your bride; recognize that at any moment she has the right to say, "I'm dissatisfied with you. Get away from me." Regard her thus and nine years after your marriage she'll still inspire in you the same poetic feeling she did as a bride; no, it will be even more poetic and more ideal in the good sense of that word. Acknowledge her freedom just as openly and formally, with no reservations, as you recognize your friends' rights to value or spurn your friendship. Then, ten years or even twenty after your marriage, you'll be just as dear to her as you were when you were a bridegroom. (354)[39]

In short, the narrator tells the reader that true love is possible between men and women only when all inequality is removed, when a man and a woman approach each other not as master and servant, nor as owner and property, but as autonomous human beings.

Although the narrator has purportedly given the reader the true secret of love, his digression does not end the discussion of the subject in the novel. The secret of true love has been revealed to the reader, but the characters must still work out the question for themselves. Even after they have united into a happy union, Vera Pavlovna and Kirsanov attempt to define the essence of love. True to his materialistic and utilitarian theories, Kirsanov attempts to define love in terms of its usefulness to his organism. For example, in response to Vera Pavlovna's question about what her love has brought him, Kirsanov answers: "It gives my nerves a strong, constant, healthy stimulus that inevitably leads to the development of my entire nervous system. . . . Therefore, both my intellectual and moral strength grow as a result of my love" (355–56).[40] Vera Pavlovna's and Kirsanov's conversation continues this discussion of the beneficial influence of love on the human organism and leads to a discussion of love throughout history. It is in this conversation that the reader is informed that love is essential to the health and happiness of human beings and that, moreover, the reason for much unhappiness in the past was precisely due to the lack of and the misunderstanding of true love (356–57). The question of love as understood through the ages and the corresponding human unhappiness is treated further by Vera Pavlovna shortly thereafter in the first half of her fourth dream.

Although these discussions seem to have powerful force, they, too, are only a part of the story, for the discussion of love continues. The topic resurfaces in the story of Katerina Polozova's love for Solovtsov and her subsequent marriage to Beaumont/Lopukhov and even reappears in the winter picnic scene. Despite the numerous discussions, however, love is never quite defined exactly in *What Is to Be Done?* The reader is informed by the different expositions of the characters and of the narrator what love is not, what is necessary for love, and what love does for its participants, but the reader is never told exactly what love is. In effect, Chernyshevskii stresses that love is essentially something that must be felt, intuited; it cannot be grasped so easily in the abstract. The net result is to define love as something basically indefinable, while simultaneously acknowledging it as of the utmost importance for human existence. In the words of Joe Andrew, "the novel ends up by being a eulogy to the positive, life-giving power of love and physical love in particular."[41]

THEORY VERSUS INTUITION

The dichotomy between men and women presented in the novel parallels and is directly tied to another dichotomy, namely that between rationality and intuition/emotion. This seems somewhat surprising given the oft-cited truism in scholarship that Chernyshevskii was a cold rationalist, a worshiper of reason, who either misunderstood or denigrated the importance of human emotions, and, because of this, attempted to impose a theory (materialism/utilitarianism) upon human behavior.[42] The characters of the novel are often viewed as paragons of reason who reflect first, then act, never doing anything spontaneous or irrational.[43] They are viewed as mere marionettes used by Chernyshevskii to express his ideology. Chernyshevskii's supposed allegiance to materialism/utilitarianism will be discussed later. Here, we turn to the more general question of whether Chernyshevskii's novel preaches the subordination, if not the abolition, of human emotion/intuition. Was Dostoevskii correct in viewing Chernyshevskii's novel as an attempt to impose a theory upon life?

The dichotomy between rationality and emotion/intuition appears early in the novel, shortly after Vera Pavlovna's first prolonged conversation with Lopukhov. She is puzzled by the correspondence between her views and his:

> "How strange," thinks Verochka. "I myself had pondered and anticipated all that he said about the poor, about women, and about love. Where did I get it from? Was it from the books I read? No, it's not the same: books contain hesitations and reservations. It's all so extraordinary and improbable, like a wonderful dream, only it won't come true. But to me it always seemed so simple, simpler than anything else, the most ordinary thing, impossible to be without, sure that it would be, the surest of all! I considered these books the very best there were. Take George Sand, for instance—she's so kind and upstanding, but in her books it's all only dreams. (103)[44]

Moreover, Vera Pavlovna goes on to say that authors of books do not even believe the radiant visions they draw up, implying that books are not to be trusted as oracles or truth:

> Or take Dickens. He has it, but he really doesn't expect it to happen; he merely desires it because he himself is so kind, but he knows that it can never be. Why don't they know that this is impossible to do without, that this really must be accomplished, that it certainly will be—so that no one will ever be poor or unhappy again? Isn't this what they're all saying? No, they feel sorry, but they really think things will always stay just the way they are—maybe a little better, but still much the same. (103–4)[45]

Here Chernyshevskii has already introduced a theme that runs consistently throughout *What Is to Be Done?* It is the contrast between book learning (theory) and intuition. Vera Pavlovna clearly relates that she has intuited much of what she knows; she has not learned it from books. Moreover, the narrator comments extensively on this fact, indicating that this attribute is something to be valued in Vera Pavlovna.[46] For example, one page later, after Vera Pavlovna has fallen asleep, the narrator gives his own assessment: "No, Verochka, it isn't strange that you've pondered all this and have taken it to heart, you simple girl, you who've never even heard the names of those who've begun to teach this way and who've proven that this must come to pass, that it certainly will, that it can't help but be. It isn't strange that you understood and took to heart those ideas that your books couldn't present clearly to you. Your books were written by people who studied these ideas when they were still just ideas; they seemed astonishing and exhilarating; but nothing more" (104).[47] Here the narrator sets up a contrast between the simple girl, Verochka, and the learned writers of progressive ideas.[48] It is significant that the narrator states that Vera Pavlovna not only intuits these ideas without the aid of books, but that she intuitively understands these ideas far better than the authors of such books. The reader is provided with a clear indication that the narrator (and, at least implicitly, the author) considers intuited knowledge superior to that obtained through reading and abstract theorizing.

The dichotomy appears again when Vera Pavlovna is discussing the living arrangements for her marriage with Lopukhov. Lopukhov is struck by the fact that she has come up with these ideas on her own: "But all joking aside, what you describe really is the best way to arrange our life. But where did you come up with these ideas? I recognize them, and I even remember where I read them. But you couldn't have seen any of those books and there were no such details in the ones I lent you. Did you hear them from someone? From whom? Surely I'm the first decent person you've ever met?" (147).[49]

Lopukhov is a man who acts according to books and only according to books. As such, he relates to the rest of the world in such a manner and is simply at a loss to explain the "spontaneous generation" of an idea. In his view, the only way to expand one's knowledge is through reading and study. Vera Pavlovna, however, states quite clearly that she intuited it all based on practical experience: "My dear, is it really all that hard to arrive at these ideas independently? I have observed family life" (147).[50] It is Vera Pavlovna's capacity to intuit combined with her capacity for action that gives her the decided advantage over the men in the novel. Whereas the men must take time to reflect and to reason, and thus tend toward passivity, Vera Pavlovna is clearly the most active, forceful personality in the novel.

Vera Pavlovna's spontaneity and intuition are explicitly endorsed, but the male characters' emphasis on theory is often a source of amusement for the narrator. For example, in the scene of the Sunday outing (chapter 3, section 6) the narrator flippantly treats the learned discourse that the male participants engage in: "Needless to say, it was difficult for the uninitiated to tolerate these investigations for more than a few minutes. Even one of the debaters, the romantic, couldn't stand more than an hour and a half; he ran off to join the dancers" (203).[51] Likewise, in the "theoretical conversation" the narrator reproduces Kirsanov's and Lopukhov's overly elevated language and their abstract manner of formulating the most basic human situations. In the conversation Kirsanov insists on retreating into further and further abstraction, even using the term *abstract hypothesis* in his arguments against Lopukhov. In one paragraph alone Kirsanov uses the term *abstract hypothesis* four times, while also using similar terms, such as *hypothetical conclusion* or *in the abstract* (256).[52] The narrator's flippant attitude toward the male characters and their discourse is apparent when one page later the narrator turns Kirsanov's own terminology against him: "Kirsanov sat there examining his fingers as if each one stood for an abstract hypothesis" (257).[53]

Throughout *What Is to Be Done?* learning from books is given second rank to intuition, to one's own inner thoughts and feelings. When Vera Pavlovna does go astray in her actions, it is as a direct result of the influence of theory. Regarding her activity with the sewing cooperative, for example, Chernyshevskii is careful to alert the reader that Vera Pavlovna's involvement with the co-op is due precisely to the influence of theory. When outlining her plan of action to the young women in her establishment, Vera Pavlovna reveals that she is doing this under the influence of books, of theory. She consistently refers to certain "good people" (*dobrye liudi*) and their ideas, revealing that this idea is not her own, but an alien one (189). With time Vera Pavlovna comes to realize this deficiency in her actions when she states that her work in the co-op is an "artificial task" (343). Vera Pavlovna clearly realizes that she has been acting according to theory, not her own feelings, when she says: "Is the workshop really a part of my personal life? It's a cause, not my own, but someone else's. I work at it not for myself but for others" (343).[54] Moreover, Vera Pavlovna indicates how unfulfilling her work with the co-op has been, stating that she needs a cause that her life could seriously hinge upon (345). Lest the reader misunderstand the importance of Vera Pavlovna's confession, the narrator adds his own commentary apropos Vera Pavlovna's new inspiration resulting from her married life with Kirsanov: "Thoughts began to arise within her and assume a practical necessity that had been known to her on a theoretical level but had never really affected her inner life. What one can't do, one doesn't even contemplate seriously" (346).[55] Vera Pavlovna's involvement with the sewing co-op is a deed born of an abstract idea that can in no way provide true satisfaction for her. It is only with the newfound happiness of her personal life[56] that Vera Pavlovna can begin to find truly fulfilling activity: "Yes, now Vera Pavlovna has found her life's work, one she could never have conceived of before. . . . The following ideas were those that Vera Pavlovna now began to consider actively and that served as the motivation for her activity" (346).[57] In contrast to the abstract idea of the co-op, Vera Pavlovna decides to undertake the more practical idea of becoming a doctor. Vera Pavlovna's decision to study medicine is not based on a theoretical consideration; that is, it is not something she obtains by reading a book. Chernyshevskii demonstrates via Vera Pavlovna's interior monologue that her decision to become a doctor is born of practical necessity and practical observation of Russian life. She makes this decision in large part because she, as a woman, intuitively understands the position of women in general: "It's very important indeed to have women doctors. They would prove very useful to all women. It's much easier for a woman to talk to another woman than to a man. How much unhappiness, suffering, and death could be avoided! I must try!" (347).[58] In addition, the exclamatory tone of the final two sentences suggests that this is indeed a cause that Vera Pavlovna takes seriously and considers urgent. It, unlike her co-op, is something that she could seriously hinge her life upon.

In these passages regarding Vera Pavlovna, the reader is given a positive example of what the author considers an essential element in behavior: intuition. Indeed, if we did not know of Chernyshevskii's immense respect for books, for learning, we might be tempted to draw an anti-intellectual interpretation from the novel. But we must remember that within the novel Vera Pavlovna reads and accepts much of what she reads without any harmful results. It is not the reading of books that Chernyshevskii rejects in *What Is to Be Done?* but rather the unsophisticated, uncritical acceptance of what is in them, especially in books that are based on abstraction rather than practical experience.[59] In short, books and the theories contained in them must be subjected to the crucial test of real life, they must be evaluated. If they are accepted and followed blindly, distortion results.

The common denominator in the failings of the male characters is the attempt to live their lives according to a set of abstract principles. They try to rationalize and explain, and even deny, their actions and feelings according to a preconceived notion. Lopukhov, for example, attempts to explain love, indeed all human feeling, within the framework of his utilitarian worldview. As he later admits, he is able to relate to the world only in abstract terms: "It may seem strange, but only to someone who hasn't yet penetrated to the heart of my relations with these young people to whom I was giving so much of my time. In the first place, I had no personal relations with them; when I spent time with them, I didn't feel that I was in the company of other human beings; rather, I merely perceived several abstract types exchanging ideas" (319).[60] He acts, however, in a manner most inconsistent with his professed beliefs. And as he continues to develop in the novel he begins to turn on his former views. There is a hint of this, for example, in his theoretical conversation with Kirsanov: "But those things that are achieved through calculation, through a feeling of obligation, through an effort of will, and not through the attraction of nature, emerge stillborn. You can only destroy something that way, just as you've been destroying yourself; you can't give life" (258).[61] After his return from America disguised as Charles Beaumont, Lopukhov is indeed a new man, a striking characteristic of which is that he has dropped his former utilitarian explanation of human behavior. Implicitly at least, Lopukhov has realized that life is far too complex to be so easily explained; his theory was insufficient and he has dropped it. Not surprisingly, it is at this point that Lopukhov finds true love.[62]

The most vivid example of the poverty of the male characters' attempt to live by theory comes with regard to Kirsanov and his attempt to kill his feelings for Vera Pavlovna. The narrator's sarcastic attitude toward Kirsanov's plan shows itself from the very beginning: "His attachment was renewed, and became even stronger than before, but his struggle with it was manageable and entailed no serious torment. . . . Within this week the development of his passion has almost been arrested; in a month it will pass completely. He's very pleased with himself. He takes part in the conversation so naturally that he himself rejoices in his success; as a result of his satisfaction, the naturalness of his conduct increases all the more" (218–19).[63] The distortion, to which Kirsanov's theoretical approach leads, becomes even clearer when the narrator lets the reader eavesdrop on Kirsanov's inner psychological struggle. The reader is informed that being a participant in the affair, not an outsider, Kirsanov is having a difficult time sorting things out; his theory has begun to fail him in practice (234). Further, the reader is informed that "his feelings were inducing him to stay" (234).[64] Yet, Kirsanov comes to the conclusion that "it would be wiser to leave" (234).[65] Moreover, the narrator adds some caustic commentary, utterly belittling Kirsanov's approach: "This was a difficult and a delicate matter—to disappear from sight so that no one noticed your movements, even though all eyes were focused on you. But there was nothing else to be done. He had to do it. Besides, according to Kirsanov's theory, it shouldn't be painful, but even pleasant. The more difficult a task, the more one delights (according to egoism) in one's strength and agility at accomplishing it successfully" (235).[66]

As the narrator recounts in detail Kirsanov's ploys for distancing himself from Vera Pavlovna, a distinct tone of disapproval on the narrator's part is evident. Kirsanov's theory has transformed him from one of the honest, decent, new people into a deceitful liar. As Kirsanov is seemingly successful in his ploys, the narrator notes with condescension the perversion into which Kirsanov's theory has led him: "Kirsanov the theoretician derived immense enjoyment from the exercise, admiring his own agility. Egoists and materialists act only to satisfy themselves! Yes—and Kirsanov could swear, placing his hand on his heart, that he was acting only to satisfy himself. He rejoiced at his skill and mettle" (236).[67] Although Kirsanov may be rejoicing at his skill and mettle, all his ploys are for naught. At the end of section 18, where Kirsanov's ploys and rationalizations have been discussed with such detail, the narrator, relating the situation from Kirsanov's point of view, seems to hint that Kirsanov might be successful: "in another month . . . it would be in the bag!" (236).[68] The very next section, however, contains Vera Pavlovna's third dream, which bursts asunder all of Kirsanov's ploys. In the third dream, Vera Pavlovna's subconsciousness, her intuition so to speak, bursts forth with the truth. This dream forever shatters the Lopukhovs' family life and with it all of Kirsanov's calculated attempts to preserve it while killing his and Vera Pavlovna's attraction to one another. Kirsanov's attempts to deny his feelings, protracted and skillful as they may be, are utterly useless before the power of human emotion.

In forcing Kirsanov to continue his visits to the household (in the theoretical conversation), Lopukhov has acted very much in accordance with his utilitarian principles. He has reasoned out what the proper course of action should be (a discreet ménage à trois) and then has attempted to bring this about in practice. But he is no more successful than Kirsanov in bringing to fruition his utilitarian deliberations; concrete human feelings and reactions are too great an obstacle. In this particular case, Vera Pavlovna simply refuses to participate in the course of action he suggests. As with Kirsanov, Lopukhov also initiates the topic with Vera Pavlovna in a most abstract manner, using it as a shield against a straightforward treatment of the feelings and emotions involved. Vera Pavlovna, however, detests such abstraction: "'I won't allow you to talk to me in that way,' Vera Pavlovna said and got up. 'I won't allow you to use such obscure phrases. Have the courage to say what you mean'" (265).[69] Her response is simply to walk out. Lopukhov's plans have been dashed and he is left to ponder a new course of action. After this episode Lopukhov is worldly enough to figure out the next stage. However, despite his expectation of some sort of letter or confession from Vera Pavlovna and all his deliberation, Lopukhov is still struck by this painful blow and is "unable to collect his thoughts right away." (267).[70] If the reader keeps in mind that Lopukhov is a man who believes in and prides himself on the total calculability of each and every human action, including his own, this is a most troubling defeat for his theory. Moreover, the net result of the entire episode leaves a very clear message for the reader. Had the participants simply followed their feelings in the matter, the affair would have been a lot less painful and easier to resolve. But by trying to solve the affair by means of a theory, the male participants have made the situation much worse and almost insolvable. Thus, Lopukhov is driven to the point of faking his own suicide to cut the knot. Human emotion and behavior are not at all so reducible as he had anticipated.

The battle between the attempt to control human emotion and letting it follow its course unhindered is also played on a smaller scale in the story of Katerina Polozova in chapter 5. Polozova has fallen in love with Jean Solovtsov, a most despicable man. Her father sees Solovtsov for the cad that he is and simply forbids the relationship, claiming that it would be better for his daughter to die than be married to such a man. Kirsanov (and the narrator) even agree with Polozov on this point: marriage to Solovtsov would mean a living hell on earth for Polozova (396). Yet, Kirsanov (and the narrator) definitely part ways with Polozov over how to deal with the young woman's infatuation. Polozov subscribes to a very cold, practical point of view that allows little room for the importance of human feelings: "The old man was astonished to hear from Kirsanov that his daughter's love for Solovtsov was the cause of her illness. . . . How could she be dying of love for him? And can one really die of love? Such exaltation could not appear credible to a man accustomed to leading an exceptionally practical life and one used to regarding everything with cool common sense. Kirsanov spent a long time talking to him, but he kept repeating, 'It's the child's fantasy. She'll suffer a bit and then she'll forget'" (396).[71] Despite Kirsanov's urging to let things develop naturally, to let Polozova see for herself what a worthless fellow Solovtsov is, Polozov remains steadfast in his opposition; he simply cannot understand the power, or the complexity, of human emotion and is certain he can control it. It is interesting to note how Kirsanov finally resolves this situation. Although he is certain that given enough time he can talk sense into Polozov, Kirsanov realizes that such time is not available. Instead, he resorts to what amounts to brute force, not high-flown abstractions (400). And once Polozov's opposition has been removed, Polozova is allowed to pursue her own feelings as she sees fit. As expected, she does come to see what a rake Solovtsov is and rejects him totally (404). It is only by being allowed to follow her own, unhindered feelings that Polozova is able to make a good decision. Polozov's attempt to legislate the emotions of his daughter has precisely the undesired effect. Far from suffocating her feelings, his opposition has only helped to fan the flames (394).

The net result of the novel's concern with human emotion is very striking in view of the general interpretation of *What Is to Be Done?* Far from being a text that preaches a theory, any theory, over life, it is a text that gives primacy to life and regards distortion by theory as harmful.[72] Whether it be Vera Pavlovna's involvement with the co-op, Lopukhov's or Kirsanov's attempts to solve the love triangle, or Polozov's attempt to determine human emotion by fiat, the novel rejects all attempts to legislate human emotion and activity by means of theory as unfulfilling, distorting, even life-threatening. Moreover, the female characters in the novel are positive, superior to the male characters, in large part because they tend to follow their feelings and intuition; they do not give themselves over to a theory as the men do. The reader is left to draw the conclusion that the author supports not an abstract, theoretical approach to life, but an intuitive one based on the primacy of spontaneity and human feelings.[73] Thus, most observers have simply misread the novel on this point. *What Is to Be Done?* does not preach the subversion of life to theory.

MATERIALISM

We have seen how theory in general is treated in the novel. Let us now turn to a specific theory: materialism. Interpretation of *What Is to Be Done?* as a materialist manifesto relies heavily on the a priori assumption that Chernyshevskii was a subscriber to this philosophy, specifically that of the German vulgar materialists. I have dealt with Chernyshevskii's supposed debt to the materialist Ludwig Büchner elsewhere.[74] With regard to materialism as a whole, it is significant that Chernyshevskii never used the term to refer to himself or his worldview.[75] Whenever Chernyshevskii did use a term to describe his philosophical viewpoint, he used the term *anthropological* as defined in his essay "The Anthropological Principle in Philosophy" (1860):

> But we have almost forgotten that the term "anthropological" in the heading of our essays has still remained unexplained. What is this "anthropological principle in the moral sciences"? The reader has seen what this principle is from the very character of the essays. It is that a man must be regarded as a single being having only one nature; that a human life must not be cut into two halves, each belonging to a different nature; that every aspect of a man's activity must be regarded as the activity of his whole organism, from head to foot inclusively, or if it is the special function of some particular organ of the human organism we are dealing with, that organ must be regarded in its natural connection with the entire organism.[76]

Here Chernyshevskii explicitly rejects the concept of the dual nature of man. It is this fact that has led so many to label him a materialist.[77] But as Maurice Mandelbaum argues, materialism cannot be equated with the rejection of a theistic position:

> Thus, it is obvious that a rejection of a traditional Christian theist position is by no means equivalent to materialism.
>
> If one were to identify materialism with a rejection of mind-body dualism, then materialism was indeed not uncommon: many philosophers and philosophically oriented scientists gave up all attempts to support the view that the human mind was an entity, and that it could function independently of the human nervous system.[78]

Instead, he argues that if one defines materialism as a form of metaphysics opposed to idealism and other forms of metaphysics, then one looks in vain for materialists in nineteenth-century Europe: "Only in Germany does one find that materialism represented an important philosophic position."[79] In short, Chernyshevskii's outlook does not meet the criteria for materialism, and any attempt to apply this label to it renders the term useless.[80]

Most commentators on *What Is to Be Done?* have interpreted the novel as Chernyshevskii's paean to science and materialism. Lopukhov's and Kirsanov's fascination with science, especially physiology, and the passages in which they expound their corresponding materialist outlook are routinely identified as an exposition of Chernyshevskii's own views. Some have seen this single-minded fascination with science and materialism as the answer to the question in the novel's title.[81] It is true that Lopukhov and Kirsanov are fascinated with science and its possibilities and have adopted a materialist outlook. They both explain everything in terms of physiology and chemistry and view science and materialism as the key to changing human society. They display faith in progress, namely the fact that science's numerous advances, in and of themselves, will continue and will better human society. In effect, their answer to the question "What is to be done?" is to dedicate themselves to scientific research and to adopt a materialist worldview.

The narrator, however, never endorses the philosophy of materialism, Lopukhov's or Kirsanov's adherence to it, or their single-minded fascination with science as the panacea for all human problems. Regarding science itself, the narrator displays a rather ambivalent attitude. For example, the narrator openly questions the concept of objectivity, one of the watchwords of nineteenth-century science and materialism.[82] While commenting on the relationship between Kirsanov and the Lopukhovs, the narrator openly denies the existence of objectivity: "Isn't that always the way it is: if a person's inclined to look for something, he finds it wherever he looks. Even if there's no trace of it at all, he still finds clear evidence. Even if there's not even a shadow, still he sees not only a shadow of what he's looking for but everything he's looking for. He sees it in the most unmistakable terms, and these terms become clearer with each new glance and every new thought" (261).[83]

More important is the critique of the concept of objectivity provided by Mar'ia Aleksevna's test of Lopukhov regarding his intentions for Vera Pavlovna. The narrator comments upon her test: "But no, Mar'ia Aleksevna wasn't satisfied by her own vigilance. She went so far as to arrange a test, as if she'd studied the same rule of logic that I too learned by heart: The observation of phenomena that occur in and of themselves must be verified by experiments, conducted according to a well-formulated plan, in order to ensure the most profound insight into the mysteries of such relationships. She arranged a trial as if she'd read Saxon the Grammarian's account of how Hamlet was tested in the forest by a maiden" (114).[84] The narrator is referring to the scientific method here. The direct identification of Mar'ia Aleksevna's action as an experiment particularly stresses that the scientific method is hardly objective, that it is not something that stands above human beings and is free of them. Rather, it is very much subject to human manipulation and, as such, can be used for either good or evil. Finally, the lowering of science and its methodology is also evident when the narrator, in discussing Mar'ia Aleksevna's desire to collect information on her daughter and Lopukhov, labels it "scientific curiosity" (178),[85] again suggesting that scientific inquiry is not inherently suprahuman and positive, but can be used for either good or evil.

Finally, one should not forget that positivism, another theory celebrating the value of science, is utterly mocked, without any ambiguity whatsoever, in the form of Jean Solovtsov, an obviously negative character who insists on referring to himself as a positive sort: "But as a positive sort, I'm interested in something more substantial. I surveyed her bust" (61).[86] Solovtsov also refuses to accept anything without evidence, the hallmark of positivism: "Prove it. I'm a positive sort and cannot be convinced without proof" (62).[87] When we keep in mind that Solovtsov is referring to Vera Pavlovna and Storeshnikov's claim that she is his mistress, there can be little doubt that the association of positivism with this negative character is to its detriment. In addition, the name of August Comte, the founder of modern positivism, appears within the text of *What Is to Be Done?* as a denigrating term. At the outing in which Lopukhov is bested by the officer, the officer is "accused of Auguste Comteanism" (204).[88] In short, within the text of the novel Chernyshevskii continues his avowed disapproval of positivism.[89] Though science itself is not attacked in and of itself in the novel, neither is there evidence to argue that it is unequivocally celebrated.

In addition to these ambivalent attitudes, the narrator openly mocks the male characters' single-minded fascination with science. For example, instead of letting the characters fill the novel with their jargon, the narrator cuts them off in midstream when they are about to begin their scientific talk:

> "Meanwhile, I've finished with the optical nerve, my friend, and am about to start on the next pair. Where did you stop?"
> "I still have to finish up my work on . . ."
> Here there followed all sorts of anatomical and physiological terms. (151)[90]

Likewise, the narrator belittles the learned discussions of the main characters when he flippantly remarks that the notion of "laws governing historical progress" was "an unavoidable subject of conversation in such circles at that time." (180).[91] Moreover, in describing Lopukhov, Kirsanov, and their decision to eschew private practice for research, the narrator flippantly states:

> And so, in the name of their beloved science (they delight in abusing medicine, even though they devote all their efforts to it), they reject wealth, even prosperity, and you see, they sit in hospitals making interesting scientific observations. They dissect frogs, cut open hundreds of corpses a year, and at the first opportunity they outfit themselves with a chemical laboratory. (92)[92]

Finally, the male characters are belittled by the narrator for their continual tendency to engage in learned, scientific discussions rather than in more playful pursuits:

> But it goes without saying that for the most part they didn't listen, and even doused Lopukhov and Aleksei Petrovich with water when they got too excited over the enormous importance of mineral fertilizers. But Aleksei Petrovich and Lopukhov persevered unwavering in their learned discourse. Kirsanov didn't provide much assistance; he was more on the side of the ladies, even

> entirely so. The three of them played the piano, sang songs, and laughed until late into the night, when, exhausted, they finally managed to separate the invincible zealots of serious conversation. (180)[93]

In short, the male characters' fascination with science is never given any endorsement; rather it is gently mocked throughout the text of the novel.

In addition to this treatment, the narrator keeps his distance from materialism, consistently identifying it as the philosophy of his protagonists. For example, the narrator comments on materialism and its tendency to crude reductionism: "No spiritual travail can withstand a sufficient dose of morphine. This time two pills proved to be enough; he was becoming drowsy. Consequently, the spiritual travail was roughly equivalent in strength (according to Lopukhov's materialist viewpoint) to four cups of strong coffee. One pill would have been too little, and three would have been too much. He fell asleep, still chuckling over this comparison" (251–52).[94] Here, in addition to the flippant treatment, the narrator defines materialism as Lopukhov's viewpoint, not his own. When the narrator does express his own view, it is an explicit disavowal of materialism. In relating the story of Mar'ia Aleksevna's victory over Lopukhov at cards, the narrator states: "It was the first time he had allowed her such a triumph, and he left with her feeling very satisfied indeed, not with the money, but with the victory itself. Even those hearts that are most mired in materialism can know purely idealistic joys—which goes to show that the materialistic explanation of life is unsatisfactory" (129).[95]

The narrator's comments, scattered throughout the text, certainly do not leave the reader with the impression that Chernyshevskii is wholeheartedly endorsing a single-minded fascination with science or its sometime fellow traveler, materialism. Rather, it seems that he is gently chiding the adherents of such a worldview, providing a clear disavowal. Thus, in the end, Lopukhov's and Kirsanov's solution to the question "What is to be done?" posed in the novel's title is rejected: burying oneself in the intricacies of science and technological advancement will not by itself improve human society. Lopukhov himself evidently comes to realize this. Despite his fascination with science (that is, medicine) and materialism, he has abandoned both by the end of the novel.

Based on the various points discussed, it seems safe to conclude that Chernyshevskii rejected materialism of all types. However, one nagging concern remains: Why is there no unequivocal, extended critique of materialism and a rebuke of its adherents? The answer may lie in Chernyshevskii's ubiquitous reluctance to give any aid to the forces of reaction. For example, during the student movement of the early 1860s, Chernyshevskii, although disagreeing with the students in many respects, refused to rebuke them publicly, but defended them instead. Any reservations he had were expressed privately. Similarly, Chernyshevskii, although incredibly hostile to Darwin's emphasis on the struggle for existence, withheld public statement of his criticisms until one year before his death precisely because he did not want to aid the religious conservatives.[96]

I believe similar logic caused him to refrain from open criticism of the younger generation, which was enthusiastic about materialism, and to limit himself to the gentle chiding that can be found within the pages of *What Is to Be Done?* By using irony and a flippant narrator, he attempted to embed his rejection of materialism within the novel, while simultaneously rendering it useless to conservatives and reactionaries. This can best be illustrated by certain passages that occur later in the novel. For example, when Kirsanov uses a physiological example to illustrate a point, the narrator facetiously remarks in an aside that "(This is clearly gross materialism, I observe together with the perspicacious reader)" (355).[97] The narrator makes similar observations several times throughout Kirsanov's discourse. Such remarks are very loaded but also very difficult to decipher. While seemingly attacking Kirsanov for his materialism, the narrator's hostile attitude toward the perspicacious reader is also quite evident and clouds the issue. Thus, while counting on a careful reader to decipher the meaning of such remarks by embedding them within the context of the polemic with the perspicacious reader, Chernyshevskii renders them useless to his and the younger generation's common ideological enemies.[98]

UTILITARIANISM

Much of what has been said about materialism above also applies to the "ism" of utilitarianism. *What Is to Be Done?* is routinely cited as a work that both contains and espouses utilitarian elements. Many scholars view Chernyshevskii as propagating a philosophy of rational egoism, and *What Is to Be Done?* is often cited as the leading work in which he espoused this view.[99] Not only is this philosophy ascribed to Chernyshevskii but he is often viewed as borrowing it wholesale, with some vulgarizations, from the English utilitarians, Jeremy Bentham (1748–1832) and John Stuart Mill (1806–73).[100] The questions of Chernyshevskii's debt to the English utilitarians and of the nature of his utilitarianism in general have hardly been satisfactorily answered. It is simply assumed that Chernyshevskii must have taken his ethical theories from Bentham and Mill.[101] However, Chernyshevskii never credits either Bentham or Mill with being his source and he mentions them quite infrequently in his works.[102] When Chernyshevskii does refer to these men, his remarks are not particularly flattering and it is other aspects of their thought that form the core of his concern. For example, he thought little of Bentham's project for the judicial system, viewing it as impractical (7:505–16). Most important, however, is that Chernyshevskii is strikingly silent regarding Bentham's utilitarianism. In 1857 Chernyshevskii did review a Russian translation of *An Introduction to the Principles of Morals and Legislation* (1789), which is regarded as Bentham's major philosophical work. Chernyshevskii actually says very little about Bentham's work, most of the review being filled with quotations. When Chernyshevskii does comment, his focus is clearly on using Bentham to argue for an end to autocratic, arbitrary rule in Russia. The pleasure-pain calculus and other utilitarian concerns do not figure into his discussion (4:492–501).

As for Mill, Chernyshevskii does comment that he is the most talented of the epigones of Adam Smith and incomparably better than the French economists of the day. Having said that, however, he stresses that he does not find everything in Mill satisfactory and claims that Mill's strength lies only in the logical development of details; he is incapable of elaborating a new, full-fledged system (7:39–40). Moreover, in "The Anthropological Principle," the very document so often used to characterize Chernyshevskii as a utilitarian, he hardly treats Mill in flattering terms. He describes Mill as a man who, although talented, is at heart a coward and untrue to the principles he has expounded. Given this fact Chernyshevskii states that "neither the author of *De la Justice* nor Mill can serve as authorities in philosophy."[103] Finally, in terms of chronology it is improbable that Mill was much of a source for the supposed utilitarianism in Chernyshevskii's works *The Aesthetic Relations of Art to Reality* (1855) and "The Anthropological Principle in Philosophy" (1860), because both appeared *before* Mill's famous *Utilitarianism* (1863). Thus, for Chernyshevskii to have espoused a utilitarian philosophy, he would have had to develop it independently.[104]

Let us now turn to a brief glance at Chernyshevskii's "Anthropological Principle" and its alleged utilitarian content.[105] In this work Chernyshevskii does undertake an analysis of the motives of human behavior, arguing that "[a] man likes what is pleasant and dislikes what is unpleasant" and that "a man is good when, in order to obtain pleasure for himself, he must give pleasure to others."[106] Likewise he argues that "a man commits a bad action, that is, harms others, almost only when he is obliged to deprive them of things in order not to remain himself without the things he needs."[107] Proceeding from these basic points Chernyshevskii goes on to argue that "a man primarily loves himself" and that "people are egoists."[108] Up to this point, all Chernyshevskii has really stated is that people are subjective beings, that people act in their own interests. Moreover, what distinguishes Chernyshevskii from the utilitarians is that he is being *descriptive* not *prescriptive* here. He is not describing what should be, but what is; that is, he makes no attempt to provide a guidebook for human behavior.[109]

What has seemed particularly utilitarian in this essay is when Chernyshevskii abstracts from the individual to the general:

> Individuals regard as good the actions of other people that are beneficial for them; society holds as good what is good for the whole of society, or for the majority of its members. Lastly, people in general, irrespective of nation or class, describe as good that which is beneficial for mankind in general. . . . In such cases it is very easy to decide on which side theoretical truth lies. The interests of mankind as a whole stand higher than the interests of an individual nation; the common interests of a whole nation are higher than the interests of an individual class; the interests of a large class are higher than the interests of a small one.[110]

Chernyshevskii's argument may sound utilitarian; that is, it has seemed to many that he is invoking the pleasure-pain calculus here.[111] But this is hardly an exposition of a full-fledged ethical theory.[112] Moreover, shortly after making those statements, the real focus of Chernyshevskii's argument becomes clear:

> [T]he class which thinks of turning a national misfortune to its own advantage is mistaken from the very outset; it is dazzled by false calculations. . . . Here too it is always found that the calculations of the nation which set out to further its interests by damaging those of mankind were totally mistaken. Conquering nations have always ended by being exterminated or enslaved themselves.[113]

Here Chernyshevskii is laying the foundation for delegitimizing the rule of one class over another. Lest the reader pass this by unnoticed, Chernyshevskii then says:

> It is not for nothing that the members of the class that enriches itself to the detriment of the nation are compared to leeches; but remember what fate awaits the leeches who enjoy sucking human blood. Only rare ones among them do not encompass their own ruin by this pleasure; nearly all of them perish, and if some do survive, they are subject to severe illness, and they remain alive only thanks to the care of those whose blood they sucked.[114]

In short, "The Anthropological Principle" seems far more concerned with questioning the status quo in Russian society than it does with the propagation of a new ethical theory.[115] Although Chernyshevskii may have resorted to a utilitarian argument to give force to his radical politics, it is far from an attempt to present a full-fledged philosophical system and hardly sufficient evidence for labeling Chernyshevskii a utilitarian.[116]

It is also important to note that in the seventh article of his *Essays on the Gogolian Period of Russian Literature* Chernyshevskii flatly rejected philosophical egoism: "[I]t would be unjust to consider a cold egoist a positive man. Love and benevolence (the ability to rejoice at the happiness of those people around us and to grieve at their sufferings) are just as innate to man as egoism. Whoever acts exclusively according to the calculations of egoism, acts contrary to human nature, and suppresses in himself innate and ineradicable needs. He in his own way is just such a dreamer [*fantazer*] as he who dreams about transcendental selflessness. . . . To search for happiness in egoism is unnatural, and the lot of the egoist is not in the least enviable: he is a freak, and to be a freak is awkward and unpleasant" (3:229–30). In this passage Chernyshevskii uses the word *egoist,* the same word that appears so often in *What Is to Be Done?* Although this quite explicit rejection of egoist ethics and egoists occurs in one of Chernyshevskii's more famous works, most observers see rational egoism as the core concern of the novel.[117] It is true that Lopukhov and Kirsanov espouse a utilitarian philosophy and Lopukhov, in particular, discusses it at length in order to inculcate its principles into Vera Pavlovna. Lopukhov and Vera Pavlovna refer to his outlook as the theory of the calculation of advantage (115–16)[118] and Lopukhov is convinced that it is the solution to the problem of human ethics:

> "Yes, they are telling the truth. What we call sublime emotion or ideal aspiration—all that, in the general course of life, is completely insignificant in comparison with each person's pursuit of his own advantage. And in essence these things constitute the same pursuit of advantage." (115)[119]

> "No, Vera Pavlovna. The theory is cold, but it teaches man how to procure warmth." (116)[120]

These are strong statements indeed by Lopukhov.[121] Moreover, he suggests to Vera Pavlovna that she apply this theory to her own concrete situation: "Calculate what's the most advantageous for you" (116).[122] Such statements do leave little doubt that Lopukhov is an avowed egoist in his ethics.

Despite the long, pious statements of faith by Lopukhov and his belief in their invincibility, his theory is not presented to the reader for emulation. For example, despite his numerous attempts to teach Vera Pavlovna the principles of this theory, she is unable to accept it fully. Her reaction is that it is inhuman: "Let's assume that you're right—yes, you are right. All actions, as far as I can see, can be explained by advantage. But isn't that theory rather cold?" (115).[123] Despite Lopukhov's attempts to explain and defend his theory, Vera Pavlovna has considerable trouble in accepting it: "So this theory, whose validity I have no choice but to accept, condemns people to a cold, pitiless, prosaic life?" (116).[124] Although Vera Pavlovna pays lip service to Lopukhov's utilitarianism and says that he is right, she is simply unable to accept it fully and to internalize it. Indeed, she explicitly refers to the theory as Lopukhov's, not her own (117). Moreover, she is determined to expose any inconsistencies in Lopukhov's reasoning: "Very well. Let's see if I can trip you up with some questions about me" (116).[125] Likewise at the very end of the conversation, Vera Pavlovna still resists Lopukhov's theory by arguing for caprice (118).

In a similar vein, she admits much later in the novel that she still has never quite been able to internalize these principles:

> He [Lopukhov] was always searching for the most hidden reasons for his actions and it gave him great pleasure to subsume them to his theory of egoism. However, this habit is shared by our entire circle. My Aleksandr [Kirsanov] is also fond of analyzing himself in this same vein. If only you could hear how he explains his own behavior in regard to me and Dmitrii Sergeich over these last three years. According to him, he did everything out of egoistic calculation, for his own satisfaction. I too have adopted this habit, *but it occupies me and Aleksandr somewhat less than it did Dmitrii Sergeich.* We agree with him entirely, but he had a stronger interest in theory. To hear us tell it, we three are the greatest egoists the world has ever known. Perhaps that's even true. Perhaps there were no great egoists before us! Yes, that seems to be the case. (323; emphasis mine)[126]

Again Vera Pavlovna pays lip service to the precepts of Lopukhov's utilitarian theory, but her words reveal that she is far from an ardent advocate. The last four lines of this passage indicate an ambivalent attitude on her part, in which she views the whole thing as a bit ridiculous. In a particularly revealing passage, Vera Pavlovna seems to state that she has adopted the pose of the egoist solely to honor Lopukhov, indicating that she herself is not a true advocate: "I make this remark because Dmitrii Sergeich was so fond of such remarks. I wish to be in your good graces, my friend" (326).[127]

In addition to Vera Pavlovna's failure to adopt fully the principles of utilitarianism, there are other reasons for not viewing this theory as the message of the text. Although Lopukhov and Kirsanov make numerous utilitarian statements, the narrator *never* endorses them. Indeed, the narrator is quite careful to distance himself from those views. For example, in discussing Kirsanov's outlook on his situation, the narrator refers to it as Kirsanov's own: "according to Kirsanov's theory of egoism," "the theory that Kirsanov advocated," and "In his own terminology Kirsanov would have expressed himself thus" (234–35).[128] Thus, these passages, as heavily ideological as they are, are the views of the characters, not of the narrator. In his direct comments on egoism the narrator is quite condescending. His attitude is evident in that he deliberately misuses the word *materialism* to refer to egoism on occasion. For example, in discussing Lopukhov's meditations on how to save Vera Pavlovna from her family, the narrator uses the word *materialist* instead of *egoist:* "A materialist thinks exclusively about advantage, and indeed he was considering only that. Instead of lofty poetic and sublime visions, he was concerned with the sort of amorous fantasies appropriate to a crude materialist" (149).[129] In addition to this deliberate misuse of terms, the two concepts are often uttered in the same breath by the narrator: "Egoists and materialists act only to satisfy themselves!" (236).[130] Thus, throughout the novel, the two "isms" are consciously interlinked by the narrator as inseparable. By linking the two "isms" together in this way, the narrator forces the reader to reject both if he rejects either.

Furthermore, the utter ridiculousness of the utilitarianism of the male characters is demonstrated at several points. For example, the narrator leads the reader to understand that utilitarian theory paralyzes the male characters:

> "So that's all there is to it, Aleksei Petrovich. I understand that it entails a large risk for you. It'll all be all right if we make it up with her parents, but what if they press a lawsuit? Then there could be trouble for you, and there probably will be. But . . ." Lopukhov couldn't come up with a single "but." How indeed can you persuade a person to place his head in a noose for your sake?
>
> Mertsalov thought about it for a long time, he too trying to come up with a "but" *to authorize himself to run such a risk;* but he couldn't come up with a single one either. (156; emphasis mine)[131]

Mertsalov's subscription to a utilitarian ethic has clearly paralyzed him and prevents him from doing good. If he is left to follow the dictates of his theory, Vera Pavlovna cannot be saved from ruin. The philosophical dead-end in which Mertsalov has been placed combined with the narrator's sardonic attitude leave little doubt about the poverty of this ethical theory.

The narrator further mocks the characters' utilitarian deliberations in numerous asides throughout the novel. For example, when Lopukhov finally realizes that his wife is in love with his best friend, he has to devote much thought to finding a solution. In commenting on these deliberations, the narrator remarks: "But now, having dispensed with his own point of view (as an egoist he always thought of himself first, and about others only when there was nothing left of his own to think about), he could apply himself to someone else's point of view, namely hers" (249).[132] Likewise, in relating Kirsanov's deliberations on how to distance himself from Vera Pavlovna the narrator takes a rather condescending attitude, making light of Kirsanov's spiritual travail: "But there was nothing else to be done. He had to do it. Besides, according to Kirsanov's theory, it shouldn't be painful, but even pleasant. The more difficult a task, the more one delights (according to egoism) in one's strength and agility at accomplishing it successfully" (235).[133]

The high point of the exposition of utilitarian ethics in *What Is to Be Done?* comes in the theoretical conversation (chapter 3, section 22) between Lopukhov and Kirsanov in which the two men attempt to come to a solution for the love triangle. Their discourse is filled with one utilitarian formulation after another. Lopukhov and Kirsanov duel with each other, both using their utilitarian theory, replete with the necessary examples, to try to defeat the other. This in itself calls the utilitarian theory into question, particularly any claims it might have to objectivity or universality. That is, using the same theoretical formula, Kirsanov and Lopukhov come to widely different solutions to the problem. Moreover, it is significant that the crisis is not solved by utilitarian theory, but by force, clearly demonstrating the poverty of utilitarianism. That is, Lopukhov tires of the debate and simply threatens to tell Vera Pavlovna unless Kirsanov does what Lopukhov wants him to do (257).

After the conclusion of this theoretical conversation, the narrator appends some remarks that Lopukhov and Kirsanov would have said had they had the opportunity. In those supposed remarks, Lopukhov and Kirsanov again use the same formulations, the same phrases. For example, each uses the phrase "It's pleasant to observe as a theorist the tricks that egoism plays in practice" (258).[134] However, despite this similarity in approach, both men again come to very different conclusions, with each accusing the other of having his actions twisted by egoism so that he acts the role of a man acting nobly (258–59). The narrator then adds a rather caustic remark: "But neither Lopukhov nor Kirsanov had the opportunity to become a theoretician and to make these pleasant observations. The practical aspects of this matter weighed on both of them rather heavily" (259).[135] Here the narrator indicates that the ethical theory held by Lopukhov and Kirsanov is a mere intellectual exercise that does little to help these men in practice.

Finally, after the exchange of letters between the former medical student (that is, Lopukhov) and Vera Pavlovna, the narrator remarks on the utilitarian formulations contained in them. The letters, especially Lopukhov's, are filled with utilitarian formulations, especially egoistic self-justification. The letters, along with Lopukhov's diatribe in chapter 2 and the theoretical conversation, are the main evidence of those who insist on viewing *What Is to Be Done?* as a utilitarian tract. However, what is often ignored is that the narrator's remarks immediately following the letters greatly delegitimize their content:

> These letters, absolutely sincere, were really somewhat one-sided, as Vera Pavlovna noticed herself. Of course, both correspondents tried to lessen the strength of the painful shocks they'd suffered. Oh, these people are so clever! I've often heard from them, that is, from them and people like them, things that made me laugh in the middle of their emotional assurances that "it was nothing at all, really nothing." Naturally, I laugh both when these assurances are made to me by a stranger and when they're made in private conversation. But when the same thing is said to someone who needs to hear it, then I always go along and agree that it really was "nothing at all." An honorable man is such an amusing creature! I've always laughed at every honorable man with whom I've been acquainted.
>
> Such an amusing creature, even to the point of absurdity. Take these letters, for instance. My friendship with ladies and gentlemen of this type has made me somewhat accustomed to these tricks of theirs. (328)[136]

Again, the narrator does display a rather condescending attitude to the egoistic deliberations of the characters. His tone is one of an indulgent parent or mentor, patiently tolerating the misguided actions and views of beloved children.

From these and other passages in *What Is to Be Done?* it is quite clear that the narrator does not at all endorse utilitarianism, but rather distances himself from it at every opportunity. It is within this context that we now turn to several key passages in the novel in which the narrator seemingly professes an adherence to utilitarianism or at least justifies it. To begin with, there is the section in which there appears a certain Madame B., whom Lopukhov visits in the hope of getting Vera Pavlovna a position as a governess. At first, Madame B. is quite happy with the prospect of hiring Vera Pavlovna. But when she hears that a rich suitor is pursuing her, she changes her mind, fearing trouble from Vera Pavlovna's family. In due course she attempts to justify her actions by resorting to utilitarian formulations. Lopukhov gives credence to this fact when he says that she is absolutely right; he accepts her utilitarian self-justification: "Oh, if only I didn't know that you were absolutely right. Yes, how splendid it would be if you were wrong. I'd tell her that we couldn't agree on terms or that you weren't to my liking, and that's all there was to it. She and I could continue to hope that we'd find another opportunity for deliverance. But now, what can I possibly tell her?" (133–34).[137] Madame B.'s utilitarian self-defense is so convincing that Lopukhov gives up the hope of finding any position for Vera Pavlovna.

In the passage that follows this scene, the narrator openly disagrees with Lopukhov regarding Madame B., noting that she "was not absolutely right in the way grown-ups are when they prove to children that they can't reach out and touch the moon." Instead, he notes that she could have hired Vera Pavlovna had she really wanted to do so. Furthermore, in an apparent defense of Madame B. and her utilitarian position the narrator says: "Nevertheless, Madame B. would have incurred a great deal of trouble, and perhaps even a few unpleasant exchanges. She would have had to ask favors of various people, whose services it might have been better to reserve for her own needs, not for those of others. Who is obligated, and what reasonable person would wish to behave any differently? We have no right whatever to condemn Madame B" (134).[138] Although the narrator states literally that we are not to condemn Madame B., the ironic and sarcastic tone of the passage is quite evident to the reader, forcing precisely such a condemnation of Madame B. and her utilitarian self-justification for her actions.[139]

In a passage that appears remarkably out of character, the narrator seems to endorse Lopukhov's way of thinking: "Lopukhov found that his theory provided an infallible means for analyzing the movements of the human heart; I must confess that I agree with him entirely on this point. During the long years that I've relied upon this theory as true, it's never led me astray and never once refused to reveal the truth to me, however deeply this truth was concealed by some human action. The truth is that this theory itself is not so easily embraced. One has to have lived and thought in order to be able to grasp it" (251).[140] This passage seems to conflict with the narrator's numerous other comments on utilitarianism. However, it seems clear that the narrator is speaking tongue-in-cheek here. For example, these remarks are followed by the scene in which Lopukhov takes morphine, accompanied by the narrator's caustic commentary. Furthermore, the theoretical conversation follows in the very next section. Here Lopukhov's theory does not prove infallible; indeed, it does not work at all. Despite all his deliberation, guided by his infallible theory, he fails to solve the situation rationally and has to resort to the extreme measure of a faked suicide. Thus, this passage is no way an endorsement of utilitarianism.

In addition to these facts, there are many other elements in the novel that must lead one to conclude that *What Is to Be Done?* is not a utilitarian text. For example, despite Lopukhov's emphasis on the calculation of advantage as the motive force of man's behavior, he does not really live up to those principles. In applying his theory to his own situation he states to Vera Pavlovna: "I persuaded my father to let me enter the Medical Academy instead of taking a post in the civil service. How did this come about? My father and I realized that doctors live much better than low-ranking civil servants or even department heads, which was as high a rank as I could reach. That's the reason I wound up in the Academy and why I stayed there: for a big hunk of bread. Without that calculation I would neither have entered the Academy nor remained there" (115).[141] As is her wont, Vera Pavlovna again resists Lopukhov's utilitarianism by asking, "But surely you loved your studies in the gymnasium and then you came to love medical science?" Lopukhov, however, remains true to his utilitarian theory: "Yes, but that was icing on the cake. It may even be useful for achieving success. But while you can get along without icing, you can't manage without cake. Love for science was only a result of the process, not its motive. My real motive has always been one and the same: advantage" (115).[142]

Lopukhov's pronouncements are uttered with such force that most have concluded that they must be Chernyshevskii's own views. However, there is a remarkable inconsistency between Lopukhov's words and his actions. Despite his insistence on a "big hunk of bread" as his motivation, the narrator reveals that Lopukhov is actually guided by an ideal: "And so, in the name of their beloved science . . . , they reject wealth, even prosperity" (92).[143] Thus, even before Lopukhov gives up his medical career to save Vera Pavlovna, he has already chosen a relatively austere career path. While paying lip service to getting a "big hunk of bread," he has already chosen a path of poverty: that of a research scientist. This simply does not go with his professed utilitarian principles or his analysis of his own personal situation. In short, while professing to follow an abstract theory, Lopukhov clearly acts differently in practice.[144]

Lopukhov's utilitarianism is also called into question by his relationship with Mar'ia Aleksevna. Mar'ia Aleksevna finds nothing objectionable in

Lopukhov's numerous utilitarian pronouncements, both those spoken directly to her and those that she hears while eavesdropping. Mar'ia Aleksevna comes to conclude that she and Lopukhov think exactly alike. Indeed, she even hopes that he will instill his way of thinking into Vera Pavlovna (118). This identification of Lopukhov's theory with Mar'ia Aleksevna's way of thinking is potentially very dangerous for Lopukhov. That is, since Mar'ia Aleksevna is an obviously negative character, does this not reflect badly upon Lopukhov? The narrator himself meets this problem head on. To begin with, the narrator indulges in commentary on the fact that Mar'ia Aleksevna's approval of Lopukhov's ideas has put her in a comic situation. He notes that she is a most vigilant person and that had there been any reason to suspect Lopukhov, she most assuredly would have noticed it. The narrator begins the string of ambiguities by saying, "But he really did behave himself in precisely the way that Mar'ia Aleksevna thought only a person of her own ilk would" (119).[145] The narrator further notes that, "Yes, Mar'ia Aleksevna was quite right to realize that she and Lopukhov had a great deal in common" (120).[146]

The remarks in this section are greatly complicated by the fact that the narrator speaks with such evident irony and also intentionally mixes terms (again using *materialist* to refer to *egoist*). Furthermore, this section is made completely ambiguous when the narrator makes remarks such as "I understand how much Lopukhov is compromised in the eyes of my enlightened public by Mar'ia Aleksevna's sympathy for his way of thinking" (120).[147] Finally, this complicated situation is taken to a new level when Chernyshevskii indulges in a few attacks on his perceived opponents: "Indeed, as has been demonstrated by the conversation between Lopukhov and Verochka, his way of thinking would appeal much more to people of Mar'ia Aleksevna's ilk than to the eloquent advocates of various sublime ideals. . . . The similarity between their views was so great that enlightened and high-minded novelists, journalists, and others instructors of our public have long since proclaimed: 'People such as Lopukhov are no different from Mar'ia Aleksevna and her ilk.' If such enlightened and high-minded writers have thus understood people such as Lopukhov, can we really condemn Mar'ia Aleksevna for not seeing in him anything but what our best writers, thinkers, and teachers have seen?" (120).[148] As these passages show, the narrator engages in so much irony that it is hard to determine where he actually stands. Is Lopukhov's way of thinking the same as Mar'ia Aleksevna's, and if so, is he to be condemned for it?

The narrator seems to indicate that their way of thinking is not exactly the same, that Mar'ia Aleksevna's understanding of advantage was different from Lopukhov's (121). However, he further complicates this issue by suddenly blaming Lopukhov for being a materialist:

> But everything I say is intended to excuse Mar'ia Aleksevna for not managing to sniff out what sort of man Lopukhov really was, and not as an excuse for Lopukhov himself. It would not be appropriate to exonerate him; the reasons will be made clear soon enough. While not exonerating him, some people might wish to excuse him out of love for their fellow man; they should not do so. For example, they might use the excuse that he was a medical student who studied natural science, and that this predisposed him to a materialist point of view. But that kind of excuse is very poor. There are any number of sciences that predispose one to this view. . . . In other words, Lopukhov does not escape blame. (121–22)[149]

This passage is notable for several details. First, the narrator has switched from a discussion of Lopukhov's egoism to a discussion of his materialism, demonstrating that for the narrator the two are intertwined. Moreover, the narrator's sarcasm is abundantly clear: although he has appropriated the discourse of his ideological enemies and seemingly agrees with it in its condemnation of Lopukhov, it is clear that he is speaking tongue-in-cheek. Yet, as we know, the narrator never endorses materialism or utilitarianism, so this passage can hardly be in support of such theories. Indeed, this passage is a classic example of Chernyshevskii's continual attempt to chide the younger generation without aiding the conservatives and reactionaries.

The solution to this problem comes in the distinction the narrator continually makes between Lopukhov as a person (and the other characters) and Lopukhov's purported way of thinking. In other words, it is Lopukhov's decency as a person that the narrator approves of and loves while refusing to endorse his theories. This also explains the real difference between Mar'ia Aleksevna and Lopukhov: it is their basic character that separates them. The narrator hints at this in his sarcastic discourse when he says:

> Compassionate people who do not seek to exonerate him could say in his defense that he's not completely devoid of several praiseworthy characteristics: he made the firm and conscious decision to refuse any material rewards and honors for the work he did for others, finding that the best reward was pleasure in the work itself. And when he met a young woman who was so pretty that he fell in love with her, he decided to treat her with a chaste regard, purer than that with which many brothers regard their own sisters. But, in reply to this defense of his materialism, it must be stated that no man is completely devoid of redeeming characteristics, and that materialists, whatever they are, are still materialists; and by that very fact alone it is resolved and proved that they are base and amoral people who cannot be excused, because to do so would constitute a display of indulgence toward their materialism. Therefore, without exonerating Lopukhov, no excuse is possible. (122)[150]

Again, the narrator, while seemingly agreeing with the critics, is speaking with evident irony. We are to infer that it is possible to exonerate Lopukhov without endorsing materialism. The reference again to the fact that Lopukhov has renounced any material rewards, greatly contrasts with his insistence on a "big hunk of bread" as his sole motivation. Thus, it is clear that what guides Lopukhov is an underlying sense of decency, an ideal, some would say, and this is clearly what the narrator endorses, not his materialism or utilitarianism. As such, there is very little evidence in the text of *What Is to Be Done?* to argue that Chernyshevskii openly advocates and propagates a utilitarian ethical philosophy.

Chapter Four

Rakhmetov and Revolutionary Asceticism

NEAR THE END of chapter 3 in *What Is to Be Done?* the main narration is broken off to give the reader a twenty-page discussion of a peculiar man, Rakhmetov. Rakhmetov plays almost no role in the plot proper. In the rough draft he does not even appear, and his one action (to show Vera Pavlovna Lopukhov's note indicating the suicide is a fake) is performed by another character.[1] In the final version only some forty pages are devoted to him, occupying about one-tenth of the text.[2] Yet despite this rather innocuous role, Rakhmetov has become one of the most infamous characters in Russian literature, and certainly the most discussed character of the novel. His adoption of strict asceticism and his incredible feats, such as sleeping on a bed of nails, have inspired many while scandalizing others. It is to this enigmatic character that we now turn.

PREVIOUS INTERPRETATIONS OF RAKHMETOV

Briefly stated, twentieth-century scholarship has interpreted Rakhmetov as Chernyshevskii's answer to the call for a positive hero in Russian literature and as his model for the young generation to follow. Many have even argued that Chernyshevskii presents the reader with an ideal in Rakhmetov. Soviet scholars, for example, interpreted Rakhmetov as Chernyshevskii's attempt to present a positive image of the professional revolutionary engaged in underground activity.[3] Correspondingly, many have argued that Chernyshevskii meant Rakhmetov as a model for emulation and that, therefore, Chernyshevskii preached the precepts of revolutionary asceticism.[4] N. P. Zhdanovskii provides a concise summary of the Soviet interpretation:

> Rakhmetov is not simply a "new man." This is the embodiment of the ideal of the revolutionary, as Chernyshevskii understood him, and therefore, is indisputably the central figure of the novel *What Is to Be Done?*
>
> Chernyshevskii uses the image of Rakhmetov to assert and propagandize the idea of revolutionary duty, of selfless devotion to the interests of the masses.[5]

Soviet scholars argued that Rakhmetov is the answer to the question posed in the novel's title, What is to be done?[6] Basing themselves on Plekhanov's statement that "in each of the prominent Russian revolutionaries there was a huge share of Rakhmetovism,"[7] Soviet scholars traced a direct line from Rakhmetov to later Russian revolutionaries, especially the Bolsheviks. As a result, many Soviet scholars claimed that it is Rakhmetov who is the main character of the novel[8] and, furthermore, that his image, based on the Russian reality of the time, is a great achievement in Russian realism.[9] Soviet scholars considered Rakhmetov so important a figure that several pedagogical works appeared to give students the proper understanding of this "great theoretician and practical person of the revolutionary movement."[10]

Western scholars have generally followed their Soviet counterparts, although they have been far from enthusiastic about the character. Most Western scholars agree that Rakhmetov is a straightforward, positive image presented by Chernyshevskii for emulation.[11] Many even agree with Soviet scholars that he is the main character of the novel.[12] Western scholars also agree that Chernyshevskii preaches the precepts of (revolutionary) asceticism by means of this character[13] and that Rakhmetov is a model of the subsequent revolutionaries, especially the Bolsheviks.[14] Western scholars do occasionally stress other aspects of the character,[15] but where Western scholars really differ is in the interpretation of Rakhmetov as a literary character. Most see him as an abysmal failure because of his hyperbolic characteristics and treat him as evidence that Chernyshevskii was utterly untalented as a writer. For example, Ernest Simmons argues that "no more boring, dull, flat, two-dimensional, unreal hero has ever been created in serious fiction since Richardson's Sir Charles Grandison."[16] Whatever reservations an observer might have, scholars of the twentieth century have been unanimous in their interpretation of Rakhmetov as Chernyshevskii's positive hero.

Twentieth-century views, however, do not at all correspond with how observers of the nineteenth century, particularly Chernyshevskii's contemporaries, viewed Rakhmetov. The nineteenth-century Russian displayed much more ambivalence about the character. It is true that Rakhmetov's image found some resonance among the younger generation. For example, there is the case of Nikolai Ishutin, who consciously emulated Rakhmetov by getting a job on a Volga River steamboat.[17] Likewise, Sergei Nechaev is said to have imitated Rakhmetov's ascetic habits by sleeping on bare boards and eating only bread.[18] However, most contemporaries did not seem to view Rakhmetov as someone to emulate. When one enthusiastic young lad attempted to do just that, he quite amazed his compatriots: "Having become acquainted with my new comrades I happened to hear strange references about one of the members of the former male circle. He was spoken of with good-natured irony and at the same time with a sort of special respect. They joked about him, but at the same time they were perplexed by how to treat him. They recounted, while laughing, that, having read Chernyshevskii's *What Is to Be Done?* he set up some kind of bed of nails, wanting to train himself for torture. It was clear that this person did not confine himself to ordinary limits."[19]

These isolated examples, however, were only a minor part of the reaction to the novel.[20] Most young Russians were far more taken with the adventures of Vera Pavlovna with her two husbands and the setting up of the sewing co-op. Although the incidence of cooperative ventures and fictitious marriages increased due to the novel's influence, few consciously tried to imitate Rakhmetov. Even in the long litany of attacks against the novel in the press, Chernyshevskii's opponents concentrated more on the "debauchery" of the three main characters than on the image of Rakhmetov.[21] Moreover, Russian contemporaries considered Rakhmetov so ridiculous that he could not be taken seriously: "This Rakhmetov is so holy and stupid that he could hardly frighten anyone."[22]

The nineteenth-century reaction to Rakhmetov is perhaps best exemplified by the discussions of the first critics of the novel. In general, those critics paid only scant notice to Rakhmetov, sometimes mentioning him only in passing, if at all. For example, in his critique of *What Is to Be Done?* Nikolai Strakhov was far more concerned with the absence of tragedy and suffering in the lives of the new people. As for Rakhmetov, Strakhov has remarkably few comments, merely noting that Rakhmetov, who is transformed within the span of six months, is an example of how the new people acquire their wisdom far too easily and far too quickly. For Strakhov, the essence of the section on Rakhmetov and of the novel as a whole is the simple, cold, almost inhuman denial of suffering.[23] This is all that Strakhov has to say about Rakhmetov. Rakhmetov simply does not possess any major significance for him, and Strakhov clearly did not view him as Chernyshevskii's great ideal or the center of the novel.

Similar to Strakhov, Nikolai Leskov had little to say about Rakhmetov; indeed, he makes not a single comment. Leskov's review is far from an in-depth one and he himself was careful to stress that he was writing only a letter. Yet it is noteworthy that the character who has so often attracted the attention of twentieth-century scholars did not merit a single remark from Leskov. Moreover, Leskov is interesting in that he gave *What Is to Be Done?* a nonradical reading. Far from providing a revolutionary utopian program, Leskov saw Chernyshevskii's goals as fully achievable and, moreover, advanced in a peaceful, gradual manner. Leskov was so certain of his reading that he carefully distinguished Chernyshevskii from the majority of nihilists, giving Chernyshevskii the label of a nihilist-gradualist.[24] Leskov's comments are valuable in that they show that a nonrevolutionary reading of the novel is possible and, consequently, that Rakhmetov does not necessarily have to be interpreted as Chernyshevskii's ideal of the ascetic revolutionary.

Shortly after *What Is to Be Done?* appeared in 1863, Afanasii Fet, with the help of Vasilii Botkin, prepared a review of the novel for M. N. Katkov's journal *Russkii vestnik*.[25] Although Fet offers an extended discussion of the novel, like Strakhov, he has relatively little to say about Rakhmetov. When he does address the character of Rakhmetov, Fet does not take him very seriously. After recounting Rakhmetov's adventures, Fet labels Rakhmetov absurd, so absurd that he is harmless. Fet asks what harm there is in Rakhmetov's giving away his land, pulling a barge, and sleeping on nails.[26] Fet's only real concern is with Rakhmetov's contribution to the doctrines expounded in the text.[27]

In contrast to Strakhov, Leskov, and Fet, Chernyshevskii's fellow radicals, Dmitrii Pisarev and Nikolai Shelgunov, provide far more remarks regarding Rakhmetov. Pisarev notes that Rakhmetov plays a secondary role in the novel and argues that Chernyshevskii introduces him only to show that the three main characters are really ordinary people.[28] Moreover, Pisarev goes on to castigate Rakhmetov for his asceticism, arguing that his behavior is illogical: it is incompatible with the progressive goal of achieving a happy life for all.[29] Pisarev almost seems to retreat from this harsh condemnation of Rakhmetov when he says that there are moments when such people are indispensable and irreplaceable. However, he is careful to state that such moments are rare and very short and that in normal times, when routine reigns, there is no application for the strength of the Rakhmetovs and they busy themselves with petty matters such as gymnastics.[30] Commenting on Rakhmetov's feat of sleeping on a bed of nails, Pisarev says, "Obviously all such fancies come from superfluous energy which cannot find wide or useful enough application."[31] In short, Pisarev found Rakhmetov to be a very problematic character and did not at all interpret him as a positive image to be emulated.

Finally, there are the extensive comments of Shelgunov regarding Rakhmetov. In his evaluation of the novel as a whole Shelgunov is very harsh in that he criticizes Chernyshevskii for making the same mistake as all novelists: he draws heroes, not simple mortals.[32] It is in this respect that he makes his numerous comments apropos Rakhmetov. For Shelgunov, Rakhmetov is an ambiguous character. He does approve of Rakhmetov's utilitarianism and his theory of labor.[33] However, he sees Rakhmetov as an eccentric and disapproves of his feat of sleeping on a bed of nails and his strange dietary habits. Shelgunov further argues that there is an irreconcilable dichotomy in Rakhmetov between his theory and his aristocratic origins. Despite his attempts at living like the common man, Rakhmetov can never become one, and thus his activities become ridiculous.[34] It is important to note that Shelgunov does argue that Rakhmetov *could* be a model if he were stripped of his eccentricities and the dichotomy were removed. It is perhaps this observation that might best lead us to a reevaluation of Rakhmetov. According to Shelgunov, it is certain *drapirovki* (drapings) that ruin the perception of Rakhmetov as a positive ideal.[35] Shelgunov is quite correct in this statement and it is to those *drapirovki*, especially the narrator's characterization and attitude toward Rakhmetov, that I now turn.

A REEVALUATION

Rakhmetov displays many extreme, absurd qualities that are hard to accept in a character that is a positive hero or an ideal. For example, his sleeping on a bed of nails has caused more than a few heads to shake (288). Chernyshevskii's detractors, as in the case of Fet, cite this episode as an example of the absurdities of the author and the lack of any artistic ability on his part.[36] Chernyshevskii's supporters have had particular difficulty in dealing with this scene. Both Pisarev and Shelgunov were clearly disturbed by it, which did much to lower Rakhmetov in their estimation. How could Chernyshevskii have created something so obviously ridiculous?[37] One answer, championed by Soviet scholars, has been to claim that Chernyshevskii is warning his radical colleagues to prepare themselves for the torture of the Tsarist prisons.[38] If this answer were not enough, some Soviet scholars have tried to make a direct connection between the bed of nails and the fact that Chernyshevskii was on a hunger strike while he was working on this section of the novel.[39] However, no one has convincingly explained away this most disturbing scene, and the question remains: can one really believe that Chernyshevskii expected his reader to accept and to imitate a character who slept on a bed of nails?[40] The answer may lie in the manner in which Rakhmetov is treated within the actual text.[41]

In the section entitled "A Peculiar Man" (chapter 3, section 29), where Rakhmetov is described in detail, he is treated in an irreverent, almost disrespectful manner, often mocked and abused by the narrator.[42] For example, the narrator states about people such as Rakhmetov: "I used to laugh at those particular individuals, my intimate friends, when I was alone with them. They either got angry or didn't, but they also used to laugh with themselves. In fact, there was a great deal that was very amusing about them: everything of importance about them was amusing, everything that characterized them as a breed apart. I love to laugh at such people" (274).[43]

Whenever the narrator refers to Rakhmetov, he continually notes that he finds him both amusing (*zabavnyi*) and ridiculous (*smeshnoi*).[44] Indeed, the narrator stresses that everything about Rakhmetov is ridiculous. For example, in describing the scene in which Rakhmetov shows Vera Pavlovna the note, the narrator says: "If an onlooker had been present, no matter how sensitive his heart, he couldn't have refrained from laughing at the solemnity of this entire procedure, in particular at the ritual ceremoniousness of this finale. It was undoubtedly ridiculous" (297).[45] In addition to these terms, the very title of the section in which Rakhmetov appears, "A Peculiar Man," conveys that the narrator views him as a bit strange and eccentric.[46] The narrator continually uses the word "peculiar" (*osobennyi*) to refer to Rakhmetov and his outlook while describing his transition into a peculiar man (279–80; LP 205–6). In conjunction with the ludicrous activities described in this paragraph by the narrator, including Rakhmetov's feat of reading for three consecutive days, such language displays hardly a reverential tone, but a negative, condescending attitude toward this character.

The narrator also characterizes Rakhmetov as eccentric and even juvenile when describing his transition into a peculiar man. The narrator uses the phrase "Это ему засело в голову" (It became lodged in his head; LP 205) to describe his decision to acquire and maintain great physical strength. This phrase is slightly negative in that it denotes a certain rigidity. That is, the decision to become a peculiar man has entered Rakhmetov's mind and become a fixed idea. It further denotes that Rakhmetov has become peculiar for its own sake. Combined with the negative designation "rigorist" (204, 279; LP 143, 205) given to Rakhmetov, the latter is clearly depicted as an inflexible eccentric acting according to an abstract idea. In addition, Rakhmetov's strange behavior is clearly treated by the narrator as the half-baked idea of an adolescent. For example, when Rakhmetov decides to take up gymnastics, the narrator uses the term *vzdumal* to describe it (LP 204).[47] This term too has a slightly negative connotation, denoting that his actions are not at all well considered or planned, and making Rakhmetov appear all the more flighty, eccentric. Thus, Rakhmetov's actions are not at all held up by the narrator for emulation. Rather they are treated as absurdities and, at least, implicitly rejected.[48]

Rakhmetov is characterized as absurd in other ways. For example, when he first comes to see Vera Pavlovna he searches for something to read. He settles upon Sir Isaac Newton's *Observations on the Prophecies of Daniel and the Apocalypse of Saint John.* Often too much is read into this choice by Rakhmetov.[49] However, this scene is meant merely to characterize Rakhmetov as a ridiculous, peculiar man. Immediately after Rakhmetov claims that the book is worth studying, the narrator states: "And with pleasurable zeal he sat down to read a book that has hardly been read by anyone but its original proofreaders for a hundred years or so. Anyone else would have found this book as tasty a dish as sand or sawdust. But Rakhmetov considered it a delicious morsel" (274).[50] Far from containing any great allegorical meaning, this passage fits quite well with the narrator's incessant characterization of Rakhmetov as an absurd individual.

Soviet scholars, in arguing that Rakhmetov is Chernyshevskii's positive hero, often point to the personal acquaintance between Rakhmetov and the narrator. This shows, they argue, that both are engaged in underground revolutionary activity.[51] That Rakhmetov is involved in some activity is not in dispute. However, those lines where the narrator acknowledges that he is personally acquainted with Rakhmetov do not do Rakhmetov any credit. For example, when the narrator first meets Rakhmetov, his attitude to the latter is hardly one of respect or reverence: "He arrived after I did. I was the only one present whom he didn't know. As soon as he came in he took Kirsanov aside; glancing at me, Rakhmetov uttered a few words. Kirsanov answered him with equally few words and was then released. A minute later Rakhmetov sat down directly across from me . . . he began to stare at my face with all his might. I was annoyed" (284).[52] The narrator is so put off by Rakhmetov that he uses the rather strong word *chudak* to describe him (LP 209).[53] Moreover, in this scene the narrator clearly wants to avoid Rakhmetov's acquaintance and is vexed by him: "At that time I didn't desire any new acquaintances, nor did I appreciate his persistence" (285).[54] When Rakhmetov finally succeeds in speaking to the narrator, the narrator refuses to take part in whatever activity Rakhmetov has suggested. The conversation that takes place between the two does not end on a good note, with Rakhmetov stating that the narrator is "either a liar or a worthless fellow" (286).[55] Rakhmetov is so strange, however, that the narrator is unable to get angry: "He himself was so peculiar that it would have been absurd to take offense; I could only laugh" (286).[56] Thus, contrary to Soviet speculations, Rakhmetov and the narrator are not cofighters for the cause; rather, the narrator has quite explicitly rejected Rakhmetov, dismissing him as an eccentric.

That Rakhmetov is characterized as ridiculous and eccentric is hardly in doubt. Rather, the motivation behind this characterization is the issue. Arguably, Rakhmetov follows in the long tradition of seemingly foolish men beginning with Jesus Christ.[57] As Christ appeared ridiculous to the masses, so too may Chernyshevskii have meant Rakhmetov. Or Rakhmetov's ridiculous qualities are arguably within the Russian tradition of the holy fool, in which such saintly characters are a bit eccentric, if not demented.[58] Contributing to this possibility is the fact that Rakhmetov is surrounded with numerous biblical (or near-biblical) quotations and religious motifs that seem to give him a religious aura.[59]

The most immediate religious model for Rakhmetov can be found in the *Life of Aleksei, a Man of God,* which Chernyshevskii, as the son of a priest and a former seminarian himself, undoubtedly knew very well.[60] In this *zhitie,* Aleksei is born the son of wealthy Roman citizens. His parents proposed the traditional lifestyle for him, sending him to school and marrying him to a girl of royal blood. But on his wedding night, Aleksei returns his ring to his spouse and leaves Rome for Syria. Once in Syria, Aleksei sells all his belongings and distributes the money to the poor. He spends his time in beggar's clothing, distributing all the alms he collects to the poor. Aleksei leads his life in vigil and fasting. After seventeen years abroad, Aleksei returns in disguise to his father's house. There he is lodged but treated badly by the servants. Aleksei, of course, bears this treatment gladly, with rejoicing. So he passes seventeen more years. When his end draws near, he leaves a parchment for his parents, in which he divulges his identity.[61]

Rakhmetov's own story, especially his giving up of all personal wealth and his adoption of an ascetic lifestyle in devotion to a cause, follows the pattern of Aleksei's *Life* very closely.[62] Rakhmetov and his story have all the hallmarks of medieval hagiography. Rakhmetov is given an extended genealogy, which was common for the medieval saint. Also, like a traditional ascetic he drinks no wine, follows a special diet, needs no rest, and rejects women.[63] Moreover, he subjects himself to self-mortification of the flesh, as when he sleeps on a bed of nails. These and many other characteristics leave little doubt that Chernyshevskii patterned Rakhmetov, at least in part, on the medieval, ascetic saint.[64] Thus, because of the host of religious imagery and hagiographical patterns, many have argued that Chernyshevskii presents the reader with a modern-day, secular saint who is to be emulated.

If the matter were left to rest there Rakhmetov could easily be interpreted as Chernyshevskii's reintroduction of the ascetic hero into Russian literature.[65] However, there are other elements surrounding Rakhmetov, besides his appearance as ridiculous, that lead one to question whether he is meant to be a positive hero. First, there are minor hints scattered throughout the sections on Rakhmetov that give an indication that he is to be rejected. For example, as we have seen, Pisarev found Rakhmetov's undertaking of gymnastics a wasteful enterprise. Chernyshevskii too apparently had little use for gymnastics. In "The Anthropological Principle," he states: "To avoid a subjective disturbance in the organism, to avoid sicknesses that are the result of inaction, to avoid ennui, the society man must create fictitious activity in place of normal activity. He lacks motion that has an objective rational purpose, so he 'takes a constitutional,' i.e., spends as much time putting one foot in front of the other as he ought to do in walking to work. He has no physical work to do, so he spends as much time 'doing gymnastics for the benefit of his health' . . . as he ought to spend on physical work."[66] In other words, Rakhmetov, whose social origin is quite high, has to create activity to keep himself occupied. The reference to gymnastics clearly places him within the tradition of the superfluous man, a type for which Chernyshevskii and the other radicals of the 1860s had nothing but contempt.

Another clue that Rakhmetov is to be rejected is that he is a member of the gentry. The narrator goes into great detail outlining Rakhmetov's genealogy, tracing it as far back as the thirteenth century, and is quite detailed about the wealth that Rakhmetov's family possesses. Traditionally, that genealogy is viewed as lending force to this positive hero by giving him the most impressive of backgrounds.[67] Chernyshevskii's hostility to the gentry is well known and hardly needs further elaboration. Within the novel itself, the narrator shows that the gentry is corrupt and hopeless.[68] Even the terrible Mar'ia Aleksevna is treated more kindly than the members of this class. Bearing this fact in mind, his origin is an indelible stain upon Rakhmetov.[69]

Further challenging Rakhmetov's viability as a positive hero is the fact that his grandfather was associated with the liberal Speranskii (276). This association is usually viewed as giving Rakhmetov's genealogy more sanctity.[70] However, when one remembers Chernyshevskii's hostility to the liberals, especially at this point in his life, such a relationship is by no means certain.[71] For example, although as a young man (October 1848) he did express a rather positive view of Speranskii, calling him an "intelligent" man (1:146), by September 1856 Chernyshevskii's attitude had changed sharply.[72] Moreover, by 1861, when the liberal-radical split had become irreversible, Chernyshevskii dismissed Speranskii as an "impractical dreamer" (7:812) who was given to "coarse self-delusion" (7:826). Summing up Speranskii's life and career, Chernyshevskii concluded thus:

> All such people are ridiculous, their delusions are petty. But they can be harmful to society when they are under delusions in serious matters. In their enthusiastic fussiness on a false path they can seem to achieve a certain success and thus sidetrack many who because of this apparent success decide to go along this same false path [which leads to nothing but phantasmagoria]. In this regard Speranskii's activity can be called harmful. [By means of his mistaken passion he enticed many to that same useless waste of strength on the application of means which did not correspond to the matter. Because of his work he gave several years of our history a false tint. There are people who take his activity as evidence that ideas about serious transformations existed. In fact, his work was set to serve only as a useless theoretical game and was discontinued by the first feeble impulse toward real significance.] (7:827)[73]

It is particularly significant that Chernyshevskii uses the word "ridiculous" (*smeshny*), the same word so often used with regard to Rakhmetov, to describe people like Speranskii. Moreover, Chernyshevskii explicitly states that Speranskii's ridiculousness is quite harmful. Thus, although Speranskii is often fondly remembered by Western scholars as a liberal reformer along Western lines, such was not Chernyshevskii's view. Speranskii's tenure was clearly viewed by Chernyshevskii as a harmful period in Russian society. Thus, the fact that his grandfather is associated with Speranskii must be viewed as most damaging to Rakhmetov.

Rakhmetov is often cited by Soviet scholars as having an organic tie to the people and being devoted to their welfare. One Soviet scholar claims that the leitmotif of Rakhmetov's life is service to the people.[74] In this regard, it is argued, Rakhmetov's social origin does not hinder him. Rather, he shows the only true path for the nobleman: to break with his own class.[75] Despite Soviet assertions to the contrary, however, Rakhmetov is far from close to or devoted to the people.[76] For example, Kathryn Feuer may be correct when she argues that Rakhmetov does not free his serfs but *sells* them.[77] The text is not entirely clear on this point because Chernyshevskii's narrator feigns ignorance: "[H]e received only about 400 souls and 7,000 desiatinas of land. No one knew how he'd disposed of the souls and 5,500 of his desiatinas" (276).[78] The reader is told that Rakhmetov kept 1,500 desiatinas for himself and later sold them (287). However, the fate of the serfs is never mentioned, though it is explicitly stated that he sold part of his land. This is indeed a glaring omission, and the reader can safely assume that Rakhmetov either sells or gives away his serfs, but he does not free them.[79] For someone supposedly dedicated to the cause and to the people, this is a most hypocritical act that Chernyshevskii obviously could not have approved of.

In addition, the very scene in which Rakhmetov sleeps on his bed of nails also subtly displays his hypocrisy regarding the people. This supposed lover of the common people has been torturing his landlady for months with his odd behavior. This act alone has frightened the poor landlady: "The next morning Rakhmetov's landlady came running to fetch Kirsanov in great alarm: 'Mr. Doctor, I don't know what's become of my tenant. He hasn't come out of his room for some time. The door's locked. I looked through the crack and saw him lying there covered with blood. I began yelling, but he called through the door, "It's nothing, Agrafena Antonovna." What kind of nothing? Save him, Mr. Doctor, I fear for his life! He's so hard on himself'" (288).[80] Moreover, despite the numerous claims that Chernyshevskii is trying to hint at something of great importance here,[81] the narrator's sympathy seems to be on the side of the distressed landlady. Rakhmetov does make his famous statement, "A trial. . . . It's necessary. Improbable, of course, but in any case necessary. Now I know I can do it" (288).[82] But the narrator then says: "Besides those things that Kirsanov saw, it was obvious that the landlady could tell a great many more interesting stories about Rakhmetov; but she was a simple-hearted and simply attired old woman who doted on him. It was impossible to get anything more out of her. This particular time she'd come to fetch Kirsanov simply because Rakhmetov allowed her to do so in order to calm her down. She wept bitterly at the idea that Rakhmetov might have wanted to kill himself" (288–89).[83]

Rakhmetov is devoted to his cause no matter what the consequences, including the infliction of distress on a simple-hearted old woman. It is the motivation behind his devotion that betrays Rakhmetov's ultimate shortcoming. As Marcia Morris argues, "the most salient details of Rakhmetov's life are all indicative of his efforts to improve himself, and only himself." Despite the assumption that Rakhmetov works for the cause of the people, in fact, he never "undertakes anything remotely connected with this task."[84] His quest for acquiring great physical strength, for example, is pure vanity: "It inspires respect and love of the common people" (279).[85] Rakhmetov is motivated, rather, by his search for perfection. In other words, he has given himself over to an abstraction and thus alienated himself from society.

Vera Pavlovna's attitude toward Rakhmetov is also a valuable clue to deciphering the character and his purpose in the novel. Until Rakhmetov comes to her to deliver the letter, Vera Pavlovna's attitude is almost entirely negative. She refers to him as terrible (*uzhasnyi*) and as the narrator states: "He held himself very removed from Vera Pavlovna. She found him boring; he never joined her circle of friends" (272).[86] It is true that during their conversation, Vera Pavlovna finds Rakhmetov to be more human than she thought (300). However, one should take note of the fact that on this evening, Rakhmetov has dropped his ascetic habits for the most part. He has eaten and drunk his fill and otherwise let himself go. It is due only to this that Vera Pavlovna's opinion of him softens, which suggests that Rakhmetov is not a bad person, but that his ascetic outlook is ridiculous and dehumanizing. Moreover, an explicit rejection of Rakhmetov's ascetic path is made by Vera Pavlovna later in the novel. Although Rakhmetov's dedication may be admirable, Vera Pavlovna is clearly aware that it is exceptional and impractical for most people to follow: "The Rakhmetovs are a different breed. They identify with the common cause to such an extent that it becomes their own necessity, filling their lives. It even comes to replace their personal life. But that's beyond us, Sasha. We're not eagles, like he is. Personal life is the only thing that's indispensable to us" (343).[87] The fact that the main (and narrator's favorite) character of the novel explicitly rejects Rakhmetov's path seriously calls into question whether he is Chernyshevskii's positive hero.

Adding to these facts is the considerable distance between the narrator and Rakhmetov maintained in *What Is to Be Done?* Similar to his treatment of the views expressed by Lopukhov and Kirsanov, the narrator distances himself from those of Rakhmetov. After Rakhmetov has become a peculiar man, the narrator is careful to give Rakhmetov's formulations as direct quotations. For example, regarding Rakhmetov's justification for the adoption of an austere lifestyle, it is Rakhmetov himself who explains his reasoning (281). Also when using key words of Rakhmetov's vocabulary, such as *nuzhno* (LP 214), the narrator is always careful to place them in quotation marks (*kavychki*), thus stressing that they are not his own. In short, the narrator never endorses any of Rakhmetov's formulations and is quite careful to distance himself from them. Thus, there is no cause to attribute Rakhmetov's views either to the narrator or to the author.

The views espoused by Rakhmetov are not those of Chernyshevskii and, in fact, are often polar opposites.[88] They differ, for example, regarding love. Rakhmetov, as part of his austere philosophy, renounces love to devote himself fully to his cause. After his conversion he states, "I shall not touch any women" (280)[89] Rakhmetov is tempted by the young widow whose life he saves. When she confesses her love and proposes marriage, he refuses, however, so as not to tie his hands: "You must see that people like me have no right to bind their destiny to someone else's" (290).[90] Rakhmetov is certain that love will inhibit his activity and doom him to failure.[91] Such a view is in stark contrast to Chernyshevskii's thinking, in which love played a very large role. He considered love and marriage a necessary spur to human activity; without them, a man is doomed to fail.[92] As a strong supporter of women's emancipation, Chernyshevskii found marriage in its contemporary form abominable. Despite this fact, however, he considered love so important in human life, that he argued that it is impossible not to get married.[93] This outlook is also expressed in the novel itself, where the topic of love and marriage is given an inordinate amount of attention and defined as one of, if not the, basic prerequisite of human existence.[94] If Feuer is correct that "the test of successful love between men and women" is crucial for Chernyshevskii, then Rakhmetov has failed miserably.[95] In short, Rakhmetov's ascetic philosophy is not at all Chernyshevskii's and is not held up for emulation.

Chernyshevskii's and Rakhmetov's views are also diametric regarding sex. Rakhmetov has renounced not only love but also the sexual act. When the young widow accepts his decision not to marry she asks him to love her at least for the moment. Rakhmetov refuses that also, stating: "No, I can't do that. I must suppress any love in myself: to love you would mean to bind my hands. They're already bound, and it will take me some time to untie them. But I'll manage. I must not love" (290).[96] In short, Rakhmetov will let nothing get in the way of his devotion to the cause. This view contrasts with Chernyshevskii's own, which regarded sex as an essential part of the human condition and abstinence as harmful, especially for women.[97] Chernyshevskii's view finds some expression in *What Is to Be Done?* for the novel is saturated with numerous references to the sexual act that are presented with apparent narrative approval.[98] Again Rakhmetov's outlook is at odds with the views of both the narrator and the author.

Rakhmetov is also a questionable positive hero in that he is clearly a subscriber to the principles of utopian socialism. This is best exemplified by his interest in Vera Pavlovna's co-op. Rakhmetov fully approves of it and is interested in its survival.[99] For example, he berates Vera Pavlovna for her decision to leave the co-op and get away: "The position requires rather rare ability. I'll bet ten to one that there's really no one to replace you and that your departure would destroy the whole enterprise. Is that fair? You'd be subjecting the well-being of some fifty people to almost certain, inevitable ruin. And for what? For some small personal convenience! Is that right? What tender solicitude to your own insignificant comfort, yet what indifference to the fate of others! How do you like this view of the whole affair?" (298–99).[100] Such views do not at all coincide, however, with those of Chernyshevskii at the time he wrote the novel.[101] Rakhmetov is explicitly identified with views to which we know Chernyshevskii was hostile. Moreover, within the novel itself, utopian socialism is rejected in that Vera Pavlovna's co-op comes under a subtle critique from Chernyshevskii; it is not endorsed. In short, Rakhmetov differs greatly from his creator on a key ideological issue.

There is also a wide ideological gap between Chernyshevskii and Rakhmetov regarding materialism and utilitarianism. Rakhmetov, as part of his process of becoming a peculiar man, becomes enamored of the many "isms" of the time. In this regard, Kirsanov serves as his mentor. The reader is told that Rakhmetov wept the first night he heard Kirsanov speak, and it is Kirsanov, the confirmed materialist and utilitarian, who provides Rakhmetov with the names of the proper books to read (279–80). In addition, Rakhmetov clearly invokes the utilitarian pleasure-pain calculus when he berates Vera Pavlovna for her actions regarding the co-op: "You would have provided the defenders of darkness and evil with an argument against your own sacred principles. I'm not even talking about the fact that you might have destroyed the well-being of some fifty people. *What do fifty people matter? You could have harmed the cause of all mankind and betrayed the idea of progress!* That, Vera Pavlovna, in ecclesiastical language is called a sin against the Holy Spirit" (301–2; emphasis mine).[102]

In contrast to Rakhmetov's logic, *What Is to Be Done?* actually reverses the pleasure-pain calculus, giving primacy to the interests of the few or even of one over those of the many. For example, many (Lopukhov, the Mertsalovs, even Julie) risk themselves or expend effort to aid Vera Pavlovna. Moreover, as we have seen in the previous chapter, *What Is to Be Done?* is a text that rejects materialism and utilitarianism. Rakhmetov's identification with those philosophies can only be to his detriment. Furthermore, Rakhmetov clearly has given power to an abstraction (that is, to the idea of progress) over human beings. Rakhmetov clearly does not care so much about the fifty people involved in the co-op, but only about an abstract goal.

In conjunction with this Rakhmetov clearly endorses the concept of self-sacrifice to an abstract goal. That he has committed himself to it is all too evident: "In general one sees such disagreeable things; how can one help being a gloomy monster? Only now, Vera Pavlovna, that you've had the chance to see me in a mood that I'd like to be in all the time, and since we've been so open with one another, let it remain our secret that I'm really not a gloomy monster because I enjoy it. It'll be easier for me to fulfill my obligations if others don't notice that I'd like not only to do that, but also to enjoy life. Now people don't try to distract me or take up my time by forcing me to refuse their invitations" (300–1).[103] However, he also demands this of Vera Pavlovna. For Rakhmetov, her petty feelings and concerns are not of the slightest importance.[104] Rather, she must subdue these and subordinate herself to the good of the whole. She is obligated, according to Rakhmetov, to serve the cause no matter what the cost, including her own personal happiness. In short, not only does Rakhmetov impose theory on life, but he demands that Vera Pavlovna do the same. It is precisely this type of self-sacrifice and suppression of feeling that Chernyshevskii rejects most forcefully in this novel.

Rakhmetov is a very questionable character indeed: there is very little that supports him as the positive hero, but there is much evidence to reject him. The question still remains, however, why Chernyshevskii included such a character in his novel in the first place. There are two answers to this question. The first answer lies, I believe, in a specific ideological point that Chernyshevskii is trying to make. This answer is hidden and must be inferred by the reader to a large degree. Hints appear in one-line statements by the narrator to the effect that the female reader and common reader will know why Rakhmetov has been introduced (292, 294). Although not the positive hero or an ideal to be emulated, Rakhmetov does play a very important part in Chernyshevskii's message. In short, Rakhmetov is part of Chernyshevskii's answer to the question "What is to be done?" or, more accurately, Rakhmetov's story is what is not to be done.

To better understand Rakhmetov's role in *What Is to Be Done?* we must examine the real-life model on which he was closely based. Although several sources have been suggested as the real life model of Rakhmetov, the most likely is Pavel Aleksandrovich Bakhmetev (born 1828), who was from Chernyshevskii's native region of Saratov.[105] Chernyshevskii and Bakhmetev were personally acquainted in Saratov, probably as early as 1846. According to what sources there are on this mysterious man, he was a member of a wealthy family, known since the fifteenth century, who might be described as a repentant (penitent) nobleman. He sold his estate, including his serfs, in 1857 for about 15,000 rubles. Bakhmetev arrived in Petersburg and spent an evening in May 1857 walking with Chernyshevskii, leaving Russia shortly afterward. He arrived in London, where he visited Herzen and gave him a considerable sum of money (800 pounds sterling) to be used for the cause of the revolution. After this point, he went to the South Pacific (variously reported as the Marquesas Islands, Australia, the Sandwich Islands, New Zealand) to found a new social order, based on utopian socialist principles, and was never heard from again.[106]

The similarities between Rakhmetov and Bakhmetev are very striking, from their surnames to the many events in their respective biographies.[107] Moreover, several of Chernyshevskii's contemporaries, especially his relatives, were convinced that Chernyshevskii based his character on the adventures of Pavel Bakhmetev. His sister-in-law, E. Pypina, for example, wrote: "Nikolai Gavrilovich knew a lot about him which we did not even suspect."[108] Likewise, Herzen believed that Rakhmetov's story was based largely on the adventures of Bakhmetev.[109] And, if we are to accept S. G. Stakhevich's memoirs as accurate, then Chernyshevskii explicitly accepted such an identification: "In my novel I called the peculiar man Rakhmetov precisely in honor of this Bakhmetev."[110]

All the evidence certainly seems to demonstrate that Chernyshevskii based his character Rakhmetov in large part on Bakhmetev. The real question is what Chernyshevskii does with this material. Soviet scholars have traditionally argued that Chernyshevskii chose Pavel Bakhmetev on which to model Rakhmetov because he approved of Bakhmetev's activities in the cause of the revolution. Evidence of such an opinion on Chernyshevskii's part is not forthcoming, however. Bakhmetev's name is mentioned only twice in Chernyshevskii's collected works and then only in passing (14:40, 71). There is no extended discussion of Bakhmetev and, consequently, no endorsement of his activities. In view of the fact that Chernyshevskii probably knew Bakhmetev personally since 1846, this is somewhat remarkable. If Chernyshevskii had the high opinion of Bakhmetev that is so often assumed, one would expect more references to him.

There is evidence, however, that Chernyshevskii held a negative opinion regarding Bakhmetev. Stakhevich, in discussing Chernyshevskii's trip to London in 1859, seems to convey that Chernyshevskii had a very condescending attitude toward Bakhmetev: "Perhaps it was during this same meeting with Herzen that Nikolai Gavrilovich heard from him about the Saratov landowner Bakhmetev who sold off his estates, went abroad and left at the disposal of Herzen a significant sum of money made from this sale, asking him to use this money for the cause of the revolution. . . . He added details, calling them amusing, about how this eccentric (that is, Bakhmetev) went into Herzen's place with some kind of bundle in his hands, how he unwrapped the napkin in which packets of money were tied up, how several packets slipped out and scattered on the floor."[111] This description treats Bakhmetev as far from a heroic figure. Rather, like the character based on him, he is treated as an eccentric.

In creating Rakhmetov, Chernyshevskii was responding to a particular social phenomenon that we today call the repentant, or penitent, nobleman. Such young people felt guilt for the fact that they had been born of the gentry. In an attempt to atone for their guilt, they would break with their own class, including their own families, and devote themselves to the people, to the cause. This phenomenon manifested itself in many ways: most popular of course was either to give away all their money or to use it to support others less fortunate than themselves. Few stopped there though: many put themselves through the most rigid of demands all in the attempt to expiate their guilt. And most important, they viewed themselves as owing some sort of debt to the people. They felt that they had acquired an education and refinement at the people's expense and that they must give something back. As a result they were obsessed with helping the people (*narod*) even when their help was not at all desired.

Chernyshevskii, who it must be remembered was not of the gentry himself, had very little use for the repentant noblemen,[112] and the concepts of self-sacrifice and duty ran counter to many of his own notions.[113] He felt that for all their dramatic displays, these people were useless in the revolutionary cause. He was put off by the young revolutionaries who made a public show of their devotion to the cause, seeing it as all glitter and little substance.[114] For example, when speaking of the revolutionary M. D. Muravskii, he expressed a remarkable amount of contempt for his type: "He belongs to the category of those straightforward revolutionaries who do not know how, and do not even want, to take into consideration circumstances of time and place. In the critical moments of national life these people will carry their banner through the scene of action; this they know how to do and will do. But critical moments are rare and short. Before them and after them it is necessary to give up these people as hopeless: it is impossible to get anything from them or at least very little. Saintly babies: they are saintly it is true, but they are also babies."[115]

It is the reference to these types of people as "saintly babies" that explains the rather odd combination we have in Rakhmetov; that is, he seems to many a secular saint. Chernyshevskii no doubt noticed that penitent noblemen like Pavel Bakhmetev had many of the same qualities as the medieval ascetics. Beyond mere outward similarities, there was a strong similarity in their respective philosophies. Both philosophies preached the notion of some sort of debt or duty and both preached a life of suffering, denial, and martyrdom on earth in the hopes of bringing about the future paradise. The definitions of this future paradise of course were different, but a man like Chernyshevskii, who always stressed living for the here and now, could not have helped but notice the basic similarity between the two philosophies.

It is for this reason that Rakhmetov is introduced into the novel. Rakhmetov is meant as a parody of a particular type: the ascetic who gives up everything for some sort of cause, be it religious or secular. It is precisely for this reason that Chernyshevskii uses so many hagiographical devices. The language, imagery, and events of the *zhitie* of a medieval ascetic were so familiar to his readers, especially his radical compatriots, many of whom were former seminarians, that few were likely to miss the connection. By combining the traits of Pavel Bakhmetev, a type easily recognizable in Russian society of the time, with the commonplaces of hagiography, Chernyshevskii created a very powerful image of an ascetic that was easily identifiable. Moreover, he took some of those traits to such absurd extremes that few readers, who were in the know, could mistake the purpose of this character. The religious imagery is not meant to sanctify Rakhmetov, as has often been argued, but rather to make him readily identifiable as a specific type. In this sense, Rakhmetov's story is not neohagiography, but antihagiography.

Despite the multitude of evidence to the contrary, scholars have persisted in seeing Chernyshevskii's positive hero in Rakhmetov. Largely responsible for this is Chernyshevskii's fervent desire not to aid the forces of reaction and conservatism in any way. No matter what his opinion of the members of the younger generation, Chernyshevskii would not openly condemn them in print, but defended them from the slanderous attacks of their enemies. A hint at such attacks is expressed by Rakhmetov himself when he says to Vera Pavlovna, "You know it's said that people of our kind hold nothing sacred. We're capable of any violence and villainy" (304).[116]

In response to this perceived hostility Chernyshevskii provides an ardent defense of the younger generation in his polemic with the perspicacious reader apropos Rakhmetov:

> Such was the scheme devised by Lopukhov; Rakhmetov was merely his agent. You see, my dear sir, O perspicacious reader, what schemers these noble young are, and how egoism plays in their souls. It's different from yours, dear sir, because they take their satisfaction elsewhere. They take their greatest satisfaction in having people whom they respect regard them as noble; to achieve this end, my dear sir, they work hard and devise all sorts of schemes no less diligently than you do in pursuit of your goals. Only your goals are different, and so the schemes you devise are not the same. You devise schemes that are worthless and harmful to others; they devise schemes that are honest and useful to others. (309–10)[117]

Likewise, at the end of the section entitled "A Peculiar Man" the narrator says the following about people like Rakhmetov:

> There are only a few of them, but through them everyone's life will flourish. Without them life would wither and go sour. There are only a few of them, but they make it possible for all people to breathe; without them people would suffocate. There's a great mass of honest and good people, but there are very few people like them. But these few people are within that mass, as theine is in tea, as bouquet is in fine wine. They are its strength and its aroma. They are the flower of the best people, the movers of the movers, the salt of the salt of the earth. (293)[118]

These are strong words and have been accepted at face value by twentieth-century scholars as evidence that Rakhmetov is Chernyshevskii's positive hero. However, this passage is not quite the endorsement of him that many scholars think. The positive words that are so often cited regarding Rakhmetov come only within the context of the narrator's polemic with the perspicacious reader:

> So you see, O perspicacious reader, it isn't to you but to another part of the public that I admit that people like Rakhmetov are ridiculous. To you, O per-

> spicacious reader, I shall say that these people aren't bad people. Otherwise, you might not understand that for yourself. Yes, they're not bad people. There are only a few of them, but through them everyone's life will flourish. (293)[119]

Within this very defense the narrator admits openly that Rakhmetov is ridiculous and defends him only with regard to certain hostile circles. Moreover, the narrator's stress that "they're not bad people" is quite clearly directed at defending their character. Nothing is said in defense of their philosophy. In fact, despite the defense of the members of the younger generation, the narrator acknowledges his disagreement with their chosen path and explicitly disavows it: "Yes, people like Rakhmetov are ridiculous, very amusing indeed. I say that for their own benefit, because I feel sorry for them. I say it to those noble people who are so fascinated by them: 'Don't follow their example, O noble people,' I say, 'because the path to which they summon you leads to no personal joys.' But the noble people don't listen to me. They reply, 'No, it's not barren, it's rich—and even if barren here and there, still it doesn't take long to get past those places; we'll have the strength to reach other places that are rich in endless joy'" (292–93).[120]

This is not the only disavowal of revolutionary asceticism in the novel. At the very end of chapter 3, after Rakhmetov has been dismissed from the novel, the narrator directly addresses the reader regarding this philosophy. Here, he again disavows revolutionary asceticism and encourages the reader to live and enjoy life: "Come up out of your godforsaken underworld, my friends, come up. It's not so difficult. Come out into the light of day, where life is good; the path is easy and inviting. Try it: development, development. Observe, reflect, read those books that tell you about the pure enjoyment of life, and about the fact that man can be kind and happy. Read them: such books gladden the heart. Observe life: it's so interesting. Reflect: it's so fascinating. That's all there is to it! *No sacrifices are needed, no deprivations required—they're all unnecessary. Desire to be happy—that's all.* Only desire is needed" (313; emphasis mine).[121] This passage comes at the very end of the sections devoted to Rakhmetov; that is, directly after the reader has been given the long story of Rakhmetov's revolutionary ascetic journey. No more striking contrast and no more striking rejection than this is to be had. In view of the evidence delegitimizing Rakhmetov as a positive hero and the explicit disavowals provided, Rakhmetov's story is clearly what is not to be done.

META-NARRATIVE TREATMENT

We have seen that Chernyshevskii has an ideological purpose in mind when introducing Rakhmetov into the novel. But this is not the entire story, for Chernyshevskii also introduces him for literary reasons. Chernyshevskii purposely introduces the question "Why is this character, who is practically unnecessary from the point of view of plot, introduced and given space?" The answering of that question forms a large part of Chernyshevskii's polemic with conventional Russian literature and aesthetics. Unfortunately, however, that aspect of the text has largely been ignored in the discussion of Rakhmetov.

The three sections devoted to Rakhmetov are filled with numerous meta-narrative discussions of the character. In the first of them, the narrator, no doubt anticipating the charges of implausibility, claims to know Rakhmetov and people like him, although they are rare. It is there that the narrator makes his famous statement that he has met only eight such people in his lifetime.[122] Throughout section 29, the narrator continually stresses that he is personally acquainted with Rakhmetov. To emphasize the point he uses such phrases as "we learned it all later" (276)[123] or "none of us knew" (277).[124] All this serves to create the illusion that Rakhmetov is, as Soviet scholars loved to phrase it, a person whom one could easily meet walking down Nevskii Prospekt. The illusion is further strengthened by the narrator's telling of his first meeting with Rakhmetov and their subsequent conversation (285–86). The narrator describes the encounter in detail, relating such facts as his vexation and confusion at being confronted with such a strange person. When the narrator relates some of the content of the conversation that later follows, the reader is left with the illusion that this character is indeed based on a living, breathing human being.

Toward the end of section 29 this illusion is given one last bit of support. The narrator directly addresses the perspicacious reader apropos Rakhmetov. In that address, the narrator states his purpose in describing such a character in detail—to show that such people do exist in the world: "Yes, he was an extraordinary man, a specimen of a very rare breed. I haven't described a specimen of this breed in such detail merely in order to instruct you, O perspicacious reader, in the appropriate way (unknown to you) to treat such people. You'll never get to see even one example of this breed. Your eyes, O perspicacious reader, aren't constituted so that you can perceive such types. They're invisible to you. Only honest and bold eyes can see them. This description serves merely so that you'll know, even if only by hearsay, what kind of people exist on this earth" (292).[125] However, at the end of that paragraph the narrator adds one very important sentence: "As for what purpose this description serves the female reader and the common reader, well, they themselves know" (292).[126] It is this last sentence that is perhaps the key to understanding Rakhmetov as a whole. As we have seen, the addresses to the perspicacious reader are the least trustworthy passages in the novel. They form a part of Chernyshevskii's game with conventional literature and aesthetics and cannot be taken too literally. The last sentence greatly stresses that fact and alerts real readers that they are not to take anything the narrator says to the perspicacious reader at face value.

Thus, this passage in its entirety begins to undermine the illusion that Rakhmetov really does exist. That fact is strongly emphasized in the very next section (30), where Rakhmetov performs his one action. Before the actual action of the section begins, the narrator engages in a dialogue with the perspicacious reader. The perspicacious reader begins the dialogue by positing that Vera Pavlovna will now fall in love with Rakhmetov and begin a new love triangle. The narrator then informs him that nothing of the sort will happen and further informs him of exactly what will happen with Rakhmetov: he will talk with Vera Pavlovna, leave, and play no more role in the novel (293).

It is at this point that Chernyshevskii's polemic with conventional literature and aesthetics reaches its culmination, for the narrator openly taunts the perspicacious reader to guess *why* a character such as Rakhmetov has been introduced: "But why then was he introduced and described in such detail? Well, my perspicacious reader, wouldn't you like to guess the reason? You'll be told why a few pages hence, following the conversation between Rakhmetov and Vera Pavlovna. As soon as he takes his leave, I'll explain it all to you at the end of this chapter" (293–94).[127] This challenge serves several functions. First, it stresses that Rakhmetov is a literary construct, not a real person. It also demonstrates once again that statements to the perspicacious reader are not particularly trustworthy. On the previous page the narrator has just told the perspicacious reader that Rakhmetov has been introduced so that he (the perspicacious reader) will know that such people actually do exist. This passage, through both its emphasis on Rakhmetov as a literary construct and its further challenge to guess why he is in the novel, greatly delegitimizes the first answer provided by the narrator.

This passage demonstrates that Rakhmetov is introduced as a deus ex machina; his presence in the novel is seemingly unmotivated by literary concerns. The narrator is obviously aware of this fact (and so is the author). Yet the narrator hardly seems concerned with it and certainly does not try to hide it. Instead, he throws down the gauntlet at conventional literature and challenges the perspicacious reader to guess why Rakhmetov is introduced. The challenge turns particularly vicious when the narrator states:

> You may want to guess now what you'll be told then. It's not hard to guess if you've even the least notion of art, about which you so love to blather. But how could you guess? Well, I'll prompt you with more than half the answer: Rakhmetov has been introduced to fulfill the principal, most fundamental requirement of art, and exclusively to satisfy it. Well, well, can you guess now? At least you can guess what this requirement is, what was needed to satisfy it, and how it was satisfied by the introduction of Rakhmetov, even though he has no influence or importance in the rest of the story. Come now, guess! My female reader and the common reader who doesn't go on at length about art already know the answer. But you, my wise male reader, you too must try to

> guess! You can have as much time as you need; for that purpose I'll put a long, thick black line between sections. See what good care I take of you? Pause over it and reflect as to whether you will or won't be able to guess the answer. (294)[128]

After Rakhmetov performs his action in section 30, section 31, entitled "A Conversation with the Perspicacious Reader Followed by His Expulsion," is devoted entirely to a discussion of why Rakhmetov appears in the novel. This section is a masterpiece of meta-narrative. The first three paragraphs, for example, do much to convey the tone and content of this section:

> Now tell me, O perspicacious reader, why Rakhmetov was introduced, if now he's gone and will no longer appear in my story? You've already been told that he has no role whatever in the action. . . .
>
> "That's not true," interrupts the perspicacious reader. "Rakhmetov is a principal character: he carried the note in which . . ."
>
> "You're very poor, my dear, in those aesthetic deliberations you so love," I reply, interrupting him. "In that case would you also consider Masha a principal character? At the beginning of the story she also delivered a letter that horrified Vera Pavlovna. And what about Rachel? She gave Vera money for those goods, and without it Vera Pavlovna wouldn't have been able to leave. Is Professor N. an important character because he recommended Vera Pavlovna as a governess to Madame B., and otherwise there would have been no scene upon her return from Konnogvardeiskii Boulevard? Perhaps even the boulevard is a principal character? Without it there would have been no possibility of either meeting on it or returning from it." (307–8)[129]

Throughout this section, Chernyshevskii introduces and lays bare many of the traditional devices of conventional literature.[130] For example, when the perspicacious reader responds that Rakhmetov is introduced to bring a verdict upon Vera Pavlovna and Lopukhov and to converse with Vera Pavlovna, the narrator responds: "Oh, you're so dumb, my dear sir! You've got it all backward. Was it really necessary to introduce a special character so that he could express his opinion of the others? Perhaps your great literary artists introduce characters in their works and discard them according to those considerations, but I, although only a poor writer, understand nevertheless the requirements of true art somewhat better than that. No, my dear sir, Rakhmetov wasn't needed for that at all! How many times have Vera Pavlovna, Lopukhov, and Kirsanov expressed their opinions of their own actions and relationships? They're not stupid people; they can decide for themselves what's good and what's bad, and have no need for any prompting" (308).[131] This passage continues for another two pages, in which the narrator informs the perspicacious reader that Rakhmetov functions merely as Lopukhov's instrument (308–9).

From this point, the narrator switches from questioning the reader about Rakhmetov's purpose to questioning the reason the conversation between Rakhmetov and Vera Pavlovna is introduced: "Now, dear sir, here's a question for you. Why have I included this conversation between Rakhmetov and Vera Pavlovna? Do you understand that if I choose to convey a conversation between them instead of Lopukhov's or Vera Pavlovna's thoughts, then it was essential to convey not merely the thoughts that made up their conversation but also the conversation itself? Why was it necessary to convey that conversation? Because it took place between Rakhmetov and Vera Pavlovna. Now do you understand? You still don't? You're a fine one! Not too bright, are you?" (310).[132] In further playing with the perspicacious reader, the narrator leads the perspicacious reader to guess that Rakhmetov is not introduced to give the conversation but rather that the conversation is introduced to characterize Rakhmetov (310–11).

Now that the perspicacious reader has seen the light, that is, now that he knows that Rakhmetov has not been introduced to converse with Vera Pavlovna, the narrator continues to press him about why Rakhmetov is in the novel: "Now do you understand, my perspicacious reader, that while many pages were devoted to a direct description of Rakhmetov's character, many more served exclusively to make you better acquainted with an individual who is not at all a principal character in the novel? Tell me now why this figure was presented and described in such detail" (311).[133] It is at this point that the narrator feigns exasperation with the perspicacious reader and says he will speak with the general public instead and, moreover, that he will speak seriously (311). In the passages that follow, the narrator outlines many of the basic rules of artistry and explains why he has introduced Rakhmetov. The narrator states that he has introduced Rakhmetov to give the public a sense of proportion. That is, he is worried that the public will think too highly of the three main characters and worship them. Thus, he has introduced a gigantic figure like Rakhmetov to make his real heroes seem down-to-earth (312–13).

Many observers have taken these passages quite literally, as direct expressions of both Chernyshevskii's aesthetic principles and his reason for introducing Rakhmetov into the novel.[134] However, I would argue for a far more critical look. In particular, the assertion by the narrator that he will speak seriously, following as it does on the heels of a conversation with the perspicacious reader, is extremely suspect. It seems intended to alert the reader to quite the opposite. In these passages, rather, Chernyshevskii plays with and mocks the devices of conventional literature and, in this regard, they cannot be taken too literally. Thus, I would argue that *none* of the reasons given by the narrator for Rakhmetov's existence in the novel are trustworthy. All the purported reasons he offers are maxims of conventional aesthetics, and he introduces the "answers" to belittle them. The discussions with the perspicacious reader, the embodiment of the aesthetes, show that Rakhmetov is introduced, in large part, to belittle and play with the devices of conventional aesthetics and its self-appointed defenders. In short, far from being the great positive hero intended for emulation, Rakhmetov is a mere device to aid the author in his polemic against an outmoded aesthetics.

CHERNYSHEVSKII AND THE QUESTION OF ASCETICISM

We have seen above that there is much evidence calling into question Rakhmetov's status as a positive hero and that there is an explicit disavowal of his chosen path. We now turn to the question of how (revolutionary) asceticism is treated in the remainder of the novel. This question is quite relevant because *What Is to Be Done?* has been labeled "an ascetic book, a sort of manual of the devout life for Russian nihilists."[135] Despite this evaluation, however, throughout the novel the narrator is careful to stress that one should enjoy life, that one should live for the here and now. For example, in describing why Julie leads an unhappy life, the narrator makes it clear that it is due to self-denial: "Nevertheless, upon returning to her senses, she sees that she has no freedom herself. She must please others and constrain herself—and it's all very painful" (104).[136] Likewise, the narrator seems to address Vera Pavlovna directly, saying, "What's strange in your wanting to be a free and happy person? That desire is neither a very puzzling discovery of science nor a great feat of heroism" (104).[137] The narrator goes on to state that asceticism, although he does not use the actual word, is bad; that for a person to think about the happiness of others, he must first think about his own happiness: "What's really strange, Verochka, is that there are people who don't share this desire, who have completely different ones; perhaps it's they who will find those ideas strange, my friend, with which you can fall asleep the first night of your being in love, that from thinking about yourself, your beloved, and your love, you should begin to think that all people should be happy and that one must work to bring this about soon. But, while you don't know how strange it is, I know that it isn't strange at all, that it alone is natural and humane. It's simply humane: 'I feel joy and happiness' means 'I want everyone to be joyful and happy.' It's humane, Verochka, that both of these ideas are one and the same" (104–5).[138]

These and other statements demonstrate that the narrator does not hold an ascetic outlook, but quite the opposite.[139] In this regard the narrator stands very close to the actual author. In his other works Chernyshevskii consistently took a stand against any philosophy of asceticism, especially when it was intended to mask exploitation.[140] For example, Chernyshevskii states of the Jesuits and their like: "the goal of preaching asceticism is to inculcate in the unhappy and the hungry the idea that they will have to be hungry eternally and that they should be happy that such is their fate" (4:629).[141] Chernyshevskii attacked "the more or less official doctrine of Western civilization that self-denial and self-sacrifice were good goals." Rather, "man is destined, according to Chernyshevsky, to be happy and fulfilled."[142] Chernyshevskii so stressed that one should live for the here and now that one author has even labeled him a hedonist.[143]

Chernyshevskii's polemic with asceticism is also quite evident in the course of events in the novel. When he is first introduced, Lopukhov, like Rakhmetov, leads a Spartan existence, fully devoted to his work. Upon entering his room, Vera Pavlovna is shocked by the extent of his ascetic habits. It is this fact that forces her to realize that she and Lopukhov actually have little in common (246–47).[144] Moreover, it is made clear that Lopukhov, like many of the male characters, is not quite able to enjoy life like the female characters do: "But it goes without saying that for the most part they didn't listen, and even doused Lopukhov and Aleksei Petrovich with water when they got too excited over the enormous importance of mineral fertilizers. But Aleksei Petrovich and Lopukhov persevered, unwavering in their learned discourse. Kirsanov didn't provide much assistance; he was more on the side of the ladies, even entirely so. The three of them played the piano, sang songs, and laughed until late into the night, when, exhausted, they finally managed to separate the invincible zealots of serious conversation" (180).[145] This passage also demonstrates that Kirsanov is a bit of an exception. Unlike Lopukhov, Mertsalov, and Rakhmetov, he tends to join in with the more entertaining pursuits of the women. It is this fact that makes him a far better match for Vera Pavlovna, and it is significant that it is he who becomes her true companion for life, not Lopukhov. By rejecting Lopukhov for Kirsanov, Vera Pavlovna also rejects asceticism for a more fulfilling life.

In stark contrast to Lopukhov and Rakhmetov, the female characters live anything but an ascetic lifestyle. Vera Pavlovna sleeps late, likes a lot of cream in her tea, and has a fascination with buying new boots. The narrator even devotes an entire section (chapter 3, section 5) to describing in detail Vera Pavlovna's sybaritic behavior. For three pages the narrator revels in the details of Vera Pavlovna's love of cream and boots. The language of that section, moreover, is very affectionate, childlike. The use of diminutives (*Verochka, chasten'ko;* LP 139–41) in particular gives this section a very warm tone. Toward the end of the section, the narrator sums up Vera Pavlovna's love of luxury: "Vera Pavlovna really enjoys this free, open, and active life, which is not without its sybaritic side—luxuriating in her soft, warm bed, as well as savoring real cream and pastries with cream" (202).[146] The narrator does seem to cast a bit of a cloud on this when he states: "Can life really be any better in this world? Vera Pavlovna thinks not. Yes, and for someone in her early youth it could scarcely be better" (210).[147] However, this is not a condemnation by the narrator of Vera Pavlovna's luxuriating. Rather, it is a sober warning that life has some hard times ahead. And, if anything, it is an implicit admonition for her to enjoy things while she can.

Vera Pavlovna's love of fun and relaxation is made explicit in other passages throughout the novel. For example, it is clear that she loves to dance. When the narrator ironically says, "Yes, to Verochka's shame it must be admitted that she was an ordinary young girl who loved to dance" (98),[148] it is obvious that he is not condemning Vera Pavlovna for her passion but condones it. In addition to this passion, two outings, and all the enjoyment therein, are described in detail by the narrator (chapter 3, section 6; chapter 5, section 23). Vera Pavlovna also spends a lot of time luxuriating on her couch (244–45). However, she is never condemned by the narrator for any of this.[149] Rather, he seems to relish relating her sybaritism. In describing Vera Pavlovna's marital life with Kirsanov, for example, the narrator adopts her tone and point of view: "How nice it is to take a bath every morning! At first the water is so very hot, then the hot's turned off, the other faucet's turned on, and the cold water starts to trickle in. Slowly, imperceptibly, the water in the bath begins to cool. How splendid! A half hour, sometimes more, sometimes a whole hour goes by, and she still doesn't want to leave her bath" (350–51).[150] Moreover, in this marital bliss, Kirsanov waits on Vera Pavlovna hand and foot:

> In any case, her sweetheart takes upon himself the established duty of attending to morning tea.
>
> There really was no other way. Sasha was absolutely right when he said that it should be so organized, because it was very pleasant to have one's morning tea, that is, mostly cream warmed by the addition of a small amount of very strong tea, in bed. Sasha would fetch the tea service. Yes, that occurred more often than his having to come in with it, and he would officiate while she lounged in bed. After drinking her fill, she'd continue to recline, now no longer in bed, but on her little sofa. It was so wide, but most of all it was very soft, almost like a featherbed. She'd rest until ten or eleven o'clock. (351)[151]

In short, Vera Pavlovna is hardly the paragon of ascetic behavior, yet the narrator clearly approves of her and her behavior in this regard.[152] The conclusion to be drawn does indeed seem to be that living for the moment, enjoying life, is part of the answer to the question of what is to be done.

What is perhaps the key issue in determining whether *What Is to Be Done?* is an ascetic book is sex. Chernyshevskii is often seen as a sexual prude who was unable to deal with that aspect of human life. In large part, that interpretation is dependent upon a reductionist view of Vera Pavlovna's first, fictitious marriage.[153] Several scholars have argued that by means of the first marriage, Chernyshevskii is attempting to present his readers with a model of behavior. Dennis Reinhartz, for example, argues that for Chernyshevskii, true love was founded upon mutual respect, a spiritual commodity, and not mere upon physical sex. He further states that Chernyshevskii mechanized the man-woman relationship to the extent of omitting almost completely the human side of this marriage. In large part, Reinhartz bases his argument on the apparent fact that Vera Pavlovna's first marriage was never consummated.[154] There is serious doubt, however, whether Vera Pavlovna's and Lopukhov's marriage is actually fictitious, and whether it is by any means offered as a model.

Vera Pavlovna and Lopukhov marry so that she can escape from her family. In addition, the fact that the young newlyweds sleep in separate bedrooms has often given rise to the notion that it is an asexual relationship, a mere marriage of convenience. Despite those outward signs, the narrator uses the word "love" (however defined) to describe their feelings for each other. For example, shortly after the two have met, the narrator refers to Lopukhov as Vera Pavlovna's "beloved" and further states that Lopukhov is in love with her (105). In addition, there are other indications that the two do have some affection for each other: they sometimes refer to each other as "my friend" and switch to the informal "thou" (*ty*) when speaking to each other alone (127, 143; LP 78, 92). Moreover, as Naumova argues, though it is undoubted that Lopukhov is offering a fictitious marriage to Vera Pavlovna, his agitation, his shaking voice, show that he is in love with her.[155] It can be argued that the offer of a fictitious marriage is merely a cover, however in line with his feminist and utilitarian convictions it may be, that Lopukhov uses to keep from revealing that he is actually in love with her. After their wedding, both Vera Pavlovna and Lopukhov continue to state that they love each other and do express concern about each other's welfare. It is not a marriage entirely without feeling. In addition, it is not entirely certain that the marriage remains platonic. That an erotic element is present is evident when Lopukhov insists on serving as Vera Pavlovna's dressing maid after her second dream (188). Moreover, although it is rather late in the day, the marriage is presumably consummated after the third dream. In her anguish after the third dream Vera Pavlovna rushes into her husband's room. She obviously spends the night there because it is explicitly stated: "The next morning Dmitrii Sergeich had no need to summon his wife to tea: she was already there, snuggled up next to him" (243).[156] Finally, as Naumova argues, the third dream itself lets us know that the two had relations even before she is found in his room (242).[157] Vera Pavlovna's and Lopukhov's marriage does not follow the pattern of a true fictitious marriage, but, idiosyncratic though it may be, it is an authentic marriage.[158]

Chernyshevskii's purpose in introducing Vera Pavlovna's first marriage is not to offer a positive model. The obvious question arises that if this marriage is so ideal, then why does it fail? Rather, Chernyshevskii seems to question the notion that first love is always an occasion for marriage. As Naumova correctly argues, although Vera Pavlovna and Lopukhov are indeed in love, it is a youthful, immature love. It is first love for both of them.[159] As such the marriage does not last, but falters as the participants realize that they are not truly suited to one another. Although it does fail, this marriage is a learning experience for both characters and prepares them for their more fulfilling and happier second marriages. As a result of their first experience both Vera Pavlovna and Lopukhov mature and come to the realization that marriage must be based not on gratitude and mere friendship, but on the compatibility of natures. The fact that both Lopukhov and Vera Pavlovna are involved in happy, successful marriages, including the erotic component of marriage, by the end of the novel, indicates that the first marriage is not to be taken as a positive ideal. Rather, it is to be viewed only as a stage in their development, a stage that could have been avoided, moreover, had not external circumstances forced the two to enter into marriage. That is, in addition to arguing that marriage must be a matter of choice for the participants, not their parents, Chernyshevskii argues for a restructuring of the courtship ritual that would allow a young couple to test the nature of their relationship before entering the binding contract of marriage.

As we have seen, Rakhmetov rejects sex totally, fearing it will compromise his dedication to the cause. That, of course, opposes the author's own views.[160] Rather, Chernyshevskii's attitude toward sex finds its expression in the behavior of the three main characters. When Lopukhov is first introduced into the novel, he has views quite similar to those of Rakhmetov. In his conversations about his "fiancée" (that is, a symbol for the cause, for the revolution), he says that "she" has cured him of the desire to be in the company of women (100). At that point, Lopukhov believes, like Rakhmetov, that one has to be an ascetic to be devoted to the cause; that is, that revolution and women do not mix. However, Lopukhov comes to change his mind in that respect. He marries Vera Pavlovna and is obviously very attached to her. Moreover, when their marriage ends, Lopukhov does not return to his former ascetic outlook, but ends up in a second, happier marriage to Katerina Polozova. The fact that Lopukhov's ascetic views are introduced so early in the novel and that he himself comes to reject them does indicate that the author also rejects such an outlook.

A more explicit, positive treatment of sex can be found in the numerous references to the sexual act in the novel.[161] Although Vera Pavlovna's first marriage is relatively passionless, her second is not. In passages that were no doubt absolutely shocking by nineteenth-century standards, Chernyshevskii provides clear references to Vera Pavlovna's and Kirsanov's eroticism. In chapter 4, Vera Pavlovna's and Kirsanov's conversation is interrupted by a subchapter boundary, obviously meant to indicate they are engaging in the unprintable (344). Moreover, when their conversation continues, it is clear that there is no denial of the flesh:

> "Sasha, you didn't even let me get to what I wanted to talk about," Vera Pavlovna began some two hours later, when they sat down to tea.
>
> "I didn't let you? Am I to blame?"
>
> "Of course you are."

> "And who started fooling around?"
> "Well, aren't you ashamed?"
> "Of what?"
> "That it was I who started fooling around. Fie! To compromise a modest woman so by your indifference."
> "Indeed? And I thought that you preached equality. If that's true, then there's equality of initiative."
> "Ha, ha, ha! What learned talk! Are you really accusing me of illogicality? Don't I try to maintain equality of initiative as well? Well, Sasha, now I'm taking the initiative in resuming the serious conversation that we interrupted."
> "Take it, but I refuse to follow your lead. Now I'll take the initiative and continue to interrupt. Give me your hand."
> "But Sasha, we must finish talking."
> "We'll have time for that tomorrow. Right now, as you see, I'm much too interested in investigating this hand." (344–45)[162]

The fact that this passage hints at a woman's right to initiate the sexual act not only indicates that Chernyshevskii is not at all a sexual prude and does not preach sexual asceticism, but also deals forthrightly with that area of human life.[163]

Finally, perhaps one of the most memorable of references to eroticism, which belies the notion that the novel preaches asceticism, occurs in Vera Pavlovna's fourth dream: "As for the rest: that's my secret. In the hall you saw how their cheeks glowed and their eyes sparkled. You saw how they came and went. When they leave, it's I who lures them away. The room of each man and woman is my sanctuary. Within those walls my mysteries are inviolable. The curtained doors and thick carpets absorb every sound. Silence and mystery prevail. They return: it's I who brings them back from my kingdom of mysteries into the realm of light entertainment. I reign here" (378).[164] The reader is provided here with a vision of the future in which sexual freedom reigns.[165] In short, Chernyshevskii's novel is anything but a manual for an ascetic lifestyle. Rather, insofar as it has a message, it encourages quite the opposite.

As we have seen, there is abundant evidence *within the novel itself* that overwhelmingly indicates that Rakhmetov is not to be taken as positive, that his actions are not held up for emulation by the author. Rather, this episodic character is introduced only to make a specific ideological point and to aid the author in his battle against a stale set of aesthetic norms. Rakhmetov's ascetic philosophy, as striking as it may be, is clearly at odds with the views of the author himself and with the attitude expressed throughout the remainder of the novel. Rakhmetov's story is an intrusive insertion into the text motivated by polemical concerns; he is not the center of the novel. As such, Rakhmetov is not Chernyshevskii's contribution to Russian literature's search for a positive hero. Rather, his chosen path, with all its self-imposed deprivations, is precisely what is not to be done.

Chapter Five

Utopianism, Co-ops, and Dreams

CHERNYSHEVSKII AND THE UTOPIAN SOCIALISTS

Chernyshevskii is often viewed as heavily influenced by the utopian socialists, especially Fourier, and treated as a propagandizer of their ideas.[1] N. G. O. Pereira, for example, argues that Chernyshevskii's use of Blanc, Fourier, and Owen represented a major innovation for the time and place and that he popularized those authors in Russia through his articles in *Sovremennik*.[2] Leonard Schapiro argues that Chernyshevskii was a supporter of cooperative, or phalanstery, socialism, which he had learned from Fourier.[3] With regard to *What Is to Be Done?* itself, many scholars have viewed Vera Pavlovna's sewing cooperative and her fourth dream as straightforward expositions by Chernyshevskii of the ideas of the utopian socialists.[4] A. P. Skaftymov, for example, argues that Chernyshevskii propagates the ideas of Saint-Simon, Fourier, and Owen.[5] Brodskii and Sidorov concur, arguing that there are close parallels between *What Is to Be Done?* and the ideas of Owen and Fourier.[6] Richard Stites expresses the general opinion succinctly when he argues that the details presented in the fourth dream are taken straight from Fourier.[7]

Chernyshevskii is generally viewed as a consistent utopian socialist from his student days until the creation of *What Is to Be Done?*[8] Several scholars, though cognizant of the fact that Chernyshevskii was hostile to utopian socialist ideas at the time he wrote the novel, argue that Vera Pavlovna's sewing co-op and her fourth dream betray a lasting attachment by Chernyshevskii to the ideas of those men. Emily Klenin, for example, argues that "there remains in the text of *Čto delat'?* significant testimony to Černyševskij's continued faith in Leroux's ideas."[9] Likewise, Adam Ulam argues that the utopian socialism in *What Is to Be Done?* is "obviously a throwback to his [Chernyshevskii's] youthful infatuation with Fourier."[10] Thus, Chernyshevskii is viewed as never having transcended his early infatuation with utopian socialism.

Chernyshevskii's intellectual debt to the utopian socialists is far from certain, however. It is true that during his student days in Saint Petersburg

Chernyshevskii occasionally wrote with admiration of the French socialists. For example, closely observing the events of the year 1848 he writes: "It seems that I belong to the extreme party, the ultra; Louis Blanc especially, after Leroux, fascinates me" (1:66). Somewhat later Chernyshevskii was even more unreserved in his admiration. For example, on October 12, 1848, he writes regarding Proudhon and Louis Blanc: "I have not finished, but the strength of mind of these gentlemen struck me and I confess that I am decidedly their follower and there remains for me only to read them in the original. I am completely devoted to them and respect them" (1:146). Likewise, Chernyshevskii proclaims his enthusiasm for the French socialists in a letter to M. I. Mikhailov of May 15, 1850: "I am becoming more and more firm in the ultrasocialist mode of thinking. The main objects of my worship are Louis Blanc (whom I have barely read), to whose followers I belong, Proudhon, Feuerbach, etc." (14:198). Despite these early statements of admiration, however, Chernyshevskii's passion for the French socialists quickly faded. Due to the events of 1848–49, Chernyshevskii became disillusioned with all the leftist parties of the French political scene, including the socialists. Chernyshevskii was even to turn on the hero of his youth, Louis Blanc, for accepting a government post.[11]

A striking example of Chernyshevskii's disillusionment with the French radicals can be found in his later treatment of Proudhon. As we have seen, during his student days Chernyshevskii expressed his utmost respect for Proudhon. That admiration would be more than counterbalanced, however, by Chernyshevskii's later hostile statements regarding the French thinker. For example, in "The Anthropological Principle in Philosophy" (1860) Chernyshevskii reproaches P. L. Lavrov for using Proudhon as a source in his pamphlet "Essays on Problems of Practical Philosophy" (1860). Chernyshevskii states of Proudhon that although he is familiar with German philosophy, he is behind the times because he learned his concepts from Hegel.[12] Chernyshevskii further states of Proudhon's system that it "consisted of a combination of Hegel's philosophy and the concepts of the French philosophers, which often lacked scientific spirit. . . . [One] too often sees that this mind was shackled by views that lacked scientific foundation. The result of these unfavourable conditions was obscurity."[13] Chernyshevskii concludes his discussion of Proudhon by arguing that he cannot serve as an authority in philosophy and that he cannot be regarded as representative of the views that modern science has developed.[14]

Although Chernyshevskii seems to have restrained himself somewhat in his public statements regarding Proudhon, his private ones reflect an extreme animosity toward him. For example, writing in November 1873 he states: "One of the progressive idiots who had a very strong influence on all idiots without distinction was Proudhon. . . . He was an ignoramus and a lout who without analysis shouted all sorts of nonsense which wandered into his head from wherever: from the newspaper, from an idiotic book, from a clever one. He was unable to make a distinction due to a lack of education. And now he is one of the oracles of people of all kinds of opinions" (14:550). Thus, as can be seen in the case of Proudhon, any affection Chernyshevskii displayed for the French utopians during his student days had long been replaced by an unremitting antipathy. Writing in 1858 Chernyshevskii seems to settle accounts with those French socialists for whom he had once shown any sympathy:

> In fact, these terrible people were: Pierre Leroux, a weak-sighted man of timid appearance, bashful and quiet to the point that he appeared more like a sheep in man's clothing. Considérant, the mildest creature in the world after Pierre Leroux; a man who made complete submissiveness to any government the general principle of his actions and who did not have any hatred for the moderate Republicans or even for Guizot, and thought day and night about how to reconcile and assure all. Louis Blanc, who never took part in the movements of the masses but, on the contrary, always sought to restrain them; a man brilliant in the faculty but completely incapable of practical demagogy whether because he loathed any sort of violence and disorder or due to weakness of character. Proudhon, a man with a firm character but with very calm opinions; a man who despite evident sharpness of expression could have been a minister of Frederick II or Joseph of Austria and who was not suspected of any kind of designs or intrigues even by his enemies. (5:958)

It seems clear that although Chernyshevskii displayed some admiration for figures such as Blanc, Leroux, and Proudhon in his student days, those men held no attraction for him at the time he wrote *What Is to Be Done?* With those men there is at least some basis for arguing for a lingering influence. Regarding other utopian socialists, however, Chernyshevskii never seems to have expressed any admiration. For example, Saint-Simon is often cited as a source for the utopian socialist elements in the novel and, at least implicitly, is viewed as an intellectual mentor of Chernyshevskii. Yet Chernyshevskii was consistently critical of Saint-Simon and his followers. For example, writing in 1857 Chernyshevskii states of Saint-Simon's ideas that "the times of this system, truly dreamy [*mechtatel'nyi*] and impractical, passed long before 1847" (4:330). Chernyshevskii provides a more thorough discussion of Saint-Simon in 1860 in his article "Iiul'skaia monarkhiia." There he stresses the dreamy character of Saint-Simon and his school: "The first manifestations of new social aspirations always have a character of enthusiasm, of dreaminess, so that they are more similar to poetry than to serious science. Such was the nature of Saint-Simonism" (7:156). Chernyshevskii is critical of Saint-Simon's teachings because they reflect the idealized views of an aristocrat (7:157). Chernyshevskii regards Saint-Simon as an aristocrat, obviously with good intentions, engaging in mere philanthropy (7:159). Summing up Saint-Simon's teachings Chernyshevskii claims that "this naive fantasy enchanted no one" (7:161). Dealing with specific faults of Saint-Simon's system Chernyshevskii states that "his whole theory arises from false ideas about the role that supposedly belonged to Catholicism" and argues that although Saint-Simon presented his system as opposed to Catholicism, his system is merely a refurbished Catholicism (7:163). Chernyshevskii dismisses Saint-Simon as a naive enthusiast who was "exalted by false stories about the previous philanthropy of the Papacy" (7:164). Chernyshevskii seems to have been quite consistent in his opinion of Saint-Simon. In a letter of 1876 he refers to Saint-Simon as "a brilliant, but very ignorant thinker" (14:651). Chernyshevskii did view Saint-Simon as an intelligent man, but never expressed any enthusiasm for his socialist teachings.[15]

Finally, we come to Charles Fourier, the source so often cited for Chernyshevskii's utopian socialism. Unlike Proudhon, Leroux, and Blanc, Chernyshevskii was not particularly impressed by Fourier during his student days. He makes several diary entries in late 1848 stating that he is engaged in reading Fourier. However, in those entries Chernyshevskii is clearly struck by the oddities of Fourier's system. In November, for example, he states regarding Fourier's discussion of cosmogony that "the examples and applications of ideas seem strange or almost ridiculous to me." Chernyshevskii does go on to say that "the basis of the idea is, it seems, positively correct," but the impression of Fourier's ideas as strange remained (1:183). Chernyshevskii's ambivalent attitude continued. Writing in December he states that Fourier has a strong, independent mind, but he labels the results reached by Fourier "strange" (1:187). He further states about Fourier's "O libre arbitre": "It is as if you are reading some kind of mystical book of the Middle Ages or of our schismatics. There is a lot (that is, not a lot, but simply a few, because in all there is little) of healthy thoughts, but an infinitude of oddities" (1:188).[16] Chernyshevskii's opinion of Fourier at this time was that Fourier was an intelligent man who did have something new to say, but: "It seems to me a strange thing that a man with such oddities and limitations in his interpretations and reasonings should be placed as the head of a school. . . . His claims are so limited and clearly accidental and not independent, . . . and the whole second volume echoes the arguments of Gogol's madman" (1:195).[17]

Those statements were made by Chernyshevskii in his private diary. In his public statements he also describes Fourier as unsatisfactory. Although on one occasion he does refer to Fourier as a first-class thinker (9:355), Chernyshevskii is careful to distance himself from Fourier's views. In his comments to his translation of Mill's *Principles of Political Economy*, Chernyshevskii provides a small discussion of Fourier and his legacy, noting that in contrast to Saint-Simonism, Fourierism gave more attention to the economic side of life. When summing up, however, Chernyshevskii clearly finds Fourierism lacking: "We want to say that Fourierism still has too encyclopedic or philosophical a nature and that the socialist movement in its further development should have acquired an appearance more individual or special than that which is to be had in Fourierism" (9:829). At a later date Chernyshevskii repeated this formulation, making it quite clear that he thought Fourierism had no place in the radical movement: "That is impossible. Whoever likes Fourierism will not like communism. This can be compared with gastronomical tastes: whoever is accustomed to the exquisite dishes of French cooking will make a wry face if you begin to treat him to our *shchi* and *kasha*."[18]

In sum, by the time Chernyshevskii wrote *What Is to Be Done?* he had clearly broken with the utopian socialists, with whom he had previously sympathized. Moreover, the most oft-cited source of Chernyshevskii's supposed utopian socialism, Charles Fourier, was not regarded highly by Chernyshevskii at any time. Yet, there are elements of *What Is to Be Done?* that must be classified as utopian socialist. In addition to the lengthy description of Vera Pavlovna's co-op and the depiction of the future society in her fourth dream, smaller elements, such as Lopukhov's photograph of Owen (247)[19] and his bringing of Considérant's *Destinée sociale* to Vera Pavlovna (112), provide a consistent utopian socialist undertone to the novel.[20] It seems quite clear that the impetus for Vera Pavlovna's plans comes directly from the reading of utopian socialist works (189). Keeping in mind that the author is unquestionably dismissive of utopian socialism, the question then becomes, What is the artistic purpose of those elements?

VERA PAVLOVNA'S CO-OP

Vera Pavlovna's sewing cooperative has long attracted the attention of scholars as Chernyshevskii's prescription for the future, as his answer to the question in the novel's title.[21] The meticulous detail in which the co-op is described is ritually cited as evidence that Chernyshevskii fully endorsed that course of action.[22] It has even been suggested that Chernyshevskii was so supportive of co-ops that he ruined his novel out of the desire to propagandize. Žekulin, for example, claims that those sections are far too long and unnecessary and contribute to *What Is to Be Done?*'s failure as a novel.[23]

Many Soviet scholars, in particular those who based themselves on Lenin's pronouncements on Chernyshevskii, long stressed the utopian character of this part of the novel. Skaftymov, for example, notes the similarities between the formulations of Western utopian socialists such as Fourier and Owen and the principles on which Vera Pavlovna's co-op is founded.[24] He argues that the process of the transition to a socialist structure is shown by Chernyshevskii in the description of the sewing co-op and further argues that Chernyshevskii's belief that it was possible to create socialist forms in the conditions of a capitalist social structure was undoubted utopianism.[25]

In other words, Chernyshevskii never made the final transition to scientific socialism and always remained a utopian.[26]

Finally, basing themselves on one passage in the text of the novel, many scholars have stressed that the radiant vision of the future that appears in Vera Pavlovna's fourth dream is a direct result of phenomena such as her co-op:

> "You know that I require nothing too difficult. Why, you yourself are doing something for me, in my own way! Is it really so hard?"
> "No."
> "Of course not. Remember your own dressmaking establishment? Did you have many resources? Any more than others?"
> "No. We had no resources to speak of."
> "But now your seamstresses have ten times more comfort. They enjoy life twenty times as much and experience unpleasantness a hundred times less than others who had the same resources as you. You've proven that even in your own time people can lead a free and easy life. One has only to be rational, to know how to organize, and to learn how to use resources most advantageously."
> "Yes, yes. I know that."
> "Let's see how people live only a short time after they've come to understand what you've long understood." (375–76)[27]

This passage does indeed make the explicit claim that the radiant future is tied to ventures similar to Vera Pavlovna's sewing co-op, and most scholars have thus simply linked the two together as part of Chernyshevskii's grand utopian vision.[28] It is generally assumed that the entire novel has been subsumed to the call of the future[29] and that Chernyshevskii has abandoned all subtlety, any attempt at artistry, for the sake of propagandizing utopian socialist principles.[30]

The question of Chernyshevskii's own attitude toward the co-op is indeed a very tricky one. It is created by his main character, a character with whom he obviously sympathizes and definitely holds in the highest esteem of all the characters. Yet, as we have discussed, the narrator's attitude toward his main characters is not entirely uncritical. Although obviously approving of those characters as people, we have seen that the narrator does disagree with and distance himself from their ideas. Vera Pavlovna is no different: the narrator disagrees with her, corrects her, and on occasion stresses her naïveté. The narrator expresses great admiration toward Vera Pavlovna as a person, but has some reservations about her ideas. This attitude can be found quite clearly in references to her co-op.

In the description of Vera Pavlovna's co-op provided in *What Is to Be Done?* there is very little to indicate that the narrator approves of the undertaking in and of itself. For example, when the topic is first introduced into the novel it is Vera Pavlovna herself who elaborates on the venture. The exposition of the planned co-op is presented as verbatim conversation between Vera Pavlovna and Lopukhov. The narrator does not comment or interfere in any way: rather, he lets Vera Pavlovna tell her own story (172–74). When the verbatim conversation ends and the third-person narration returns, the facts are given in a dry, laconic manner, with neither narrative commentary nor the flippancy so often accompanying it. In relating the account of the early formation of the co-op, the narrator limits himself to a recounting of the bare facts and little else (174).

Likewise, when the narrator himself undertakes a description of the history of the co-op, he refrains from any sort of endorsement. The narrator does stress that Vera Pavlovna begins her enterprise in a most nondescript manner; that is, he notes that there is nothing extraordinary in the manner in which she acted (188–89). However, the narrator retreats from a direct exposition of the principles on which Vera Pavlovna founds her co-op. Rather, the basic principles of the co-op are outlined in a monologue by Vera Pavlovna, not by the narrator (189–91). Only after the basic ideology of the co-op has been expressed by the main character does the narrator provide a third-person narration of the first three years of the co-op's history (191–96). There too, the narrator relates just the bare facts. When the co-op's basic history is finished, however, the more familiar narrator, the one who comments extensively, returns. For example, in relating some of the unpleasant events of the co-op, and the unhappy love affairs of some of the young women in particular, the narrator digresses into an allegory about smallpox (197–98). After the basic outline of the utopian socialist principles has been provided by a character, the familiar narrator returns, apparently no longer fearing too close an identification with those principles.

The distance between the narrator and the actual details of the co-op is maintained throughout the novel. For example, the last description of the co-op, which comes after Kirsanov's visit to the police, is provided by the young Katerina Polozova (380–86). In this case the author relies on the inserted genre of a personal letter to maintain the distance of his narrator from the undertaking. Thus the narrator does not even relate the details at all; rather, they are provided as the verbatim transcription of a character's description, without any authorial or narrative commentary. Chernyshevskii has kept his narrator as distant as possible from the rapturous description of the co-op the letter provides.

In her letter Polozova expounds in great detail the inner operations of the co-op, even providing copies of its budgets. There can be little doubt that young Polozova is very enthusiastic about the whole affair and that her description embodies many utopian socialist formulations. However, it cannot be stressed enough that this dithyramb to the sewing co-op is provided from the point of view of a character, not the narrator. This character, moreover, is young and naive, and can in no way share an identical viewpoint with the narrator. Chernyshevskii has constructed the positive, enthusiastic descriptions of the sewing co-op so that they must be attributed not to his narrator (or to himself) but only to his characters.

An important feature of the sewing co-op as it functions in the novel is its identification with the female characters during the early stage of their development as budding social activists. Their involvement in the co-op represents not the culmination of their development but only a particular, rather early stage. Involvement in the sewing co-op is undertaken by these characters while they are very young and still rather naive. Vera Pavlovna, for example, establishes the co-op about five months after she marries Lopukhov. During this early stage she believes forcefully in the co-op and works enthusiastically. However, as she matures and loses some of her naive illusions, her enthusiasm for the undertaking wanes. As she tells Kirsanov, she needs her own cause, something that she cannot live without. The co-op, for all the enjoyment it brought her, was merely a passing fancy: "Is the workshop really a part of my personal life? It's a cause, not my own, but someone else's. I work at it not for myself but for others, though perhaps also from my own convictions" (343).[31] Vera Pavlovna's enthusiasm for the enterprise cools even more after her husband's visit to his new acquaintance (380). By the end of the novel Vera Pavlovna is in the midst of leaving the co-op altogether to take her medical exams (431.) As she leaves her first husband for Kirsanov, so too does she leave the co-op for a medical career; the co-op no longer has any hold on her. The only person in the novel who still holds to the idea of the sewing co-op is the younger and less-experienced Katerina Polozova.

When describing both Vera Pavlovna and Polozova during the early stages of their development, the narrator presents them as naive, dreamy enthusiasts. For example, the narrator describes Vera Pavlovna's hopes for the future of her co-op as follows: "Vera Pavlovna took the greatest possible pleasure in the workshop when explaining to someone that the entire system was organized and maintained by the girls themselves. With these explanations she was trying to convince herself of what she wanted to believe; namely, that the workshop could function without her, that other workshops of the same sort could appear completely independent of theirs, even—Why not? It would be splendid! Best of all!—even without any supervision from someone outside the seamstresses' ranks, but entirely as a result of the ideas and skills of the seamstresses themselves. That was Vera Pavlovna's fondest dream" (199).[32]

Despite this fond dream and her attempts to convince herself of its viability, however, Vera Pavlovna is quite aware that the co-op cannot survive on its own. In her conversation with Rakhmetov, for example, she admits as much: she had planned to leave the co-op in the hands of another director, Mertsalova. When Rakhmetov rebukes her, arguing that the co-op would fail utterly without her guidance, Vera Pavlovna does not object, but pleads guilty (298–99). Finally, when Vera Pavlovna is on the verge of abandoning the co-op for good, it is not left to the seamstresses themselves, but rather in the hands of Katerina Polozova. In short, Vera Pavlovna consistently, if implicitly, acknowledges that despite the hopes of her dream (that is, theory), daily reality does not allow its translation into practice: the co-op is simply unable to survive on its own.

It is the dreamy quality of Vera Pavlovna and Katerina Polozova that links them directly with the Western utopians. As we have already seen, Chernyshevskii rejected the Western utopians, especially Saint-Simon, precisely for their tendency to enthusiasm, naïveté, and dreaminess. Similar terminology appears in the description of Vera Pavlovna and Katerina Polozova. For example, the narrator uses the word "dream" (*mechta*) to describe Vera Pavlovna's hopes for her co-op. Vera Pavlovna is a good-hearted, but incredibly naive young woman given to utopian visions. The narrator continues the use of this word *mechta* (and its variants) so that the reader never forgets Vera Pavlovna's essential naïveté. For example, he states that she and Mertsalova "were already dreaming that in two years or so, instead of two sewing cooperatives, there might be four or five, then even ten or twenty" (379)[33] Again the use of the word *mechtali* together with the somewhat unrealistic numbers of future co-ops they envision stresses the essentially naive, utopian nature of these young women.

The emphasis on a dreamy nature is even stronger regarding young Katerina Polozova. In the sections of chapter 5 where Polozova is described in detail, the narrator constantly stresses her inclination for dreaming (*mechta*) and her tendency to live in that manner:

> Thus Katia relaxed and began to enjoy complete freedom at home. For Katia that meant that no one would interfere with her reading or dreaming. She had very few friends, only two or three close ones, but there was no end of suitors. Polozov had only one daughter and—one shudders to think—four million rubles!
>
> But Katia read and dreamed, while the suitors despaired. She was already seventeen. So she read and dreamed, but didn't fall in love. (389)[34]

In this passage, the narrator uses the verb *mechtat'* three times to describe young Katerina Polozova. She is a young woman who has no practical experience at all, but lives entirely in her own imaginary world, fostered by the novels she reads. Likewise, in describing her passion for Jean Solovtsov, the narrator stresses that her love for him is all due to her inclination for dreaming: "Katerina Vasil'evna fell in love with Solovtsov because of his letters; she was dying of a love based solely on her dreams. From this it's perfectly clear that she was very romantically inclined at the time. The boisterous life of the vulgar society that filled Polozov's house was in no way conducive to exalted idealism. In other words, this characteristic arose from her own nature. All that boisterousness had oppressed her for some time; she preferred to read and dream" (406).[35] In short, an essential component of Katerina Polozova's character is a tendency to live in a fantasy world.

Finally, Polozova is characterized as a dreamer (*mechtatel'nitsa*) in two ways. First, she envisions herself as a Romantic heroine based upon the novels she has read: "She was a dreamer, but her dreams were gentle, like her character; they contained as little brilliance as she did herself. Her favorite writer was George Sand, but she imagined herself not as Lelia, Indiana, Cavalcanti, or even Consuelo; in her dreams she was either Jeanne or more often Geneviève. Geneviève was her favorite heroine" (407).[36] As Charles Corbet and Emily Klenin have observed, Polozova is attracted to the least "political" of Sand's various heroines.[37] That is, Polozova is at this time a naive, young woman with hardly any practical experience and barely any conception of social issues. However, as the narrator states, she does begin to turn to more serious thoughts. For example, she begins her development as a social activist by engaging in philanthropy, only to become disillusioned and to realize the utter futility of such activity (407). Although Polozova attempts to envision other avenues of activism, she remains essentially a dreamer: "She also loved to ponder the enviable fate of Miss Nightingale . . . who, at the end of the war, returned to her homeland with hundreds of men whom she'd saved and continued to take care of the infirm. . . . These were her dreams; Katerina Vasil'evna wished to see them fulfilled. Her fantasy carried her no further than these thoughts about Geneviève and Miss Nightingale. Can one say that she possessed a genuine fantasy? Can she really be called a dreamer?" (407–8).[38] The choice of Florence Nightingale as a model of behavior is far from a radical, revolutionary one. Despite the obvious feminist implications, Polozova (herself quite wealthy) chooses a model that essentially repeats the pattern of upper-class philanthropy à la Saint-Simon.

Polozova's qualities of dreaminess, naïveté, and enthusiasm follow her into the field of social activism and influence her views. It is this fact that first makes philanthropy seem so attractive to her and explains her subsequent infatuation with Vera Pavlovna's co-op. It also explains why she remains infatuated with the co-op at a later age than Vera Pavlovna did. There is little doubt that she is a naive (read: utopian), idealistic young woman who is only beginning the journey to radicalism. Presumably, Polozova will follow a line of development similar to that of Vera Pavlovna and also come to reject the co-op (and with it utopian socialism) as insufficient. Thus, although the reader is presented with characters who are clearly utopian in their ideology, their personality, or both, the text is constructed so that the reader must interpret this utopianism as an early, by no means sufficient, stage of the development of the characters. It is presented not as a positive model to be followed, but as a mere fancy that will pass.

A clear-cut rejection of co-ops as an appropriate method of revolutionary activity is presented by Chernyshevskii near the end of chapter 4. Chernyshevskii adopts a structure designed precisely to undermine the radiant vision of the future society presented in Vera Pavlovna's fourth dream. In the fourth dream it is stated that the future society is the direct result of ventures such as Vera Pavlovna's. It is this fact that is often cited as evidence of a continuous, consistent strain of utopian socialism running throughout the novel.[39] However, what has often been missed is that *immediately* after this dream is presented, there is a section that deals with the further development of the sewing co-op and the accompanying negative consequences.

In section 17 of chapter 4 Kirsanov has the pleasure to make a new acquaintance, occasioned by his wife's sewing co-op. In the published version of the novel, this section has been greatly shortened. The situation is not altogether clear, but Chernyshevskii himself probably reduced the section before submitting it to the investigative commission for fear that its strong ideological content would endanger the novel's publication.[40] The intent of the section is still quite clear, but its reduced size and the deletion of the verbatim discussion between Kirsanov and his new acquaintance have caused many an inattentive reader to miss the import of this section.[41] In the published version, for example, section 17 covers a mere two pages, but in the rough draft, the full version covers approximately eight pages. The content of Kirsanov's conversation with his new acquaintance fills only one paragraph in the published version, but in the rough draft, the conversation fills approximately four to five pages and is far more explicit.

In the published version, Kirsanov makes the acquaintance of a man (whom the reader is supposed to infer is a government official) and discusses the name of the shop that Vera Pavlovna's enterprise has opened on Nevskii Prospekt—*Au bon travail:*

> About three months after the store opened, Kirsanov received a visit from a colleague with whom he was slightly acquainted. He told Kirsanov a great deal about various medical cases. . . . In conclusion he said that one of his acquaintances wished to meet Kirsanov. Kirsanov agreed to this request. The encounter was amiable; their conversation touched on many subjects including the new shop on Nevskii. Kirsanov explained that it had been opened purely for commercial reasons. They spoke at length about the sign hanging over it. Was it really a good idea to include the word *travail?* Kirsanov said that *travail* means work, and that "Au bon travail" meant a store that filled its orders well. They discussed whether it wouldn't be better to replace that motto with some surname. Kirsanov explained that his wife's Russian surname would be bad for business. At last he offered the following solution. His wife's first name was Vera, which in French is *foi:* would it do to replace "Au bon travail" by "A la bonne foi"? That would have only the most innocent meaning, "a conscientious shop," and the owner's name would actually appear on the sign. After some discussion it turned out that this would indeed

be acceptable. Kirsanov managed to direct the conversation to such questions with particular zeal; in general he succeeded so well that he returned home feeling very satisfied. (379–80)[42]

The obvious sarcasm with which this scene is presented is meant to alert the reader that something very important is going on.[43] One is to infer that Kirsanov comes away from the conversation anything but satisfied. Vera Pavlovna's undertaking has obviously attracted the unwanted attention of the government authorities. And, as a further paragraph demonstrates, this attention continues: "Kirsanov's new acquaintance continued to visit and afforded him a great deal of pleasure" (380).[44]

This scene is even more caustic and far more explicit in the rough draft. Throughout that version, the narrator continually refers to the official as an "enlightened man," indicating his hypocrisy. When the conversation turns from the usual pleasantries to the heart of the matter, it is clear that the government is concerned with Vera Pavlovna's seemingly socialist enterprise. The enlightened man begins by trying to disarm Kirsanov: "We will speak frankly, Aleksandr Matveevich. Why can't enlightened people be fully open among themselves? I myself am a socialist in spirit and I read Proudhon with satisfaction. But . . ." (LP 660).[45] The direct link of Vera Pavlovna's co-op to utopian socialism is introduced here by the enlightened man, but Kirsanov parries the blow, stating: "Allow me to say a few words so that no misunderstandings remain between us. You said: 'also a socialist.' This 'also,' probably, refers to me. Why do you think I am socialist? Perhaps not at all. Besides the socialists there are the protectionists, Say's followers, the followers of Rau's historical views; there are followers of a multitude of different trends in political economy. In order to consider a person among the followers of one of them one needs to have some reasons" (LP 660).[46] In response, the enlightened man argues that Kirsanov is to be classified a socialist on the basis of his wife's store. Kirsanov continues to resist the identification:

> "This arrangement is allowed by followers of all trends, when they are speaking seriously. Some of them—and even now there are only very few—attack it, when they are conducting a polemic against followers of some other trend, depending on necessity. But they attack it only when they conduct a polemic. In a mild, purely scholarly exposition absolutely none of those writing about political economy dare not to acknowledge its safety and usefulness for society. If I speak incorrectly, I ask you to show me at least one example to the contrary." (LP 660)[47]

Kirsanov's response is most interesting in that he argues there is really nothing socialistic about the enterprise and certainly nothing revolutionary.[48]

Despite Kirsanov's reassurances, the enlightened man is far from convinced, and his paranoia reaches new heights when he turns to the question of the name of Vera Pavlovna's shop:

> "Mr. Kirsanov, we are not here for scholarly arguments. You will agree that I have no time for them. Mrs. Kirsanov's store has a harmful tendency, and I would advise her, and in particular you, to be more careful."
>
> "If it is harmful, then you should close it and prosecute us. But I would be curious to know in what way is it harmful."
>
> "Why, in every way. Let's begin with the sign. Just what is this *Au bon travail?* It is a revolutionary slogan."[49]
>
> "In translation this means 'a store of good work.' I do not understand what kind of revolutionary meaning there is in that a fashion store promises to fill orders well."
>
> "That is not the meaning of these words. They mean that all stores should be arranged in such a manner; only then will it be good for the working class. And the word *travail* itself, it is clear, is taken from the socialists. This is a revolutionary slogan." (LP 660–61)[50]

Interestingly, Kirsanov goes so far as to try to convince him that the enterprise is a purely commercial one. Finally, as a way of mollifying the enlightened man, Kirsanov proposes a name change that seems far less threatening to Russian society:

> "This is what comes to my mind. The inconvenient word *travail* is present on the sign and it must be replaced by the name of my wife. This is the requirement of the public welfare?"
>
> "Yes."
>
> "I find it possible to fulfill this requirement, the importance of whose foundations I fully value, and to avoid the worst of two evils: the terrible blow the store would suffer if a name with the ending *-off* were placed on it. My wife's name is Vera. This can be translated into French by the word *Foi.* If the word *bon* is left, limiting the change only to the degree necessitated by the word *travail,* then the new sign would be: *A la bonne foi.* Strictly speaking, this is 'a conscientious store' but in the French inscription there would even be a nuance of a conservative meaning. *Foi* is Faith, [which is] as if in opposition to tendencies of a negative character." (LP 662)[51]

In this scene, Chernyshevskii lets no chance for vicious satire pass by: although Kirsanov's suggestion would indeed give the new sign a hint of conservatism, the enlightened man insists on several minutes to consider this "important question." If this were not enough the narrator goes on to relate in a most sarcastic tone the Kirsanovs' reaction to this meeting: "For a fairly long time Vera Pavlovna and her husband found themselves a source of frequent pleasure in reflections about how society—one could say, social organization—was saved from danger by exchanging the word *travail* with the word *foi* and the corresponding change in the gender of the adjective on one of the many thousands of signs on Nevskii Prospekt" (LP 663).[52]

The net result of this rather humorous, caustic scene, in addition to being an exercise in literary revenge by Chernyshevskii against his captors, is the dashing of all of Vera Pavlovna's and Mertsalova's hopes. Before Kirsanov's visit to the official, Vera Pavlovna and Mertsalov continue to fantasize in the same tones as the fourth dream: "Natasha Mertsalova and Vera Pavlovna were already dreaming that in two years or so, instead of two sewing cooperatives, there might be four or five, then even ten or twenty" (379).[53] But as the narrator states in the published version, after the visit the two have had to clip the wings of their dreams and have given up any hope of any further development of the co-op (380). Government interference has simply made this impossible: Vera Pavlovna and Mertsalova are left only to rejoice in the fact that the co-op has continued to exist (380).

Again, this situation is far more explicit in the rough draft. There, the narrator describes in detail the Kirsanovs' coming to grips with the realization that the co-op will not be allowed to develop further:

> But, in essence, it was not at all a laughing matter. The store got off easy this time, of course. But all the same it was clear that it was necessary to keep restraining oneself, to force one to forget about oneself [and] that now—at least for a long time—there was no use thinking about the development of the enterprise, which was so asking to go forward. The highest possible happiness for a long time would consist in continuing to exist, having resisted the expansion of the business for many months, probably more than a year. This was hard, of course. But to tell the truth, was it really unforeseen? It was even good that the matter had succeeded in developing thus far without obstacles: obstacles could have appeared much earlier. It was also good that obstacles appeared only in a restraining and not a destructive manner: in truth one could have expected destruction also. (LP 663)[54]

The narrator goes on to state that surveillance of the co-op's activities continues, and in a rather sarcastic passage the narrator hints that Kirsanov has been subjected to much unpleasantness on account of the co-op: his medical career is threatened by his wife's activities (LP 664). The narrator stresses that, in essence, Vera Pavlovna's enterprise exists purely on the indulgence of the state. It can be destroyed at any time and is hardly in a position to challenge. As a result, the Kirsanovs are on their way to a realization that ventures such as the co-op are not the answer to the question of what is to be done.[55]

When one remembers that this scene comes *immediately* after the radiant vision presented in Vera Pavlovna's fourth dream, no more decisive a rejection of that vision, especially its faith in the future of cooperative ventures, could be found. In constructing *What Is to Be Done?* in such a manner, Chernyshevskii attempts to make a concrete ideological statement: to show the younger generation that such ventures are doomed to failure. The copious detail with which the venture is described is meant to indicate that despite the observance of all possible measures, the venture cannot succeed due to state interference. Likewise, the remarkable ease with which Vera

Pavlovna at first succeeds is meant to drive the point home that, even if all goes well, such ventures are doomed: the state will simply not allow them to succeed. Thus, although not unremittingly hostile to cooperatives, and certainly still approving of the concept of communal labor, Chernyshevskii attempts to show that they are by no means sufficient to bring about the desired changes in society; something more is needed.

As is well known, many young Russian readers took the presentation of the co-op in *What Is to Be Done?* as a sort of how-to manual and founded numerous co-ops throughout Russia. Such was not Chernyshevskii's intention and, indeed, he was aware of the danger of the manner of subtle exposition he chose. For example, in the published version, his narrator stresses that he is not really describing a cooperative in and of itself, but only because it relates to his character: "I choose to omit many details here, because I'm not really describing the workshop, merely mentioning it insofar as it's necessary to characterize Vera Pavlovna's activity. If I dwell on some particulars, it's only because I want to show how she led the way step by step, and how she patiently, indefatigably, and resolutely maintained her own rule: not to issue pronouncements, but to consult, explain, offer cooperation, and assist in carrying out the decisions reached by the entire group" (193).[56]

It might be objected that the narrator is speaking tongue-in-cheek here because he does go on to enumerate many details of the co-op and that despite the disclaimer he really is propagating utopian socialism under the guise of describing a character's activity. However, a comparison of the rough draft with the published version reveals that Chernyshevskii clearly worried about being misinterpreted on this point. In a passage near the end of the rough draft, well after all descriptions of the co-op, the narrator claims that Vera Pavlovna, in reality, did not found a co-op at all: "There is in the story one more feature made up by me: the co-op. In fact Vera Pavlovna did not trouble herself over the building of a co-op. I did not even know such co-ops as I have described: there are none of them in our amiable fatherland. In fact it took the form of something like a Sunday school—or closer to the truth—like a free daily school not for children but for adults. But for the course of the story itself, it is all the same. It seemed to me that instead of something more or less well known, it was better to describe something little known among us" (LP 714).[57]

In this passage, we see Chernyshevskii using many of the devices described in chapters 1 and 2. His narrator continues the illusion that Vera Pavlovna is an actual human being, whom he knows personally, while undercutting the illusion of reality by proclaiming he made up something. But more important is the attempt to persuade the reader that the narrator is engaging in naked didacticism. These statements occur shortly after his claim that he is not really writing a novel, but only describing his acquaintances (see chapter 1). The reference to describing something not well known in Russian society under the pretext of educating it seems designed to irritate those readers opposed to any sort of didacticism.[58] This passage is clearly designed to provoke the negative reaction of a hostile reader.[59] However, Chernyshevskii may have realized that he was playing with a two-edged sword. It is perhaps the fear that readers might take him too literally on this point that led him to cut the passage from the published version. Despite this deletion, Chernyshevskii obviously failed: instead of taking the novel as a rejection of such ventures, the younger generation took it as an endorsement. His subtlety has been lost on his contemporaries and many modern scholars alike.

DREAMS

As many observers have noted, Vera Pavlovna's four dreams form a major element of *What Is to Be Done?* Anatolii Lunacharskii, in outlining the basic structure of the novel, gave the dreams as much value as any of the characters.[60] Vera Pavlovna's fourth dream has become (in)famous and is generally treated as the most spectacular example of utopian socialism on Russian soil. In this regard, Chernyshevskii is (dis)credited with creating a significant utopian vision of the radiant future in Russian literature.[61] Some, such as Tamarchenko, regard the fourth dream as the most important exposition of socialist ideas in the novel.[62] Common to much of the commentary on the dreams is the basic assumption that they directly, without any hint of subtlety, reflect the political views of Chernyshevskii himself. Michael Katz, for example, claims that they are not dreams at all; rather, they are mere political allegories, "naive allegories" according to Northrop Frye's terminology.[63]

The dreams of *What Is to Be Done?* have long been problematic, especially for Chernyshevskii's supporters. With the utter naïveté of the radiant vision presented in the fourth dream usually being attributed to Chernyshevskii himself, the dreams have often served as a source of embarrassment and conflict for some of his friends and supporters.[64] And in the same vein, the dream sequences were often used as a source of mockery by his detractors. This dichotomy has continued among scholars of the twentieth century, with detractors using the fourth dream to ridicule the novel, whereas supporters of Chernyshevskii struggle to find some extenuating explanation. Indeed, many have had trouble with the idea that such a sharp and intelligent man as Chernyshevskii could fall into such utter naïveté. Volodin and Shakhmatov, for example, express this consternation quite clearly: "With such a summons concludes the story of the light(-haired) beauty of 'Vera Pavlovna's Fourth Dream'—the story of the wonderful coming kingdom, where there is 'any happiness which anyone needs,' where 'all live as well as possible,' where 'to each and everyone there is full freedom, unrestricted freedom.' And these words were written by one of the most sober thinkers of nineteenth-century Russia, who spoke ironically, repeatedly and maliciously, apropos all sorts of 'fantasies' and 'idylls' regarding the organization of social life!"[65] Some scholars, in an attempt to rescue Chernyshevskii from himself or to at least explain the paradox, have argued that it was merely due to his being imprisoned in a cold, dark cell. No doubt, they argue, that such bright visions were consolation to a man trapped in such conditions.[66]

The reason for consternation and confusion among observers of Chernyshevskii is the a priori assumption that Chernyshevskii presents his vision, or daydream (*mechta*), to his readers in the thin disguise of a character's dream (*son*). The situation with Vera Pavlovna's dreams, as with so much else in the novel, is by no means clear, however. Chernyshevskii's hostility toward utopian socialism, with which the fourth dream is rife, alone should cause one to question the notion that the dreams are mere political allegories clumsily inserted by the author to propagate his ideology. Because the ideological content of the fourth dream is clearly inimical to Chernyshevskii's own views, there is serious question about whether anything in those dreams can be attributed directly to Chernyshevskii. Instead, a more detailed study of the dreams is in order to determine their function and significance in the text.

Although it is Vera Pavlovna's fourth dream that is traditionally associated with utopian socialism, I first turn to an analysis of the preceding dreams, for they provide the key to understanding and interpreting the last. All of Vera Pavlovna's dreams show a definite pattern; there is an underlying consistency in their structure that cannot be ignored. In all of Vera Pavlovna's dreams the overt presence of the narrator, so evident throughout the rest of the novel, is conspicuous by its absence. The irony, flippancy, narrative digressions, and so forth that the reader has come to expect are entirely absent from those sections. For example, the first dream is about one and a half pages long, with very little narrative presence. Most of the dream is constructed as quoted conversation: that of Vera Pavlovna and that of the bride. What little narrative presence exists is pure laconic third-person narrative, indicating a change in speaker or action, such as "And Verochka has a dream." In addition, this third-person narrative is related in Vera Pavlovna's language and from her point of view. Finally, there is absolutely *no* commentary by either the narrator or the author. In short, the manner in which they are presented and the views they reflect all indicate that the dreams are indeed Vera Pavlovna's own. All of Vera Pavlovna's dreams (and Mar'ia Alekseevna's dream) follow this same basic pattern. Thus, there is no structural basis for attributing the content of the dreams to either Chernyshevskii or his narrator; it belongs exclusively to the characters.

In his study of Vera Pavlovna's dreams, Michael Katz argues that they do not in any way help to characterize Vera Pavlovna's inner world, that they are not genuinely psychological. Rather, he argues, Chernyshevskii uses these so-called dreams as mere device to avoid the censor.[67] Katz discusses the first dream in this regard, arguing that it is clearly a dream of liberation, described in religious language and imagery, and that it anticipates Chernyshevskii's great utopian vision.[68] There is much in this dream that begs for ideological interpretation. Its feminist content is self-evident and hardly needs commentary. And there is little reason to dispute Katz's claim that the first dream is one of (feminine) liberation. However, it is not at all clear that this dream in anyway corresponds to the author's own views. That is, there is little evidence to support the assertion that the first dream represents a straightforward, point-by-point exposition of Chernyshevskii's own ideological views.

The incredible naïveté and simplicity with which the first dream is presented seem to indicate that it is merely the vision of a seventeen-year-old character, and not that of actual author (age thirty-four at the time of writing the novel). This fact is reflected in the very title to the dream: whereas her other three dreams are entitled "Vera Pavlovna's . . . ," this dream uses the affectionate diminutive for a child in its title, "Verochka's First Dream." Moreover, there is a consistent effort to avoid too close an identification with the dream by the author. For example, the narrator is careful to distance himself from the contents of the first dream. Although the cellar that appears in the dream becomes a major symbol for Vera Pavlovna, a close reading reveals the narrator never adopts that symbol as his own. The first mention of the word outside the dream itself is given by Vera Pavlovna when describing the dream to Lopukhov. The narrator does use the word "cellar": subsequently, but he is careful to place it in quotation marks (*kavychki*) or to refer to it as *her* (Vera Pavlovna's) "cellar." For example, the narrator states, "By the third day her 'cellar,' as she called it, seemed twice as unbearable as before" (154).[69] Thus, the text is constructed so that the exceedingly naive vision presented in the first dream can be attributed only to the young Vera Pavlovna.

Despite the claim that there is nothing psychological to Chernyshevskii's artistic method, the first dream does much to characterize Vera Pavlovna and her psychology.[70] The extremely optimistic and simplistic vision in it corresponds quite well to what one might expect of a young woman trapped in Vera Pavlovna's situation. Moreover, the dream plays an important role in the story in that the first hint of the solution to Vera Pavlovna's problem is given: she subconsciously realizes she must marry the right person to escape her family. Not only does the dream foreshadow the events to come, but arguably it is an important part of the action: it is under the stimulus of this dream that Vera Pavlovna is prepared to accept Lopukhov's solution to her dilemma. In addition, on the very next day, Vera Pavlovna mentions the dream to Lopukhov. She describes the dream to him and makes it clear that she had such a dream in the expectation of her prompt liberation from her family: "I was so excited that I couldn't get to sleep until two o'clock this morning. And when I did, I had such a wonderful dream! I dreamed that I was being liberated from a stuffy cellar, that I'd been paralyzed and was cured, and then I ran out into a field with many other girls who'd also been freed from cellars and cured of their paralysis. It was so much fun to run around in that spacious field. But my dream hasn't come true. I thought I wouldn't be returning home" (135).[71] Moreover, it is just such a vision of liberation that makes her situation at home all the more unbearable. Without the vision given in the dream, Vera Pavlovna may have been able to endure the few months remaining until Lopukhov finished his studies (154). But once given a glimpse of freedom in her dream, Vera Pavlovna is unable to wait and her marriage to Lopukhov (and the ensuing difficulties) is hastened. In short, the first dream forms an integral part of the text and is far from a mere authorial insertion, clumsily introduced to propagate an ideological point.

Before proceeding to Vera Pavlovna's second dream, it is important to note that Vera Pavlovna is not the only one whose dreams are recounted in the novel: the reader is also presented with the dream of her mother, Mar'ia Aleksevna. The night after Lopukhov has foiled Mar'ia Aleksevna's plans for Vera Pavlovna, Mar'ia Aleksevna has a dream that might be described as consolatory (166–67). Before going to bed, Mar'ia Aleksevna is extremely upset: all her plans for wealth have been ruined. However, as a sort of compensation for this fact, she dreams of Vera Pavlovna as married to a very wealthy Lopukhov. In the dream Vera Pavlovna and Lopukhov spend money as if there were no end to it. This pleases Mar'ia Aleksevna very much, even if it mystifies her somewhat.

Few would suggest that the content of this dream in any way corresponds to Chernyshevskii's own views or that it is meant as some sort of political allegory. The content of the dream corresponds very well to what one would expect from a money-loving woman like Mar'ia Aleksevna who has had her fond hopes dashed. Moreover, as with Vera Pavlovna's dreams, there is no intrusive narrative presence in the dream. It is given in a dry, laconic, third-person narrative, with lots of direct quotation and without authorial or narrative commentary. In terms of both structure and content, Mar'ia Aleksevna's dream is precisely a dream, not a political allegory inserted by the author. Chernyshevskii was quite capable of constructing true literary dreams that reflect the inner world of his characters.

Vera Pavlovna's second dream comes after she has already been freed from her "cellar." It occurs one night after the Lopukhovs have visited Mar'ia Aleksevna, followed by the visit of their friends, which includes long discussions of politics, history, and other serious topics. In a well-known phenomenon, Vera Pavlovna's dream continues those conversations. The dream repeats the pattern of the real conversations, in which the men tend to engage in overly intellectualized, boring discussions while the women gravitate to lighter, more entertaining topics and pursuits.

Vera Pavlovna's second dream has long been regarded by Western and Soviet scholars as the consummate embodiment of Chernyshevskii's philosophical views. Lopukhov's and Mertsalov's discussion of good dirt versus bad dirt, especially statements such as "movement is reality" or "movement is life" (181),[72] have long been cited as evidence of the novel's propagation of materialism. Francis Randall, for example, argues that the image of seeds growing in different soils in the second dream expresses Chernyshevskii's materialist convictions about the importance of chemical nutrients to the growth of living things and the importance of scientific nutrition for human welfare. In addition, he argues that the seeds are a perfect image for fooling the censor: that is, the rotten soil is the existing social and political institutions that will have to be replaced by the healthy soil of future rational institutions of society and government, in which fully developed human beings can grow.[73] Most scholarship views the second dream as only an allegory encapsulating the ideological views of the author.[74]

In addition to the absence of any narrative presence that would indicate an endorsement by the narrator, the second dream is constructed as a subtle criticism of the views expressed by Lopukhov and Mertsalov. Lopukhov and Mertsalov appear first in the dream and outline in detail their materialist viewpoint. Their discourse is rich with the scientific jargon and catchwords of the day. However, they do not maintain the field but are interrupted by Vera Pavlovna, who demands a change in activity: "Vera Pavlovna goes up to both of them and says, 'Enough of your analyses, identities, and anthropologisms. Gentlemen, please talk about something else so I can participate in your conversation; or better still, let's play a game'" (182).[75] This interruption perfectly illustrates the dichotomy that runs throughout the novel, with the men given to overly intellectualized, bookish behavior, while women are much more in tune with the world and their own feelings. Moreover, if we remember that women are always better than men in this novel, Vera Pavlovna's interruption and comments are a criticism of Lopukhov and Mertsalov and, consequently, the materialist views they express.[76]

The views expressed by Lopukhov and Mertsalov, particularly those concerning the impossibility of putrid, "phantasmic" dirt ever producing anything healthy without "drainage," are also directly contradicted within the dream itself. As the dream progresses, Mar'ia Aleksevna appears to inform Vera Pavlovna that she is good because of the former's vileness.[77] Mar'ia Aleksevna shows Vera Pavlovna what would have happened if she (Mar'ia Aleksevna) had remained a good woman. Mar'ia Aleksevna claims that Vera

Pavlovna is what she is due to her (Mar'ia Aleksevna's) machinations: "'Not a peep! Do they live well, I ask you! Are they good people? Do you want to become like them? Silence. Don't turn your mug away! You listen to me, Verka, listen to what I have to say. You're learned now, educated with money that I stole. You dream about the good, but if I hadn't been so wicked, you wouldn't even know what the good is! Do you understand? *Everything* comes from me! You are *my* daughter, understand? *I* am your mother.' Verochka weeps, trembles, and shudders" (186).[78]

All this directly contradicts the statement made by Lopukhov and Mertsalov to the effect that bad can give rise only to bad. Although Mertsalov is quite capable of defeating Serge in those terms, Mar'ia Aleksevna, using the clear-cut example of Vera Pavlovna, overturns his arguments.[79] The second dream is constructed on the principle of dialogue, with each character expressing different, even contradictory views. In the exchange of discourses given in Vera Pavlovna's second dream, it is Mar'ia Aleksevna's explanation that wins out over the rigid determinism of Lopukhov and Mertsalov, indicating that their philosophy is far from adequate.[80] The fact that Lopukhov's and Mertsalov's views are presented as inadequate within the dream itself casts serious doubt upon the assumption that their views can be identified as Chernyshevskii's own. Likewise, although Mar'ia Aleksevna's point of view appears victorious in the dream, it is very unlikely that the views expressed by such a negative character could be endorsed by Chernyshevskii. Thus, we are left with little else to attribute to him in terms of allegory. Rather than presenting the monologic discourse of the author, the second dream represents a dialogue; one, moreover, that reflects Vera Pavlovna's internal struggle.

What is most important about the second dream is not ideology or philosophy but psychology. That is, this dream is concerned with and accurately reflects Vera Pavlovna's internal psychological struggle. To begin with, the dream starts out as many ordinary dreams do: it continues the events that occupied Vera Pavlovna before she went to sleep. But once the dream begins, it takes unexpected turns, very much like the chaotic process so common to actual dreams. Serge appears out of nowhere and Vera Pavlovna's mother arrives on the scene to defend herself. This part of the dream is key to understanding Vera Pavlovna's internal struggle. She is tormented with the knowledge that she has arisen from the most vile of circumstances and yet, to all appearances, is a rather decent person. Such a struggle is intensified by her husband's rigid determinism, which tells her she must be bad because she grew up in bad circumstances. In this regard, the appearance of the "Bride of her Bridegrooms" after Mar'ia Aleksevna provides much-needed consolation and reassurance for Vera Pavlovna. It is the "Bride" who assures her that her origins are not to be held against her and, moreover, that people such as Mar'ia Aleksevna are needed in such circumstances if any progress is to be made at all (187). Although one may be tempted to see only political allegory in the dream, particularly in the "Bride's" discourse, it depicts little more than Vera Pavlovna's internal psychological struggle and her final self-rationalization of who and what she is.[81] Even well after the dream is over, Vera Pavlovna is still somewhat bothered by the question of how she came to be what she is (221). The second dream is Vera Pavlovna's own, her attempt to come to terms with herself, and thus a literary dream, not a mere political allegory.

Of Vera Pavlovna's four dreams, the third has traditionally received the least treatment in the critical literature. It seems devoid of overt didacticism (although in terms of plot it is arguably the most important of all the dreams[82]) and thus occasions fewer comments from most observers of Chernyshevskii, who are concerned primarily with content.[83] At the same time, however, the third dream occasionally serves as a rare source of recognition of Chernyshevskii's abilities as a writer. For example, the third dream is sometimes cited as the only place in the novel where Chernyshevskii achieves recognizable human feeling.[84] The Russian critics Vail' and Genis even argue that the third dream is a fine work of psychological analysis. They argue that, although the third dream reads as if copied from Freud's *The Interpretation of Dreams* and is followed by a psychoanalytically correct dialogue the next morning, this "exceptionally interesting and even mysterious phenomenon" is clearly all Chernyshevskii's own achievement.[85]

Vera Pavlovna has this dream as she is coming face to face with the fact that she and her husband are not really suited for each other and that she is attracted to her husband's best friend. Before the dream this possibility occurs only at the subconscious level:

> "What about Vera Pavlovna?"
> "No, she hasn't noticed anything, either."
> "Has she noticed anything in herself?"
> "No, Vera Pavlovna hasn't noticed anything in herself, either. But she does have a dream." (236)[86]

The third dream begins with a scene from a typical evening at home: Vera Pavlovna has gone to her room after drinking tea with her husband. Then begins a series of free associations that lead to the appearance of an unnamed "guest." The guest commands Vera Pavlovna to read her diary, which, in reality, she never wrote. Against her will Vera Pavlovna reads the diary and is forced to realize that she does not truly love her husband, that they are not well matched. Instead, she realizes that her attachment to him is mere friendship combined with gratitude for saving her from the "cellar." Vera Pavlovna resists this realization as much as possible: she even refuses to read further. However, Vera Pavlovna cannot escape her own subconscious: the guest finishes reading the diary for her. Vera Pavlovna interrupts her, cursing her guest, and wakes up from the excitement caused by the dream.

The third dream plays an extremely important role in the plot of the novel. First, up to this point, it is not entirely clear whether the Lopukhovs' marriage has been consummated. However, Vera Pavlovna is so distraught by the dream that she rushes into her husband's arms. Although it is never stated openly, the references to her husband's caresses, Vera Pavlovna's unprecedented presence in her husband's room, and her worries about what her maid will think all seem to indicate that the marriage has been consummated at this point. Frightened by the implications of the third dream the young couple draw closer together for a while: Vera Pavlovna tries to force out any doubts and Lopukhov forces himself to spend more time with her. But the significance of the third dream is so powerful that it cannot be ignored. The characters continue to talk about it for many months afterward: it has frightened Vera Pavlovna and she cannot get it out of her mind.[87] It is the powerful effect of the dream on his wife that forces Lopukhov to subject their relationship to a thorough analysis. As a result, he comes to realize that they are not truly suited to each other and, moreover, that she is in love with his best friend. This realization, conditioned by the third dream, prompts Lopukhov to take the rather extreme action of faking his suicide to free his wife.[88] As Lopukhov later stresses in a letter to Vera Pavlovna, it was precisely the third dream that forced him to realize what was going on (314).

What several observers have found interesting in the third dream is Chernyshevskii's capturing of recognizable human emotion and the chaotic thought process.[89] At the beginning Vera Pavlovna's rather frivolous thoughts fly from one topic to another (237–38). When the dream takes a more serious turn, an interesting psychological phenomenon occurs when Vera Pavlovna reads a diary that, in reality, she never wrote. Yet as she reads the pages of the diary, she recognizes the facts and the feelings expressed to be quite correct. They correspond perfectly to her past and to her thoughts, both conscious and subconscious, of that time. Subconsciously Vera Pavlovna has long recognized that she and Lopukhov do not actually love each other as husband and wife; now she is forced to deal with that fact openly. Within the dream itself, Vera Pavlovna does her best to resist the implications of her diary. But because the words on those pages reflect her true thoughts and feelings, she cannot deny them forever: she does come to the realization that she and her husband are not well matched. Vail' and Genis are quite correct in their estimation of the originality of this dream.[90]

In arguing that the dreams in *What Is to Be Done?* are not transparent, simplistic political allegories, I do not wish to give the impression that there is no point to them. The third dream, for example, is part of a larger didactic point regarding love that Chernyshevskii attempts to make in the novel. It is this one subject, far more than any other, that forms the primary concern of the author. For example, an important component of the novel is a stress on the need for compatibility in relationships: two decent people do not necessarily make a happy union. Something more than mere decency of character is necessary for a happy union based on love. It is this that Vera Pavlovna recognizes in the third dream: a union based solely on decency of character or gratitude is not a healthy one and is bound to falter (242). In addition, the third dream is also crucial to Chernyshevskii's emphasis on the primacy of human emotions. Throughout the novel, Chernyshevskii continually hints at his displeasure with the notion of living according to a theory, the overrationalization of human actions. The third dream is part of Chernyshevskii's loud proclamation that one cannot hide from one's own emotions, no matter what theory (or convention) demands. We have seen that fact in relation to Vera Pavlovna, who tries to ignore her feelings, but whose subconscious forces her to confront them. An even more vivid example of the irresistibility of human emotions is present in Kirsanov's maneuvers.

For years Kirsanov has felt an irresistible attraction to Vera Pavlovna, the wife of his best friend. Acting as both a decent fellow and an adherent of utilitarianism, he does his best to distance himself from the Lopukhovs in the hope that with time, this passion will disappear. Lopukhov's illness, something not foreseeable according to theory, forces Kirsanov back into the lives of the Lopukhovs (217–18). The narrator recounts in detail, accompanied by a healthy dose of irony and sarcasm, Kirsanov's rather pathetic attempts to kill the renewed attraction he feels for Vera Pavlovna before she or Lopukhov realizes anything (233–36). As the narrator notes, Kirsanov takes satisfaction in his various maneuvers, in his "art": "This maneuver was a difficult one. Week after week it was necessary to drag out this about-face and move as slowly and smoothly as the hour hand on a clock. Look at it as attentively as you please, you won't see it budge, but it goes about its business very quietly all the same, moving ever so slowly away from its previous position. On the other hand, Kirsanov the theoretician derived immense enjoyment from the exercise, admiring his own agility. Egoists and materialists act only to satisfy themselves! Yes—and Kirsanov could swear, placing his hand on his heart, that he was acting only to satisfy himself. He rejoiced at his skill[91] and mettle" (236).[92]

In addition to having the narrator voice irony and sarcasm, the author drives the point home by placing Vera Pavlovna's third dream in the very next subchapter (less than a half-page away). Due to the impact of this dream on Vera Pavlovna (something unforeseen by either Vera Pavlovna or Kirsanov), all of Kirsanov's various skillful maneuvers, which have extended over several years, fall like a house of cards. Vera Pavlovna and Lopukhov are forced to confront the mutual attraction that exists between her and Kirsanov. In one fell swoop the unpredictability of human emotion smashes conscious, rational deliberation. No more definite a rejection of the attempt to manipulate or conceal human emotions can be found in the novel.

As we have seen regarding the dreams prior to Vera Pavlovna's fourth, Chernyshevskii uses dreams to give further insight into his characters' personality. Mar'ia Aleksevna's dream, for example, demonstrates that she is not purely evil or hateful. She does want her daughter to do well: she is comforted by the prospect of a wealthy Vera Pavlovna. Nonetheless, her dream also demonstrates that Mar'ia Aleksevna is a woman who has been ruined by her harsh circumstances and who knows how to act only in harmful ways. Vera Pavlovna's dreams correspond well to the various stages of her development and reflect the inner struggles she undergoes along the way. These dreams are indeed the true dreams of the characters and not mere political allegories inserted by the author to fool the censor. This point cannot be stressed enough for the fourth dream: despite its seeming propagation of utopian socialist principles, it continues the pattern established in the previous dreams.

Of all the dreams in the novel, Vera Pavlovna's fourth dream is by far the most infamous. It is routinely seen as Chernyshevskii's vision of the radiant future, his prophecy and his legacy to the young generation: "Vera Pavlovna's fourth dream represents the culmination of all her dreams and the fullest incarnation of Chernyshevskii's utopian vision."[93] Many scholars interpret the various elements of the fourth dream as an actual blueprint provided by Chernyshevskii.[94] Evaluations of this dream have varied widely, in large part depending upon the political views of the commentator. For example, Soviet scholars generally commended Chernyshevskii for creating a bright inspiring vision of the radiant future.[95] On occasion, Soviet scholars did feel the need to apologize for its utopian elements, but in the official Soviet view, the dream was long considered a great accomplishment by Chernyshevskii.[96] Non-Soviet scholars, in contrast, have generally evaluated and dismissed the dream as thinly disguised propaganda, as an example of Chernyshevskii's willingness to subordinate literature to the demands of ideology. Vail' and Genis, for example, though praising the third dream so highly, label the fourth "primitive and sugary."[97] Whatever the evaluation of the fourth dream's literary merits, however, most scholars are agreed in accepting its content as a straightforward exposition of Chernyshevskii's own views.[98]

As we have seen earlier, although the fourth dream may embody many of the principles of utopian socialism, Chernyshevskii was irreconcilably hostile to that ideology at the time he wrote the novel; the utopian socialist views expressed in *What Is to Be Done?* do not at all correspond to his own views. In addition to his explicit condemnations of utopian socialism and socialists, prior to writing *What Is to Be Done?* Chernyshevskii made several explicit rejections of the possibility of predicting the future. For example, in his comments on Mill's *Principles of Political Economy*, Chernyshevskii asserts that the point of departure for all discussions about the future is the present. He does not deny that guesses and hypotheses are relevant, but argues that one cannot forget that they are just that: guesses and hypotheses. They are not facts but "only inferences from signs indicating the near realization of well-known facts. But it is impossible to worry too much about that which is still not here when there are already facts coming into being which demand the full force of our attention. Thoughts about the future, even if the fairly close future, have only a small degree of practical importance in comparison with circumstances whose influence man is already undergoing in the present" (9:217–18).

Although Chernyshevskii is sometimes viewed as attempting to predict the actual date of the coming revolution in *What Is to Be Done?* he argues quite explicitly that such a task is impossible: "If slavery lasted for several centuries due to the force of routine after it ceased to be a convenient form of production, then the form of hired labor in the advanced countries of Europe, perhaps, will last for a fairly long time—perhaps several decades, or perhaps several generations. In questions about the future one can definitively see only the goal toward which something is moving by necessity of its development, but it is impossible to guess with mathematical exactness how long is necessary for the achievement of this goal" (9:222). As can be seen, Chernyshevskii does argue that it is possible to discern a goal toward which human society is moving. Indeed, he even seems to argue that a goal is necessary to some degree (9:353, 828). But he stresses this can be done only in limited fashion and only on the basis of analysis of the present. He is adamant that no one can predict the future: "Fantasy is a very weak capability; it is unable to depart from reality. It is unable to create for its pictures not even one element, except those given to it by reality. . . . All theories of the radical improvement of human life are based on this concept. With time, of course, reality will present data for more perfect ideals. But at the present time no one is able to describe in distinct form for others or even to imagine it for himself another social structure which would have as its basis a higher ideal" (9:465).

These quotations demonstrate that during his publicistic career Chernyshevskii remains quite consistent to the approach he outlines in *The Aesthetic Relations of Art to Reality*, in which he denies the possibility of man's stepping outside his own time and space.[99] Yet the image presented in Vera Pavlovna's fourth dream appears quite inconsistent with the legacy of his publicistic work. Despite Chernyshevskii's statements that it is not possible to discern the details of the future, the novel gives the reader a detailed picture of the radiant future. Did the experience of isolation in a cold, dark cell make Chernyshevskii forget who he was and his principles, and lead him to embrace what amounts to blatant idealism?[100] Or is it possible that the image in the fourth dream is not presented as a blueprint or as the author's political allegory, but serves some other, more artistic purpose?

Like all of Vera Pavlovna's other dreams, the fourth is motivated by events within the text itself. Prior to the dream, Vera Pavlovna and Kirsanov have numerous conversations on the status of women and the concept of love. Just before the fourth dream begins, Vera Pavlovna mentions her reading of Boccaccio's *Decameron.* In the conversation that ensues, the concept of love throughout the ages is discussed: "In the same way many of our customs and manners will seem crude and dirty in much less than five hundred years. But that's beside the point. I'm talking about those wonderful stories where Boccaccio seriously depicts passionate, sublime love. Those stories show his great talent best. Here's what I meant to say, Sasha. He depicts love very well and vividly, but judging from his work, one can see that in those days people didn't understand the tenderness of love as we do now. Love was not felt so strongly then, even though it's been said that his age was one when love was enjoyed most fully. No, no matter what, people didn't enjoy love then even half as much as we do now. Their feelings were too superficial, their rapture too weak and momentary" (357–58).[101] Vera Pavlovna is clearly concerned with the problem of how women and the concept of love have been perceived in human history. It is precisely this line of thinking that appears in the beginning of the fourth dream and conditions much of it. The first half of the fourth dream is not the author's "sweeping tableau of the evolution of humanity in the pseudo-apocalyptic style of Lamennais, Ballanche, and the French Social Romantics of the 1830s,"[102] but merely the continuation of Vera Pavlovna's deliberations before she lay down to sleep. Thus, the first half of the dream is perfectly motivated by the events leading up to it.

The second half of this dream is very triumphant, enthusiastic, and bright. A vivid description of two future societies, one in the nearer future, the other in the more distant, is given to the reader. The celebratory tone of this description, with its incredible naïveté, is very hard to miss.[103] Moreover, it appears that the reader is commanded to strive for the radiant future when the beauty in the dream tells Vera Pavlovna: "[N]ow you know what the future will be. It's radiant and beautiful. Tell everyone that the future will be radiant and beautiful. Love it, strive toward it, work for it, bring it nearer, transfer into the present as much as you can from it. To the extent that you succeed in doing so, your life will be bright and good, rich in joy and pleasure. Strive toward it, work for it, bring it nearer, transfer into the present as much as you can from it" (378–79).[104] In this passage, combined with the undoubtedly Fourieristic basis of the organization of the future societies,[105] it would seem that Chernyshevskii has betrayed every principle he held dear at this stage in his life and openly embraced idealism and utopian socialism. However, if the structure of this dream is examined in close detail, there is very little reason to assign either the views expressed or the triumphant tone to Chernyshevskii.[106]

In the fourth dream, as in the previous dreams, the ironic, sarcastic narrator, to whom the reader has become accustomed, is conspicuously absent. The fourth dream begins with the rather laconic, dry description that Vera Pavlovna is dreaming. The narration remains in the third person but switches to Vera Pavlovna's point of view, with all its enthusiasm and naïveté. As the dream progresses, the third-person narration is gradually replaced by the monologues of the two beauties, with the last part formed entirely by the monologue of the older beauty. Much of the actual content of the fourth dream is narrated by those new narrators.[107] The usual narrator, the one that stands closest to the actual author, is totally absent from the fourth dream. Thus, in terms of narrative structure, there seems little reason to argue that Chernyshevskii is expressing his own views here. Rather, it seems clear that Chernyshevskii takes great care to distance both himself and his usual narrator from the fourth dream.[108]

As discussed previously, the subsection of the novel that immediately follows the fourth dream is the one that deals with the further development of the cooperative and Kirsanov's new acquaintance. The narrator does not at all endorse, or even comment on, the fourth dream or its contents. Instead, Chernyshevskii deftly creates this scene to provide a most striking contrast to the naive, rapturous image presented in the fourth dream. The fact that the future society depicted in the dream is explicitly linked to Vera Pavlovna's co-op indicates to the reader that this naive image is clearly delegitimized. Moreover, these two sections play a key part in Vera Pavlovna's development as a budding radical activist. By the time of the fourth dream she has clearly reached the heights of utopianism. Her naive enthusiasm cannot go higher and she is primed for disillusionment. The uninvited attention of the government authorities is the catalyst that shatters her many naive illusions and prepares her for a more radical outlook. The rapturous heights achieved in the fourth dream are artistically necessary to demonstrate the depth of Vera Pavlovna's disillusionment and her corresponding change in activity.

Regarding the actual content of the fourth dream, many scholars have been correct in individual observations. Katz's observation that the two rows of dots in subsection 7 of the dream symbolizes revolution is correct,[109] as is the frequent observation that most of the details of the future society are borrowed straight from Owen and Fourier. The observation that the entire vision presented in the second half of the dream is naive and utopian is quite to the point. The problem is not in the interpretation of the various details, however, but in to whom to attribute this image: Vera Pavlovna or Chernyshevskii himself. It is on this issue that a major reevaluation of *What*

Is to Be Done? began to take place in the last two decades. For example, N. Naumova argues that the themes of the co-op and the depiction of the future society are interlinked and that only the organizer of the co-op could see several details of the fourth dream.[110] In a similar vein, Iu. K. Rudenko argues that it is not Chernyshevskii himself who gives this vision of the future society; it is not given as a reality but only as a fantasy, the fantasy of Vera Pavlovna.[111] Finally, Anatolii Lanshchikov asks a very important question: should we really equate the dream-vision of a young woman just beginning social activity with that of the much older, experienced author of the novel? As he states: "If we consider *What Is to Be Done?* an artistic work nevertheless, then we have no bases for seeing in her dreams the encoded foresights of the author himself without the risk of destroying the logic of character of the main heroine."[112] In terms of narrative structure the fourth dream is clearly presented as Vera Pavlovna's image, not the author's, and should be treated as such.

The frequent observation that the fourth dream is hopelessly naive, simplistic, and utopian is actually quite correct. What most scholars have missed is that this is precisely the point. This dream is Vera Pavlovna's own and is being used in part by Chernyshevskii to characterize her. The vision in the second part of the dream is the result of Vera Pavlovna's milieu: she has been reading the classics of utopian socialism and has associated with people espousing similar views.[113] As Lanshchikov stresses, it is important that Vera Pavlovna is introduced to the works of Considérant, a disciple of Fourier. Moreover, it must be remembered that Lopukhov, who introduces her to utopian socialist works, is himself an ardent admirer of Owen. Vera Pavlovna is clearly presented as an adherent of utopian socialism. She has not yet disavowed that ideology by the time of the fourth dream. Keeping this fact in mind, what else is one to expect of her but a highly utopian image, with the accompanying naïveté?[114] Such a worldview serves to characterize Vera Pavlovna as a young woman, who for all her positive qualities, still has a way to go in terms of her ideological development. Her naive faith is soon to be shattered by both Kirsanov's visit regarding her shop and the events of the winter picnic scene.

Therefore, we see that the primary reason for the utopian socialist elements present in *What Is to Be Done?* is for purposes of characterization. The radical youth of the time was infatuated with the ideas of utopian socialism and the portrait given in *What Is to Be Done?* is what one might reasonably expect of the younger generation.[115] In this regard, the characters' attachment to the ideas of Western utopian authors corresponds to certain stages of their development. They are most infatuated with those ideas when they are younger, more naive. As they mature, such ideas hold far less attraction for them, as Vera Pavlovna's decision to abandon the co-op for a medical career illustrates. In presenting utopian socialist views in conjunction with the materialist and utilitarian views of his main characters Chernyshevskii merely attempts to present the milieu in which they lived. To give such a depiction, extended and kind as it may be at points, is in no way an endorsement. For Chernyshevskii, just as for any other writer, to love one's characters is not the same as identifying with them.

In addition to serving artistic functions, Chernyshevskii's presentation of the utopianism of the younger generation makes a concrete ideological point. It seems clear that the high expectations expressed by Vera Pavlovna regarding her co-op, a quintessential utopian socialist enterprise, and the hyperbolic imagery of the fourth dream are destined for the deflationary treatment brought on by Kirsanov's conversation with the enlightened man. Besides accurately depicting the younger generation, Chernyshevskii's treatment of their utopianism contains the clear, if gently expressed, message that such views are misguided. Far from advocating or propagating utopian socialism, Chernyshevskii's seeks to combat its influence upon the younger generation. Even before the appearance of *What Is to Be Done?* several cooperative ventures, founded on utopian socialist principles, had already appeared in Saint Petersburg. It was this proliferation of utopian ideas that Chernyshevskii was attempting to combat, without, as was his constant concern, giving anything of use to the conservatives and reactionaries.

Thus, there is remarkably little reason to assign the utopian socialist elements of *What Is to Be Done?* to Chernyshevskii himself. *What Is to Be Done?* cannot be interpreted as an attempt by Chernyshevskii to propagate utopian socialist ideology. All the evidence in the novel itself points against this interpretation and it is quite clear that Chernyshevskii himself was hostile to utopian socialism at the time he wrote the novel. Chernyshevskii does not offer a picture of a future society as a blueprint for society to follow. Thus, all criticism of Chernyshevskii as naive, simplistic, utopian, and so forth is simply beside the point. Rather, the problem lies in literary criticism's inability to appreciate Chernyshevskii's artistic subtlety and the fact that *What Is to Be Done?* is a literary work incorporating several different, often conflicting, layers of consciousness and is not the mere transparent diatribe of its author.

Conclusion

STRESSING THE ARTISTIC nature of *What Is to Be Done?* may give the impression that the novel is free of radical ideology, but such is not the case. Chernyshevskii was a radical and the novel very much reflects that. As many scholars have noted, the novel is filled with subversive references. Some of those references are so daring, it is amazing that the novel ever saw the light of day. The presence of details such as Lopukhov's fake suicide, his avoidance of the police by fake documents, and the necessity of keeping his American citizenship when he returns all give *What Is to Be Done?* a consistent, subversive flavor.[1] Allegories, such as the term "bride" for revolution and the two rows of dots in Vera Pavlovna's fourth dream, leave the reader with no doubt that the creator of this text had a radical, subversive outlook. The text also contains allegorical asides that are extremely radical in their implications. For example, in a thinly veiled hint at the necessity of revolution, the narrator states: "Someday people will be rid of this kind of smallpox as well; the remedy is already available, but people still prefer not to swallow it, just as they chose not to adopt any cure against smallpox for years and years" (198).[2] Granted that such statements reflect a radical worldview, but do the various details really tell us anything that we do not already know? Would we not think of Chernyshevskii as a radical without those details? And, more important, do they in any way form a positive program?

Many scholars, looking at these and other details, have interpreted *What Is to Be Done?* as a positive program presented by Chernyshevskii to his readers.[3] They argue that the novel is constructed around the principle of answering the question in its title, "What is to be done?" and that Chernyshevskii meant for his readers to imitate the characters and their actions.[4] The conclusions reached, however, have often been quite varied, because, of the many elements in the novel, one is usually singled out and proclaimed as Chernyshevskii's political program. Thus, some suggest that the message of the novel is rational egoism, others suggest the revolutionary ascetic path of Rakhmetov, yet others suggest utopian socialist principles, and so forth. Likewise, on the level of personal behavior, *What Is to Be Done?*

is sometimes viewed as a text that encourages fictitious marriages, communal living, and so forth. As we have seen, none of those forms the positive content of the text. Either they perform a purely descriptive function or are part of Chernyshevskii's polemic with his predecessors. Quite often the "isms" attributed to Chernyshevskii are the targets of his polemical thrust, not posited models. The novel does contain positive content, such as a stress on the primacy of human emotion and the need for true love in human relations. However, of what is traditionally considered a political program, there is actually very little.

Although the title of the novel may presume a positive answer, that is, a detailed exposition of what is to be done, *What Is to Be Done?* is actually constructed on the principle of negation. Answers are offered to the question of what is to be done, but the proposals are rejected. In other words, the novel is the story of what is not to be done. This principle is most evident and easy to discern with regard to the negative characters. For example, Serge's solution is actually a pure nonsolution: he states that there is nothing to be done and passively withdraws from the world at large. When Julie asks him to help save Vera Pavlovna from Storeshnikov, he answers: "Calm down, Julie. That's impossible. If it isn't he, it'll be someone else—it's all the same. Look here, Jean is already hoping to win her over for himself. And there are thousands like him, you know. When a mother decides to sell off her daughter, you can't protect her from everyone. As we Russians say, there's no use beating your head against a brick wall. We're a clever people, Julie. You see how serene my life is, having accepted this Russian principle?" (63).[5] Serge's solution is tinged with hypocritical self-righteousness. He sees the evil all around him and refuses to do anything about it. Yet he commits no evil himself. In other words, Serge accepts the dirty world around him while attempting to take the moral high ground by not getting dirty himself. This is in contrast to the answer proposed by Mar'ia Aleksevna and Julie. Both argue that because the present world is indeed vile, the best that can be done is to reconcile oneself to it and try to turn things to one's own advantage. For example, Julie suggests to Vera Pavlovna that she marry the disgusting Storeshnikov and make him her slave (73–75). Whereas all these negative characters accept the world as it is, Mar'ia Aleksevna and Julie differ from Serge in their active approach, particularly in their willingness to get dirty.

The obviously negative answers are presented quite early in the novel and, not surprisingly, they are rejected. Once those "solutions" are dispensed with, the narrative takes up solutions that are more explicitly political. Various possibilities of activity are offered to the reader by the actions or philosophies of Vera Pavlovna, Kirsanov-Lopukhov, and Rakhmetov. Lopukhov and Kirsanov present the reader with a single-minded fascination with science (and the materialistic and utilitarian theories often associated with it), whereas Rakhmetov demonstrates the path of revolutionary asceticism. However, one by one each of those solutions is rejected. Even Vera Pavlovna's cooperative venture (that is, utopian socialism), although receiving the most gentle treatment of all the solutions, is also clearly rejected in the end. What is seemingly offered as a possible solution is ultimately shown to be unsatisfactory, insufficient, or, in Rakhmetov's case, completely misguided. Thus, the positive political program that is so often attributed to the novel is nowhere present.

Once that fact is recognized, it should be clear that *What Is to Be Done?* is not built upon the imposition of "what should be" upon "what is," as has often been argued.[6] Chernyshevskii does not try to create an abstract image and impose it upon his reader for emulation. In this regard, the term "positive hero," though accurate for Chernyshevskii's novel, should be used only in a limited sense. Chernyshevskii's use of the positive hero consists not in the creation of abstract, idealized images, but in presenting the reader with a cast of characters who are ordinary, yet worthy of respect.[7] They are positive characters in the sense that they are not negative or unworthy. *What Is to Be Done?* is not a prescriptive offering of idealized images completely divorced from reality, but is merely a descriptive portrayal of the milieu of the younger generation in Russia of the 1860s.

A similar myth about the politics of *What Is to Be Done?* is that it argues that the end justifies the means. Contemporary observers such as Dostoevskii interpreted it in this manner. Likewise, Soviet scholars, seeing in that interpretation an affinity with Bolshevik ideology, also accepted it.[8] Kirsanov's offer of poison to Katerina Polozova is regarded as an example of Chernyshevskii's supposed philosophy. As we have seen, however, the manner in which the text is constructed gives us no basis for assuming that the characters' actions and words correspond to the author's precepts. Moreover, supporters of that interpretation have conveniently ignored Chernyshevskii's emphatic condemnation of such a philosophy: "But I want to take the opportunity to express proper ideas . . . about the famous, foul principle, which is ascribed to the Jesuits and truly belongs to them, but was not thought up by them and does not belong to them alone, but to all those people, who love to behave badly—to all scoundrels. [This is] 'the end justifies the means,' which implies: a good end, bad means. No, it cannot justify them because they are not all means for it: a good end cannot be achieved by bad means. The nature of the means must be the same as the nature of the end. Only then can the means lead to the end. Bad means are suitable only for a bad end; but for a good end only good means are suitable" (684).

Key to understanding *What Is to Be Done?* is whether the novel is, in sum, optimistic or pessimistic. The majority of observers, arguing that *What Is to Be Done?* depicts what should be and basing themselves on certain elements of the text, such as Vera Pavlovna's fourth dream, assert that the novel is uniformly optimistic in its outlook. Lotman, for example, argues that the novel is filled with bright optimism because the personal fortunes of the heroes turn out well and many episodes have an idyllic character.[9] The excessive optimism ascribed to the novel is often argued as giving the novel an unrealistic, cardboard nature.[10] As Plimak argues, however, there is a consistent pessimistic or gloomy undertone that permeates the novel.[11] For example, he refers to one of the narrator's statements that can hardly be interpreted as optimistic: "This type appeared quite recently but now it's propagating quickly. It was engendered by its epoch; it's an emblem of it, and (shall I say it?) it will vanish together with it all too quickly. Its fate was to appear not that long ago and to vanish very soon. . . . A few years later, perhaps not even years, but a few months later, they'll be cursed, driven from the stage, hissed at, and insulted. . . . But won't even one of them be left on stage? No" (212).[12] Here the narrator sees not a bright future, but sorrow for the new people. Far from ordaining them for happiness, they are destined to disappear quickly and in an unpleasant manner. Bearing that in mind, can one really label the outlook of the novel excessively optimistic?[13]

That statement by the narrator comes near the middle of the novel and seems to be contradicted by another near the end: "Indeed, they do live in peace. They live harmoniously and amicably, quietly and boisterously, playfully and industriously" (431).[14] Likewise, in the next subsection (that is, the beginning of the winter picnic scene) the narrator further states: "They live cheerfully and amicably. Working and resting, they enjoy life and contemplate the future, if not without concern, then with the firm and absolutely well-founded confidence that the further they advance, the better it will be" (431).[15] If taken in isolation, those statements by the narrator do seem to confirm that the characters are leading completely happy lives and that the outlook for the future is optimistic: things are certain to get better.

But are those statements to be taken literally? Is this the end of the story? A hint to the contrary is provided by the narrator himself when he states, "But it doesn't follow that my story is at an end" (431).[16] More important is the context in which the narrator's statements are made: Vera Pavlovna and Katerina Polozova discuss the prospects of the future and do not seem overly optimistic. Vera Pavlovna laments that the sewing co-ops cannot be expanded further. Katerina Polozova expresses relief that she does not have to worry about providing for her son. Something is weighing heavily on the minds of the two characters. This becomes evident when Vera Pavlovna asks Polozova, "We'll continue to live in peace and quiet, won't we?" (431).[17] A silent Polozova, pushed by Vera Pavlovna for an answer, finally responds, "It doesn't depend on my yes or no, but to please you I'll say it: Yes, we will" (431).[18] It is at this point that the narrator interjects the statement, "Indeed, they do live in peace." As can be seen, there is a gloomy undertone to the characters' conversation. In this context the narrator's statements have an ironic ring to them. Moreover, the second statement occurs at the beginning of the winter picnic scene, far from ending the discussion, but actually opening it.

It is the reintroduction of a gloomy undertone, a nonoptimistic resonance, that characterizes the end of the novel. In this regard the final part of the novel, the winter picnic scene and chapter 6, constitutes a key to understanding the message of the novel. Likewise, the main characters continue to develop throughout the novel, reaching a culmination in the winter picnic scene. Thus, this scene is critical to understanding the novel as a whole. That is not evident, however, from the treatment it has received in the West. The first to translate the novel into English, Benjamin Tucker, was simply at a loss about its significance: "The pages which follow, in conclusion of this story, the translator does not pretend to understand. He cannot identify the new characters introduced or connect them with the story, nor can he fathom the purpose of their introduction. Whether they conceal some moral so revolutionary that the author from his prison cell did not dare avow it more openly, or whether the mystery is a device on his part to carry over the interest of the reader to the sequel which he undoubtedly intended to write, or whether the explanation is something different from either of these, the reader must determine for himself."[19]

Although confessing to bewilderment, Tucker did attempt to remain true to the novel and included this section in his translation. However, subsequent editors were quite unceremonious in their treatment of the novel's conclusion. In 1961 a new edition of Tucker's translation was published by Vintage Press. The conclusion was considered so incomprehensible that it was decided to delete it entirely. In the introduction to that edition, E. H. Carr justified the decision, stating, "It ends in a bewildering and incomprehensible Walpurgis Night of Reason, with a nameless Woman in Black leading the abstemious revels, and in the half-mocking promise of a second part—which was, of course, never written."[20] Although Michael R. Katz attempted to rectify the situation in 1982 with the publication of a new translation of the conclusion, in the same year, a new edition of *What Is to Be Done?* appeared that repeated the editorial decision of 1961.[21]

Due to such cavalier treatment, the winter picnic scene has not attracted much, if any, critical attention from Western scholars, rarely receiving more than a passing remark.[22] Despite Katz's publication of the conclusion, it has still generated remarkably little attention. In general, Western scholars are comfortable with established interpretations regarding the novel, the sewing cooperative, and the fourth dream in particular, and have not undertaken any further analysis that might question them. The winter picnic scene, however is the culmination of the novel, not Vera Pavlovna's co-op, nor her fourth dream.[23] It is in that scene that Vera Pavlovna and the other main characters reach the final stage of their development. It cannot be ignored without greatly distorting the meaning of the novel.[24]

In contrast to their Western counterparts, Soviet scholars consistently viewed the winter picnic scene as *the* scene of the novel. Soviet scholars, though always viewing Rakhmetov's story as the most important in terms of ideology, emphasized that in terms of the main characters' development, the winter picnic scene is the most important point. It is there, the Soviets argued, that the three main characters and Katerina Polozova actually decide to become underground, professional revolutionaries: they see the necessity of following Rakhmetov's path, the path of revolutionary asceticism.[25] Thus, Soviet scholars argued, the new people make the transition to becoming extraordinary, or higher, people and it is in the winter picnic scene (and in chapter 6) that the answer to the question "What is to be done?" is provided.[26]

A major focus of Soviet analyses of this scene is the interpretation of exactly who are the Lady in Black and her husband (who appears in chapter 6). The inability to determine for certain who those characters represent caused one of the most intense polemics in Soviet scholarship on Chernyshevskii. Many Soviet scholars chose to see the Lady in Black as the young widow saved by Rakhmetov and her husband as Rakhmetov himself. In this regard, the note Chernyshevskii sent to Pypin and Nekrasov on the same day he completed the novel, plus certain passages of the text, functioned as evidence. Others, however, identified the Lady in Black as Chernyshevskii's wife, Olga Sokratovna, and the young man of thirty as Chernyshevskii himself. Supporters of this interpretation relied on the correspondence between certain passages of the text and passages in Chernyshevskii's diary relating to his wife.[27] Despite the intense nature of the discussion, Soviet scholars did not essentially differ on the meaning of the conclusion as a whole. After years of debate about the problem, Iu. K. Rudenko postulated that the fascination with identifying the Lady in Black and the young man of about thirty was actually harmful to an understanding of the novel. He argued that, even if one could pin down exactly who those characters represent, it would not enrich understanding of the scene but only impoverish it.[28] Moreover, the net result of Soviet research was to prove that the young man of about thirty cannot be either Rakhmetov or Chernyshevskii himself, and, consequently, the Lady in Black cannot be Ol'ga Sokratovna or the young widow.[29] In short, the Lady in Black and her husband are composite images meant to represent anyone who has undertaken political activity; the search for models in this case is a fruitless, sterile one.[30]

Soviet scholars were correct when they emphasized that the winter picnic scene is important in the characters' development. Up to that point in the novel, the characters have pursued activities that, although unconventional in many respects, are not particularly revolutionary. As Soviet scholars often phrased it, up to that point they have been pursuing the progressivist, evolutionary path of social change.[31] As we have seen, however, regarding the fate of the co-op, the characters are primed for a change in their outlook. Vera Pavlovna and Kirsanov have been forced to confront the fact of a state hostile to even seemingly innocuous enterprises such as a cooperative. Moreover, the dark turn in the conversation between Vera Pavlovna and Katerina Polozova indicates that something serious has been looming in the background.[32]

It is in the winter picnic scene, however, when confronted with the Lady in Black's unfortunate situation (that is, that her husband is suffering on account of his political activity), that the characters are forced to part openly with their illusions and make a conscious choice. As they observe the distress of the Lady in Black the characters come to realize that such a fate, if they persist in the direction in which they have been tending, could befall them: "The ladies, at least, exchanged quite anxious private glances five or six times. Twice Vera Pavlovna whispered furtively to her husband, 'Sasha, what if this happens to me?' The first time Kirsanov couldn't think of anything to say; the second time he did and answered, 'No, Verochka, this can't happen to you.' 'It can't? Are you sure?' 'Yes.' And twice Katerina Vasil'evna whispered furtively to her husband, 'This can't happen to me, can it Charlie?' The first time Beaumont only smiled, neither cheerfully nor soothingly; the second time he too answered, 'In all likelihood, it can't—in all likelihood' " (436).[33]

The male characters' attempts to reassure their wives that such a fate is not likely reflects a lack of resolve to some degree. The question posed is a rather painful one that they would prefer to avoid. However, it is one that cannot be avoided. When the Lady in Black returns, she informs those around her of the dangers involved in political activity for both the activist and his or her loved ones. She transmits that message via the songs she sings. Those songs are all quotations of various lines of poetry, especially Lermontov's, which, although written for entirely differently circumstances, acquire an entirely new radical meaning when combined as a whole in the Lady in Black's monologue.[34] The Lady in Black stresses that if one marries, one must do so without deception.[35] In other words, the budding political activist must inform the future spouse of the possible dangers (440–42). The Lady in Black informs the characters that if they enter the arena of political activity, they must do so in a sober, realistic manner.[36]

In the whirlwind of new characters and the apparent revelry of song that are presented in the winter picnic scene, it is perhaps easy to lose the main track. The reader almost loses sight of the main characters, who play only a minor role in this section, forgetting in the process that this is their story. In many ways, that is the point of this section. Only a reader skilled in the nuances of Aesopian language is expected to decode it. The Lady in Black and the cast of new characters are provided precisely to deflect the unwanted attention of certain readers away from the story of the main characters. Despite the apparent revelry and the new characters, however, it is the main characters who are the real subjects of this scene. They demonstrate a greater political awareness and increasing dedication in this scene. Although at first they recoil and express some reservation, they demonstrate much more boldness as the Lady in Black continues her performance. Finally, the characters put aside their doubts and fears and are ready for the final step: "('Forget what I told you, Sasha, listen to her!' whispers one of them and squeezes his hand. 'Why didn't I tell you that? Now I'll say it,' whispers the other.)" (442).[37] It is only here, a few pages before the end of the novel, that the characters finally embrace a revolutionary outlook, with all the risks and possible unhappiness that entails.[38] Of what that consists cannot be stated by the author, of course, but it is clear that the main characters have taken a qualitative step in their development: an important threshold has been crossed.[39]

Thus, it is clear that the winter picnic scene is heavily political and rife with allegory. That this scene is an important part of the novel and essential to understanding the development of the main characters is not in doubt. However, too much should not be made of the scene. For example, the attempts by Soviet scholars to read a detailed political program into the scene (and chapter 6) are not at all well founded.[40] Even for the most reasonable of Soviet assertions, that is, that the characters have decided to follow the path demonstrated by Rakhmetov, there is remarkably little evidence.[41] However, there is little that would enable one to argue that they set down any path in particular. Beyond statements such as that one should marry without deception, the Lady in Black provides no other advice: this, in itself, is the end-all of her monologue. Moreover, although it is clear that the characters have parted with their illusions and realized the necessity of some type of political, revolutionary activity, what that entails, how and what the characters are to do, who is to lead the activity, and so forth, are all left totally unsaid. There is no political program provided in the winter picnic scene.

Likewise, in chapter 6 ("Change of Scene"), which consists of only one page, no program is provided either. The main characters do not appear at all. Whatever they may have realized is left unsaid and not presented to the reader. Instead, the Lady in Black, now in pink, and her husband have been reunited. That this short chapter hints that a revolution has occurred between chapters 5 and 6 goes almost without saying. The very name of chapter 6, "Change of Scene," combined with the freeing of the husband of the Lady in Black make it evident. Moreover, the abrupt ending of the novel is obviously one more hint at something that simply could not be described: revolution. Chapter 6 can certainly be interpreted as a call to action by the author.[42] However, it is very general in nature, providing no specifics for the reader. Thus, we see that there is no real answer provided to the question posed in the novel's title, and certainly no prediction of the actual date of the revolution, as has been suggested by some.[43] As Volodin et al. demonstrate, Chernyshevskii was a sober analyst of the historical process; he could not have seriously expected such a quick victory.[44] If anything, chapter 6 most probably represents little more than one last act of defiance by Chernyshevskii against his tsarist captors. Thus, rather than providing a how-to manual with a set of ready-made answers for his readers, Chernyshevskii merely poses the question while exhorting his reader to find an answer to it.[45] How and what was to be done are left totally unsaid by the author. Rather, Chernyshevskii invites the reader to provide his or her own answer.

Appendix: Plot Summary

THE FOOL

The novel begins in medias res with an unnamed gentleman taking a hotel room. He is not there the next morning but has left a suicide note that explains the events of the previous night.

THE FIRST CONSEQUENCES OF THE FOOL'S DEED

A young woman is sewing and singing when news of the suicide is given to her. It greatly upsets her.

CHAPTER ONE

The story turns to the prehistory of the young woman, Vera Pavlovna. A brief account of her childhood and family situation is presented. Her mother, Mar'ia Aleksevna, does her best to see that Vera Pavlovna is well brought up, but her basic purpose is to sell her daughter to a rich or noble suitor. The action proper begins when the landlord's son, Storeshnikov, begins pursuing Vera Pavlovna. Vera Pavlovna's mother wants to marry her off to the young rake. Vera Pavlovna refuses, which causes numerous trials and tribulations.

CHAPTER TWO

Lopukhov is introduced into the action as Vera Pavlovna's brother's tutor. Lopukhov's behavior pleases Mar'ia Aleksevna, so he is invited to Vera Pavlovna's seventeenth birthday party. There he and Vera Pavlovna talk for the first time. She informs him of her terrible situation vis-à-vis her parents and Storeshnikov.

Lopukhov tries to find an escape for Vera Pavlovna by arranging a job for her. He is unsuccessful and informs her of the one way out: marriage. After laying out the ground rules, Vera Pavlovna agrees. Lopukhov and Vera

Pavlovna marry in secret. Three days later, Vera Pavlovna abandons her mother, telling her she is married.

CHAPTER THREE

The Lopukhovs' life goes well. Vera Pavlovna decides to open a sewing co-op. The narrator gives the history of Vera Pavlovna's co-op.

Slowly, tension mounts as an attraction between Vera Pavlovna and her husband's best friend, Kirsanov, begins to develop. This tension is interrupted when Kirsanov meets an old flame, Nastia Kriukova. The grief over Kriukova's death brings Vera Pavlovna and Kirsanov closer together.

Vera Pavlovna has her third dream, in which she realizes that she and Lopukhov are not suited for each other and, moreover, that she has feelings for Kirsanov. To solve the situation Lopukhov stages the fake suicide developed at the beginning of the novel.

CHAPTER FOUR

Now free, Vera Pavlovna enjoys her new marital life with Kirsanov. After some time Vera Pavlovna announces her decision to become a doctor. The Kirsanovs' marital bliss is interrupted by the unwelcome attention of the authorities to Vera Pavlovna's co-op.

CHAPTER FIVE

New characters are introduced: Katerina Polozova and an American, Charles Beaumont (that is, Lopukhov). Beaumont and Polozova fall in love and marry. They become close acquaintances with the Kirsanovs and both couples settle in adjoining apartments.

The winter picnic scene: the Beaumonts and the Kirsanovs go on an outing during which they participate in some revelry and evidently make the decision to become political activists.

Notes

PREFACE

1. See N. G. Chernyshevskii, *Polnoe sobranie sochinenii* (Moscow: 1939–53). These comments are based on conversations with the Russian scholar Iurii K. Rudenko, held in the summer of 1993. Rudenko has worked extensively with Chernyshevskii's manuscripts and informs me that the distortions are many. In addition, there are also cases of omission. For example, the editors felt the need to delete a passage from one of Chernyshevskii's letters in which he comments on Pushkin and other writers (15:91). The editors do at least mark the deletion by ellipsis points.

2. Among the more egregious transgressions is the fact that Soviet scholars felt the need to "correct" Chernyshevskii's literary texts on occasion.

3. N. G. Chernyshevskii, *Chto delat'?* (Leningrad: 1975). This edition was prepared by T. I. Ornatskaia and S. A. Reiser. According to Ornatskaia and Reiser, p. 6, it contains over 100 corrections of the *PSS* version.

4. The text of this edition was reprinted three years later in a three-volume collection of Chernyshevskii's literary works: N. G. Chernyshevskii, *Izbrannye proizvedeniia v trekh tomakh* (Leningrad: 1978). For any scholar who wishes to work on Chernyshevskii's other literary works, this is the edition to be used. Unfortunately, even within this edition, the text of *Prolog* is not completely trustworthy. As Rudenko informs me, the publisher did not allow them to go back to the original manuscripts, but only to use the comments of E. L. Efremenko, who criticized the *PSS* text of the novel. Despite this defect, this is the best text available for *Prolog*. The third volume of this edition contains the texts of several of Chernyshevskii's literary works that were unpublished in his lifetime. Those texts were checked against the manuscripts and are authoritative. For Efremenko's criticisms, see "Publikatsiia khudozhestvennykh proizvedenii N. G. Chernyshevskogo," in *Voprosy tekstologii* (Moscow: 1957), 189–223.

5. Chernyshevskii's cousin, A Pypin, stated that the novel was published "without any cuts." In addition, I. Borisov stated that "the censorship of the Third Section corrected it very little." Both quoted in A. A. Dem-

chenko, *N. G. Chernyshevskii. Nauchnaia biografiia. Chast' tret'ia. 1859–1864* (Saratov: 1992), 212.

6. See S. A. Reiser, "Nekotorye problemy izucheniia romana *Chto delat'?*" in the LP edition, 782–833. See also T. I. Ornatskaia, "Roman N. G. Chernyshevskogo *Chto delat'?* (K istorii teksta)," *Russkaia literatura,* no. 3 (1977): 115–27; Tamara Ivanovna Ornatskaya and Galina Silina, "*What Is to Be Done?* Deciphering the Manuscript," *Soviet Literature* 10 (1975): 131–33.

7. Nikolai Chernyshevsky, *What Is to Be Done?* translated by Michael R. Katz, annotated by William G. Wagner (Ithaca: Cornell University Press, 1989). Translation copyright © 1989 Cornell University. Used by permission of the publisher, Cornell University Press. This translation is by far the best one available and a valuable resource for scholars working on Chernyshevskii. I do have some individual reservations, which will be noted where relevant.

8. In direct quotations from other scholarly works and in bibliographic citations, I preserve the system of transliteration of the original.

9. N. G. Chernyshevsky, *Selected Philosophical Essays* (Moscow: 1953).

INTRODUCTION

1. Nor do I intend to provide a biography of Chernyshevskii because this information is easily available in other sources in English. For a concise account, see Francis B. Randall's entry on Chernyshevskii in the *Handbook of Russian Literature.* Extended studies of Chernyshevskii are: William F. Woehrlin, *Chernyshevskii: The Man and the Journalist* (Cambridge: 1971); Francis B. Randall, *N. G. Chernyshevskii* (New York: 1967); N. G. O. Pereira, *The Thought and Teachings of N. G. Černyševskij* (The Hague: 1975); Irina Paperno, *Chernyshevsky and the Age of Realism: A Study in the Semiotics of Behavior* (Stanford: 1988). See also the chapters devoted to Chernyshevskii in Franco Venturi's *Roots of Revolution* (New York: 1960) and E. Lampert's *Sons against Fathers* (Oxford: 1965). For works in Russian, see Iu. M. Steklov, *N. G. Chernyshevskii. Ego zhizn' i deiatel'nost'. 1828–1889,* 2 vols. (Moscow-Leningrad: 1928); A. A. Demchenko, *N. G. Chernyshevskii. Nauchnaia biografiia,* 4 parts (Saratov: 1978–94).

2. A brief discussion of Lenin's admiration for Chernyshevskii can be found in Leonard Schapiro, *Russian Studies* (London: 1986), 214–17. See also Randall, pp. 143–45.

3. Soviet scholars did have to exercise caution with regard to interpreting Chernyshevskii's legacy. His credentials as a great revolutionary, a proto-Bolshevik, could not be questioned. When the Soviet scholar Pokrovskii interpreted Chernyshevskii as a proto-Menshevik rather than a proto-Bolshevik, it provoked a rebuke from Stalin (Randall, 148).

4. James P. Scanlan provides numbers on Soviet dissertations in his articles. Writing in 1967, for example, he estimated that 400 Soviet dissertations had been written on Chernyshevskii. In 1985 he put the number at 600 dissertations. See James P. Scanlan, "Nikolaj Černyševskij and Soviet Philosophy," *Studies in Soviet Thought* 7, no. 1 (1967): 2; James P. Scanlan, "Nikolaj Chernyshevsky and the Philosophy of Realism in Nineteenth-Century Russian Aesthetics," *Studies in Soviet Thought* 30 (1985): 1.

5. Lenin never wrote a specific work devoted to an analysis of Chernyshevskii, but he turned to him frequently in his writings. For a convenient collection of Lenin's statements, see I. I. Skvortsov-Stepanov, ed., *Lenin o Chernyshevskom* (Moscow-Leningrad: 1928).

6. Nikolay Valentinov, *Encounters with Lenin* (London: 1968), 63–64.

7. G. V. Plekhanov, *N. G. Chernyshevskii* (Saint Petersburg: 1910). Individual parts of Plekhanov's works on Chernyshevskii are reprinted in the two-volume collection G. V. Plekhanov, *Literatura i estetika* (Moscow: 1958).

8. See his "[O romane Chernyshevskogo *Chto delat'?*]," *Literatura i estetika,* 2:175–81. Iurii Rudenko discusses Plekhanov's analysis extensively, arguing that Plekhanov often did little more than repeat the arguments of Chernyshevskii's contemporaries. See Iu. K. Rudenko, *Chernyshevskii-romanist i literaturnye traditsii* (Leningrad: 1989), 11–12. See also U. A. Gural'nik, *Nasledie N. G. Chernyshevskogo-pisatelia i sovetskoe literaturovedenie* (Moscow: 1980), 29–32, who also finds Plekhanov's study of Chernyshevskii inadequate. Both Rudenko and Gural'nik provide valuable summaries of Soviet scholarship on Chernyshevskii. See also Randall's discussion, pp. 143–48, which covers the attitude of the early Soviet political figures toward Chernyshevskii.

9. A. V. Lunacharskii, *Stat'i o Chernyshevskom* (Moscow: 1958). An English translation of one of these articles appears in Anatoly Lunacharsky, *On Literature and Art* (Moscow: 1973), 22–70. Gural'nik, p. 38, views Lunacharskii's work as a step forward in the study of Chernyshevskii. Rudenko, p. 14, argues that Lunacharskii was the first person to view Chernyshevskii as a truly great writer.

10. A. P. Skaftymov, "Roman *Chto delat'?*" in *N. G. Chernyshevskii. Sbornik. Neizdannye stat'i, materialy, vospominaniia* (Saratov: 1926), 92–140; *Zhizn' i deiatel'nost' N. G. Chernyshevskogo*, 2nd ed. (Saratov: 1947). See also A. P. Skaftymov, *Nravstvennye iskaniia russkikh pisatelei. Stat'i i issledovaniia o russkikh klassikakh* (Moscow: 1972). Other valuable works published in the Saratov publications include those by Vasilii Gippius: "Chernyshevskii—stikhoved," in *N. G. Chernyshevskii. Sbornik. Neizdannye stat'i, materialy, vospominaniia* (Saratov: 1926), 73–91; "Neizdannaia stat'ia Chernyshevskogo," in *Nikolai Gavrilovich Chernyshevskii 1828–1928. Neizdannye teksty, materialy i stat'i* (Saratov: 1928), 101–3.

11. Rudenko, p. 15, is rather critical of Skaftymov's work, citing methodological mistakes. It is true that Skaftymov operates under the basic assumption that *What Is to Be Done?* is lacking as an artistic work. Despite this fact, in his early articles he does offer several valuable discussions.

12. As Randall, p. 146, notes, Stalin was also an admirer of Chernyshevskii; under his rule, the canonization of Chernyshevskii was completed.

13. For a particularly crude example of sloganeering, see N. V. Vodovozov, *Roman N. G. Chernyshevskogo "Chto Delat'?"* (Moscow: 1953). On p. 17 Vodovozov takes time out for a propaganda aside when he argues that the radiant vision provided in Vera Pavlovna's fourth dream corresponds to contemporary Soviet reality.

14. Gural'nik notes, p. 46, that during the 1930s, 1940s, and 1950s, Chernyshevskii was studied primarily for his theoretical views and his novels were used mainly for this purpose. He also refers, p. 76, to the "inertia" of this period, stating that it relied on dogmatic explanations of Chernyshevskii's legacy. In a pointed criticism directed at Soviet scholarship, he also claims that this inertia continued into the present.

15. S. A. Reiser, "Legenda o prototypakh *Chto delat'?* Chernyshevskogo," *Trudy Leningradskogo bibliotechnogo instituta imeni N. K. Krupskoi. Kafedra literatury* 2 (1957): 115–25, questions the long-held belief that the novel was based on the Sechenov-Bokov-Obrucheva circle. In his articles, Bukhshtab subjects the belief that the young man of about thirty who appears in the last chapter of the novel is Rakhmetov to critical analysis. See B. Ia. Bukhshtab, "Zapiska N. G. Chernyshevskogo o romane *Chto delat'?*" *Izvestiia Akademii Nauk SSSR. Otdelenie literatury i iazyka* 12, no. 2 (1953): 158–69; B. Ia. Bukhshtab, "K voprosy o siuzhete romana Chernyshevskogo *Chto delat'?*" *Izvestiia Akademii Nauk SSSR. Otdelenie literatury i iazyka* 15, no. 5 (1956): 444–56.

16. G. Verkhovskii, *O romane N. G. Chernyshevskogo "Chto delat'?"* (Iaroslavl': 1959); A. Lebedev, *Geroi Chernyshevskogo* (Moscow: 1962). In his summation of Lebedev's work, Gural'nik argues that it held a lot of promise but finished weakly. He does state, however, that it remains one of the most significant works on Chernyshevskii (Gural'nik, 83–89).

17. See especially the works of Rudenko and Verderevskaia: Iu. K Rudenko, "N. G. Chernyshevskii kak khudozhnik: belletristicheskie opyty 1840-kh godov," *Russkaia literatura,* no. 1 (1970): 101–20; Iu. K. Rudenko, "Problema chitatelia v romane N. G. Chernyshevskogo *Chto delat'?*" in *Russkaia literatura XIX–XX vekov,* ed. I. G. Iampol'skii (Leningrad: 1971), 61–76; Iu. K. Rudenko, *Roman N. G. Chernyshevskogo "Chto delat'?" Esteticheskoe svoeobrazie i khudozhestvennyi metod* (Leningrad: 1979); N. A. Verderevskaia, "O 'prototipicheskoi versii' v izuchenii khudozhestvennykh proizvedenii Chernyshevskogo," in *N. G. Chernyshevskii. Stat'i, issledovaniia i materialy* (Saratov: 1968), 5:117–28; N. A. Verderevskaia, *Stanovle-*

nie tipa raznochintsa v russkoi realisticheskoi literature 40–60kh godov XIX veka (k probleme tipologii zhanra, siuzheta i obraza) (Kazan': 1975). Another work worthy of note is N. Naumova, *Roman N. G. Chernyshevskogo "Chto delat'?"* (Leningrad: 1972).

18. One should not conclude that all of the work of the 1970s was of a uniformly high quality. In Gural'nik's words, the "inertia" of the past did continue throughout the period.

19. See, for example, T. Iu. Dubrovina, "Khronotop v romane N. G. Chernyshevskogo 'Chto delat'?" in *Iz istorii russkoi literatury i literaturnoi kritiki* (Kishinev: 1984), 54–60; E. A. Podshivalova, "O khudozhestvennom khronotope v romane N. G. Chernyshevskogo *Chto delat'?*" in *Problema avtora v khudozhestvennoi literature. Mezhvuzovskii sbornik nauchnykh trudov* (Izhevsk: 1983), 61–69.

20. It also provides some interesting information on the past. The Gural'niks discuss an intriguing episode regarding the publication of Chernyshevskii's collected works. Apparently, Chernyshevskii's "Znamenie na krovle" was considered to be too apocalyptic, that is, a prediction of the destruction of the world by atomic bombs, and thus was not included in the thirteenth volume, where it belonged. See U. A. Gural'nik and Iu. U. Gural'nik, "Roman *Chto delat'?* segodnia. Opyt sovremennoi interpretatsii," in *"Chto delat'" N. G. Chernyshevskogo. Istoriko-funktsional'noe issledovanie* (Moscow: 1990), 236–37. "Znamenie na krovle" was subsequently included in the sixteenth, supplementary volume of the collected works.

21. These remarks are based on personal observation from 1992 and 1993: whereas editions of *What Is to Be Done?* and *Prolog* were once common fare, they have now disappeared entirely from bookstores. Likewise, few publications analyzing Chernyshevskii's literary works have appeared in the post-Soviet period. The major exception to this rule is Chernyshevskii's home town of Saratov, where some post-Soviet scholarship has managed to appear. For example, parts 3 and 4 of A. A. Demchenko's *N. G. Chernyshevskii. Nauchnaia biografiia* appeared in 1992 and 1994. The year 1994 also saw the appearance of the collection *N. G. Chernyshevskii. Istoriia. Filosofiia. Literatura.*

22. Randall, 152–58, provides a summary of Western treatment of Chernyshevskii up to 1967. See also Michael R. Katz and William G. Wagner, "Introduction: Chernyshevsky, *What Is to Be Done?* and the Russian Intelligentsia," in *What Is to Be Done?* by Nikolai Chernyshevsky (Ithaca: 1989), 1–36. For a Soviet view of Western scholarship see A. Sigrist, "Fal'sifitsirovannyi Chernyshevskii: stereotipy i novatsii," *Voprosy literatury*, no. 1 (1971): 130–45. See also the chapters devoted to Western scholarship in *N. G. Chernyshevskii v obshchestvennoi mysli narodov zarubezhnykh stran* (Moscow: 1981).

23. The most well known is Thomas Garrigue Masaryk, *The Spirit of Russia: Studies in History, Literature, and Philosophy* (New York: 1955),

2:1–52. Masaryk's study originally appeared in German in 1913. Some Western political figures, such as leaders of the German Social Democrats, did devote some attention to Chernyshevskii. See Karl Kautski, "Tchernichewsky et Malthus," *La Revue Socialiste*, no. 10 (1880): 425–32 and no. 11 (1880): 458–65; A. Bebel, "Ein idealistischer Roman," *Neue Zeit* 3 (1885).

24. See, for example, Jack Abraham Posin, "Chernyshevsky, Dobrolyubov, and Pisarev, the Ideological Forerunners of Bolshevism" (Ph.D. diss., University of California, 1939).

25. One exception to this exaggerated hostility is the work of David Hecht, which appeared in the 1940s.

26. Adam B. Ulam, *The Bolsheviks* (New York: 1965), 54–70. See also Simon Karlinsky, "The True Father of Bolshevism," *Saturday Review*, September 4, 1976, p. 45. Karlinsky states, for example, "It is because of the ideas Chernyshevsky formulated in the 1860s that today's Communist societies are puritanical in sexual matters and simplistically utilitarian in their approach to the arts."

27. Western studies of nineteenth-century Russian literature typically do not devote space to Chernyshevskii.

28. See, for example, G. Žekulin, "Forerunner of Socialist Realism: the Novel 'What to do?' by N. G. Chernyshevsky," *Slavonic and East European Review* 41 (1963): 467–83. In his study, first published in 1958, Mathewson argues for a direct link between Chernyshevskii and Socialist Realism. Mathewson repeats this assertion in the preface to the second edition: "I have insisted on the heavy contribution of Belinsky, Dobrolyubov, and Chernyshevsky made to the genesis of socialist realism. I still think this is so[.]" See Rufus W. Mathewson Jr., *The Positive Hero in Russian Literature*, 2nd ed. (Stanford: 1975), xiv.

29. Randall, 158–61.

30. Woehrlin, 314–19.

31. Pereira, 85. Pereira further argues that the novel should be read and studied merely because it inspired the younger generation.

32. In addition to obvious geopolitical causes, a contributing factor in the negative perception of Chernyshevskii by Western scholars is probably Nabokov's *The Gift*. Although first published in 1937–38, chapter 4, containing the lampoon of Chernyshevskii, was omitted due to the objections of the editorial board of *Sovremennye zapiski*. Chernyshevskii, despite the attempts of the Bolsheviks to claim him as their own, remained a respected figure among the liberal and radical intelligentsia of the Russian diaspora. However, a second, complete edition of *The Gift* appeared in 1952, with a complete English translation appearing in 1963. Simon Karlinsky, the author of a rather harsh appraisal of Chernyshevskii, certainly read *The Gift*. See his "Vladimir Nabokov's Novel *Dar* as a Work of Literary Criticism: A Structural Analysis," *Slavic and East European Journal* 8, no. 3 (1963): 284–90.

33. Scholars who devoted entire monographs to Chernyshevskii tended to be much more balanced in their observations. See Woehrlin, Pereira. Venturi provides a valuable chapter on Chernyshevskii in his *Roots of Revolution.* Lampert also provides a nonhostile treatment of Chernyshevskii, for which he has often been criticized. For an example of the criticism that Lampert has received, see Joseph Frank's chapter "Sons against Fathers," *Through the Russian Prism* (Princeton: 1990), 201–8. In the field of philosophy, James P. Scanlan provides a balanced treatment of Chernyshevskii in his articles. See Scanlan, 1967 and 1985; James P. Scanlan, "Nicholas Chernyshevsky and Philosophical Materialism in Russia," *Journal of the History of Philosophy* 8, no. 1 (January 1970), 65–86. See also Dennis Reinhartz, "N. G. Chernyshevsky on Aesthetics and Art: The Role of the Artist in a Revolution" (Ph.D. diss., New York University, 1971).

34. Michael R. Katz, "English Translations of *What Is to Be Done?*" *Slavic Review* 46, no. 1 (1987): 125–28. As Katz discusses, all the men involved had a clear political agenda in translating Chernyshevskii into English. Although their intentions were to acquaint the American public with Chernyshevskii and his radical politics, the hideous translations they produced had precisely the opposite affect, discouraging American readers from taking up Chernyshevskii.

35. Katz, 126. If these distorted translations were not bad enough, the scholarly commentary accompanying them has been distinguished by its sloppiness and ignorance of the basic facts (Katz, 128–30).

36. Randall states in his preface, pp. 7–8: "Less than half the American and British born Russian specialists seem to have read *What is to be Done?* in any language, and scarcely one in twenty seems to have read anything else by the man save for a few anthologized excerpts and bits quoted by other writers." I can add, based on my own experience, that through the years the situation has not improved appreciably.

37. Even a cursory glance at most scholarship on Nabokov's *The Gift* quickly reveals that most specialists have not done their homework. Most bibliographies reveal only one of the flawed translations of *What Is to Be Done?* and few, if any, secondary works. Russian-language sources are particularly absent.

38. Scholars concerned with the rise of the "women's question" in Russia began to turn to Chernyshevskii's novel, noting its immense importance for generations of young women. See, for example, Richard Stites, *The Women's Liberation Movement in Russia: Feminism, Nihilism, and Bolshevism* (Princeton: 1978); Barbara Alpern Engel, *Mothers and Daughters: Women of the Intelligentsia in Nineteenth Century Russia* (New York: 1983). See also Joe Andrew, *Women in Russian Literature, 1780–1863* (London: 1988). This is paralleled in other areas of Chernyshevskii's legacy, particularly his philosophy and aesthetics. See, for example, Scanlan, 1985;

James P. Scanlan, "Chernyshevsky and Rousseau," in *Western Philosophical Systems in Russian Literature: A Collection of Critical Studies* (Los Angeles: 1979), 103–20; Edward J. Brown, "So Much Depends . . . Russian Critics in Search of 'Reality,'" *Russian Review* 48 (1989): 353–81; Frederick C. Copleston, S. J., *Philosophy in Russia from Herzen to Lenin and Berdyaev* (Notre Dame, Ind: 1986), 101–11; Edward Wasiolek, *Fathers and Sons: Russia at the Crossroads* (New York: 1993).

39. Katerina Clark, *The Soviet Novel: History as Ritual* (Chicago: 1981), 49–56. Gary Saul Morson, *The Boundaries of Genre: Dostoevsky's Diary of a Writer and the Traditions of Literary Utopia* (Austin: 1981), 99–104; Emily Klenin, "On the Ideological Sources of *Čto delat'?*: Sand, Družinin, Leroux," *Zeitschrift für slavische Philologie* 51, no. 2 (1991): 367–405. In addition to Irina Paperno's monograph, see also her articles, "The Myth of Reality in N. G. Černyševskij's Works and Life," in *Myth in Literature* (Columbus, Ohio: 1985), 154–69; "The Novel Myth: N. G. Chernyshevskii's *What Is to Be Done?*" in *Issues in Russian Literature Before 1917* (Columbus, Ohio: 1989), 133–49.

40. Chernyshevsky, 1989. Old attitudes toward Chernyshevskii's novel will probably die hard, however. For example, Edward Acton states with regard to this translation: "This new version is therefore in a class of its own. It offers the complete text, erotic passages and all. Michael Katz's translation is . . . fluent and engaging. . . . Indeed at times it is almost too good, giving Chernyshevskii's style unfamiliar grace and panache." See *Revolutionary Russia* (June 1990): 118. Katz recently made another contribution to the study of Chernyshevskii with his translation of the novel *Prologue.*

41. V. G. Smolitskii, *Iz ravelina. O sud'be romana N. G. Chernyshevskogo "Chto delat'?"* 2nd ed. (Moscow: 1977), 60. Smolitskii presents a useful account of both Chernyshevskii's stay in the fortress and the events surrounding the writing and publication of *What Is to Be Done?*

42. Chernyshevskii, as was his usual practice since his student days, wrote much of the rough draft in a cipher that included elements of the Greek, Latin, and even Arabic alphabets in addition to the Russian (Smolitskii, 47). Chernyshevskii's cipher subsequently proved difficult to decipher. As a result the first publication of the rough draft in 1929 proved to be faulty. See the LP edition, p. 5; Tamara Ivanovna Ornatskaya and Galina Silina, "*What Is to Be Done?* Deciphering the Manuscript," *Soviet Literature* 10 (1975): 131–33.

43. This particular incident has always been a source of wonder for scholars and even novelists: the tsarist authorities themselves helped to recover the manuscript of one of the world's most subversive literary works.

44. Smolitskii, 67–68. See also the notes on the text in the LP edition, p. 834.

45. Joseph Frank, *Dostoevsky: The Stir of Liberation, 1860–1865* (Princeton: 1986), 285.

46. Quoted in E. Bushkanets, "Tsarskaia tsenzura i *Chto delat'?* Chernyshevskogo," *Ogonek,* no. 39 (September 1951): 24.

47. See Frank, 1986, p. 286, for an exposition. Feuer, p. ix, offers the explanation that perhaps the censors were unable to plow through it and did not know what it said.

48. According to Smolitskii, the commission ordered that if nothing suspicious was found in the novel, then it should be sent for publication in accordance with the usual rules (Smolitskii, 61–62).

49. Frank, 1986, 286.

50. His two reports, dated April 24 and May 15, 1863, appear in N. A. Bukhbinder, "Tsenzura o *Chto delat'?* N. G. Chernyshevskogo," *Katorga i ssylka,* no. 44 (1928): 44–50.

51. Likewise, I. Borisov, who worked in the *Alekseevskii ravelin* while Chernyshevskii was in prison, claimed to have read the manuscript for *What Is to Be Done?* He is at least the third person on record as having read it before it reached Beketov. See Borisov's memoirs, "Alekseevskii ravelin v 1862–65 gg.," *Russkaia starina* 108, book 12 (December 1901): 576.

52. Naumova, 8.

53. Richard L. Brown, "Chernyshevskii, Dostoevskii, and the Peredvizhniki: Toward a Russian Realist Aesthetic?" (Ph.D. diss., Ohio University, 1980), 66. Brown's discussion is directed at the relationship between the censors and the journals as a whole. However, his discussion is easily applicable to the particular incident of *What Is to Be Done?*

54. Smolitskii, 66–67. Chernyshevskii's remarks on this can be found in his *PSS* (1:732).

55. Dobroliubov attributed Beketov's liberalism to his stupidity (Smolitskii, 66).

56. Perhaps contributing to his difficulties was his personal philosophy regarding works under consideration. Beketov did not like to cut up a work; he believed that is was better simply to reject the work entirely. Thus, Beketov probably found himself in a difficult, all-or-nothing situation (Smolitskii, 67).

57. Smolitskii, pp. 65–66, stresses that Chernyshevskii had become very skilled at dealing with the censor during his many years of publicistic work.

58. This device does seem to have been partly successful. When he read the first part submitted by Chernyshevskii, Przhetslavskii saw nothing dangerous in it. Indeed, he characterized it simply as a response to Turgenev's *Fathers and Sons.* When the third chapter was submitted, Przhetslavskii began to change his mind, seeing in it blasphemy and the destruction of the idea of marriage. However, he was partly disarmed by the fact that

he apparently thought that it was the end of the novel. Naumova, p. 10, argues that it was precisely the novel's design that fooled the censors. In her view, the novel's idea is revealed step by step, and the answer posed in the novel's title is answered only when the very last line has been read. Similarly, L. M. Lotman argues that Chernyshevskii had an amazing ability to feel the reader. Lotman argues that Chernyshevskii counted on the difference in the perception of the reader reading the novel in parts (that is, the censor) from the perception of the reader, before whose eyes the novel appeared as a whole. See Lotman, "Ideino-khudozhestvennye printsipy beletristiki Chernyshevskogo 1860–1870-kh godov," in *N. G. Chernyshevskii. Estetika. Literatura. Kritika* (Leningrad: 1979), 74.

59. Turgenev's stories were originally passed by the censor and published separately. However, when he wanted to publish them all together in book form, the censor refused, seeing in the whole a criticism of serfdom.

60. This note appears in the LP edition, p. 744. An English translation appears in the 1986 Ardis edition of *What Is to Be Done?* pp. xxxvii–xxxviii.

61. For a discussion, see B. Ia. Bukhshtab, "Zapiska N. G. Chernyshevskogo o romane *Chto delat'?*" *Izvestiia Akademii Nauk SSSR. Otdelenie literatury i iazyka* 12, no. 2 (1953), 158–69. See also Smolitskii, p. 64.

62. Iurii Rudenko argues that the censor thought the novel so tendentious and so inartistic that it could only discredit the author and the left in general. He also adds that there might have been a second motivation in the government's decision to allow the novel's publication: it considered the novel harmless and thought it could reconcile the left by letting Chernyshevskii publish. See Rudenko, 1971, p. 61. See also Paperno, 1988, p. 27.

63. T. I. Ornatskaia, "Roman N. G. Chernyshevskogo *Chto delat'?* (K istorii teksta)," *Russkaia literatura,* no. 3 (1977): 115–16.

64. Likewise, contrary to normal procedure, Chernyshevskii was not presented with the censor's prohibitions and given a chance to rewrite the text. A further indication of some type of government plot may also be seen in the fact that Chernyshevskii was not allowed to see the published version of his novel when it appeared. Ornatskaia, p. 116, doubts that Chernyshevskii ever saw a published version of his own novel.

65. Smolitskii, p. 68, notes that the scandal in the censor's office started immediately after the appearance of the final installment on May 30, 1863. On June 14 Beketov asked to retire. But in a letter of June 21, 1863, to Nekrasov, he stated that he had been ordered to retire. His letter appears in *Literaturnoe nasledstvo* 51–52 (1949): 110.

66. The government also took revenge on Chernyshevskii by giving him an extremely harsh sentence at his trial.

67. Beketov, although somewhat worried for a time, did receive his full pension of 1,500 rubles per year. Moreover, he received a one-time payment of 500 rubles. His attitude during the time period shortly after the

appearance of the novel hardly seemed one of great distress at having let this dangerous work through. Rather, most of his concerns in the period following this incident are incredibly mundane. Smolitskii, 68–70.

68. Ulam argues that it is unreasonable to credit the tsarist authorities with such discernment and such touching faith in the literary taste of the younger generation. See Adam B. Ulam, *In the Name of the People* (New York: 1977), 136.

69. Demchenko, part 3, 214.

70. According to Petr Tkachev, *What Is to Be Done?* was the "gospel of Russian radicalism." Quoted in Abbott Gleason, *Young Russia* (Chicago: 1983), 296.

71. Smolitskii, pp. 84–85, discusses the government's unsuccessful measures.

72. M. P. Sazhin, *Vospominaniia* (Moscow: 1925), 23. Herzen, commenting on the young Russians arriving abroad, stated, "The young Russians who arrived after 1862 were almost all out of *What Is to Be Done?*, with the addition of a few Bazarovian traits." See his *Sobranie,* vol. 20, book 1, 337. Reverence for Chernyshevskii was also demonstrated by the numerous pictures of him discovered by the Third Section: "Photographic portraits of various sizes of Chernyshevskii are found in the majority of the searches conducted." Quoted in V. N. Shul'gin, *Ocherki zhizni i tvorchestva N. G. Chernyshevskogo* (Moscow: 1956), 94.

73. Quoted in Stites, p. 98.

74. E. N. Vodovozova, *Na zare zhizni* (Moscow: 1964), 2:189.

75. Quoted in Stites, p. 97. Tsitovich's remarks can be found in his *Chto delali v romane "Chto delat'?"* 4th ed. (Odessa: 1879).

76. Quoted in S. E. Shatalov and A. S. Kurilov, *Nikolai Gavrilovich Chernyshevskii* (Moscow: 1978), 37.

77. See, for example, the comments of A. Nezlobin: "Every Nadechka, Iulechka got married according to *What Is to Be Done?*, set up the well-known 'neutral room' with some *stolonachal'nik* and called each other—she him: 'my dear,' and he her: 'my friend.'" Quoted in N. L. Brodskii and N. P. Sidorov, *Kommentarii k romanu N. G. Chernyshevskogo "Chto delat'?"* (Moscow: 1933), 102.

78. Stites, 105–7. See also Olga Matich, "Dialectics of Cultural Return: Zinaida Gippius' Personal Myth," in *Cultural Mythologies of Russian Modernism* (Berkeley: 1992), 60–67. Matich notes that in her personal life, Gippius very much modeled herself on many aspects of Vera Pavlovna's first marriage.

79. Paperno, 1988, p. 31; Adam B. Ulam, "Party Girl," *New York Times Book Review,* January 31, 1993, p. 12.

80. For a discussion, see Stites, pp. 109–11.

81. Vodovozova, vol. 2, p. 199, recounts such an episode.

82. See Gleason, pp. 304–7. See also B. M. Sivovolov, "Roman N. G. Chernyshevskogo *Chto delat'?* v sotsial'noi praktike sovremennikov (O zhenskom trude po memuarnym istochnikam)," in *Roman N. G. Chernyshevskogo "Chto delat'?" (K 100-letiiu vykhoda v svet). Sbornik statei* (Shakhty: 1963), 91–104.

83. Gleason, 296, 304.

84. Shul'gin, 94. Shul'gin argues that in the 1860s there was not a single significant trial in which Chernyshevskii's works—especially *What Is to Be Done?*—did not figure.

85. See Smolitskii, p. 83; N. G. O. Pereira, "Chernyshevsky's *What Is to Be Done?* as a Statement of Social Utopia," *Rocky Mountain Social Science Journal* 9, no. 3 (1972): 42. Several officials, among them Count Murav'ev, wanted to bring Chernyshevskii back to Saint Petersburg to stand trial for plotting the tsar's assassination. However, Chernyshevskii was already safely isolated and cooler heads prevailed. The government contented itself merely by blaming Chernyshevskii and his novel for having a destructive influence. This claim was a part of the official sentence pronounced upon the Karakazovites.

86. Hans Kohn, *The Mind of Modern Russia* (New Brunswick, N.J.: 1955), 140. Kohn posits that Rakhmetov and his travels around the Russian countryside were a source of inspiration for the younger generation.

87. A concise summary of this reaction is provided in the commentary to the novel in Chernyshevskii's *PSS* (11:705–11).

88. There is very little evidence in the novel for such a view, yet contemporaries made these charges nevertheless. Nikolai Berdiaev would later defend Chernyshevskii from such charges, labeling him a modern-day saint and his detractors hypocrites. In contrast to the contemporary reaction, Berdiaev interpreted *What Is to Be Done?* as a text that is supportive of marriage and the family. See Nicolas Berdyaev, *The Russian Idea* (Westport, Conn.: 1979), 105–10; Nicolas Berdyaev, *The Origin of Russian Communism* (Ann Arbor, Mich.: 1960), 46–53.

89. Quoted in Stites, p. 96. Tolstoi's review, "Lzhemudrost' geroev Chernyshevskogo," appeared under the name Rostislav in issue 138 (1863).

90. *Domashnaia beseda,* no. 8 (1864): 212–13.

91. Stites, 96–97. Solov'ev provided a review of the novel, entitled "Zhenshchinam," in *Epokha* (December 1864): 15–24. Such views on the novel were also presented to foreign readers by D. K. Schedo-Ferroti in his *Aus der Literatur des Nigilismus. Kritische Beleichtung des Tschernyscheffskyschen Romans "Was tun?"* (Braunschweig: 1871). Schedo-Ferroti was an agent of the Russian government who consistently denounced the "nihilists" in the foreign press. For further discussion, see M. G. Zel'dovich, "Zabytyi epizod bor'by vokrug romana N. G. Chernyshevskogo *Chto delat'?*" in *N. G. Chernyshevskii. Stat'i, issledovaniia i materialy* (Saratov: 1961), 2:96–115.

92. Bukhbinder, 50.

93. Tsitovich, 19. Stites, p. 97, provides a small discussion of this rather amusing work. As Stites describes it, Tsitovich's book is "a deliberate effort to distort and discredit the meaning of the book, by means of a dubious exegesis of the Russian law codes."

94. Tsitovich, 54.

95. Turgenev, *PSS,* 5:113, 128.

96. Ibid., 5:129.

97. See, for example, the commentary to his *PSS,* 7:389–92.

98. Ibid., 34:65.

99. Quoted in B. P. Koz'min, *Iz istorii revoliutsionnoi mysli v Rossii* (Moscow: 1961), 24.

100. Koz'min, 26–28. For an example of the extremely hostile split that developed at this time, see V. Zaitsev, "Glupovtsy, popavshie v *Sovremennik,*" *Russkoe slovo,* no. 2 (1864): 34–42.

101. M. E. Saltykov-Shchedrin, *Sobranie sochinenii* (Moscow: 1968), 6:324.

102. Koz'min, 30.

103. For a contemporary's discussion, see N. N. Strakhov, "Schastlivye liudi," *Iz istorii literaturnago nigilizma. 1861–1865* (Saint Petersburg: 1890), 316–18.

104. Charles A. Moser, *Antinihilism in the Russian Novel of the 1860's* (The Hague: 1964), 29. See also I. P. Viduetskaia, "Roman *Chto delat'?* v otsenke revoliutsionno-demokraticheskoi kritiki," in *"Chto delat'?" N. G. Chernyshevskogo. Istoriko-funktsional'noe issledovanie* (Moscow: 1990), 78–106.

105. Strakhov, for example, stated: "What did Mr. Shchedrin say or want to say in the course of the year? Why did he attack the novel *What Is to Be Done?*" Strakhov's comments appeared in "Zametki letopistsa. Poslednie dva goda v peterburgskoi zhurnalistike," *Epokha,* no. 10 (1864): 9. See the commentary to Saltykov-Shchedrin's *Sobranie,* 6:712–13.

106. Saltykov-Shchedrin, 6:527–28. In these discussions, he refers to Chernyshevskii by the circumlocution "the author of *What Is to Be Done?*"

107. Saltykov-Shchedrin, vol. 19, book 1, 194.

108. In a letter of July 14, 1867, Herzen asks S. Tkhorzhevskii to send him a copy of the Geneva edition of the novel. *Sobranie,* vol. 29, book 1, 144.

109. Ibid., 157.

110. In another letter to Ogarev, he writes, "What a pity that Chernyshevskii's novel is written in the language of the scholarly anteroom,—in it there is an infinitude of good" (ibid., 159). See also pp. 160, 163, 167. In another letter, p. 326, Herzen teases Ogarev for not completing a rereading of the novel, asking him if he fears disenchantment.

111. Ibid., 185.

112. Emma Goldman, *Living My Life* (New York: 1970), 1:26. In the episode Goldman relates, it is clear that the reading of *What Is to Be Done?* was a symbol of revolutionary commitment. Her new acquaintance, Alexander Berkman, doubted that such a young woman had managed to find and read the novel. Goldman, p. 28, presents *What Is to Be Done?* as a key moment in her radicalization.

113. This information was provided by Paul Avrich for Edward J. Brown, 1989, p. 374. See also Dennis P. Reinhartz, "Russian Nihilism and American Anarchism: A Brief Encounter," *Madison College Studies and Research* 31 (March 1972): 48–52.

114. Peter Kropotkin, *Ideals and Realities in Russian Literature* (New York: 1915), 281. Kropotkin's opinion was based on the novel's importance in the revolution; he questioned *What Is to Be Done?*'s value in terms of artistry.

115. For example, see Ulam, 1965, p. 54. Ulam labels Chernyshevskii "the real source of Bolshevism."

116. The major exception is young Maksim Gor'kii. Gor'kii especially disliked Rakhmetov. See his *Istoriia russkoi literatury* (Moscow: 1939), 228. Gural'nik excuses Gor'kii by arguing that Gor'kii's views were the result of the times in which he lived (U. A. Gural'nik, 41).

117. G. V. Plekhanov, "[O romane Chernyshevskogo Chto delat'?]," 175.

118. For further discussion see Schapiro, pp. 214–17.

119. Valentinov, 63–64. Lenin's comments came in response to Valentinov's negative remarks regarding *What Is to Be Done?* See also Valentinov's article, "Chernyshevskii i Lenin," *Novyi zhurnal* 26 (1951): 193–216, and 27 (1951): 225–49.

120. *What Is to Be Done?* was one of the texts proclaimed as a forerunner (not a prototype) of Socialist Realism by the Soviet regime. This lofty status, combined with Lenin's unabashed love for the novel, led Soviet scholars to proclaim it a masterpiece of realism. See Clark for a study of the genesis of Socialist Realism, including the part played by *What Is to Be Done?*

121. A convenient listing of the various translations of *What Is to Be Done?* can be found in the LP edition, pp. 862–67.

122. N. S. Travushkin, *Chernyshevskii v gody katorgi i ssylki* (Moscow: 1978), 305–6. Travushkin provides a useful summary of reactions to Chernyshevskii and his novel abroad during his later years. Tucker's translation began to appear in *Liberty* on May 17, 1884. It was published as a separate book in 1886. According to Travushkin both Tucker's translation and also the one by Dole and Skidelsky went through several editions, evidently selling very well.

123. Annegret J. Wiemer, "Corpus Ex Machina: Nikolai Chernyshevsky's *What Is to Be Done?* (1863) and Mary Bradley Lane's *Mizora* (1880/81)," *Neophilologus* 79, no. 2 (April 1995): 187–96.

124. Quoted in M. Chistiakova, "Lev Tolstoi i Frantsiia," *Literaturnoe nasledstvo* 31–32 (1937): 1011. Le Provost bought a copy of the second edition (1888) of the 1886 English translation by Dole and Skidelsky. Tolstoi never responded to Le Provost's letter.

125. For recent discussions see Wasiolek, pp. 39–41; Joseph Frank, *Dostoevsky: The Miraculous Years, 1865–1871* (Princeton: 1995), 67–69. See also Jane Barstow, "Dostoevsky's *Notes From Underground* Versus Chernyshevsky's *What Is to Be Done?*" *College Literature* 5 (1978): 24–33.

126. One should not conclude, however, that Dostoevskii was an "enemy" of Chernyshevskii. Although it has long been popular to set up a polarity between Dostoevskii and Chernyshevskii, the issue is very complicated. For his part, Dostoevskii insisted that he liked Chernyshevskii personally and that Chernyshevskii never offended him with his convictions. See his *PSS*, 21:25, 29. For an opposing view see Derek Offord, "Dostoyevsky and Chernyshevsky," *Slavonic and East European Review* 57, no. 4 (1979): 509–30.

127. Derek Offord argues that Razumikhin is Dostoevskii's fictional response to Rakhmetov. He notes that Dostoevskii even confuses the two names at one point in a rough draft of a scene in *Crime and Punishment*. Derek Offord, "The Causes of Crime and the Meaning of Law: *Crime and Punishment* and Contemporary Radical Thought," in *New Essays on Dostoevsky* (Cambridge: 1983), 47.

128. For further discussion, see A. I. Volodin et al., *Chernyshevskii ili Nechaev* (Moscow: 1976), 229–36; P. S. Reifman, "Tri romana," in *Puti razvitiia russkoi literatury. Literaturovedenie* (Tartu: 1990), 87–101. There are also those who claim that Dostoevskii parodied Chernyshevskii himself in his story "Crocodile." Dostoevskii denied this. For his comments see his *PSS*, 21:24, 26–30.

129. Hugh McLean, *Nikolai Leskov: The Man and His Art* (Cambridge: 1977), 126–28. McLean argues that the third part of *Nekuda* is directed against the Znamenskii Commune, organized by V. Sleptsov. According to McLean, Leskov had nothing but contempt for buffoons like Sleptsov, but greatly appreciated the moral beauty of people such as Chernyshevskii.

130. N. S. Leskov, "Nikolai Gavrilovich Chernyshevskii v ego romane *Chto delat'?*" *Sobranie sochinenii* (Moscow: 1958), 10:15. This first appeared in *Severnaia pchela* no. 142, (1863) under the name of Nikolai Gorokhov. This essay was in part an answer to F. M. Tolstoi's (Rostislav) hostile review.

131. Ibid., 10:15, 21–22. Throughout this essay, Leskov also attacks many of Chernyshevskii's detractors. He holds blindness and cowardice responsible for Chernyshevskii's negative reputation. He also attacks those who reacted negatively to *What Is to Be Done?* saying, "there is nothing to be said" about such people. As might be expected, Leskov's defense of Chernyshevskii was less than well received by official Russia and the essay was not allowed to be reprinted.

132. Strakhov, 1890, 309–42. This article was supposed to appear in Dostoevskii's *Epokha* but did not for reasons not entirely clear. See Strakhov's comments, p. 342.

133. Ibid., 315.

134. Ibid., 318.

135. Ibid., 338.

136. Quoted in Linda Gerstein, *Nikolai Strakhov* (Cambridge: 1971), 59.

137. N. V. Shelgunov, "Russkie idealy, geroi i tipy," in *Shestidesiatye gody* (Moscow-Leningrad: 1940), 176.

138. Ibid., 177.

139. Ibid., 178. Shelgunov, pp. 180–84, goes on to discuss the character Rakhmetov, whom he views as an eccentric flawed by an irreconcilable dichotomy in his personality. Shelgunov's comments on Rakhmetov will be discussed in more detail in chapter 4.

140. Ibid., 184.

141. Ibid., 185.

142. Ibid.

143. This article first appeared in *Russkoe slovo* under the title, "A New Type." It was given the title "Thinking Proletariat" in the first edition of his collected works, which appeared in 1867. The fact that Pisarev's article appeared at all is a minor miracle. Its publication greatly upset the government and the journal received a stern rebuke for printing a work that "rejects the concept of marriage and carries through the theory of socialism and communism." See the notes to Pisarev's *Selected Philosophical, Social and Political Essays* (Moscow: 1958), 704. The article "Thinking Proletariat" appears on pp. 624–75 of this edition.

144. Pisarev, "Thinking Proletariat," 626.

145. This last fact was a rather clever attempt on Pisarev's part to acquaint more readers with the actual content of the novel.

146. Pisarev, "Thinking Proletariat," 630.

147. Ibid., 635–40.

148. Ibid., 648.

149. Ibid., 667. The only character that Pisarev finds questionable is Rakhmetov. Pisarev is less than satisfied by Rakhmetov's eccentricities and concludes that he was placed in the novel only to show that the three main characters are very ordinary people.

150. One other work that might be described as criticism was written by A. Fet with the help of V. Botkin. This article was refused for publication by *Russkii vestnik* in 1863. It is not of particularly high quality and consists mostly of a plot summary and accusations of immorality similar to those that appeared in the Russian press in short reviews. This article is printed in *Literaturnoe nasledstvo* 25–26 (1936): 477–544.

151. Rudenko, 1989, p. 8, argues that Strakhov ended up defeating his own argument: instead of discrediting the novel, he actually showed that it was innovative. Rudenko overstates his case here, for although Strakhov does find the "tendency" of the novel repulsive, he is fairly balanced in his aesthetic judgments of the novel. Strakhov's article was long treated in a hostile manner by Soviet scholarship. For a reevaluation, see G. N. Antonova, "N. N. Strakhov o romane *Chto delat'?*" in *N. G. Chernyshevskii. Stat'i, issledovaniia i materialy* (Saratov: 1978): 8:48–60.

152. For example, see Gleason, pp. 295–96.

CHAPTER ONE

1. Chernyshevskii's other works specifically devoted to this topic are his review of Aristotle's *Poetics,* his own review of *Aesthetic Relations,* the essay "Vozvyshennoe i komicheskoe," and the essay "Kriticheskii vzgliad na sovremennye esteticheskie poniatiia." All these works appear in volume 2 of his *PSS.*

2. René Wellek, *A History of Modern Criticism: 1750–1950,* vol. 4, *The Later Nineteenth Century* (New Haven: 1965), 241. Wellek is quite critical of Chernyshevskii's aesthetics but argues that these essays demonstrate that Chernyshevskii "had the makings of an intellectual historian."

3. Chernyshevskii's public defense drew quite an audience, which was ecstatic over the work. See James P. Scanlan, "Nikolaj Chernyshevsky and the Philosophy of Realism in Nineteenth-Century Russian Aesthetics," *Studies in Soviet Thought* 30 (1985): 5.

4. William F. Woehrlin, *Chernyshevskii: The Man and the Journalist* (Cambridge: 1971), 179.

5. Edgar H. Lehrman, ed. and trans., *Turgenev's Letters* (New York: 1961), 70–71.

6. A. V. Knowles, ed. and trans., *Turgenev's Letters* (New York: 1983), 51. The appearance of Chernyshevskii's dissertation sparked an intense round of debate in Russian intellectual circles. See Charles A. Moser, *Esthetics as Nightmare: Russian Literary Theory, 1855–1870* (Princeton: 1989), 4–16; George Genereux, "The Crisis in Russian Literary Criticism: 1856—The Decisive Year," *Russian Literature Triquarterly,* no. 17 (1982): 117–40.

7. Quoted in Joe Andrew, *Russian Writers and Society in the Second Half of the Nineteenth Century* (London: 1982), 36.

8. Isaiah Berlin, introduction to *Roots of Revolution,* by Franco Venturi (New York: 1960), xxiii. Berlin's views also appear in his *Russian Thinkers* (New York: 1978), 224–31. Many other scholars have drawn a similar conclusion and deny Chernyshevskii any aesthetic sensibility. See Victor Terras, *Belinskij and Russian Literary Criticism: The Heritage of Organic Aesthetics* (Madison: 1974), 245; N. G. O. Pereira, *The Thought and Teach-*

ings of N. G. Černyševskij (The Hague: 1975), 40; Joseph Frank, *Through the Russian Prism: Essays on Literature and Culture* (Princeton: 1990), 68; Wellek, 239.

9. Abbott Gleason, *Young Russia* (Chicago: 1983), 103.

10. Victor Terras, p. 237, for example, dismisses Chernyshevskii's aesthetics, saying that his argument "is that of a man who is not only uninterested in art, but who actually has never bothered to find out what art is. It is the argument of a man unfamiliar with aesthetic experience."

11. Herbert E. Bowman, "Art and Reality in Russian 'Realist' Criticism," *Journal of Aesthetics and Art Criticism* 12, no. 3 (1954): 387. See also Francis B. Randall, *N. G. Chernyshevskii* (New York: 1967), 38–41; Terras, 236; Joseph Frank, *Dostoevsky: The Years of Ordeal, 1850–1859* (Princeton: 1983), 244; Richard L. Brown, "Chernyshevskii, Dostoevskii, and the Peredvizhniki: Toward a Russian Realist Aesthetic?" (Ph.D. diss., Ohio University, 1980), 74–75. Brown demonstrates how several passages in Chernyshevskii's writings on aesthetic matters have clear sociopolitical implications. However, I think he overstates the case, p. 70, when he says that Chernyshevskii "was from the beginning interested almost exclusively in the practical matters of social reform, and all his writings on art are bound up with his social philosophy." Many Soviet scholars have also taken such a view of Chernyshevskii's aesthetics. Skaftymov, for example, says, "Problems of aesthetics served Chernyshevskii as material for propaganda of the general principles of a materialist worldview." See Aleksandr Pavlovich Skaftymov, *Zhizn' i deiatel'nost' N. G. Chernyshevskogo*, 2nd ed. (Saratov: 1947), 24.

12. For reevaluations of Chernyshevskii's aesthetics see Scanlan; Edward J. Brown, "So Much Depends . . . Russian Critics in Search of 'Reality'" *Russian Review* 48 (1989): 353–81; Frederick C. Copleston, S. J., *Philosophy in Russia from Herzen to Lenin and Berdyaev* (Notre Dame, Ind.: 1986); and Edward Wasiolek, *Fathers and Sons: Russia at the Crossroads* (New York: 1993). This is not a uniform trend by any means. For example, Moser takes a consistently negative view of Chernyshevskii's aesthetics. E. Brown, p. 380, while arguing for a reevaluation of Chernyshevskii's publicistic legacy, states that *What Is to Be Done?* fails as art.

13. Dennis Reinhartz, "N. G. Chernyshevsky on Aesthetics and Art: The Role of the Artist in a Revolution" (Ph.D. diss., New York University, 1971), 146.

14. Wellek, 1965, 245. Wellek, p. 244, also states: "Chernyshevsky's attitude toward his Russian contemporaries was defined in many reviews during the next years: one hesitates to call the bulk of these articles literary criticism."

15. Terras, 236. See also Kathryn Feuer, "What Is to Be Done about *What Is to Be Done?*" in *What Is to Be Done?* by N. G. Chernyshevsky (Ann

Arbor, Mich.: 1986), viii, who states that Chernyshevsky engaged in "crusading radical journalism—frequently under the guise of literary criticism."

16. Ralph Matlaw, introduction to *Belinsky, Chernyshevsky, and Dobrolyubov: Selected Criticism* (New York: 1962), xv.

17. Sometimes Chernyshevskii is viewed as attacking Turgenev in this essay. For example, Terras, p. 230, claims that Chernyshevskii reproached Turgenev for failing to produce a positive hero. However, a careful reading of the essay shows that Chernyshevskii reproaches not Turgenev but Russian society.

18. This article appears in Matlaw's collection, pp. 108–29. See p. 110.

19. The complete title in the original is "Russkii chelovek na Rendezvous. Razmyshleniia po prochtenii povesti g. Turgeneva 'Asia.'" Compare this title with that of Chernyshevskii's review of Tolstoi's early works: "Detstvo i Otrochestvo. Sochinenie grafa L. N. Tolstogo. Spb., 1856. Voennye rasskazy grafa L. N. tolstogo. Spb., 1856," or with his review of Aristotle's *Poetics:* "O poezii. Sochinenie Aristotelia. Perevel, izlozhil i obiasnil B. Ordynskii. Moskva, 1854." It seems quite clear that the omission of Turgenev's name and the title of his story from the title and the creation of an entirely new title were very much a device to signal Russian readers that what follows is not pure literary criticism.

20. In his large body of work, Chernyshevskii demonstrated considerable acumen in his views and statements. For example, Chernyshevskii revered Gogol although he was quite aware of the latter's conservative views. It was precisely as an *artist,* not as a social activist or champion of the oppressed, that Chernyshevskii admired him (Woehrlin, 164). Woehrlin argues that this was something of a rarity for Chernyshevskii: "very few Russian writers who strayed as far from Chernyshevskii's conception of the true path were treated so generously." Wellek also notes that Chernyshevskii's view of Gogol's political evolution is surprisingly sympathetic, although he still concludes that Chernyshevskii did not fully understand him (Wellek, 243). See also his "Social and Aesthetic Values in Russian Nineteenth-Century Literary Criticism (Belinskii, Chernyshevskii, Dobroliubov, Pisarev)," in *Continuity and Change in Russian and Soviet Thought* (Cambridge: 1955), 390.

21. Matlaw, xv.

22. Those who have a negative view of Chernyshevskii's aesthetics tend to ignore this article. Terras, for example, does not discuss it. Those that do discuss it have treated it as some sort of intellectual fluke by an otherwise incapable man. Matlaw, for example, states: "Ironically, this man who had little use for literature first used the term 'interior monologue' in an important passage of this review" (xv). For an excellent discussion of the term "interior monologue," see Gleb Struve, "*Monologue Intérieur:* The Origins of the Formula and the First Statement of its Possibilities," *PMLA* 69, no. 5 (1954): 1101–11. Despite Struve's conclusive analysis, other scholars were

resistant to his conclusions. René Wellek, 1955, p. 390, for example, while admitting that there seems to be no other alternative than Chernyshevskii as the originator of this term, argues that it is improbable that he could have invented it.

23. One of Chernyshevskii's biographers states about this review: "One can hardly reproach the author of these lines, . . . with contempt for artistry or with aspiring to bind the artist with some aesthetic canons, albeit new ones." See Anatolii Lanshchikov, *N. G. Chernyshevskii,* 2nd ed. (Moscow: 1987), 156.

24. Struve, 1106. Chernyshevskii grasped that Tolstoi's ability must be due in large part to introspection and self-analysis. Regarding this observation Struve states: "Here again Chernyshevsky gave proof of his perspicacity, for he had no knowledge of Tolstoy's diaries and his constant self-searching."

25. David Rampton, *Vladimir Nabokov. A Critical Study of the Novels* (Cambridge: 1984), 73. Although Rampton's book is primarily a study of Nabokov, he has a fine section on Chernyshevskii and calls into question many of the traditional myths about the man. Regarding this particular review, he surmises that Nabokov ignored it when writing *The Gift* out of the assumption that Chernyshevskii wrote it merely to flatter Tolstoi. It is true that Chernyshevskii admits this in a letter to Nekrasov. (14:329–30). However as Rampton, p. 72, states: "Yet what is so interesting about this review is not why he wrote it but what he says in it." Kathryn Feuer, p. viii, concurs: "That Chernyshevsky acknowledged that he'd flattered Tolstoy to keep him for the journal should not detract from his critical achievement here."

26. This is perhaps the most discussed aspect of Chernyshevskii's aesthetics and I will not go into great detail here. Discussions can be found in Copleston and Scanlan, 1985.

27. N. G. Chernyshevsky, *Selected Philosophical Essays* (Moscow: 1953), 132–33.

28. Ibid., 134.

29. Traditionally, the label "Feuerbachian" has been applied to Chernyshevskii's philosophy, including his aesthetics. This is in large part due to the preface to the third edition of *Aesthetic Relations,* which Chernyshevskii prepared in 1888. Here Chernyshevskii states that he "wished merely to interpret Feuerbach's ideas in application to aesthetics" (Chernyshevsky, 416). However, the issue is far from clear because Chernyshevskii had a tendency to deny almost any originality in his theoretical writings. Most Western scholars have been more than happy to take him at his word and view him as a mere popularizer (and a vulgarizer) of other people's ideas. However, with regard to Feuerbach, it seems that Chernyshevskii had formulated most of his ideas, especially those regarding aesthetics, independently. When he later read Feuerbach it was more a case of discovering a

like-minded thinker. For further discussion see James P. Scanlan, "Nikolaj Černyševskij and Soviet Philosophy," *Studies in Soviet Thought* 7, no. 1 (1967): 20–23. In a later article, Scanlan argues that Rousseau is an important source of Chernyshevskii's aesthetics. See James P. Scanlan, "Chernyshevsky and Rousseau," in *Western Philosophical Systems in Russian Literature: A Collection of Critical Studies* (Los Angeles: 1979), 103–20. Woehrlin, p. 147, and Wellek, 1965, pp. 238–39, also call into question the connection with Feuerbach. Woehrlin claims that Chernyshevskii's ideas are all his own, but Wellek claims that Chernyshevskii's real philosophical sources must be the German materialists Vogt, Moleschott, and Büchner.

30. Chernyshevsky, 282. This passage is interpreted by Moser, p. 9, as an example of Chernyshevskii's disrespect for both aesthetics and art. However, it seems clear that the phrase "if it is still worth our while to discuss aesthetics" is merely a rhetorical device designed to jolt the reader. Chernyshevskii obviously considers it worthwhile to discuss aesthetics: this passage is followed by almost 100 pages devoted to the topic.

31. Chernyshevskii did not mention the name of Hegel in this essay, later claiming that it was inconvenient to use that name. As a result, he chose an epigone of Hegel, F. Th. Vischer, and his *Aesthetik oder Wissenschaft des Schönen* as the object of his attack. See Chernyshevsky, 416.

32. Chernyshevsky, 331–32.

33. Ibid., 287.

34. Ibid., 379.

35. To this one should add that, in addition to "nature," Chernyshevskii understood reality as the complex sum of human perceptions, thoughts, and practical deeds. Chernyshevskii makes this clear in his own review of *Aesthetic Relations:* "Reality embraces not only inanimate nature, but also human life, not only the present, but also the past, insofar as it has expressed itself in deeds, and also the future, insofar as it is prepared by the present. The deeds of Peter the Great belong to reality; Lomonosov's odes belong to it no less than his mosaic pictures. . . . Thought is not the antithesis of reality, because thought is engendered by reality and strives to realize it, and is therefore an integral part of reality" (ibid., 393–94).

36. Wasiolek, 34–35, 78. Wasiolek further argues, "We are likely to have been so schooled in the sacredness of 'culture' that such opinions are automatically dismissed as nonsense. Yet it is difficult to respond with persuasive arguments to Chernyshevsky's reasoning." V. V. Zenkovsky, *A History of Russian Philosophy* (New York: 1953), 1:333–34, also concludes that Chernyshevskii was in the mainstream of Russian aesthetic thought. Moser, pp. 102–3, and Terras, 230, 232, also note that there is actually a great deal of common ground between Chernyshevskii and his opponents in the field of aesthetics.

37. Terras, p. 261, for example, argues that as a straightforward materialist, Chernyshevskii "refused to single out the aesthetic fact from among

the rest of human experience." Likewise, Wellek, 1965, p. 239, states, that for Chernyshevskii, "The purely aesthetic is dismissed as mere sensual pleasure, trivial at its best, reprehensible at its worst."

38. Chernyshevsky, 319.

39. Ibid., 320.

40. Ibid., 411.

41. See Scanlan, 1985, for another discussion of many of these misconceptions.

42. Wellek, 1955, 389.

43. Chernyshevsky, 282.

44. Ibid., 301. The title of F. Th. Vischer's work, *Aesthetik oder Wissenschaft des Schönen,* which serves as Chernyshevskii's target, clearly indicates that aesthetics is to be considered the science of the beautiful.

45. Chernyshevsky, 423.

46. Ibid., 423–27.

47. In his own review of *Aesthetic Relations* he states, "His [Chernyshevskii's] attitude towards the system of aesthetics, the inadequacy of which he tries to prove, is by no means hostile; he admits that it contains the germ of the theory that he himself is trying to build" (ibid., 395).

48. Copleston, 105. See also Vasilii Gippius, "Chernyshevskii—stikhoved," in *N. G. Chernyshevskii. Sbornik. Neizdannye stat'i, materialy, vospominaniia* (Saratov: 1926), 73–91.

49. Terras, 241.

50. Pereira, 40–41.

51. Chernyshevsky, 370.

52. See his discussion, ibid., 369–71. See also Scanlan, 1985, who provides a discussion of Chernyshevskii's conception of form and its place in his aesthetics. He argues, p. 11, that Chernyshevskii gives a special meaning to the form-content distinction in his aesthetics: he employs the distinction to differentiate between the material that a work of art addresses and the artist's manner of treating that material. The material or content consists of real people in real historical situations; that is the reality of which art is a reproduction, and there can be no art without this anchor in the existing world. The "form," on the other hand, is everything added by the artist: it consists in the explanation, the evaluation, and sometimes the imaginative projection that the artist brings to the subject, thereby investing the work with moral and "scientific" significance.

53. Woehrlin, p. 158, does note that Chernyshevskii did respect form and that he occasionally gave some attention to it.

54. Gippius, p. 81, calls into question Chernyshevskii's methodology in his campaign to change the system of Russian versification. Despite this criticism, however, Gippius views Chernyshevskii's thought as "bold and

fruitful." Chernyshevskii's comments appear in his "Sochineniia A. S. Pushkina" (2:424–516).

55. Gippius, p. 82. The work in question is his review of P. Leont'ev's *Propilei* (2:544–79).

56. Wellek, 1955, 390.

57. Gippius, p. 85, states: "As we can see, Chernyshevskii the 'Nihilist' and 'destroyer of aesthetics' displays much greater poetic sharpness than, for example, a representative of 'pure' art such as Turgenev who, in the interests of moderation and accuracy, 'forced Tiutchev to button himself up and Fet to clean his trousers' (his words). That is, according to his rights as editor he mutilated their rhythmically and semantically bold verses which had broken free from fixed patterns."

58. Bowman, 388.

59. Chernyshevsky, 364. See also Scanlan, 1985, p. 3, for further discussion of this common misunderstanding of Chernyshevskii's views.

60. Chernyshevsky, 365.

61. Ibid., 368.

62. Ibid., 367.

63. Ibid., 441–42.

64. It is true that Chernyshevskii attacks what he considers to be false idealization. For example, he states, p. 442, "if by idealization is meant 'ennobling' the objects and characters depicted, it will be tantamount to primness, pompousness, false dramatization." Chernyshevskii takes a similar stance while defending the technique of idealization in his review of Avdeev's fiction (2:218).

65. Compare with Moser's interpretation, p. 136, of Chernyshevskii as a man "inclined to see fantasy as abnormal, a faculty which came into play only when people were in extraordinary states."

66. See also pp. 128, 132, 682.

67. Bowman, 388, 391. Similarly, Rufus W. Mathewson Jr., *The Positive Hero in Russian Literature,* 2nd ed. (Stanford: 1975), 71, claims that Chernyshevskii denies the writer the right to manipulate experience at all. He further states, pp. 72–73: "The principle of selectivity, first invoked by Belinsky, is the only substitute Chernyshevsky offers for invention, manipulation, and all formal organizing techniques, which are suspect in his eyes because they embellish, rigidify, or otherwise falsify life."

68. Chernyshevsky, 373. Chernyshevskii, p. 340, does make statements such as "the power of the 'creative imagination' is very limited." However, once placed in their polemical context, these statements become quite clear: Chernyshevskii is merely denying the notion that the imagination gives man the ability to transcend reality and establish contact with another, supernatural one. Chernyshevskii also discusses this issue in his own review, pp. 388–90.

69. Zenkovsky, p. 333, comes to a similar conclusion. He states: "He [Chernyshevskii] does not oppose *day-dreaming,* but he opposes aesthetic sentimentalism. In so far as day-dreaming and even fantastic constructions occur in real life, they possess true value as a living part of reality. But, in so far as we cultivate dreams and *oppose* them to reality, in so far as we retreat into an *artificial* and invented world—i.e. retreat from reality—we lose contact with beauty."

70. Joseph Frank, 1990, p. 68, disagrees: "Just as Marx had learned from Feuerbach that religion was the opium of the people, Chernyshevsky had arrived at the same conclusion about art: it could only be tolerated as a substitute, until what is depicted could be obtained in reality." He also states, 1983, p. 246, that, "It is also clear that, if Chernyshevsky's ideas are accepted, art is left without any independent value or stature."

71. Chernyshevsky, 379.

72. Ibid., 409. As stated, recently there has been some reevaluation of Chernyshevskii's aesthetics and his very concept of art. Richard L. Brown demonstrates that far from rejecting art, Chernyshevskii merely sought to establish it on a new, nonidealistic basis (R. Brown, 64–94). Likewise, James P. Scanlan, 1985, p. 2, concurs, noting that Chernyshevskii "seeks not to disparage those relations [between art and reality] but to identify and recommend them. The 'aesthetic' elements Chernyshevsky approves may be different from those recommended by others, but his position is far from amounting to the wholesale rejection of art."

73. Terras, p. 243, for example, says that Chernyshevskii's "program for Russian literature was . . . one of competent, positivistic 'case studies.'" Likewise, Mathewson, pp. 73–74, argues that Chernyshevsky put a new set of restrictions on art, just as bad as the demands of tragedy were.

74. Chernyshevsky, 372.

75. Ibid., 372.

76. Ibid., 369.

77. Ibid., 373.

78. Ibid., 369–70.

79. Regarding the dissertation, Wasiolek, p. 35, comes to a similar conclusion, noting that Chernyshevskii argues against a narrow definition of art—art confined to painting, poetry, and music. Copleston, p. 106, concurs: "He [Chernyshevskii] goes on to maintain that a definition of the content of art solely in terms of beauty is too narrow" and that the "fine arts can concern themselves with anything which is of interest to the human being." He further states, p. 107: "Chernyshevsky did not claim that art is superfluous, that it served no useful purpose or purposes in life. On the contrary, he maintains that it does serve useful purposes, meeting human needs. He rejects the idea of art for art's sake, but this does not mean that he rejects art. Its existence is justified by human nature and human needs."

80. Quoted in Matlaw, p. 104.

81. Chernyshevskii made other statements along these same lines. In a letter to Nekrasov (1856), for example, he states: "The freedom of poetry is . . . in not constraining one's talent by arbitrary pretensions and writing about that toward which one's heart lies. Fet would be unfree if he took it into his head to write about social questions; he would produce only rubbish. . . . Gogol' was completely free when he wrote 'The Inspector General'—his talent was inclined to 'The Inspector General.' But Pushkin was unfree when, under the influence of the Decembrists, he wrote 'Ode to Freedom' and so forth, and free when he wrote 'To the Slanderers of Russia' or 'Ruslan and Liudmila.' . . . Freedom consists of each person doing what his nature demands" (14:314). As Venturi notes, Chernyshevskii made these statements in defense of artistic freedom against Nekrasov's "civic tendencies." See Franco Venturi, *Roots of Revolution* (New York: 1960), 141.

82. Woehrlin, pp. 173–74, looking at the same materials, draws a different conclusion. He does note the existence of this review but dismisses it, saying: "The article concluded with an appeal for artistic autonomy, which in the context of Chernyshevskii's other reviews strikes one as an unintended irony."

83. Other examples could easily be added. For example, in his discussion of Avdeev's fiction, Chernyshevskii argues that art should not have to depict just "heroes," that it can depict ordinary beings if it chooses (2:156). It is also worth noting that in his own fiction, Chernyshevskii consciously sought to expand the boundaries of art. In one of the variants of the foreword to his unfinished novel, *Povesti v povesti,* Chernyshevskii discusses both the idea of a novel without love and a novel in which the author's position is hidden, indiscernible (12:683–84).

84. Mathewson, p. 73, views this expansion of art's boundaries with suspicion: "By demeaning formal discipline, Chernyshevsky has opened literature to alien material, and at the same time diminished literature's ability to digest it."

85. Lunacharsky, 47. Wasiolek, p. 35, comes to a similar conclusion, noting that Chernyshevskii argued against a canonized and untouchable view of art that was mystical, idealistic, and unquestioned.

86. Frank, 1983, p. 246, for example, sees Chernyshevskii as "telling the artist that his chief task is to fulfill the social needs of the moment—whatever these needs may happen to be in the opinion of the critic." Frank, 1990, p. 77, also argues that Chernyshevskii saw no other role for literature (and art in general) except that of social propaganda to enlighten the masses. Likewise, Gleason, p. 100, argues that in his master's dissertation, "he coolly denied the importance of technical aesthetic questions and advocated an art that would pose vital moral and political questions." It is Terras, pp. 242–43, however, who provides the harshest assessment when he says that Cherny-

shevskii argued for a literature that made a point of serving a distinct tendency and that for Chernyshevskii, "literature merely 'filled orders' which it received from society, for the public's judgment was far superior to that of most literary men (poets, critics, editors)." Pereira, pp. 41–43, and Woehrlin, pp. 153–54, also see Chernyshevskii as attempting to ideologize and subordinate literature.

87. Chernyshevsky, 374–75.

88. Quoted in Pereira, p. 43. In the full passage Chernyshevskii explicitly identifies the supporters of pure art as deceivers or pretenders in their support of their theory (3:301).

89. Chernyshevskii was quite consistent in viewing all areas of human activity as inherently subjective. For example, in his "The Anthropological Principle in Philosophy" he argues that all political theories and all philosophical doctrines are created under the powerful influence of the social context to which they belong (Chernyshevsky, 50). Chernyshevskii dismissed the notion of objectivity as nonsense.

90. See Reinhartz, p. 48, and R. Brown, pp. 87–88, for further discussion. See also Gary Saul Morson, "Introduction: Literary History and the Russian Experience," in *Literature and History* (Stanford: 1986), 15–21.

91. Evgenii Lampert, *Sons Against Fathers: Studies in Russian Radicalism and Revolution* (Oxford: 1965), 210, states: "Now it is odd to find that this work gives no support to the view that Chernyshevsky turned art into a vehicle of propaganda, made didacticism an artistic—or unartistic—dogma, and dealt a death-blow to all aesthetics, as Pisarev insisted with acclamation." He also states, p. 221: "But all this does not add up to the idea, attributed to Chernyshevsky, that the arts, and literature in particular, are a mere code of behaviour for the people. Nothing could be further from the truth. Not only did he believe that artistic effect can only be achieved by working through particular and intimate experiences, but that didacticism and moralizing turn art into an abstraction. He was completely opposed to every kind of rigidity. He laid stress on Belinsky's resistance to preaching in literature and assailed any tendency among writers to reduce art as well as life to a system."

92. Matlaw, 104–5. As clear as this passage is, many have misinterpreted it. René Wellek, 1955, p. 391, for example, says: "But it is typical of Chernyshevskii and his audience that after praising Tolstoy's moral purity, Chernyshevskii suddenly turns to an embarrassed defense of Tolstoy's theme of childhood. *Childhood,* he says, at great length, is about a child and not about issues such as war and social reform, but it is still worth reading." Obviously, Wellek did not read this review as closely as he should have.

93. Quoted in Lunacharsky, p. 31. The letter is found in *PSS* (14:321–29).

94. Lunacharsky, 31.

95. It is perhaps relevant that Chernyshevskii's friend and colleague, Nikolai Dobroliubov, explicitly stated that blatant didacticism was both unnecessary and harmful. See Moser, pp. 93–94.

96. Terras, 238. Woehrlin, p. 178, also labels Chernyshevskii's aesthetics utilitarian.

97. Chernyshevsky, 367.

98. Compare also his remark: "Man does not exist for art or science (as many of the great philosophers, including Aristotle, thought); science and art must serve to benefit man" (ibid., 430).

99. Ibid., 432–33.

100. Ibid., 329.

101. Andrzej Walicki, *A History of Russian Thought from the Enlightenment to Marxism* (Stanford: 1979), 194.

102. Chernyshevsky, 408–9.

103. See U. A. Gural'nik, *Nasledie N. G. Chernyshevskogo-pisatelia i sovetskoe literaturovedenie* (Moscow: 1980), 179, and Reinhartz, p. 125, for further discussion. Gural'nik notes that this is a typical trick used by Chernyshevskii's detractors.

104. A. A. Fet, "*Chto delat'?* Iz rasskazov o novykh liudiakh. Roman N. G. Chernyshevskogo," *Literaturnoe nasledstvo,* 25–26 (1936): 489–90.

105. N. S. Leskov, "Nikolai Gavrilovich Chernyshevskii v ego romane *Chto delat'?*" *Sobranie sochinenii* (Moscow: 1958), 10:15. Leskov uses this reasoning to excuse Chernyshevskii for any artistic failures of the novel. Most twentieth-century Western scholars, however, have seen in Chernyshevskii's action a continuation of his alleged degradation of art.

106. G. V. Plekhanov, "[O romane Chernyshevskogo Chto delat'?]," *Literatura i estetika* (Moscow: 1958), 2:179. His exact statement is: "Vera Pavlovna's love for Lopukhov and Kirsanov is only an outline [*kanva*] along which are arranged other, more important thoughts of the author."

107. Iu. K. Rudenko, *Chernyshevskii-romanist i literaturnye traditsii* (Leningrad: 1989), 7, attributes the beginning of this interpretation to Leskov, but Gural'nik, pp. 29–30, attributes it to Plekhanov. Subscribing to this interpretation is not necessarily dependent upon the commentator's evaluation of Chernyshevskii. Many who have rated Chernyshevskii very highly subscribe to the notion that he turned to fiction only out of force of circumstances. Georg Lukács, for example, argues that if Chernyshevskii had not been imprisoned, he would never have written a single novel. See George Lukács, "Tschernyschewskijs Roman 'Was Tun?'" *Der russische Realismus in der Weltliteratur* (Berlin: 1952), 98.

108. Moser, 1989, 145–47.

109. For a discussion of these youthful attempts, see Iu. K. Rudenko, "N. G. Chernyshevskii kak khudozhnik: belletristicheskie opyty 1840-kh godov," *Russkaia literatura,* no. 1 (1970): 101–20.

110. N. Naumova, *Roman N. G. Chernyshevskogo "Chto delat'?"* (Leningrad: 1972), 3–5. Pereira sounds a similar note when he argues that Chernyshevskii's ability to write *What Is to Be Done?* in less than four months demonstrates that the idea must have been gestating in his mind for a long time. See N. G. O. Pereira, "Chernyshevsky's *What Is to Be Done?* as a Statement of Social Utopia," *Rocky Mountain Social Science Journal* 9, no. 3 (1972): 35. There is some possibility that Chernyshevskii actually began *What Is to Be Done?* before he went to prison. Chernyshevskii's son, Mikhail, claimed that Chernyshevskii had worked on the manuscripts for *What Is to Be Done?* while living in Saratov before his return to Saint Petersburg. Likewise, E. Pypina, the wife of his cousin A. Pypin, claims to have read the novel in manuscript before he went to prison. See A. P. Skaftymov, "Roman *Chto delat'?*" in *N. G. Chernyshevskii. Sbornik. Neizdannye stat'i, materialy, vospominaniia* (Saratov: 1926), 94–96. Skaftymov gets his information from N. M. Chernyshevskaia-Bystrova. Skaftymov, though reporting these facts, concludes that Chernyshevskii's contemporaries were simply mistaken. He argues that there could not have been drafts of the novel before Chernyshevskii went to prison. Further contributing to this possibility, however, are the remarks of O. A. Przhetslavskii, who reports that Chernyshevskii began work on the novel and published the first part before he went to prison. Przhetslavskii's reporting is filled with obvious factual errors and has led to its being dismissed out of hand. We know, for example, that *What Is to Be Done?* was not published until well after Chernyshevskii was arrested and placed in prison. However, because there are indeed references to the existence of an earlier manuscript of *What Is to Be Done?* from other sources, perhaps Przhetslavskii's remarks do have some factual basis behind them. See "Vospominaniia O. A. Przhetslavskago," *Russkaia starina* 14, no. 3 (September 1875): 154. At the present there is no independent proof of the novel's existence before Chernyshevskii's arrest, but if such were to be true, this indeed would show that Chernyshevskii's turn to literature was not at all motivated by necessity of circumstance.

111. Chernyshevskii wrote much more than we have manuscripts for. While in Siberia he wrote constantly but often destroyed what he had created, probably out of security concerns. Most of this material is not even known to Western scholars. Except for the novel *Prolog*, these materials have been ignored by most Soviet scholars.

112. This evidence is indeed most troubling for Chernyshevskii's detractors and usually it is ignored. Moser, in trying to come to grips with many statements Chernyshevskii made after he wrote *What Is to Be Done?* explains things as follows: Chernyshevskii had a contemptuous attitude toward art in all his published works before 1862. However, once he started to write *What Is to Be Done?* he began to discover the artistic process and its values. Moser argues that after 1862 Chernyshevskii's statements on art

are far less extreme (44–45). The problem with Moser's argument, however, is that it ignores the attempts at fiction Chernyshevskii made in the 1840s; *What Is to Be Done?* was not his first literary endeavor.

113. "У меня нет ни тени художественного таланта. Я даже и языком-то владею плохо. Но это все-таки ничего: читай, добрейшая публика! прочтешь не без пользы. Истина—хорошая вещь: она вознаграждает недостатки писателя, который служит ей. Поэтому я скажу тебе: если б я не предупредил тебя, тебе, пожалуй, показалось бы, что повесть написана художественно, что у автора много поэтического таланта. Но я предупредил тебя, что таланта у меня нет,—ты и будешь знать теперь, что все достоинства повести даны ей только ее истинностью" (LP 14).

114. A major exception is Rudenko, who argues that Chernyshevskii hid his own views from the reader by using the cyclical structure of the novel. See Iu. K. Rudenko, "Printsip tsiklizatsii v khudozhestvennoi sisteme N. G. Chernyshevskogo (K postanovke voprosa)," in *Problemy poetiki russkogo realizma XIX veka* (Leningrad: 1984), 187.

115. Gleason, 295.

116. G. Žekulin, "Forerunner of Socialist Realism: The Novel 'What to do?' by N. G. Chernyshevsky," *Slavonic and East European Review* 41 (1963): 473.

117. Other evidence sometimes used to argue that Chernyshevskii regarded art only as a propaganda medium is his testimony before the investigative commission: "For a long time I have planned . . . to apply myself to literature. But I am convinced that people of my character must do this only in their later years. . . . A novel is destined for the great mass of the public. It is a writer's most serious undertaking, and so it belongs to old age. The frivolity of the form must be compensated for by the solidity of the thought" (quoted in Venturi, p. 178). This passage, especially the phrase "the frivolity of the form," is often cited as evidence of Chernyshevskii's lack of respect for form and his disrespect for art. However, I would submit that anything said by Chernyshevskii before the investigative commission should be treated with great caution. The same applies to his letters: he was quite aware that his correspondence was being monitored. At the most basic level, he was doing his best to save his skin. In addition, the numerous statements Chernyshevskii made during this period all seem designed to mislead the authorities. For example, Chernyshevskii also testified to the investigative commission that his diaries were not diaries but merely material for a novel. Few have taken this statement seriously and most have recognized it as that of a man in a difficult situation. See N. A. Alekseev, ed., *Protsess N. G. Chernyshevskogo* (Saratov: 1939), 295, for Chernyshevskii's statements.

118. "неразборчива и недогадлива" (LP 12).

119. "всегда будешь за двадцать страниц вперед видеть развязку каждого положения" (LP 13).

120. *What Is to Be Done?* is built around the principle that things are not what they seem. The reader is given a signal to this effect early in the novel, in the first minichapters. In interpreting the actions of the unknown gentleman (that is, Lopukhov) the crowd labels him a fool (*durak*). As the reader learns, however, Lopukhov is in fact doing something quite clever. See L. M. Lotman, "Ideino-khudozhestvennye printsipy belletristiki Chernyshevskogo 1860–1870-kh godov," in *N. G. Chernyshevskii. Estetika. Literatura. Kritika* (Leningrad: 1979), 87. Lotman argues that the word *durak* is made into a concept similar to the word "idiot" in Dostoevskii's *The Idiot.* See also Emily Klenin, "On the Ideological Sources of *Čto delat'?* Sand, Družinin, Leroux," *Zeitschrift für slavische Philologie* 51, no. 2 (1991): 383.

121. "отгадывать недосказанное" (LP 14).

122. Gary Saul Morson, *The Boundaries of Genre: Dostoevsky's Diary of a Writer and the Traditions of Literary Utopia* (Austin: 1981), 101–2. Morson further states: "Using 'Aesopian language,' the Russian phrase for this kind of hidden political allegory, Chernyshevsky's text invites an esoteric, as well as an exoteric, reading. *What is To Be Done?,* therefore, relies on yet another kind of double encoding, this one with the censor as dupe and the readers—or more accurately, some readers—as partners in deceit. In short, reading becomes a form of complicity, which is to say, a political act."

123. Ibid., 102.

124. Nikolaev argues that undoubtedly the investigative commission was expecting something fiery, but after reading the first two subchapters, which promised a family drama or an adventure story, they perceived the rest in a similar tone. See P. Nikolaev, "Revoliutsionnyi roman," in N. G. Chernyshevskii, *Chto delat'?* (Moscow: 1969), 6. Przhetslavskii seems to have found nothing dangerous in the first parts of the novel: "Therefore, the content of the novel is in general not reprehensible." Quoted in N. A. Bukhbinder, "Tsenzura o *Chto delat'?* N. G. Chernyshevskogo," *Katorga i ssylka,* no. 44 (1928): 44.

125. Klenin, 381–84.

126. "«я знаю, что этот застрелившийся господин не застрелился»" (LP 12).

127. From Przhetslavskii's second report in Bukhbinder, p. 49.

128. Chernyshevskii later stated: "An open declaration of Turgenev's hatred for Dobroliubov was, as is well known, the novel *Fathers and Sons*" (1:737). In addition to the scandal over *Fathers and Sons,* Chernyshevskii's feud with Turgenev went back to 1855 and was common public knowledge.

129. Henry Gifford, *The Hero of His Time: A Theme in Russian Literature* (London: 1950), 183. The connection between the two novels is a given in the scholarship. For a recent discussion, see Wasiolek, pp. 39–40.

For studies devoted specifically to this question, see V. A. Mysliakov, "*Ottsy i deti* v vospriiatii Chernyshevskogo," *Russkaia literatura,* no. 2 (1978): 36–53, and H. Günther "Turgenevs *Väter und Söhne* und Černyševskijs *Was tun?*" *Zeitschrift für Slawistik* 34, no. 5 (1989): 674–83.

130. Gural'nik, 64. See also N. A. Verderevskaia, *Stanovlenie tipa raznochintsa v russkoi realisticheskoi literature 40–60kh godov XIX veka (k probleme tipologii zhanra, siuzheta i obraza)* (Kazan': 1975), 108–9. Verderevskaia argues that there is no evidence of any direct polemic between *What Is to Be Done?* and *Fathers and Sons.* She goes so far as to suggest that Chernyshevskii may not have been very familiar with Turgenev's novel, which appeared shortly before he was arrested. She further notes that Turgenev's earlier novels are far more relevant for discussion, especially *On the Eve* (see pp. 106–9). Joe Andrew also argues that *What Is to Be Done?* is directed at *On the Eve,* particularly Elena's question "What is there to do in Russia?" See Joe Andrew, *Women in Russian Literature, 1780–1863* (London: 1988), 155–56.

131. Quoted in Bukhbinder, p. 44.

132. Quoted in I. P. Viduetskaia, "Roman *Chto delat'?* v otsenke revoliutsionno-demokraticheskoi kritiki," *"Chto delat'?" N. G. Chernyshevskogo. Istoriko-funktsional'noe issledovanie* (Moscow: 1990), 80–81. See also Mysliakov, p. 47.

133. Randall, 121.

134. Petr Vail' and Aleksandr Genis, *Rodnaia rech'* (Tenafly, N.J.: 1990), 126.

135. Irina Paperno, *Chernyshevsky and the Age of Realism: A Study in the Semiotics of Behavior* (Stanford: 1988), 221.

136. Iu. K. Rudenko, *Roman N. G. Chernyshevskogo "Chto delat'?" Esteticheskoe svoeobrazie i khudozhestvennyi metod* (Leningrad: 1979), 19. Dealing with the question of why a novel seemingly so bad could be so popular, he argues that the answer must lie within the text itself: "The question of the 'artistry' of the novel, persistently discussed *within* the text, is one of the most important *artistic principles,* organizing the novel as a whole."

137. Rudenko, 1979, 8. Although other Soviet scholars, such as Naumova, have come close to this conceptual breakthrough, it is Rudenko who openly states that the deliberate cultivation of an inartistic appearance and of didacticism is the organizing principle of *What Is to Be Done?* Rudenko's analysis is quite valuable, although he limits himself primarily to a discussion of the three minichapters at the beginning of the novel and does not use all the information available to support his view. See also V. V. Shcheulin, "N. G. Chernyshevskii i voprosy iazyka i stilia," in *Roman N. G. Chernyshevskogo "Chto delat'?" (K 100-letiiu vykhoda v svet). Sbornik statei* (Shakhty, 1963), 112–13, who argues that the roughness and carelessness of Chernyshevskii's style is the result of an intentional awkwardness.

138. Rudenko, 1979, 7.

139. Ibid., 13–14. Moser, p. 145, makes a similar observation but comes to the conclusion that Chernyshevskii is doing this to undermine and question the very existence of art.

140. Klenin, 384.

141. *Molotov* appeared in *Sovremennik,* no. 10 (1861). Chernyshevskii had with him in prison the issues of *Sovremennik* in which *Molotov,* and also Pomialovskii's earlier work, *Meshchanskoe schast'e,* had appeared. Those works are republished in N. G. Pomialovskii, *Meshchanskoe schast'e. Molotov* (Moscow: 1957).

142. Joseph Frank, *Dostoevsky: The Stir of Liberation, 1860–1865* (Princeton: 1986), 164.

143. Several members of the old generation, the so-called aesthetes, reveled in calling Chernyshevskii "the one who smells of bedbugs" (*pakhnushchii klopami*) or "the bedbug-stinking gentleman" (*klopovoniaiushchii gospodin*). This term for Chernyshevskii was apparently coined by Grigorovich, although Turgenev became enamored of it. Turgenev declared that he would call Chernyshevskii by no other name. See his letters of July 1855 and the accompanying commentary in I. S. Turgenev, *Pis'ma v trinadtsati tomakh,* in *Polnoe sobranie sochinenii i pisem v dvadtsati vos'mi tomakh* (1961), 2:290, 293, 574, 577. See also Tolstoi's letter to Nekrasov of July 2, 1856, in his *Polnoe sobranie sochinenii* (Moscow-Leningrad: 1949), 60:74. It is unclear whether this term actually refers to Chernyshevskii's body odor or simply to his seminarian origins. Grigorovich claimed to be able to spot a seminarian, even in the communal bath, because of the distinctive smell of oil and soot that would invariably emanate from him (Pereira, 60). Grigorovich's remarks are recorded in A. Ia. Panaeva, *Vospominaniia* (Moscow: 1956), 265.

144. Turgenev, Grigorovich, Botkin, and Druzhinin gathered in 1855 for a house party at which they composed a comic skit belittling Chernyshevskii. This "bit of tasteless malice, not even very funny," as Kathryn Feuer, p. ix, has described it, was reworked and published by Grigorovich in September 1855 as "The School of Hospitality." For further discussion of this episode, see Michael Pursglove, *D. V. Grigorovich: The Man Who Discovered Chekhov* (Brookfield, Vt: 1987), 53–55; and Charles A. Moser, *Antinihilism in the Russian Novel of the 1860's* (The Hague: 1964), 86–88. See also V. P. Meshcheriakov, *D. V. Grigorovich—Pisatel' i iskusstvoved* (Leningrad: 1985), 54–61. Chernyshevskii demonstrates in a letter from November 1862 that he was well aware that he was the intended target of this work (14:462).

145. Quoted in Nikolai Bogoslovsky, "Great Russian Scholar and Critic," *International Literature,* no. 10 (1939): 51–52. In the letter, Chernyshevskii also states, "I am famous in Russian literature for negligence of

style. Naturally, this was only scorn for style. When I want, I know how to write in any of the good sorts of style" (14:616).

146. Chernyshevskii had already demonstrated a keen awareness of the type of reaction he provoked as early as his master's dissertation. He easily anticipated the opposition of certain circles and attempted to answer it beforehand with his own review of the work.

147. Rudenko, 1979, 20–21.

148. Ibid., 9. See also his 1989 book, especially chapter 3, "'Uchitel'nyi' roman Chernyshevskogo i traditsiia 'romana s otstupleniiami,'" pp. 117–43. Along a similar line, Ishchuk notes that there are numerous references in the novel to Western authors who were considered "tendentious." See G. I. Ishchuk, "Nekotorye problemy iskusstva v romane N. G. Chernyshevskogo *Chto delat'?*" in *Roman N. G. Chernyshevskogo "Chto delat'?" (K 100-letiiu vykhoda v svet). Sbornik statei* (Shakhty: 1963), 79–80.

149. Rudenko, 1979, 9.

150. See Julia Alissandratos, "Hagiographical Commonplaces and Medieval Prototypes in N. G. Chernyshevsky's *What Is to Be Done?*" *St. Vladimir's Theological Quarterly* 26, no. 2 (1982): 107.

151. Ibid., 104. There can be little doubt that, as a former seminarian, Chernyshevskii was familiar with the literature of medieval Russia. See also Paperno, pp. 196–218, who discusses in great detail the numerous biblical and other religious references that occur in the novel.

152. Naumova, for example, answers the question with a resounding NO! To make her point, she entitles one of her chapters, "Not for the Sake of the Censor."

153. I will discuss this issue in more detail in the next chapter.

154. Feuer, xxi.

155. Rudenko, 1979, p. 9, argues that the misperception of the novel Chernyshevskii tries to create is in large part dependent upon the reader's viewing the narrator as the actual author.

156. See M. V. Teplinskii, "Avtor-povestvovatel' v romane N. G. Chernyshevskogo *Chto delat'?*" in *N. G. Chernyshevskii. Stat'i, issledovaniia i materialy* (Saratov: 1978), 8:128. Although it would seem a truism of literary criticism that one must always be careful about too close an identification between the author and the narrator, such care has not been shown with regard to *What Is to Be Done?* Viewing Chernyshevskii as utterly untalented, most Western scholars have made a straightforward identification between the two. There has also been a tendency in Soviet scholarship to reduce the narrator to the actual author. In his article Teplinskii joins in the game but demonstrates that, based on evidence provided in the novel itself, the narrator cannot be the actual author.

157. Reiser seemed to dispense with this myth in 1957, but it has never quite died. See S. A. Reiser, "Legenda o prototypakh *Chto delat'?* Cherny-

shevskogo," *Trudy Leningradskogo bibliotechnogo instituta imeni N. K. Krupskoi. Kafedra literatury* 2 (1957): 115–25. By examining the chronology of the Obrucheva triangle, Reiser convincingly demonstrates that Chernyshevskii could not have known about most, if not all of the events. There is a connection here, but it seems much more likely that the participants of the triangle consciously modeled themselves on the characters of Chernyshevskii's novel. For a recent argument that Chernyshevskii modeled his characters on real people of the times, see E. Brown, p. 379. In her works, the Soviet scholar N. A. Verderevskaia seeks to answer why so many have been and continue to be fooled by a desire to seek prototypes for the heroes of the novel. She argues that Chernyshevskii intentionally creates this illusion of photographic realism to fool the reader into thinking such people do exist. See N. A. Verderevskaia, "O 'prototipicheskoi versii' v izuchenii khudozhestvennykh proizvedenii Chernyshevskogo," in *N. G. Chernyshevskii. Stat'i, issledovaniia i materialy* (Saratov: 1968), 5:124, 126; *Russkii roman 40–60-kh godov XIX veka* (Kazan', 1980), 109; *Roman N. G. Chernyshevskogo "Chto delat'?" Posobie dlia uchashchikhsia* (Moscow: 1982), 29–32. Verderevskaia's basic thesis is that Chernyshevskii uses this device to persuade the average reader that such people are not unattainable ideals but do exist and walk the streets of Saint Petersburg. This may indeed be true, but I think there is far more to this device.

158. Если б я писал роман, этим он и был бы кончен мною, но я не имею претензии писать роман,—для этого нужен был бы талант, которого у меня нет,—я просто рассказываю о жизни одной из моих добрых знакомых и людей, к ней близких, то, что мне кажется не лишенным интереса, а может быть и пользы для публики; и потому я должен прибавить еще несколько страниц.

159. This is assuming that Chernyshevskii himself removed the passage. As I pointed out earlier, we can never be quite sure who is responsible for the changes between the rough draft and the published version.

160. Chernyshevskii also states that when he wrote *What Is to Be Done?* he did not copy from reality: "When I was writing *What Is to Be Done?* . . . I saw that I was not depicting my acquaintances, I was not copying, [but] that my characters are just as invented as those of Gogol'" (12:682).

161. The reference to not reading any of the reactions was probably a sarcastic jab on Chernyshevskii's part because the authorities were keeping him in strict isolation, including keeping recent journals out of his hands. He may have had some idea of the reaction to *What Is to Be Done?* given to him during the visits from his wife, but the opportunity to study it consistently was simply not available.

162. Quoted in Pereira, p. 87.

163. Chernyshevskii also set up his hostile readers to react to the novel as immoral and plays with the fact. For example, in chapter 4 the narrator openly hints at the illegal and immoral actions the characters have been engaging in. Then the perspicacious reader interrupts with the charge of immorality, with which the narrator seemingly agrees (328–29).

164. Tolstoi's article appeared under the name Rostislav. See "Lzhemudrost geroev Chernyshevskogo," *Severnaia pchela*, no. 138 (1863).

165. Quoted in A. P. Skaftymov, "Khudozhestvennye proizvedeniia Chernyshevskogo, napisannye v Petropavlovskoi kreposti," *Nravstvennye iskaniia russkikh pisatelei. Stat'i i issledovaniia o russkikh klassikakh* (Moscow: 1972), 271. This comes from P. Kapnist's *Sobranie materialov o napravlenii razlichnykh otraslei russkoi slovesnosti* (1865), a production of the censorship.

166. Rudenko, 1979, 6.

167. It hardly needs repeating that most Western scholarship has generally repeated the formulations of Chernyshevskii's contemporaries and has rejected the novel as worthless in terms of artistic value.

168. In the published text, no names are mentioned. In the rough draft, the name Uspenskii and the titles of Pomialovskii's recent works are given (LP 356–57). Chernyshevskii may have removed those references simply for being too specific. A general statement, as exists in the final version, is far more effective.

169. "Когда я говорю, что у меня нет ни тени художественного таланта и что моя повесть очень слаба по исполнению, ты не вздумай заключить, будто я объясняю тебе, что я хуже тех твоих повествователей, которых ты считаешь великими, а мой роман хуже их сочинений. Я говорю не то. Я говорю, что мой рассказ очень слаб по исполнению сравнительно с произведениями людей, действительно одаренных талантом; с прославленными же сочинениями твоих знаменитых писателей ты смело ставь наряду мой рассказ по достоинству исполнения, ставь даже выше их—не ошибешься! В нем все-таки больше художественности, чем в них; можешь быть спокойна на этот счет" (LP 14). Klenin, 383, stresses that this passage, among many others, demonstrates that in *What Is to Be Done?* things are not at all what they seem at first glance.

170. Another relevant component of these passages is the fact that Chernyshevskii is already drawing the battle lines between himself and the aesthetes, the mainstream critics and writers of the day, who, following the traditions of German idealist philosophy, stressed only the beauty of form. Within this context we certainly have no right to take this passage as Chernyshevskii's literal denial of his own artistic ability.

171. Shcheulin, 112.

172. Žekulin, 476.

173. Ibid., 477.

174. Ibid., 478.

175. "Если бы я хотел сочинять эффектные столкновения, я б и дал этому положению трескучую развязку; но ее не было на деле; если б я хотел заманивать неизвестностью, я бы не стал говорить теперь же, что ничего подобного не произошло; но я пишу без уловок и потому вперед говорю: трескучего столкновения не будет, положение развяжется без бурь, без громов и молний" (LP 46).

176. Žekulin states, p. 479, "But, to be fair, Chernyshevsky is able to write brilliantly."

177. Ibid., 482–83.

178. Ibid., 482. Žekulin discusses every possible conflict in the novel that Chernyshevskii fails to develop. For example, in describing the theoretical conversation between Kirsanov and Lopukhov, p. 478, he states: "A conflict which, as Chernyshevsky remarks ironically, would be a godsend to every other novelist falls flat in his own hands. And he puts his finger—deliberately, it seems,—on the reason for it. Both men are men of theory and as such know in advance, as long as they stick to theory, what is going to be the result of their 'theoretical' encounter."

179. M. M. Bakhtin/P. N. Medvedev, *The Formal Method in Literary Scholarship* (Cambridge: 1985). This work originally appeared in 1928. I leave it to the Bakhtin specialists to argue over who is the actual author of this text.

180. E. Wasiolek, "Tolstoy's *The Death of Ivan Ilych* and Jamesian Fictional Imperative," *Modern Fiction Studies* 6 (1960): 323.

181. Moser, 266; Morson, 1981, 99.

CHAPTER TWO

1. Iu. K. Rudenko, "Printsip tsiklizatsii v khudozhestvennoi sisteme N. G. Chernyshevskogo (K postanovke voprosa)," in *Problemy poetiki russkogo realizma XIX veka* (Leningrad: 1984), 188–89.

2. G. Verkhovskii, *O romane N. G. Chernyshevskogo "Chto delat'?"* (Iaroslavl': 1959), 72–73.

3. As I discussed in the previous chapter, much of this can be seen as a device to fool the censor, who read the novel in parts. However, it also seems quite clear that Chernyshevskii is playing with and subverting literary tradition by means of this structure and the open references to it.

4. N. Naumova, *Roman N. G. Chernyshevskogo "Chto delat'?"* (Leningrad: 1972), 15–16. See also N. A. Verderevskaia, *Stanovlenie tipa raznochintsa v russkoi realisticheskoi literature 40–60kh godov XIX veka (k probleme tipologii zhanra, siuzheta i obraza)* (Kazan': 1975), 110.

5. Rudenko, 1984, p. 193, also sees the novel as closed, finished. M. A. Filina, however, analyzing the novel in terms of its thematics, argues that

the novel remains open and unfinished and demands a continuation. See M. A. Filina, "*Chto delat'?* Chernyshevskogo i zapadno-evropeiskaia sotsial'no-filosofskaia utopiia," in *N. G. Chernyshevskii. Estetika. Literatura. Kritika* (Leningrad: 1979), 251.

6. Lesley Singer Herrmann, "George Sand and the Nineteenth-Century Russian Novel: The Quest for a Heroine" (Ph.D. diss., Columbia University, 1979), 48; Dawn Diane Eidelman, "George Sandism and the Woman Question in Nineteenth-Century Russia" (Ph.D. diss., Emory University, 1990), 87. Herrmann and Eidelman label *What Is to Be Done?* a manual disguised as a novel.

7. For a discussion of the proliferation of terms among Soviet scholars, see U. A. Gural'nik, *Nasledie N. G. Chernyshevskogo-pisatelia i sovetskoe literaturovedenie* (Moscow: 1980), 140–41. Western scholars have also been unable to settle upon a generic designation for the novel. Moser accepts Tamarchenko's label "intellectual novel," whereas Paperno and Reinhartz call it a "utopian novel." As with the terms offered by Soviet scholars, each of these designations captures only a small part of the entire text; they fail to apply to the novel as a whole. See G. E. Tamarchenko, *Chernyshevskii-romanist* (Leningrad: 1976), 246; Irina Paperno, "The Novel Myth: N. G. Chernyshevskii's *What Is to Be Done?*" in *Issues in Russian Literature before 1917* (Columbus, Ohio: 1989), 133; Dennis Reinhartz, "N. G. Chernyshevsky on Aesthetics and Art: The Role of the Artist in a Revolution" (Ph.D. diss., New York University, 1971), 96; Charles A. Moser, *Esthetics as Nightmare: Russian Literary Theory, 1855–1870* (Princeton: 1989), 140.

8. B. Riurikov, for example, states, "Rakhmetov is the center to which all the threads of the novel converge." See B. Riurikov, *N. G. Chernyshevskii. Kritiko-biograficheskii ocherk* (Moscow: 1961), 149. P. A. Nikolaev goes even further, arguing that "this striking and original effect—a 'non-acting' character turns out to be the main one—forms one of Chernyshevskii's achievements as a novelist." See P. A. Nikolaev, "'. . . chtoby chitali vse . . . ,'" in *"Chto delat'?" N. G. Chernyshevskogo. Istoriko-funktsional'noe issledovanie* (Moscow: 1990), 10. Many Western scholars have concurred with the Soviet interpretation.

9. Francis B. Randall, *N. G. Chernyshevskii* (New York: 1967), 120, claims that it is Lopukhov who is the hero of the novel because the central decision of the novel is his.

10. Marcia Ann Morris surveys the disagreement over the hero of the novel and states: "It is perhaps symptomatic of the low artistic quality of the novel that the question of the identity of the hero is unanswerable. All of the above-mentioned characters do suggest themselves as candidates for the role, but none of them combines to a necessary degree the quality of self-assertiveness with a position of centrality in the structural design of the plot." See her "In Search of Perfection: The Ascetic Hero in Russian Literature" (Ph.D. diss., Columbia University, 1987), 219. See also her book

Saints and Revolutionaries: The Ascetic Hero in Russian Literature (Albany, N.Y.: 1993), 138. Morris is correct in her assertion that there is no clear-cut hero in terms of traditional aesthetics. However, she is quite mistaken that this fact is due to a low level of artistry. Rather, Chernyshevskii is obviously borrowing from Thackeray's *Vanity Fair*, the subtitle of which is *A Novel without a Hero.* Indeed, Chernyshevskii specifically stated in his publicistic work that Thackeray had performed a service to the world in showing that novels with "heroes" are not necessary (2:156). Thus, in *What Is to Be Done?* the reader is presented with a main character, but not a "hero."

11. Joe Andrew comes to a similar conclusion, noting that at almost every stage she generates the plot. See Joe Andrew, *Women in Russian Literature, 1780–1863* (London: 1988), 158.

12. Valentino argues that the term *Erziehungsroman* is more appropriate for *What Is to Be Done?* not *Bildungsroman.* His argument that contemporary readers perceived the novel as an *Erziehungsroman,* not a *Bildungsroman* is quite valid. I disagree with Valentino, however, that such was Chernyshevskii's intent. *What Is to Be Done?* is very much intended as a description of the growth of an individual (Vera Pavlovna) into a mature person; it is not a how-to novel. My basis for rejecting *What Is to Be Done?* as a how-to novel will be developed in the subsequent chapters. See Russell Scott Valentino, "The Rise of the Russian Tendentious Novel: Generic Hybridization and Literary Change" (Ph.D. diss., UCLA, 1993), 108–14.

13. Andrew also views *What Is to Be Done?* as a *Bildungsroman.* Like Valentino, however, he views Vera Pavlovna as reaching the high point in her development when she decides to become a doctor (159). Many scholars, both Soviet and Western, have viewed *What Is to Be Done?* as a how-to novel, although without using the term *Erziehungsroman.* See, for example, P. S. Reifman, "Tri romana," in *Puti razvitiia russkoi literatury. Literaturovedenie* (Tartu: 1990), 92.

14. As Andrew, p. 165, notes: "Perhaps the most important part of her characterisation is the fact that she is presented not as a *static image,* but as a developing personality, with a rich inner life (as represented by her dreams)." By comparison, Chernyshevskii's contemporary, N. Strakhov, argued that there was no development of the characters in the novel: "These people appear in life fully equipped, like Minerva from the head of Jupiter; not for nothing are they the representatives of the new wisdom. They evenly and gradually work their way, not once getting sidetracked, because they never have an excess of sensation nor a rush of fantasy." See N. N. Strakhov, "Schastlivye liudi," *Iz istorii literaturnago nigilizma. 1861–1865* (Saint Petersburg: 1890), 332.

15. The element of the *Bildungsroman* has been noticed by Soviet scholars. However, it is also very problematic for them. For example, Verkhovskii, p. 76, argues that as she develops, Vera Pavlovna becomes more

radical. However, this does not at all fit with his thesis, p. 72, that the novel is constructed around the principle that the younger a person is, the more radical he or she is. Presumably, Vera Pavlovna ages as she develops. Thus, according to Verkhovskii's schema she should become more conservative, not more radical.

16. What this achievement is Chernyshevskii could not, of course, relate. It simply must be inferred by the reader. The introduction of numerous new characters in this scene seems to be, at least in part, a cloaking device to fool the censor. For the careful reader, however, Vera Pavlovna and the rest have taken a decisive, if unknown, step in their radicalization. See the conclusion for further discussion.

17. A. P. Skaftymov, "Roman *Chto delat'?*" in *N. G. Chernyshevskii. Sbornik. Neizdannye stat'i, materialy, vospominaniia* (Saratov: 1926), 127.

18. V. V. Shcheulin, "N. G. Chernyshevskii i voprosy iazyka i stilia," in *Roman N. G. Chernyshevskogo "Chto delat'?" (K 100-letiiu vykhoda v svet). Sbornik statei* (Shakhty: 1963), 113–14. Shcheulin discusses an important episode in the cultural debate over stylization during the 1850s in which Chernyshevskii used stylization as a polemical weapon. Chernyshevskii, while approving of stylization, felt that some sense of proportion must be maintained. He mocked those who lost such a sense and got carried away with "speech naturalism." In a book review entitled "Novye povesti" (1855) Chernyshevskii parodied the language of such writers. This review upset Grigorovich, who responded by writing "A School of Hospitality."

19. The Russian original is: "не тронь дерма, не воняет!" (LP 20). Note also her abusive language to her husband: "'Ass! Scoundrel! Murderer! Assassin! Here's what you get!' She slapped her husband's face. 'And here!' Again. 'Let that be a lesson to you, you moron!'" (Осел! подлец! убил! зарезал! Вот же тебе!—муж получил пощечину.—Вот же тебе!—другая пощечина. Вот как тебя надобно учить, дурака!) (83; LP 43).

20. "Чать, видишь, все добрые люди крестятся!" (LP 17).

21. "Они говорят правду. То, что называют возвышенными чувствами, идеальными стремлениями,—все это в общем ходе жизни совершенно ничтожно перед стремлением каждого к своей пользе, и в корне само состоит из того же стремления к пользе" (LP 68).

22. "хороший кусок хлеба" (LP 68).

23. "Все поступки, которые я могу разобрать, объясняются выгодою. Но ведь эта теория холодна" (LP 69). Chernyshevskii also provides some stylization of the speech of the secondary characters. For example, in the second dream Mertsalov uses the Old Church Slavonic form *os'mnadtsat'* for the number eighteen instead of the Russian *vosemnadtsat'*, reflecting his seminarian upbringing (LP 125).

24. Most Western scholars have been unwilling to credit Chernyshevskii with any mastery of language. G. Žekulin, "Forerunner of Socialist

Realism: the Novel 'What to do?' by N. G. Chernyshevsky," *Slavonic and East European Review* 41 (1963): 478, for example, states of *What Is to Be Done?*: "[E]ven the language used becomes so inelegantly cumbersome as to be almost unintelligible." Kathryn Feuer claims that *What Is to Be Done?* is the rare novel that might benefit from being read in translation. See her "What Is to Be Done about *What Is to Be Done?*" in N. G. Chernyshevsky, *What Is to Be Done?* (Ann Arbor, Mich.: 1986), xxiii. Whereas Western scholars have tended to interpret Chernyshevskii's style as unintelligible, the Soviet scholar Shcheulin, p. 112, views Chernyshevskii's language as "original."

25. After this paragraph is over, the narrator goes back to the more affectionate *Verochka*.

26. "Конечно, не очень-то приняла к сердцу эти слова Марья Алексевна; но утомленные нервы просят отдыха, и у Марьи Алексевны стало рождаться раздумье: не лучше ли вступить в переговоры с дочерью, когда она, мерзавка, уж совсем отбивается от рук? Ведь без нее ничего нельзя сделать, ведь не женишь же без ней на ней Мишку дурака! Да ведь еще и неизвестно, что она ему сказала,—ведь они руки пожали друг другу,—что ж это значит?" (LP 28).

27. For a brief discussion of the occasional intrusion of the word of the other into the speech of the author, see M. V. Teplinskii, *Izuchenie tvorchestva N. G. Chernyshevskogo* (Kiev: 1981), 134.

28. This is in contrast to the general insistence in Western scholarship that Chernyshevskii was a dry, boring man devoid of any sense of humor. For example, Moser, p. 7, sums up the general view of Chernyshevskii when he states that he "lacked a sense of humor himself, and found the idea of the comic so uninteresting that he devoted but one brief paragraph to it in his essay." Randall, p. 128, in contrast, defends the novel as funny; Petr Vail' and Aleksandr Genis, *Rodnaia rech'* (Tenafly, N.J.: 1990), 122, similarly state that Chernyshevskii is no stranger to humor. It is with regard to the humor in *What Is to Be Done?* that the previous poor translations of the novel greatly affect the perception by Western readers.

29. "досталось и ему, идеально и материально досталось" (LP 108).

30. That is, Storeshnikov.

31. "—Посмотрите-ко, Михаил Иваныч, французскую-то я сама почти что разобрала: «Гостиная»—значит, самоучитель светского обращения, а немецкую-то не пойму.

—Нет, Марья Алексевна, это не «Гостиная», это Destinée—судьба.

—Какая же это судьба? роман, что ли, так называется, али оракул, толкование снов?

—А вот сейчас увидим, Марья Алексевна, из самой книги.—Михаил Иваныч перевернул несколько листов.—Тут все о сериях больше говорится, Марья Алексевна,—ученая книга.

—О сериях? Это хорошо; значит, как денежные обороты вести.

—Да, все об этом, Марья Алексевна" (LP 66).

32. See Wagner's annotations to Katz's translation, nos. 38–40, (p. 112).

33. "—Ну, а немецкая-то?
Михаил Иваныч медленно прочел: «О религии, сочинение Людвига»—Людовика-четырнадцатого, Марья Алексевна, сочинение Людовика XIV; это был, Марья Алексевна, французский король, отец тому королю, на место которого нынешний Наполеон сел.
—Значит, о божественном?
—О божественном, Марья Алексевна.
—Это хорошо, Михаил Иваныч; то-то я и знаю, что Дмитрий Сергеич солидный молодой человек, а все-таки нужен глаз да глаз за всяким человеком! . . ."
". . . Только вот что я думаю, Михаил Иваныч: король-то французский какой был веры?
—Католик, натурально.
Так он там не в папскую ли веру обращает?
Не думаю, Марья Алексевна. Если бы католический архиерей писал, он, точно, стал бы обращать в папскую веру. А король не станет этим заниматься; он, как мудрый правитель и политик, просто будет внушать благочестие" (LP 66–67).

34. See Wagner's annotations to Katz's translation, nos. 41–42 (pp. 112–13). The passage continues with more humor when Mar'ia Aleksevna is concerned about Lopukhov's possible infatuation with Catholicism and questions him to that effect. This passage is also one of Chernyshevskii's sharpest attacks on the gentry. Storeshnikov, who is of the gentry, is shown to be an ignorant fool. A. A. Fet comments on this passage in his article, stating, "Once again, let's suppose that Storeshnikov did not know of Feuerbach's atheistic work. But his assurances that the author of the book is Louis XIV, the father of Louis Philippe—in other words the assurances of our author that the Guards Officer Storeshnikov never heard about the [French] Revolution, about Napoleon I, about the taking of Moscow by the French—are not only a slander on officers or simply unsubstantiated abuse of the public, it is Herculean pillars of contempt for any common sense on the part of the reader." A. A. Fet, "*Chto delat'?* Iz rasskazov o novykh liudiakh. Roman N. G. Chernyshevskogo," *Literaturnoe nasledstvo* 25–26 (1936): 497.

35. "Мерцалов, сидевший дома один, читал какое-то новое сочинение—то ли Людовика XIV, то ли кого другого из той же династии" (LP 103).

36. M. V. Teplinskii, "Avtor-povestvovatel' v romane N. G. Chernyshevskogo *Chto delat'?*" *N. G. Chernyshevskii. Stat'i, issledovaniia i materialy* (Saratov: 1978), 8:129, interprets this as an attempt by Chernyshevskii to show that the narrator's consciousness differs from that of the author.

37. "нет никакой болезни в больной, а силы больной быстро падают. Надобно же отыскать болезнь; пользовавший врач придумал:

atrophia nervorum, «прекращение питания нервов»; бывает ли на свете такая болезнь или нет, мне неизвестно, но если бывает, то уж и я понимаю, что она должна быть неизлечима" (LP 300).

38. "Это я дарю вашей жене. Оно стоит 150 р. (85 р.), я его только 2 раза (гораздо более 20) надевала. Это я дарю вашей дочери,—Анна Петровна подала управляющему очень маленькие дамские часы,—я за них заплатила 300 р. (120 р.)" (LP 42).

39. Moser, 146–47, does precisely this.

40. "Каким образом Петровна видела звезды на Серже, который еще и не имел их, да если б и имел, то, вероятно, не носил бы при поездках на службе Жюли,—это вещь изумительная; но что действительно она видела их, что не ошибалась и не хвастала, это не она свидетельствует, это я за нее также ручаюсь: она видела их. Это мы знаем, что на нем их не было; но у него был такой вид, что с точки зрения Петровны нельзя было не увидать на нем двух звезд,—она и увидела их; не шутя я вам говорю: увидела" (LP 120).

41. "Гром изящной кареты и топот удивительных лошадей Жюли произвели потрясающее впечатление в населении 5-й линии между Средним и Малым проспектами, где ничего подобного не было видано по крайней мере со времен Петра Великого, если не раньше" (LP 120). See annotation no. 78 to the Katz translation.

42. "—А я знаю . . .

> Что это? знакомый голос . . . Оглядываюсь,—так и есть! он, он, проницательный читатель, так недавно изгнанный с позором за незнание ни аза в глаза по части художественности; он уж опять тут, и опять с своею прежнею проницательностью, он уж опять что-то знает!
>
> —А! я знаю, кто это писал . . .
>
> Но я торопливо хватаю первое, удобное для моей цели, что попалось под руку,—попалась салфетка, потому что я, переписав письмо отставного студента, сел завтракать,—итак, я схватываю салфетку и затыкаю ему рот: «Ну, знаешь, так и знай; что ж орать на весь город?" (LP 243).

43. Chernyshevskii's admiration for and debt to the French author George Sand is perhaps the most discussed aspect of *What Is to Be Done?* in the criticism. The topic was first introduced by the Soviet scholar A. P. Skaftymov in his "Chernyshevskii i Zhorzh Sand." There have been several studies devoted to Sand's reception in Russia that routinely contain a discussion of the relationship between Sand's novel *Jacques* and *What Is to Be Done?* Most of those, however, do not go beyond Skaftymov's formulations and consist mainly of comparisons between plot summaries. See, for example, Eidelman; Herrmann; Carole Sue Karp, "George Sand's Reception in Russia, 1832–1881" (Ph.D. diss., University of Michigan, 1976). See also Charles Corbet, "Réminiscences Sandiennes dans *Que Faire?* de Černyševskij," *Revue des études slaves* 43 (1976): 17–33.

44. Emily Klenin, "On the Ideological Sources of *Čto delat'?* Sand, Družinin, Leroux," *Zeitschrift für slavische Philologie* 51, no. 2 (1991): Klenin's study is a pathbreaking one that does more than merely repeat Skaftymov's formulations.

45. For a discussion of Chernyshevskii's debt to the Englishmen, see Iu. K. Rudenko, *Chernyshevskii-romanist i literaturnye traditsii* (Leningrad: 1989), 129–43. See also Reinhartz, pp. 100–1, 131–33.

46. N. L. Brodskii and N. P. Sidorov, *Kommentarii k romanu N. G. Chernyshevskogo "Chto delat'?"* (Moscow: 1933), 57. See also Rudenko, 1989, 136; Gary Saul Morson, *The Boundaries of Genre: Dostoevsky's Diary of a Writer and the Traditions of Literary Utopia* (Austin: 1981), 99.

47. Iurii Steklov, *N. G. Chernyshevskii: ego zhizn' i deiatel'nost'*, 2nd ed. (Moscow: 1928), 1:203.

48. Rudenko, 1989, 132.

49. In his publicistic work, Chernyshevskii commented on Thackeray's and Dickens's service to the world in showing that novels with heroes are not mandatory (2:156).

50. Rudenko, 1989, 134. See also A. P. Skaftymov, *Nravstvennye iskaniia russkikh pisatelei. Stat'i i issledovaniia o russkikh klassikakh* (Moscow: 1972), 240–41; Richard Freeborn, *The Russian Revolutionary Novel: Turgenev to Pasternak* (Cambridge: 1982), 246.

51. Reinhartz, 131–33.

52. Rudenko, 1989, 139. Rudenko argues that Chernyshevskii borrows much of this from Fielding.

53. Morson, p. 81, also notes this fact. Morson argues that *What Is to Be Done?* is "concerned primarily with the reconstruction of the family and only secondarily with communism." Vail' and Genis also note that the there is little true preaching in the novel and that there are no summonses or slogans (Vail' and Genis, 121).

54. It is also possible that Chernyshevskii might have saturated his novel with so many devices from English literature in an attempt to fool the censor. This would have worked on two levels. First, a work reminiscent of Victorian literature, which possessed a reputation for didacticism, would have seemed to promise the same: blatant didacticism at the expense of artistry. This, of course, would confirm the suspicions of Chernyshevskii's official readers that he possessed no talent, only "truth." Likewise, Rudenko, 1989, p. 143, argues that by orienting himself on the tradition of the English rather than on his Russian predecessors, Chernyshevskii made his novel appear inartistic to his contemporaries.

55. There have been imitators of Chernyshevskii's novel, but these epigones generally limited themselves to one specific aspect of the novel: the image of the positive hero. In the 1860s and 1870s a short-lived school sprang up in which writers tried to imitate Chernyshevskii's Rakhmetov.

For a discussion, see I. P. Viduetskaia, "Pisateli-demokraty 1860-kh—nachala 1880-kh godov i roman Chernyshevskogo *Chto delat'?*" in *N. G. Chernyshevskogo. Istoriko-funktsional'noe issledovanie* (Moscow: 1990), 37–77. During the Soviet period this aspect of *What Is to Be Done?* was held up as a prototype of Socialist Realism. For further discussion, see Katerina Clark, *The Soviet Novel; History as Ritual* (Chicago: 1981). Chernyshevskii's imitators and worshipers never attempted to imitate the entire novel; in this sense it remains a unique production in Russian literature.

56. The best exposition of this position comes in V. A. Mysliakov, "«Ottsy i deti» v vospriiatii Chernyshevskogo," *Russkaia literatura*, no. 2 (1978): 36–53.

57. Henry Gifford, *The Hero of His Time: A Theme in Russian Literature* (London: 1950), 183.

58. Andrew, 155–56.

59. See also Verderevskaia, pp. 106–9. Verderevskaia overstates her case when she suggests that perhaps Chernyshevskii was not familiar with the text of Turgenev's novel.

60. E. H. Carr, introduction to *What Is to Be Done?* by N. G. Chernyshevsky (New York: 1961), xiv. Carr's analysis is marred by his sloppiness. For example, he is mistaken when he states that Vera has no offspring from either marriage. As Randall, p. 156, points out, such a child appears on page 300 of the edition for which Carr was writing.

61. Feuer, xv. Feuer also refers to Vera Pavlovna's fourth dream as a "vision of a future with no bothersome babies or bothersome old folks." Feuer argues that the lack of children and lack of old people in *What Is to Be Done?* is in response to Turgenev's portrayal of parent-child relationships in *Fathers and Sons* as loving and positive. See Kathryn Feuer, "*Fathers and Sons:* Fathers and Children," in *The Russian Novel from Pushkin to Pasternak* (New Haven: 1983), 77–79. See also Dawn D. Eidelman, *George Sand and the Nineteenth-Century Russian Love-Triangle Novels* (Lewisburg: 1994), 51–52, who argues that "Vera appears to lack maternal instincts entirely."

62. Fet, 489. See also Strakhov, p. 320, who states, "Not once in the whole novel is the birth of a child mentioned. And even in Vera Pavlovna's female co-op, . . . there was not one instance of a birth. Thus, . . . having and raising children did not fit."

63. N. Solov'ev, "Printsipy zhizni," *Vsemirnyi trud* 1 (1867): 176.

64. For further discussion see chapter 1. See also P. S. Reifman, "Predpolagaiutsia li deti?" in *Trudy po russkoi i slavianskoi filologii. XV. Literaturovedenie* (Tartu: 1970), 357–63.

65. Her exact statement is: "Chernyshevsky was himself a mostly devoted son and a notably devoted parent, but it would be hard to guess this from the novel" (Feuer, 1986, xv).

66. Andrew, 155–60.

67. Leo Tolstoy, *The Death of Ivan Ilych and Other Stories,* trans. J. D. Duff (New York: 1960), 40.

68. Ibid., 93.

69. Some scholars have come to a different conclusion regarding Chernyshevskii's views on the family. For example, see Clark, p. 115, who states: "Many nineteenth-century utopian groups, socialists and, later, communists, sought to tear individuals away from their own families and regroup them in that higher community of the phalanstery, artel, or party. Both Chernyshevsky's *What Is to Be Done?* and Gorky's *Mother* provide object lessons in this process."

70. Victor Ripp argues that *What Is to Be Done?* stresses the importance of the family no less than Turgenev had. See Victor Ripp, *Turgenev's Russia* (Ithaca: 1980), 207. Elsewhere, he argues that "*What Is to Be Done?* is in many way the family novel par excellence." See Victor Ripp, "Turgenev as a Social Novelist: The Problem of the Part and the Whole," in *Literature and Society in Imperial Russia, 1800–1914* (Stanford: 1978), 256.

71. I am indebted to Nina Perlina for this observation. Chernyshevskii's narrator does not actually call Mar'ia Aleksevna a poet, but refers to her plans for revenge on Lopukhov as "poetry" (p. 163).

72. Fyodor Dostoyevsky, *Uncle's Dream and Other Stories,* trans. David McDuff (New York: 1989), 126.

73. See Teplinskii, 1978, p. 133, for further discussion.

74. Gural'nik, 139.

75. See "Discourse in the Novel" in his *The Dialogic Imagination* (Austin: 1981).

76. This fact has led many scholars to reject it as a work of art. See Skaftymov, 1926, p. 120. See also Morris, 1993, p. 144, who states that *What Is to Be Done?* "is part myth, part fiction; part epic, part novel; part non-naturalistic, part naturalistic; and finally, part ascetic, part worldly. Regardless of the terminology chosen, the result is the same; a mixture of generically incompatible elements." Vail' and Genis, in contrast, view this with approval: "Chernyshevskii rejected tradition and created a book composed of previously unconnected parts. . . . The very attempt is its main virtue" (Vail' and Genis, 121).

77. Naumova, 22.

78. Ibid., 44.

79. N. V. Vodovozov, *Roman N. G. Chernyshevskogo 'Chto Delat'?'* (Moscow: 1953), 12. In this melodramatic scene, Gifford, p. 189, sees Chernyshevskii as parodying "the style of Eugène Sue, Dumas, and for that matter Dostoyevsky." The fact that Chernyshevskii uses the adventure element in a highly conscious, parodic way, has been missed by many. Adam Ulam, for example, notes this and other elements in the novel and argues

that in large part the novel is addressed to adolescents. See Adam B. Ulam, *Ideologies and Illusions. Revolutionary Thought from Herzen to Solzhenitsyn* (Cambridge: 1976), 45.

80. "Я употребил обыкновенную хитрость романистов: начал повесть эффектными сценами, вырванными из средины или конца ее, прикрыл их туманом. . . . Я рассказываю тебе еще первую свою повесть, ты еще не приобрела себе суждения, одарен ли автор художественным талантом . . . моя подпись еще не заманила бы тебя, и я должен был забросить тебе удочку с приманкою эффектности. Не осуждай меня за то,—ты сама виновата; твоя простодушная наивность принудила меня унизиться до этой пошлости" (LP 12–13).

81. Morson, 99.

82. See Tamarchenko, pp. 133–35, for further discussion. See also L. M. Lotman, "Sotsial'nyi ideal, etika i estetika Chernyshevskogo," in *Idei sotsializma v russkoi klassicheskoi literature* (Leningrad: 1969), 206–7.

83. See S. E. Shatalov and A. S. Kurilov, *Nikolai Gavrilovich Chernyshevskii* (Moscow: 1978), 45. Of course, this also owes a lot to Chernyshevskii's views on the women's question; that is, he shows that a woman's life does not end with love and marriage.

84. This fact has sometimes been the source of criticism for being unrealistic or for depriving the novel of tension. See, for example, Žekulin, p. 478.

85. As Klenin notes, p. 380, in the two works in Russian literature that provide a relatively happy ending prior to Chernyshevskii, Avdeev's *Podvodnyi kamen'* and Tolstoi's *Family Happiness,* both the heroines' and the husbands' original feelings are burnt out or their happiness poisoned.

86. A Russian translation of *Jacques* appeared in *Otechestvennye zapiski* in the 1840s. However, its subject matter was considered so sensitive that the last seven chapters, where Jacques commits suicide, were not allowed to be published.

87. Reifman notes the similarities between Herzen's novel and Chernyshevskii's but interprets the relationship solely in political terms. He argues that Herzen's heroes come to such a despairing position because they place all their hopes on the heart, on love. Chernyshevskii's heroes have a different fate precisely because they do not place all their hopes on the private, personal. Love, he argues, occupies an important but not supreme place. See P. S. Reifman, *N. G. Chernyshevskii* (Tartu: 1973), 85–87.

88. In her analysis, Klenin studies Herzen's *Who Is to Blame?* and Druzhinin's *Polin'ka Saks.* As she states, p. 378, "In view of the obvious difference between the social and political orientation of *Kto vinovat?* on one hand and *Polin'ka Saks* on the other, it is striking that the two treatments of the love triangle itself are quite similar: it is disastrous for all." Klenin further argues, p. 398, that the Russian variant of the love triangle is more

tragic than Sand's novels, for example. Whereas Russian novels tended to take the consumptive-death approach for the heroine, Sand's novels lack a tragic end for the heroine. Eidelman, in contrast, argues that the solution to the love triangle presented by Sand proves to be a tragic and unsatisfactory resolution to a condition in which everyone is a victim (Eidelman, 1990, 89).

89. See N. G. Chernyshevsky, "The Aesthetic Relation of Art to Reality," *Selected Philosophical Essays* (Moscow: 1953), 304–12.

90. Mathewson argues that Chernyshevskii was opposed to the traditional concept of the tragic because he was an advocate of optimal literature and labels his position "extreme." He does note, however, that Chernyshevskii did not seek to banish tragedy from art, only to end its monopoly. See Rufus W. Mathewson Jr., *The Positive Hero in Russian Literature,* 2nd ed. (Stanford: 1975), 69–70.

91. Klenin argues, p. 380, that "[t]he triangle, then, is not destructive but regenerative." Irina Paperno takes a similar stance in arguing that *What Is to Be Done?* presents a plan for rational adultery; that is, that Chernyshevskii supported the idea of a triple union. She further argues that for Chernyshevskii, the key to bliss lies in the presence of a third party between any two people, a triangular structure at the core of any union. Likewise, regarding the living arrangement of the Kirsanovs and Lopukhovs at the end of the novel, she argues that "Chernyshevsky intended this arrangement to serve as the prototype of a new social arrangement, a harmonious paradise on earth based on the application of the principle of collectivity to all areas of human life, private and public, as presented in the picture of the communal society of the future in the fourth dream of Vera Pavlovna." See Irina Paperno, *Chernyshevsky and the Age of Realism: A Study in the Semiotics of Behavior* (Stanford: 1988), 137–38, 157–58. Although Klenin and Paperno both present brilliant analyses, I think they err in interpreting a specific element of Chernyshevskii's polemic with previous Russian literature as a model he posited for his readers to follow.

92. George Lukács, "Tschernyschewskijs Roman 'Was Tun?'" *Der russische Realismus in der Weltliteratur* (Berlin: 1952), 116.

93. This failure to construct the novel entirely around the conflict generated by a love triangle is viewed by Žekulin as a great failure on Chernyshevskii's part. He attributes this to Chernyshevskii's attempt to subordinate his art to the demands of ideology: "he misuses himself as an artist and he misuses art because he believes that art is secondary to the ideal, that the proper function of art is to serve" (478, 483).

94. See also Tamarchenko, p. 151.

95. See also the analyses presented by T. Iu. Dubrovina in her articles. See "Preodolenie tragicheskogo kak pafos romana *Chto delat'?* N. G. Chernyshevskogo," and "Bor'ba i tragicheskoe v estetike i khudozhestven-

noi praktike N. G. Chernyshevskogo," in *Literaturno-kriticheskie opyty i nabliudeniia* (Kishinev: 1982), 51–67 and 147–55. In the first article, Dubrovina argues that Chernyshevskii constructs *What Is to Be Done?* around the principle of "overcoming the tragic."

96. As Dubrovina notes, p. 147, Chernyshevskii is quite consistent on this issue both in theoretical works such as his dissertation and in his fiction.

97. Strakhov, 319. Strakhov argues that the entire novel is about how the characters avoid unhappiness and discomfort. His arguments are not supported by the text. Although the end result of the love triangle is a happy one, the characters do experience anguish and unhappiness until it is resolved. Vera Pavlovna's third dream, in particular, reveals the extent of her internal psychological struggle. Moreover, although the suffering of the characters is not dwelt upon in great detail, the narrator is careful to note that they do suffer. Regarding Vera Pavlovna's attempt to resist her love for Kirsanov, the narrator states: "The struggle was difficult. Vera Pavlovna's face grew pale" (264). Likewise, the agitation that Vera Pavlovna experiences in her difficult situation is more than adequately conveyed to the reader when the narrator describes her repeated attempts to write a note to Lopukhov (266). With regard to Lopukhov, he, too, suffers for some time because of the love triangle. As Verderevskaia argues, he does not take her love for Kirsanov so easily as it appears from a fleeting reading of the novel. See N. A. Verderevskaia, *Roman N. G. Chernyshevskogo "Chto delat'?" Posobie dlia uchashchikhsia* (Moscow: 1982), 41.

98. He states that this conflict "would be a godsend to every other novelist" (Žekulin, 478).

99. "но развязка приближалась" (LP 163).

100. This is where Katz's translation does not quite catch the ambiguity of the Russian original. Had Katz used the term "denouement" instead of "end," I think the play on words would have been more successfully conveyed.

101. Iu. K. Rudenko, *Roman N. G. Chernyshevskogo "Chto delat'?" Esteticheskoe svoeobrazie i khudozhestvennyi metod* (Leningrad: 1979), 22, argues that the narrator's commentaries and conversations with the perspicacious reader form a second layer to the novel. He terms it a "framed" narration, that is, a novel within a novel. See also Teplinskii, 1978, pp. 127–36.

102. Rudenko argues that the image of the author occupies a special place in the novel as the central structure-forming element; it is the presence of the storyteller that gives the novel unity. See Iu. K. Rudenko, "Problema chitatelia v romane N. G. Chernyshevskogo *Chto delat'?*" in *Russkaia literatura XIX–XX vekov,* ed. I. G. Iampol'skii (Leningrad: 1971), 71, 76.

103. Morson, p. 99, says of Chernyshevskii's use of this device: "'Baring' by exaggeration the devices it employs, Chernyshevsky's work can be

taken as a textbook model of the utopian genre's techniques, particularly its techniques of didactic frame-breaking."

104. "В этом вся тайна всемирной истории" (LP 65).

105. "Но забираться нам во всемирную историю будет уж лишнее: занимаешься рассказом, так занимайся рассказом" (LP 65).

106. "Полезная для проницательного читателя беседа о синем чулке, то есть о нем, оторвала меня от рассказа о том, как теперь проходит день Веры Павловны" (LP 270).

107. In constructing *What Is to Be Done?* Chernyshevskii introduces many innovative or unusual features. Many, but not all, of them are presented to the reader at an early stage in the minisection called the foreword. This foreword is of great importance due to its meta-narrative. Morson, for example, places so much value on it that he quotes it in full. See his discussion, pp. 99–104. Moser, p. 143, argues that the foreword is of "substantial theoretical interest for an understanding of what Chernyshevsky hoped to accomplish."

108. "«Содержание повести—любовь, главное лицо—женщина,—это хорошо, хотя бы сама повесть и была плоха», говорит читательница.
—Это правда,—говорю я" (LP 12).

109. "Я рассказываю тебе еще первую свою повесть, ты еще не приобрела себе суждения, одарен ли автор художественным талантом . . . моя подпись еще не заманила бы тебя" (LP 13). Rudenko, 1971, p. 72, argues that Chernyshevskii was aware that readers would not be attracted to his novel by formal considerations. Rather, they would be lured by his fame because of his work at *Sovremennik*. Thus, this reference to his name must serve some purpose, some kind of mystification. Teplinskii, 1978, p. 128, notes that in the rough draft, Chernyshevskii made this temptation even stronger by giving the narrator his first name (Nikolai) and his age (35).

110. "Я помню, как испугался я, двенадцатилетний ребенок, когда меня, никогда еще не видавшего пожаров, разбудил слишком сильный шум пожарной тревоги. . . . Я дрожал, как в лихорадке. . . . С той поры я уж и знал, что если страшно от сильного пожара, то надобно бежать туда и работать, и вовсе не будет страшно" (LP 265). This passage corresponds to an event from Chernyshevskii's own biography (Teplinskii, 1978, 136). This fact combined with the continual self-reference by the narrator has led many to conclude that the narrator of *What Is to Be Done?* is Chernyshevskii himself. Moser, p. 143, for example, argues that Chernyshevskii inserts himself as a participant, if not a character.

111. Rudenko, 1979, 16. Rudenko, in a later work (1989, 132), argues that the image of the "author" in *What Is to Be Done?* has much in common with Thackeray's *Vanity Fair.* Teplinskii, 1978, p. 128, argues that there is indeed considerable overlap between the narrator's views and those of Chernyshevskii himself. He stresses, however, that the narrator is objec-

tified to a significant degree and cannot be equated with the biographical author. Teplinskii goes on to analyze the age of the narrator and that of the heroes and shows that based on evidence found in the novel, the narrator cannot be equated with Chernyshevskii (Teplinskii, 129–30).

112. In the rough draft this claim to know the characters personally is even more explicit: "I am simply relating the life of one of my good acquaintances and the people close to her" (я просто рассказываю о жизни одной из моих добрых знакомых и людей, к ней близких) (LP 712–13).

113. Verderevskaia, 1975, 110.

114. According to Verderevskaia, 1975, p. 110, there were only two such Russian novels in the nineteenth century: *Eugene Onegin* and *What Is to Be Done?*

115. Such is the term used by Rudenko. Rudenko argues that Chernyshevskii did follow the model set by Pushkin to some extent. However, he views Gogol's novel *Dead Souls* as more of a model for Chernyshevskii than *Eugene Onegin* was (Rudenko, 1989, 126–27). Chernyshevskii had used the device of a narrator in his publicistic work at *Sovremennik.* According to Verderevskaia, to get dangerous things into print, Chernyshevskii would resort to the creation of a personage, a narrator. On one occasion, for example, Chernyshevskii creates a personage from the *narod* whose naïveté is useful in stressing certain unpleasant matters. See N. A. Verderevskaia, *Roman N. G. Chernyshevskogo "Chto delat'?" Posobie dlia uchashchikhsia* (Moscow: 1982), 12. The narrator in question is a certain Badeikin (5:571–73).

116. "Когда я рассказывал о Лопухове, то затруднялся обособить его от его задушевного приятеля и не умел сказать о нем почти ничего такого, чего не надобно было бы повторить и о Кирсанове. И действительно, все, что может (проницательный) читатель узнать из следующей описи примет Кирсанова, будет повторением примет Лопухова" (LP 146). Most scholars have taken this passage quite literally. Skaftymov, 1926, p. 122, for example, cites it as proof of Chernyshevskii's inability to give adequate, individualized portraits of his characters. Others, in contrast, argue that this is a key part of Chernyshevskii's attempt to provide a description of a new social type. Rudenko, 1979, pp. 78–79, views the remarks about not being able to differentiate Kirsanov from Lopukhov as intentional irony and mockery of the aesthetic principles of the perspicacious reader. Verderevskaia, 1982, pp. 43–45, argues that Chernyshevskii's other works demonstrate that he was quite capable of drawing individualized portraits. He chose not to do so in *What Is to Be Done?* because he is interested in the typical, not the individual.

117. "Лопухов был какой человек?" (LP 147).

118. "У Кирсанова было иначе" (LP 147).

119. "Гораздо безнравственнее,—говорю я, неизвестно, вправду ли, насмех ли над проницательным читателем" (LP 249).

120. Reinhartz, p. 100, argues that this device is traceable to two sources: the influence of Victorian authors such as Thackeray and Chernyshevskii's seminarian upbringing. Dubrovina, in contrast, argues that this is part of the principle of theatricality around which much of the novel is constructed (Dubrovina, 60). Again this device is nothing new for Chernyshevskii: he had used it in his publicistic work at *Sovremennik* (Verderevskaia, 1982, 13–15).

121. Morson, p. 101, attributes this dichotomy to the utopian genre in which he argues Chernyshevskii was working. Chernyshevskii adopts a similar division between his readers in the foreword to *Povesti v povesti.*

122. "Читатель не ограничивается такими легкими заключениями,—ведь у мужчины мыслительная способность и от природы сильнее, да и развита гораздо больше, чем у женщины; . . . читатель говорит: «я знаю, что этот застрелившийся господин не застрелился». Я хватаюсь за слово «знаю» и говорю: ты этого не знаешь, потому что этого тебе еще не сказано, а ты знаешь только то, что тебе скажут; сам ты ничего не знаешь, не знаешь даже того, что тем, как я начал повесть, я оскорбил, унизил тебя. Ведь ты не знал этого,—правда?—ну, так знай же" (LP 12).

123. Morson, p. 101, argues that Chernyshevskii divides his readers into two groups, the larger one, which he reviles, and the smaller one, which he flatters. Morson is mistaken on this point in that he omits the category of the neutral reader. For further discussion, see Rudenko, 1971, pp. 61–76.

124. "Но есть в тебе, публика, некоторая доля людей,—теперь уже довольно значительная доля,—которых я уважаю. С тобою, с огромным большинством, я нагл,—но только с ним, и только с ним я говорил до сих пор. С людьми, о которых я теперь упомянул, я говорил бы скромно, даже робко. Но с ними мне не нужно было объясняться. Их мнениями я дорожу, но я вперед знаю, что оно за меня. Добрые и сильные, честные и умеющие, недавно вы начали возникать между нами, но вас уже не мало, и быстро становится все больше. Если бы вы были публика, мне уже не нужно было бы писать; если бы вас еще не было, мне еще не было бы можно писать. Но вы еще не публика, а уже вы есть между публикою,—потому мне еще нужно и уже можно писать" (LP 14).

125. "Читательница и простой читатель, не толкующие о художественности, они знают это" (LP 216).

126. Rudenko, 1971, p. 64, argues that this reader is the stylized image of the average Russian reader, who cares little for questions of aesthetics, but reads only for entertainment. See also his discussion, 1989, p. 11.

127. See Verderevskaia, 1982, p. 15. She cites "Russkii chelovek na rendez-vous" as an example of this technique.

128. As Verderevskaia, 1975, p. 115, notes, the narrator claims in the foreword to be insolent (*naglyi*) to the public as a whole, but, in fact, is nasty only to the perspicacious reader.

129. Soviet scholars also claim that the perspicacious reader is a personification of a liberal. Chernyshevskii's antipathy toward the Russian liberals is well known and hardly in doubt. But the Soviet dichotomy assumes too much: there is nothing particularly liberal about the perspicacious reader. Most of the narrator's harangues with him concern the nature of art, not politics. Moreover, not all of the so-called aesthetes were liberals. In short, Soviet scholars tended to politicize the novel rather crudely in this respect. For Soviet discussions see Naumova, pp. 78–81, and Rudenko, 1971, pp. 69–70. Verderevskaia, in contrast, departs from this formulation in her study. She argues, 1975, p. 116, that one cannot say for sure who the perspicacious reader represents, except for the critics who will undoubtedly be hostile to the novel.

130. Tamarchenko, p. 242, argues that Chernyshevskii probably borrowed this from Gogol'. Chernyshevskii's running battle with the aesthetes has its roots in his publicistic works. For example, in his 1857 review of Tolstoi's early works, Chernyshevskii has the following statement: "But it is worth noting that people who talk a great deal about artistry are the ones who understand least what its conditions are." See N. G. Chernyshevsky, "L. N. Tolstoy's *Childhood* and *Boyhood* and *Military Tales*," in *Belinsky, Chernyshevsky, and Dobrolyubov: Selected Criticism*, ed. Ralph Matlaw (New York: 1962), 104.

131. "угадать нетрудно, если ты имеешь хоть малейшее понятие о художественности, о которой ты так любишь толковать" (LP 215). See also the narrator's statement: "You're very poor, my dear sir, in those aesthetic deliberations you so love" (Уж очень плох ты, государь мой, в эстетических рассуждениях, которые так любишь) (307–8; LP 228). The narrator's attack on the perspicacious reader reaches its summit in the sections devoted to the character Rakhmetov, which will be discussed in chapter 4.

132. Edward J. Brown, "So Much Depends . . . Russian Critics in Search of 'Reality,'" *Russian Review* 48 (1989): 379, argues that this is the salient feature of *What Is to Be Done?*

133. Donald Fanger, *The Creation of Nikolai Gogol* (Cambridge: 1979), 186–87.

134. Rudenko, 1971, 73.

135. Morson, 99. Morson's treatment is a valuable discussion of the architectonics of *What Is to Be Done?* I disagree, however, with his thesis that the key element of Chernyshevskii's novel is to make a statement about the harmfulness of novels. For example, he argues that Chernyshevskii saw the novel as "doomed Babylon's last flower" and states: "The duplicitous strategy of his work is to encourage the readers' fascination with novelistic plots and themes, and then to reproach them for that very fascination. The readers' novelistic expectations thereby become both the sign of their moral

weakness and, it is hoped, the means for their regeneration. Genre corrupts, antithetical genre purifies." Morson's analysis is in large part based upon the notion that Chernyshevskii was hostile to the very concept of art. As I have shown in the previous chapter, this was not the case. Rather, Chernyshevskii's hostility was directed at a restrictive definition of art.

136. "даже уж слишком много было чувства, не артистично" (LP 27).

137. "вообще она сохранила все свои непоэтические, и неизящные, и нехорошего тона свойства" (LP 266).

138. "неужели судьба моя как романиста состоит в том, чтобы компрометировать перед благовоспитанными людьми всех моих героинь и героев?" (LP 326).

139. Naumova, 21. Naumova, p. 20, argues that this method was used by Chernyshevskii in his publicistic work. In his "The Anthropological Principle in Philosophy," for example, she argues that Chernyshevskii constantly plays jokes upon himself, often accusing himself of lacking those very qualities that in fact constituted his strength.

140. Skaftymov, 1972, 241.

141. See also Naumova, p. 21.

142. In this respect, Chernyshevskii's foreword and many of the subsequent meta-narrative digressions bear a striking resemblance to Lermontov's introduction to the second edition of *A Hero of Our Time.* In that introduction, Lermontov insults the Russian reading public by calling it unsophisticated and takes it to task for failing to appreciate the nuances of literature. Likewise he deals with some of the criticism his novel received. Chernyshevskii, who had a very high opinion of Lermontov, undoubtedly took his cue from him. Such statements occur within the actual text of *What Is to Be Done?* and occupy far more space. However, it seems quite clear that the origin of this hostile meta-narrative can be traced to Lermontov.

143. Whether these direct statements can be trusted is a different topic that will be dealt with below.

144. "Я употребил обыкновенную хитрость романистов" (LP 12).

145. "эффектными сценами, вырванными из средины или конца ее" (LP 12).

146. "Но теперь ты уже попалась в мои руки, и я могу породолжать рассказ, как по-моему следует, без всяких уловок. Дальше не будет таинственности, ты всегда будешь за двадцать страниц вперед видеть развязку каждого положения, а на первый случай я скажу тебе и развязку всей повести: дело кончится весело, с бокалами, песнью; не будет ни эффектности, никаких прикрас" (LP 13).

147. "Если бы я хотел сочинять эффектные столкновения, я б и дал этому положению трескучую развязку; но ее не было на деле; если б я хотел заманивать неизвестностью, я бы не стал говорить теперь же,

что ничего подобного не произошло; но я пишу без уловок и потому вперед говорю; трескучего столкновения не будет, положение развяжется без бурь, без громов и молний" (LP 46).

148. "Отношения Марьи Алексевны к Лопухову походят на фарс, сама Марья Алексевна выставляется через них в смешном виде. То и другое решительно против моей воли. Если бы я хотел заботиться о том, что называется у нас художественностью, я скрыл бы отношения Марьи Алексевны к Лопухову, рассказ о которых придает этой части романа водевильный характер. Скрыть их было бы легко" (LP 71–72).

149. "Но я рассказываю дело не так, как нужно для доставления мне художнической репутации, а как оно было. Я как романист очень огорчен тем, что написал несколько страниц, унижающихся до водевильности" (LP 72).

150. For a discussion, see John Bayley, introduction to *Eugene Onegin,* by Alexander Pushkin (New York: 1979), 16.

151. V. G. Odinokov, "*Normativnost'* i psykhologizm v romane N. G. Chernyshevskogo *Chto delat'?*" in *Problemy literaturnykh zhanrov. Materialy vtoroi nauchnoi mezhvuzovskoi konferentsii 30 sentiabria-4 oktiabria 1975 goda* (Tomsk: 1975), 89–90; V. G. Odinokov, *Khudozhestvennaia sistemnost' russkogo klassicheskogo romana* (Novosibirsk: 1976), 147– 49. See also Rudenko, 1971, p. 74; 1989, p. 128. Both Rudenko and Odinokov argue that the illusion of reality is created by the narrator or storyteller but is then smashed by the actual author.

152. See, for example, V. V. Kuleshov, "Velikii russkii revoliutsioner-demokrat N. G. Chernyshevskii i nekotorye sotsial'no-ekonomicheskie problemy v ego romane *Chto delat'?*" in *Roman N. G. Chernyshevskogo "Chto delat'?" (K 100-letiiu vykhoda v svet). Sbornik statei* (Shakhty: 1963), 9–10. Kuleshov argues that new people are the bearers of the basic ideas of the author and that Chernyshevskii expresses his social ideas by means of the image of the new people. Vail' and Genis, pp. 121 and 124, resist this view somewhat, arguing that there is no true preaching in the novel.

153. With regard to the younger generation, Chernyshevskii limited himself to a defense of the young people against the unfair charges of their detractors. Chernyshevskii's defense of the younger generation should not be interpreted as complete acceptance of it and all its views and actions. Chernyshevskii was dismayed by the bloodthirsty character of "Young Russia." Instead of a public rebuke, however, he expressed his feelings by means of a messenger. See Joseph Frank, *Dostoevsky: The Stir of Liberation, 1860–1865* (Princeton: 1986), 157–58; B. P. Koz'min, *Iz istorii revoliutsionnoi mysli v Rossii* (Moscow: 1961), 272.

154. The question of the narrator and Rakhmetov will be discussed in chapter 4.

155. This topic will be discussed in far more detail in the next chapter. For a differing view, see H. Günther, "Turgenevs *Väter und Söhne* und Černyševskijs *Was tun?" Zeitschrift für Slawistik* 34, no. 5 (1989): 682.

156. "И вот они для пользы любимой науки,—они ужасные охотники бранить медицину, только посвящают все свои силы ее пользе,—они отказываются от богатства, даже от довольства, и сидят в гошпиталях, делая, видите ли, интересные для науки наблюдения, режут лягушек, вскрывают сотни трупов ежегодно и при первой возможности обзаводятся химическими лабораториями" (LP 50).

157. ". . . теперь они оба работали для докторских диссертаций и уничтожали громадное количество лягушек" (LP 50).

158. "потому-то, что я сам не таков, я и могу не совестясь выражать свое уважение к нему, к сожалению, я не себя прославляю, когда говорю про этих людей: славные люди" (LP 149).

159. "Кроме товарищей да двух-трех профессоров, предвидевших в нем хорошего деятеля науки, он виделся только с семействами, в которых давал уроки. Но с этими семействами он только виделся: он как огня боялся фамильярности и держал себя очень сухо, холодно со всеми лицами в них, кроме своих маленьких учеников и учениц" (LP 51).

160. This topic will be discussed further in the next chapter.

161. Tamarchenko, p. 241, argues that whereas his predecessors, Pushkin, Lermontov, and Gogol, tried to show the distance of their views from those of their characters, Chernyshevskii stresses in every possible way his solidarity with the heroes of his novel. He considers himself a part of their circle and expresses full agreement with their views. See also William F. Woehrlin, *Chernyshevskii: The Man and the Journalist* (Cambridge: 1971), 180, who states, "But Turgenev hit close to the mark when he implied that Chernyshevskii could not long maintain respect for true artistic detachment."

162. Morris, 1993, 137.

163. Franco Venturi, *Roots of Revolution* (New York: 1960), 179.

164. Quoted in Mikhail Bakhtin, *Problems of Dostoevsky's Poetics*, ed. and trans. Caryl Emerson (Minneapolis: 1984), 65–66. The original Russian text can be found in *PSS* (12:683–84). Bakhtin uses one of the provisional names of the novel, *The Pearl of Creation*, to refer to it.

165. Reifman argues that in the actual novel *Povesti v povesti*, Chernyshevskii does not succeed in offering true polyphony, but merely a "game of the mind." See P. S. Reifman, "Vremia v romane N. G. Chernyshevskogo 'Chto delat'?'" in *Literaturnyi protsess: vnutrennie zakony i vneshnie vozdeistviia* (Tartu: 1990), 36.

166. Bakhtin, 1984, 67. He states: "Precisely in this freedom for others' points of view to reveal themselves without any finalizing evaluations from the author does Chernyshevsky see the chief advantage of the new 'objec-

tive' form of the novel. We emphasize that Chernyshevsky saw in this no betrayal of 'his strong and fixed convictions.' Thus we can say that Chernyshevsky came very close indeed to the idea of polyphony."

167. Chernyshevskii began work on *Povesti v povesti* on July 21, 1863, about three and one-half months after completing *What Is to Be Done?* This particular variant of the foreword is dated October 10, 1863.

168. In the commentary in Chernyshevskii's *PSS,* A. P. Skaftymov does him a great injustice. Skaftymov argues that the other works Chernyshevskii wrote while in the *Alekseevskii ravelin* are devoid of the artistic merits of *What Is to Be Done?* He does cite them as important for the study of Chernyshevskii's biography, but otherwise attaches little value to them. Regarding the foreword to *Povesti v povesti,* Skaftymov attributes Chernyshevskii's desire to write an objective novel solely to the need to appear apolitical to the tsarist investigators (12:687). Even if the presence of the censor and the other authorities was solely responsible for Chernyshevskii's decision, it in no way detracts from his theoretical achievement.

169. "А впрочем, по кирсановской теории, это и не мучительно, а даже приятно" (LP 169).

170. Katz's translation leaves out in this instance the quotation marks that are to be found in the Russian original.

171. The narrator also distances himself from other key elements of Lopukhov's vocabulary, such as "fiancée" (*nevesta*), a euphemism for revolution. For example, the narrator says "it's their fiancée who provides them with these words" (Это их невеста подсказывает им такие слова) (103; LP 59). In this passage the narrator clearly states that it is their fiancée, not his. He never uses the word "our" when discussing their views.

172. One should also note that when the narrator borrows words from Mar'ia Aleksevna's vocabulary, they are not enclosed in *kavychki;* that is, Chernyshevskii did not have to worry about a misidentification of her discourse with that of the narrator.

173. "он, этот тип, зародился недавно; в мое время его еще не было, хоть я не очень старый, даже вовсе не старый человек. Я и сам не мог вырости таким,—рос не в такую эпоху" (LP 149).

174. "Я тут многое не одобряю. Пожалуй, даже все не одобряю, если тебе сказать по правде" (LP 249).

175. The differences in these views will be discussed in far more detail in the following chapters.

176. "Но как европейцы между китайцами все на одно лицо и на один манер только по отношению к китайцам, а на самом деле между европейцами несравненно больше разнообразия, чем между китайцами, так и в этом, по-видимому, одном типе разнообразие личностей развивается на разности более многочисленные и более отличающиеся друг от друга, чем все разности всех остальных типов разнятся между

собою. Тут есть всякие люди: и сибариты, и аскеты, и суровые, и нежные, и всякие, всякие" (LP 150).

177. This is significant because lack of interior monologue is one of the bases for which Edward Brown, p. 380, rejects *What Is to Be Done?* as art. Tamarchenko cites several instances of interior monologues in the novel and argues that they are built on that linguistic material, which is typical for the hero. We know not only *what* he thinks, but *how* he thinks (Tamarchenko, 140, 166).

178. "А когда бросишься в окно, как быстро, быстро полетишь,—будто не падаешь, а в самом деле летишь,—это, должно быть, очень приятно. Только потом ударишься о тротуар—ах, как жестко! и больно? нет, я думаю, боли не успеешь почувствовать,—а только очень жестко! Да ведь это один, самый коротенький миг; а зато перед этим—воздух, будто самая мягкая перина,—расступается так легко, нежно . . . Нет, это хорошо . . .

Да, а потом? Будут все смотреть—голова разбитая, лицо разбитое, в крови, в грязи. . . Нет, если бы можно было на это место посыпать чистого песку,—здесь и песок-то все грязный . . . нет, самого белого, самого чистого . . . вот бы хорошо было. И лицо бы осталось не разбитое, чистое, не пугало бы никого" (LP 89).

179. Chernyshevskii's narrator uses a different designation elsewhere in the novel, "монолог в мыслях," which Katz translates as "internal monologue" (LP 99; 151).

180. For a general discussion of Chernyshevskii's concern with the psychology of his characters, see V. G. Prokshin, "O svoeobrazii psykhologicheskogo analiza v romanakh N. G. Chernyshevskogo," in *N. G. Chernyshevskii. Stat'i, issledovaniia i materialy* (Saratov: 1968), 5:101–16. Prokshin, p. 106, argues that much of the novel is devoted to depicting the psychology of the characters, with half of the text composed of materials such as internal monologues, dreams, letters, diaries, and so forth. Tamarchenko, p. 176, argues that when it comes to psychological analysis, Chernyshevskii is on a level with Tolstoi or Dostoevskii.

181. Tamarchenko treats precisely this problem when he argues that Chernyshevskii himself feared that his preaching of a new morality would be primitively understood as a summons for the simple imitation of his heroes. Tamarchenko argues that within the bounds of the text, Chernyshevskii even warned the reader about such a mistake. See G. E. Tamarchenko, *Chernyshevskii-romanist* (Leningrad: 1976), 153. The passage to which Tamarchenko refers is: "[T]here's absolutely nothing extraordinary or charming about the idea that all husbands and wives should be separated; look here, not every decent woman conceives a passionate love for her husband's friend, not every decent man must struggle against his passion for a married woman" (ведь в этом нет решительно никакой ни крайности, не прелести, чтобы все жены и мужья расходились, ведь вовсе не каждая порядочная женщина чувствует страстную любовь к приятелю мужа, не

каждый порядочный человек борется со страстью к замужней женщине) (312; LP 232).

CHAPTER THREE

1. This topic has been well addressed by Western scholars in recent years. Scholarly works that include a discussion of Chernyshevskii are Richard Stites, *The Women's Liberation Movement in Russia: Feminism, Nihilism, and Bolshevism* (Princeton: 1978); Barbara Alpern Engel, *Mothers and Daughters: Women of the Intelligentsia in Nineteenth-Century Russia* (New York: 1983); Dawn Diane Eidelman, "George Sandism and the Woman Question in Nineteenth-Century Russia" (Ph.D. diss., Emory University, 1990). As part of the upsurge in interest in Chernyshevskii's feminism, Benjamin Tucker's translation of *What Is to Be Done?* was republished by Virago Press (London) in 1982. For a discussion of this edition, including its new preface, see Michael R. Katz, "English Translations of *What Is to Be Done?*" *Slavic Review* 46, no. 1 (1987): 125–31.

2. See Stites, p. 90, and Engel, p. 73, for a brief discussion of the details of Chernyshevskii's "private program."

3. Stites, 46. Stites gives an inaccurate picture of Chernyshevskii when he states, "'Away with these erotic questions!' was Chernyshevsky's well-known remark, and he largely ignored them until his own arrest in 1863." This statement was made by Chernyshevskii in an entirely different context (in his article "Russkii chelovek na rendez-vous") and in no way reflects his attitude toward the women's question. Stites, p. 90, also argues that it was only when faced with unlimited leisure in prison that he turned to those issues and sought answers to them.

4. Chernyshevskii's authorship of this review is not entirely certain. The editors of his collected works attribute authorship to him on two bases: (1) no else could have written it at the time; and (2) it corresponds closely to certain ideas in *What Is to Be Done?*

5. Although most scholars view *What Is to Be Done?* as a progressive text concerned with the liberation of women, George Moskos provides a harsh appraisal. He argues that Chernyshevskii constructs the text to keep Vera Pavlovna in a state of perpetual dependence on men. See his "(Dis)regarding Viéra: What Is to Be Done with Chernyshevsky?" *West Virginia University Philological Papers* 38 (1992): 49–58. See also Dawn D. Eidelman, *George Sand and the Nineteenth-Century Russian Love-Triangle Novels* (Lewisburg: 1994), 137, who argues that Chernyshevskii, like other male writers of the period, elevated women to a "terrible perfection."

6. Francis B. Randall, *N. G. Chernyshevskii* (New York: 1967), 109. See also S. M. Shibaev, "Moral'nyi oblik 'obyknovennykh liudei' N. G.

Chernyshevskogo," in *Roman N. G. Chernyshevskogo "Chto delat'?" (K 100-letiiu vykhoda v svet). Sbornik statei* (Shakhty: 1963), 37.

7. Eidelman, 1994, 63.

8. Among the more famous names are Inessa Armand and Aleksandra Kollontai.

9. Stites, 46; Engel, 74; G. Verkhovskii, *O romane N. G. Chernyshevskogo "Chto delat'?"* (Iaroslavl': 1959), 77–78.

10. Vera Pavlovna's social milieu also constitutes a point of departure. As Eidelman, 1990, p. 103, states, she was "the first female *raznochinets* to play a prominent role in the emancipation of women. She was the first woman character in Russian fiction with the pioneering task of initiating social change for women through economic independence. By establishing a sewing cooperative, the heroine traversed the bounds of limited feminism by becoming one of the 'new people in Russia.'" See also P. Reifman, *N. G. Chernyshevskii* (Tartu: 1973), 92–93.

11. I concentrate on the positive characters here, but this dichotomy is also evident among the negative characters: Julie is stronger, more assertive than Serge; Mar'ia Aleksevna, for all her negative qualities, is stronger than her weak, worthless husband.

12. "я теперь очень рад, что Наташа ободрила меня" (LP 106).

13. Engel, p. 74, for example, argues that Vera Pavlovna has to depend on men occasionally. She argues that this merely reflects the existing inequities in Russian society of the time, not prejudice on Chernyshevskii's part. Chernyshevskii's contemporary, N. V. Shelgunov, found Vera Pavlovna lacking in that she is dependent on men. See N. V. Shelgunov, "Russkie idealy, geroi i tipy," in *Shestidesiatye gody* (Moscow-Leningrad: 1940), 177.

14. Irina Paperno, *Chernyshevsky and the Age of Realism: A Study in the Semiotics of Behavior* (Stanford: 1988), p. 178, comes to a similar conclusion: "The women overtake the seemingly better informed men by embodying advanced ideas in action."

15. "мы все говорим и ничего не делаем. А ты позже нас всех стала думать об этом—и раньше всех решилась приняться за дело" (LP 117). One might also note that in Vera Pavlovna's sequence of dreams, there are many female figures, usually referred to as goddesses, but no gods. Although, the dreams must be treated as belonging only to Vera Pavlovna, this does reaffirm the consistent dichotomy of *What Is to Be Done?* in which women are constantly placed higher than men: indeed, no male counterparts are even mentioned. Kathryn Feuer, "What Is to Be Done about *What Is to Be Done?*" in *What Is to Be Done?* by N. G. Chernyshevsky (Ann Arbor, Mich.: 1986), xxii, argues that Rakhmetov may become the first male god. Based upon my arguments in the next chapter, this is not likely. Rakhmetov is a highly suspect character, in large part because he is male.

16. Some have even found fault with her. Feuer, p. ix, argues that Vera Pavlovna is often frivolous and sometimes a sexual tease. Fault-finding with Vera Pavlovna regarding her nonascetic habits has been a common theme dating back to Shelgunov. Shelgunov, p. 178, found Vera Pavlovna lacking as a positive image of the new woman because she lives like a sybarite and a spoiled child. In addition, he argues that Vera Pavlovna is anything but an advanced, liberated woman, and sees in her a woman placed on a pedestal. Soviet criticism often repeated Shelgunov's formulations, seeing in Vera Pavlovna's attachment to luxury evidence of a lower level of revolutionary consciousness.

17. Chernyshevskii's contemporary, Nikolai Strakhov, observed this aspect of the text, arguing that *What Is to Be Done?* is unlike other novels in that both (male) heroes are worthy of love. However, he uses this fact to find fault with the novel, arguing that, as a result, there are no differences among the characters. See N. N. Strakhov, "Schastlivye liudi," *Iz istorii literaturnago nigilizma. 1861–1865* (Saint Petersburg: 1890), 327.

18. Shelgunov, p. 175, stresses this aspect of the novel. See also N. Naumova, *Roman N. G. Chernyshevskogo "Chto delat'?"* (Leningrad: 1972), 29.

19. As Joe Andrew, *Women in Russian Literature, 1780–1863* (London: 1988), 158, correctly states, "The implicit polemic of the plot is that for too long women's stories have exclusively been concerned with love and marriage, with the latter more often than not being the desired end-point of their destinies, whether achieved or not."

20. Andrew, 158. Andrew, p. 159, views Vera Pavlovna's development as reaching its end point in her decision to become a doctor. As I shall argue, Vera Pavlovna continues to develop beyond this point as exemplified in the winter picnic scene.

21. See Stites, p. 46, and E. H. Carr, introduction to *What Is to Be Done?* by N. G. Chernyshevsky (New York: 1961), xiv. The statement occurs in Chenyshevskii's "The Russian at the Rendez-vous."

22. Chernyshevskii's attitude toward the family and children was discussed in the preceding chapter. His attitude toward sex is discussed in the next chapter.

23. For a differing view, see Charles Corbet "Réminiscences sandiennes dans *Que faire?* de Černyševskij," *Revue des études slaves* 43 (1976): 30. Corbet argues that whereas Sand treated love as a cardinal passion of life, Chernyshevskii treated it as a mere accessory of existence.

24. Many Soviet scholars denied that *What Is to Be Done?* had anything to do with love. For example, Riurikov argues that the novel is not a love story but a novel about the restructuring of social relations and the rebirth of man in the revolutionary struggle. See B. Riurikov, *N. G. Chernyshevskii. Kritiko-biograficheskii ocherk* (Moscow: 1961), 161. Verderevskaia takes a similar point of view when she argues that Chernyshevskii chose a

simple love story to fool the censor. See N. A. Verderevskaia, *Roman N. G. Chernyshevskogo "Chto delat'?" Posobie dlia uchashchikhsia* (Moscow: 1982), 52.

25. As Morson has observed, "N. G. Chernyshevsky's *What Is to Be Done?* is concerned primarily with the reconstruction of the family and only secondarily with communism." See Gary Saul Morson, *The Boundaries of Genre: Dostoevsky's Diary of a Writer and the Traditions of Literary Utopia* (Austin: 1981), 81.

26. Plimak makes a similar argument when he states that the themes of love and socialism are intertwined. Thus, Chernyshevskii devotes much space to the themes of love and women's liberation. See E. Plimak, "Ispytanie vremenem," *Voprosy literatury*, no. 2 (1978): 143.

27. Scholarly opinion is by no means unanimous in viewing Chernyshevskii as a denigrator of love. Many scholars have devoted substantial discussion to the importance of love for Chernyshevskii both in the novel and elsewhere. For an extended discussion, see Paperno, 1988, pp. 90, 157–58, and Naumova, pp. 29–37, 44, 47. See also Plimak, pp. 143–45; Stites, p. 94; Feuer, p. xvi; Richard Freeborn, *The Russian Revolutionary Novel: Turgenev to Pasternak* (Cambridge: 1982), 26; A. Lebedev, *Geroi Chernyshevskogo* (Moscow: 1962), 121; Irina Paperno, "The Myth of Reality in N. G. Černyševskij's Works and Life," in *Myth in Literature* (Columbus, Ohio: 1985): 155–56; V. N. Shul'gin, *Ocherki zhizni i tvorchestva N. G. Chernyshevskogo* (Moscow: 1956), 104; G. E. Tamarchenko, *Chernyshevskii-romanist* (Leningrad: 1976), 161.

28. Rakhmetov, it should be pointed out, not only fails to find love but renounces it, and thus proves himself unworthy.

29. Feuer, xxix.

30. Julie states to Vera Pavlovna: "But I know people like her very well: they have no feelings whatever that can withstand financial considerations" (Но я хорошо знаю таких людей, как ваша мать. У них никакие чувства не удержатся долго против денежных расчетов) (69; LP 31). Despite whatever good intentions she might have regarding Vera Pavlovna, Julie acts as a negative force in the novel. For example, Vera Pavlovna has the situation with her mother and Storeshnikov well under control before Julie and Serge come through the door (66). It is Julie's interference that prolongs the matter with Storeshnikov when she helps him and suggests to him that he marry Vera Pavlovna.

31. "Но жизнь—проза и расчет" (LP 35).

32. "(Верочка, это еще вовсе не любовь, это смесь разной гадости с разной дрянью,—любовь не то; не всякий тот любит женщину, кому неприятно получить от нее отказ,—любовь вовсе не то,—но Верочка еще не знает этого и растрогана)" (LP 44).

33. "Это не любовь, Вера Павловна" (LP 58).

34. "Вот, вы сами говорите, что это—лювовь. Только эта любовь—просто чувство, а не страсть. А что же такое любовь—страсть? Чем отличается страсть от простого чувства? Силою. Значит, если при простом чувстве, слабом, слишком слабом перед страстью, любовь ставит вас в такое отношение к человеку, что вы говорите: «лучше умереть, чем быть причиною мученья для него»; если простое чувство так говорит, что же скажет страсть, которая в тысячу раз сильнее? Она скажет: «скорее умру, чем—не то что потребую, не то что попрошу,—а скорее, чем допущу, чтобы этот человек сделал для меня что-нибудь, кроме того, что ему самому приятно; умру скорее, чем допущу, чтобы он для меня стал к чему-нибудь принуждать себя, в чем-нибудь стеснять себя». Вот такая страсть, которая говорит так, это—любовь. А если страсть не такая, то она страсть, но вовсе не любовь" (LP 58–59).

35. "Ведь думают, что любовь—тревожное чувство. А ты заснешь так тихо, как ребенок, и не будут ни смущать, ни волновать тебя никакие сны,—разве приснятся веселые детские игры, фанты, горелки или, может быть, танцы, только тоже веселые, беззаботные. Это другим странно, а ты не знаешь, что это странно, а я знаю, что это не странно. Тревога в любви—не самая любовь,—тревога в ней что-нибудь не так, как следует быть, а сама она весела и беззаботна" (LP 59).

36. "—Вера Павловна, за что же вы хотите разлучать наши нежные сердца?
—За то, что они нежные,—сказала Верочка, подавая руку Кирсанову, и, все еще продолжая улыбаться, задумалась: —а сумею ли я любить его, как вы? Ведь вы его очень любите?
—Я? я никого, кроме себя, не люблю, Вера Павловна.
—И его не любите?
—Жили—не ссорились, и того довольно.
—И он вас не любил?
—Не замечал что-то. Впрочем, спросим у него: ты любил, что ли, меня, Дмитрий?
—Особенной ненависти к тебе не имел" (LP 105).

37. "Они, когда соединяет их любовь, чем дольше живут вместе, тем больше и больше озаряются и согреваются ее поэзиею, до той самой поры, позднего вечера, когда заботы о выростающих детях будут уже слишком сильно поглощать их мысли. Тогда забота более сладкая, чем личное наслаждение, становится выше его, но до той поры оно все ростет. То, что прежние люди знали только на мимолетные месяцы, нынешние люди сохраняют в себе на долгие, долгие годы" (LP 271).

38. "Но вот что слишком немногими испытано, что очаровательность, которую всему дает любовь, вовсе не должна, по-настоящему, быть мимолетным явлением в жизни человека, что этот яркий свет жизни не должен озарять только эпоху искания, стремления, назовем хотя так: ухаживания, или сватания,—нет, что эта эпоха по-настоящему должна

быть только зарею, милою, прекрасною, но предшественницею дня, в котором несравненно больше и света и теплоты, чем в его предшественнице, свет и теплота которого долго, очень долго ростут, все ростут, и особенно теплота очень долго ростет, далеко за полдень все еще ростет" (LP 270).

39. "Отчего это так? А это уж секрет; я вам, пожалуй, выдам его. Хороший секрет, славно им пользоваться и не мудрено, только надобно иметь для этого чистое сердце и честную душу, да нынешнее понятие о правах человека, уважение к свободе того, с кем живешь. Только,—больше и секрета нет никакого. Смотри на жену, как смотрел на невесту, знай, что она каждую минуту имеет право сказать: «я недовольна тобою, прочь от меня»; смотри на нее так, и она через десять лет после твоей свадьбы будет внушать тебе такое же поэтическое чувство, как невеста, нет, более поэтическое, более идеальное в хорошем смысле слова. Признавай ее свободу так же открыто и формально, и без всяких оговорок, как признаешь свободу твоих друзей чувствовать или не чувствовать дружбу к тебе, и тогда,—через десять лет, через двадцать лет после свадьбы ты будешь ей так же мил, как был женихом" (LP 271).

40. "Это постоянное, сильное, здоровое возбуждение нерв, оно необходимо развивает нервную систему . . . поэтому умственные и нравственные силы ростут во мне от моей любви" (LP 272).

41. Andrew, 176.

42. See, for example, Ralph E. Matlaw, who, in referring to *What Is to Be Done?* in his introduction to *Notes from Underground and The Grand Inquisitor*, by Fyodor Dostoevsky (New York: 1960), x, states: "Here the ideas of reason, rationalism, man acting for his own advantage, the doctrine of environment, the notion of man's perfectibility and his ceaseless striving toward a perfect, harmonious society are artlessly repeated." Likewise, Joseph Frank, *Dostoevsky: The Stir of Liberation, 1860–1865* (Princeton: 1986), 32, argues that Chernyshevskii propounds a simple-minded materialism that sees man as totally subservient to the laws of nature, a materialism that left no room for the irreducible and irrational in human behavior. See also Carr, p. xi; Isaiah Berlin, introduction to *Roots of Revolution*, by Franco Venturi (New York: 1960), xxiii; Paperno, 1988, p. 107.

43. Naumova, pp. 68–69, deals with this question and argues that if this were true, it would go against one of the basic ideas of the novel. She states: "The internal spiritual struggle of such heroes is not a struggle of feeling and reason in favor of reason but a struggle of contradictory feelings. Reason helps to make a *choice*, to liberate and give strength to those *personal aspirations*, which lead to 'real' and not 'fantastic' happiness."

44. "«Как это странно,—думает Верочка:—ведь я сама все это передумала, перечувствовала, что он говорит и о бедных, и о женщинах, и о том, как надобно любить,—откуда я это взяла? Или это было в книгах, которые я читала? Нет, там не то: там все это или с сомнениями,

или с такими оговорками, и все это как будто что-то необыкновенное, невероятное. Как будто мечты, которые хороши, да только не сбудутся! А мне казалось, что это просто, проще всего, что это самое обыкновенное, без чего нельзя быть, что это верно все так будет, что это вернее всего! А ведь я думала, что это самые лучшие книги. Ведь вот Жорж Занд—такая добрая, благонравная,—а у нее все это только мечты!" (LP 59).

45. "Или у Диккенса—у него это есть, только он как будто этого не надеется; только желает, потому что добрый, а сам знает, что этому нельзя быть. Как же они не знают, что без этого нельзя, что это в самом деле надобно так сделать и что это непременно сделается, чтобы вовсе никто не был ни беден, ни несчастен. Да разве они зтого не говорят? Нет, им только жалко, а они думают, что в самом деле так и останется, как теперь,—немного получше будет, а все так же" (LP 59–60).

46. Klenin comes to a different conclusion. She argues that *What Is to Be Done?* is engaged in an intense polemical with Druzhinin's *Polinka Saks* regarding the usefulness of didactic literature. As part of her argument she states: "The history of Vera Pavlovna's consciousness-raising-through-literature shows that Černyševskij really hoped that good reading would make the reader live better." Emily Klenin, "On the Ideological Sources of *Čto delat'?*: Sand, Družinin, Leroux," *Zeitschrift für slavische Philologie* 51, no. 2 (1991): 384.

47. "Нет, Верочка, это не странно, что передумала и приняла к сердцу все это ты, простенькая девочка, не слышавшая и фамилий-то тех людей, которые стали этому учить и доказали, что этому так надо быть, что это непременно так будет, что этого не может не быть; не странно, что ты поняла и приняла к сердцу эти мысли, которых не могли тебе ясно представить твои книги: твои книги писаны людьми, которые учились этим мыслям, когда они были еще мыслями; эти мысли казались удивительны, восхитительны—и только" (LP 60).

48. Paperno, 1988, p. 178, comes to a similar conclusion: "Whereas wisdom is associated with simple young girls and women (Vera and Julie), the claims of publicly recognized men of knowledge are dismissed throughout the novel as mere semblances of real wisdom." See also Iu. M. Prozorov, "N. G. Chernyshevskii," in *Istoriia russkoi literatury XIX veka. Vtoraia polovina* (Moscow: 1987), 152, who argues that Chernyshevskii believed that women's nature is primordially high and thus Vera does not need recourse to theory like men do.

49. "шутки шутками, а ведь в самом деле лучше всего жить, как ты говоришь. Только откуда ты набралась таких мыслей? Я-то их знаю, да я помню, откуда я их вычитал. А ведь до ваших рук эти книги не доходят. В тех, которые я тебе давал, таких частностей не было. Слышать?—не от кого было. Ведь едва ли не первого меня ты встретила из порядочных людей" (LP 95).

50. “Ах, мой милый, да разве трудно до этого додуматься? Ведь я видала семейную жизнь” (LP 95).

51. “разумеется, постороннему человеку трудно выдержать такие разыскиванья дольше пяти минут, даже один из споривших, романтик, не выдержал больше полутора часов, убежал к танцующим” (LP 143).

52. “гипотетического вывода”; “в смысле отвлеченном” (LP 187).

53. “Кирсанов сидел, рассматривая свои пальцы, будто каждый из них—отвлеченная гипотеза” (LP 188).

54. “Мастерская—разве это моя личная жизнь? Это дело—не мое дело, чужое. Я занимаюсь им не для себя, а для других” (LP 261). Lebedev, p. 120, refers to this passage in his study but argues that despite Vera Pavlovna's words here, Chernyshevskii convincingly shows in the novel that her whole life is namely in the co-op.

55. “стали в ней серьезно являться, получать для нее практическую требовательность такие мысли, которые прежде были только теоретически известны ей и в сущности не затрогивали ее внутреннюю жизнь: чего нельзя делать, о том и не думаешь серьезно” (LP 264).

56. That is, her marriage to Kirsanov. In many respects, the co-op functions as a surrogate for the erotic side of marriage. Once Vera Pavlovna has attained a fulfilling relationship, she no longer needs the co-op and abandons it.

57. “Да, теперь Вера Павловна нашла себе дело, о котором не могла бы она думать прежде: . . . Вот какого рода были эти мысли, которые теперь стали живо чувствоваться Верою Павловною и служить мотивами для деятельности” (LP 263–64).

58. “Это было бы очень важно, если бы явились, наконец, женщины-медики. Они были бы очень полезны для всех женщин. Женщине гораздо легче говорить с женщиною, чем с мужчиною. Сколько предотвращалось бы тогда страданий, смертей, сколько несчастий. Надобно попытаться” (LP 264).

59. For a brief discussion of Chernyshevskii's dislike of abstractions see E. Lampert, *Sons Against Fathers: Studies in Russian Radicalism and Revolution* (Oxford: 1965), 156–58.

60. “Это может казаться странно, но только для того, кто не вникнет в сущность моих отношений к молодежи, которой я отдавал столько времени. Во-первых, у меня не было никаких личных отношений с этими молодыми людьми; когда я сидел с ними, я не чувствовал перед собою людей, а видел лишь несколько отвлеченных типов, которые обмениваются мыслями” (LP 239).

61. “Но то, что делается по расчету, по чувству долга, по усилию воли, а не по влечению натуры, выходит безжизненно. Только убивать что-нибудь можно этим средством, как ты и делал над собою, а делать живое—нельзя” (LP 189).

62. Perhaps relevant here is Tamarchenko's argument that for Chernyshevskii, without the experience of love, a person does not have the ability to deal with real people, but only abstractions. See Tamarchenko, p. 161.

63. "Привязанность возобновилась, и сильнее прежнего; но борьба с нею не представляла никакого серьезного мучения, . . . А в эту неделю уж наполовину заглушено развитие страсти; через месяц все пройдет. Он очень доволен. Он участвует в разговоре так непринужденно, что сам радуется своим успехам, и от этого довольства непринужденность его еще увеличивается" (LP 155).

64. "чувство влечет его остаться" (LP 168).

65. "Потому вернее будет удалиться" (LP 168).

66. "Тяжеловато и очень хитро это дело: уйти из виду так, чтобы не заметили твоего движения, когда смотрят на тебя во все глаза, а нечего делать, надобно действовать так. А впрочем, по кирсановской теории, это и не мучительно, а даже приятно; ведь чем труднее дело, тем больше радуешься (по самолюбию) своей силе и ловкости, исполняя его удачно" (LP 169).

67. "какое же наслаждение было Кирсанову, как теоретику, любоваться своею ловкостью на практике. Эгоисты и материалисты, ведь они всё делают собственно только в удовольствие себе. Да, и Кирсанов мог, положа руку на сердце, сказать, что он делает свою штуку в удовольствие себе: он радовался на свое искусство и молодечество" (LP 170).

68. "Еще какой-нибудь месяц, . . . и дело будет в шляпе" (LP 170).

69. "Со мною нельзя так говорить,—Вера Павловна встала,—я не позволю говорить с собою темными словами. Осмелься сказать, что ты хотел сказать!" (LP 195).

70. "не вдруг соберешься с мыслями" (LP 197).

71. "Старик изумился, когда услышал от Кирсанова, что причина болезни его дочери—любовь к Соловцову. . . . Да и вообще можно ли умирать от любви? Такие экзальтированности не могли казаться правдоподобны человеку, привыкшему вести исключительно практическую жизнь, смотреть на все с холодным благоразумием. Долго возился с ним Кирсанов, он все говорил: «Фантазия ребенка, который помучится и забудет»" (LP 305).

72. Freeborn, p. 26, comes to a similar conclusion regarding certain aspects of the novel. He argues that the appeal to reason resolves itself into a far more emotional, impassioned, and genuine summons to make the pursuit of happiness the true aim of life and states that the "plea for what Chernyshevsky calls 'development' as the clue to universal happiness is not rationally argued but emotionally proclaimed. For in the end Chernyshevsky respected the heart as much as the head."

73. In addition to the evidence presented here, Chernyshevskii also resisted the notion that human behavior and feelings were reducible and

calculable in his publicistic work. For example, in "The Anthropological Principle," Chernyshevskii critiques Mill's excessive rationalism, stating: "Why did he [Mill] do so? Simply because of his excessively strong desire that the development of social life should proceed on absolutely rational lines. This does not happen in important affairs either in the life of an individual or in the life of a nation. Only minor things are done quite coolly, calmly, deliberately and rationally." He further states: "Where passion enters, deliberation and coolness are impossible—this is a truth well known from copybook maxims. It is also well known that every important public question rouses passion." Finally he states: "[T]he impression created by an abstract idea is different from that created by a fact which affects the senses. A tangible object has a much stronger effect than the abstract conception of that object. A man who calmly considers what he will do under given circumstances rarely retains all his coolness when those circumstances actually arise, if the matter is at all important." See Nikolay Chernyshevsky, "The Anthropological Principle in Philosophy," *Selected Philosophical Essays* (Moscow: 1953), 59–61.

74. Andrew M. Drozd, "Büchner and Chernyshevskii: A Contrast of Ideas," *Germano-Slavica* 9, nos. 1–2 (1995–96): 79–102.

75. Lampert, 144. James P. Scanlan, "Nicholas Chernyshevsky and Philosophical Materialism in Russia," *Journal of the History of Philosophy* 8, no. 1 (January 1970): 71, 73, also notes that Chernyshevskii did not use the term "materialist" to describe himself and that Chernyshevskii's works prior to 1860 show relatively little trace of anything that can be called materialism. He argues that this was due to the censorship.

76. Chernyshevsky, 132–33.

77. This is Lampert's criterion, p. 144, for labeling Chernyshevskii a materialist. Lampert, pp. 299–300, rejects the label "materialist" for Vogt, Büchner, and Moleschott, arguing instead that theirs was a physiological or biological philosophy.

78. Maurice Mandelbaum, *History, Man and Reason: A Study in Nineteenth-Century Thought* (Baltimore: 1971), 21, 23. Mandelbaum also discusses the inconsistency in usage and various means of the term "materialism." In particular, the philosophical usage of the term should not be confused with the popular definition of materialism as a love of money or material things.

79. Mandelbaum, 23. Mandelbaum, p. 21, also rejects the notion that materialism can be defined as equal to the doctrine that all mental impressions resulted from the activities of the bodily organs. He argues that idealists such as Lotze acknowledged this dependence but clearly were not materialists. Rather, he defines materialism, p. 22, as a "metaphysical position. Materialists, like idealists, seek to state what constitutes the ultimate nature of reality, and are willing to distinguish between 'appearance' and that which is self-existent and underlies appearance."

80. Perhaps it is worth noting that Frederick C. Copleston in his discussion of Chernyshevskii does not use the term "materialist" to refer to him. He does state, p. 102, that "[t]he Nihilists can be described as materialists, in the sense that they rejected as fable belief in spiritual realities such as God or an immortal soul in the human being." That is, he equates materialism with the rejection of a theistic position. However, in the section specifically devoted to Chernyshevskii he avoids use of the term. See Frederick C. Copleston, *Philosophy in Russia: From Herzen to Lenin and Berdyaev* (Notre Dame, Ind.: 1986), 102–11. Charles Moser in his 1964 book *Antinihilism in the Russian Novel of the 1860s* used the term "materialist" to describe Chernyshevskii. With time, however, he obviously found the term unacceptable because in his more recent book, *Esthetics as Nightmare* (1989), he has dropped it with regard to Chernyshevskii and substituted the term "monist." With regard to Chernyshevskii's supposed philosophical mentor, Ludwig Feuerbach, many insist on the term "materialist," but many insist that it cannot be used. Feuerbach himself expressly condemned materialism. For further discussion see Mandelbaum, p. 27; Frederick Gregory, "Scientific versus Dialectical Materialism: A Clash of Ideologies in Nineteenth-Century German Radicalism," *Isis* 68, no. 242 (1977): 210.

81. See, for example, Joseph Frank, "N. G. Chernyshevsky: A Russian Utopia," *Southern Review*, New Series 3, no. 1 (1967): 77. See also Tamarchenko, p. 182, who claims that throughout the novel, Lopukhov acts as the mouthpiece of the author. He further states, p. 241, that Chernyshevskii stresses in every possible way his solidarity with his heroes: he considers himself a part of their circle and stresses full agreement with their views.

82. Frederick Gregory, *Scientific Materialism in Nineteenth-Century Germany* (Boston: 1977), 106, 210, notes that "objectivity" was the watchword of the German materialists.

83. "Это всегда так бывает: если явилось в человеке настроение искать чего-нибудь, он во всем находит то, чего ищет; пусть не будет никакого следа, а он так вот и видит ясный след; пусть не будет и тени, а он все-таки видит не только тень того, что ему нужно, но и все, что ему нужно, видит в самых несомненных чертах, и эти черты с каждым новым взглядом, с каждою новою мыслью его делаются все яснее" (LP 192).

84. "Но нет, Марья Алексевна не удовлетворилась надзором, а устроила даже пробу, будто учила «логику», которую и я учил наизусть, говорящую: «наблюдение явлений, каковые происходят сами собою, должно быть поверяемо опытами, производимыми по обдуманному плану, для глубочайшего проникновения в тайны таковых отношений»,—и устроила она эту пробу так, будто читала Саксона Грамматика, рассказывающего, как испытывали Гамлета в лесу девицею" (LP 67).

85. "научного инстинкта любознательности" (LP 121).

86. "но я как человек положительный интересуюсь более существенным. Я рассматривал ее бюст" (LP 24).

87. "Докажи. Я человек положительный и без доказательств не верю" (LP 25).

88. "уличаем в огюст-контизме" (LP 143).

89. Although Chernyshevskii is sometimes labeled a positivist, Chernyshevskii expressed nothing but contempt for the positivist philosophy of August Comte. See, for example, his remarks on Comte and Comteanism in his letter to his son (14:651–52). V. V. Zenkovsky, *A History of Russian Philosophy* (New York: 1953), 1:326, states an awareness of this fact, but concludes nevertheless that "his essential positivism is not open to question." Scanlan, 1970, p. 68, disputes his interpretation, noting that Zenkovsky misquotes Chernyshevskii and that Chernyshevskii consistently displayed a passionate dissatisfaction with Comte and his doctrines. See also Venturi, pp. 184–86, who discusses Chernyshevskii's extreme displeasure with positivist philosophy, especially that of Spencer.

90. "А я, брат, теперь с зрительным нервом покончил и принимаюсь за следующую пару. А ты на чем остановился?

—Да мне еще надобно будет кончить работу над. . . .

И пошли анатомические и физиологические термины" (LP 99)

91. "законах исторического прогресса, без которых не обходился тогда ни один разговор в подобных кружках" (LP 123).

92. "И вот они для пользы любимой науки,—они ужасные охотники бранить медицину, только посвящают все свои силы ее пользе,—они отказываются от богатства, даже от довольства, и сидят в гошпиталях, делая, видите ли, интересные для науки наблюдения, режут лягушек, вскрывают сотни трупов ежегодно и при первой возможности обзаводятся химическими лабораториями" (LP 50). In his studies on Chernyshevskii, Adam Ulam adopts a traditional approach to *What Is to Be Done?* He does come very close to a key point when he states "The author's biases, like many of his characteristics, are both disarming and frightening; they are expressed with a disingenuousness that would almost make one believe he is satirizing his own convictions." See Adam B. Ulam, *Ideologies and Illusions: Revolutionary Thought from Herzen to Solzhenitsyn* (Cambridge: 1976), 47.

93. "больше, разумеется, не слушали даже обрызгали водою Лопухова и Алексея Петровича, когда они уже очень восхитились великою важностью минерального удобрения; но Алексей Петрович и Лопухов толковали о своих ученостях непоколебимо. Кирсанов плохо помогал им, был больше, даже вовсе на стороне дам, и они втроем играли, пели, хохотали до глубокой ночи, когда, уставши, развели, наконец, и непоколебимых ревнителей серьезного разговора" (LP 123).

94. "Против морфия в достаточном количестве не устоит никакое крушение духа; на этот раз двух пилюль оказалось достаточно, вот уж одолевает дремота. Следовательно, крушение души своею силою приблизительно равнялось, по материалистическому взгляду Лопухова, четырем стаканам крепкого кофе, против которых Лопухову также было мало одной пилюли, а трех пилюль много. Он заснул, смеясь над этим сравнением" (LP 183).

95. "это в первый раз снабдил он ее торжеством и, уходя, оставил ее очень довольною—не деньгами, а собственно торжеством: есть чисто идеальные радости у самых погрязших в материализме сердец, чем и доказывается, что материалистическое объяснение жизни неудовлетворительно" (LP 81). Chernyshevskii is playing with the various meanings of materialism here, both its meaning of a love of money and its meaning as a particular philosophy.

96. See James Allen Rogers, "Russian Opposition to Darwinism in the Nineteenth Century," *Isis* 65, no. 229 (1974): 490; Daniel P. Todes, *Darwin without Malthus: The Struggle for Existence in Russian Evolutionary Thought* (New York: 1989), 37–38; Alexander Vucinich, *Darwin in Russian Thought* (Berkeley: 1988), 148.

97. "(это уж грубый материализм, замечаю я вместе с проницательным читателем)" (LP 272).

98. An answer may also lie in Lermontov's famous introduction to the second edition of *Hero of Our Time:* "[I]n a decent book open abuse cannot occur; . . . modern education has evolved a much sharper weapon—which, though almost invisible, is nevertheless lethal and which, under the guise of flattery, deals an inescapable and accurate blow" (Nabokov translation). That is to say, despite Chernyshevskii's reputation for being blatantly didactic, he was quite willing to use the subtleties of literature to get his point across and may have consciously refrained from an open statement in the spirit of Lermontov's admonition.

99. See, for example, Skaftymov, who argues that Chernyshevskii valued the hedonistic views of Bentham and Mill and tried to propagate them in the novel by means of his theory of rational egoism. A. P. Skaftymov, "Roman *Chto delat'?*" in *N. G. Chernyshevskii. Sbornik. Neizdannye stat'i, materialy, vospominaniia* (Saratov: 1926), 110.

100. See Frank, 1967, pp. 72–75; Ulam p. 34; Frederick G. Barghoorn, "The Philosophic Outlook of Chernyshevski: Materialism and Utilitarianism," *American Slavic and East European Review* 6, nos. 18–19 (December 1947): 48–52; James P. Scanlan, "Nikolaj Černyševskij and Soviet Philosophy," *Studies in Soviet Thought* 7, no. 1 (March 1967): 8–9. Occasionally other sources are cited for Chernyshevskii's supposed utilitarianism. Rufus W. Mathewson Jr., "The Hero and Society: The Literary Definitions (1855–1865, 1934–39)," in *Continuity and Change in Russian and*

Soviet Thought (Cambridge: 1955), 261, traces it to the French rationalists. N. G. O. Pereira, *The Thought and Teachings of N. G. Černyševskij* (The Hague: 1975), 37–39, while discussing Bentham and Mill also notes others such as Holbach. Lukács argues that Chernyshevskii operates within the tradition of Holbach and Helvétius but goes further in dealing with the question of rational egoism. See George Lukács, "Tschernyschewskijs Roman 'Was Tun?'," *Der russische Realismus in der Weltliteratur* (Berlin: 1952), 120.

101. See, for example, Copleston, pp. 107–8; Barghoorn, pp. 48–49; Ulam, p. 34. Scanlan, 1967, pp. 16–17, does question this traditional view to some degree. Scanlan does conclude that Chernyshevskii was a utilitarian, but he also notes that not only did he not simply borrow and vulgarize, but he actually went far beyond the Englishmen and dealt with problems they ignored. In a later article Scanlan traces many of Chernyshevskii's views to Rousseau's influence. See James P. Scanlan, "Chernyshevsky and Rousseau," in *Western Philosophical Systems in Russian Literature: A Collection of Critical Studies* (Los Angeles: 1979), 103–120. Lampert, 149–53, argues that Chernyshevskii followed Bentham to a certain degree but that he inverted Bentham's hedonistic calculus. In sum he argues that Chernyshevskii was no Benthamite.

102. This is with the exception of Chernyshevskii's translation of Mill's *Principles of Political Economy*, which appeared in *Sovremennik*. This translation and Chernyshevskii's accompanying commentary appear in volume 9 of his *PSS*. Chernyshevskii explicitly states that he does not find everything in Mill satisfactory and that Mill's system is not his. He stresses that he translated Mill's work as a public service and to spark a discussion of political economy in Russian society (9:7).

103. Chernyshevsky, 69. In one of his letters from Siberia, Chernyshevskii labels Mill, along with Darwin and Spencer, "small fry" (*meliuzga*), rating him slightly higher than Auguste Comte, whom he labels a fool (15:23). Barghoorn, p. 46, demonstrates an awareness of Chernyshevskii's opinion of Mill as a second-rate thinker. However, pp. 48–49, he views Bentham and Mill as sources of Chernyshevskii's utilitarianism all the same.

104. This would mean viewing Chernyshevskii as an original thinker, something Western scholarship, with its traditional insistence upon viewing him as a mere synthesizer and vulgarizer of the ideas of others, has not been willing to do. The exception would be Scanlan, 1967, pp. 16–17, who does view Chernyshevskii as ahead of his time in his attempt to distinguish between real and artificial desires.

105. I deal with the supposed utilitarianism of his *Aesthetic Relations* in chapter 1.

106. Chernyshevsky, 99.

107. Ibid., 101.

108. Ibid., 119–20. Although Chernyshevskii does argue that people are egoists in the sense that they are subjective beings, he did not advocate philosophical egoism; that is, the prescriptive theory that people should act only in their own interests, even at the expense of others.

109. I am relying upon a definition of "utilitarianism" as ethical theory primarily concerned with the practical question "What ought a man to do?" Utilitarianism, strictly defined, is concerned with not only the happiness of the performer of an action but also the happiness of everyone affected by it. Thus the pleasure-pain calculus figures largely into utilitarian deliberations. In short, utilitarianism is a prescriptive ethical theory concerned with producing the best possible consequences for all. In this sense, utilitarianism is distinct from egoism, which holds that man should pursue his own self-interest, even at the expense of others. For a brief overview of utilitarianism, see H[enry] R. W[est], "Philosophical Schools and Doctrines," *Encyclopaedia Britannica,* 15th ed., 30:644–46. Discussions of utilitarianism provided within the treatments of individual philosophers can be found in Frederick Copleston, *A History of Philosophy* (Garden City, N.Y.: 1985).

110. Chernyshevsky, 125.

111. See Copleston, 1986, p. 108, who argues on the basis of "The Anthropological Principle" that Chernyshevskii espoused a utilitarian ethical theory.

112. Belova argues that most scholars have misunderstood Chernyshevskii's statements. For example, she argues that Chernyshevskii did not recognize "the general good (*obshchee blago*)" but rather "the good of all (*blago vsekh*)." See N. M. Belova, "Roman N. G. Chernyshevskogo «Chto delat'?» i prosvetitel'skaia literatura XVIII veka," in *N. G. Chernyshevskii. Istoriia. Filosofiia. Literatura* (Saratov: 1994), 120.

113. Chernyshevsky, 126.

114. Ibid., 127.

115. There is nothing surprising about this. This work appeared one year before the Emancipation Proclamation and Chernyshevskii, as is well known, did everything possible to persuade educated society to produce a just settlement.

116. For a differing view see Paperno, 1988, pp. 107–8, who argues that Chernyshevskii treated the utilitarian calculus as a psychological law governing human behavior. Regarding both "The Anthropological Principle" and *What Is to Be Done?* she also states: "Chernyshevsky maintained that every act or impulse of individual human beings arises as the direct realization of the calculus of pains and pleasures, which prevails over spontaneity and emotional immediacy of any kind. Thus, determinism rules human life. . . . The role of free choice is limited, if not eliminated; with it, painful doubts about matters that cannot be controlled or accounted for are eliminated as well."

117. Lukács, p. 108, claims that it is the novel's central point. A. V. Lunacharskii, "Romany N. G. Chernyshevskogo," *Stat'i o Chernyshevskom* (Moscow: 1958), 95, argues that "rational egoism" is one of the more important doctrines of the novel. See also Philip Pomper, *The Russian Revolutionary Intelligentsia* (Arlington Heights, Ill.: 1970), 73, who argues that Chernyshevskii offered a portrait of utilitarian ethics in operation with his novel.

118. "теория расчета выгод" (LP 68–69). The term "rational egoism" is never actually used in *What Is to Be Done?* It is the creation of later observers. Although this term is often equated with utilitarianism and is meant as a distinction from pure egoism, it should be noted that Lopukhov's statements at this point in the novel amount to nothing more than pure, naked egoism, with the rational element lacking. Indeed, the narrator refers to it simply as "egoism." Be that as it may, the appellation "utilitarian" has been traditionally applied to both the characters' and the author's ethical theory.

119. "То, что называют возвышенными чувствами, идеальными стремлениями,—все это в общем ходе жизни совершенно ничтожно перед стремлением каждого к своей пользе, и в корне само состоит из того же стремления к пользе" (LP 68).

120. "Нет, Вера Павловна: эта теория холодна, но учит человека добывать тепло" (LP 69).

121. Lopukhov's statements do not at all match Chernyshevskii's own. Compare Chernyshevskii's comments on the cold egoist quoted earlier. Compare also his statement from his own review of *Aesthetic Relations:* "That is why science regards man's noble striving for everything that is lofty and beautiful as being as essential a need as eating and drinking. It also loves—for science is not abstract and not cold: it loves and hates, pursues and protects—it loves noble people who concern themselves with man's moral needs and grieve when they see how often those needs remain unsatisfied, as much as it loves those people who concern themselves with the material needs of their fellow men" (Chernyshevsky, 411).

122. "Рассчитывайте, что для вас полезнее" (LP 70).

123. "Положим, вы правы,—да, вы правы. Все поступки, которые я могу разобрать, объясняются выгодою. Но ведь эта теория холодна" (LP 69).

124. "Итак, эта теория, которой я не могу не допустить, обрекает людей на жизнь холодную, безжалостную, прозаичную?" (LP 69).

125. "Хорошо. Посмотрим, не поймаю ли я вас на вопросах о себе" (LP 70).

126. "Он постоянно отыскивает самые затаенные причины своих действий, и ему приносит удовольствие подводить их под его теорию эгоизма. Впрочем, это общая привычка всей нашей компании. Мой Александр также охотник разбирать себя в этом духе. Если бы вы послушали, как он объясняет свой образ действий относительно меня и

Дмитрия Сергеича в течение трех лет! По его словам, он все делал из эгоистического расчета, для собственного удовольствия. И я уж давно приобрела эту привычку. Только это несколько меньше занимает меня и Александра, чем Дмитрия Сергеича, мы с ним совершенно сходимся, но у него больше влечения к этому. Да если послушать нас, мы все трое такие эгоисты, каких до сих пор свет не производил. А может быть, это и правда? может быть, прежде не было таких эгоистов? Да, кажется" (LP 244).

127. "Делаю эту заметку потому, что Дмитрий Сергеич любил такие замечания. Я хочу подольститься к вам, мой друг" (LP 247).

128. "По кирсановской теории эгоизма;" "теория, которой держался Кирсанов;" "Кирсанов по своей терминологии выразился бы так" (LP 168–69).

129. "материалист, все только думает о выгодах. Он и действительно думал все о выгодах, вместо высоких поэтических и пластических мечтаний он занимался такими любовными мечтами, которые приличны грубому материалисту" (LP 97). Chernyshevskii plays on the various meanings of these terms. In particular, he uses "materialist" here, which has the popular meaning of one concerned with money or material things and thus overlaps with the term "egoist."

130. "Эгоисты и материалисты, ведь они всё делают собственно только в удовольствие себе" (LP 170).

131. "Мерцалов долго думал, тоже искал «но» для уполномочения себя на такой риск и тоже не мог придумать никакого «но»" (LP 103).

132. "А теперь, покончив свое (как эгоист, всегда прежде всего думающий о себе, и о других лишь тогда, когда уже нечего думать о себе), он мог приняться и за чужое, то есть за ее раздумье" (LP 182).

133. "а нечего делать, надобно действовать так. А впрочем, по кирсановской теории, это и не мучительно, а даже приятно; ведь чем труднее дело, тем больше радуешься (по самолюбию) своей силе и ловкости, исполняя его удачно" (LP 169).

134. "Приятно человеку, как теоретику, наблюдать, какие штуки выкидывает его эгоизм на практике" (LP 189).

135. "Но ни Лопухову, ни Кирсанову недосуг было стать теоретиками и делать эти приятные наблюдения: практика-то приходилась для обоих довольно тяжеловатая" (LP 189).

136. "Вот, хоть бы эти письма. Я к этим штукам отчасти уж попривык, водя дружбу с такими госпожами и господами" (LP 249).

137. "О, если бы я не знал, что вы правы! Да, как это было бы хорошо, если б вы не были правы. Я сказал бы ей, что мы не сошлись в условиях или что вы не понравились мне!—и только, и мы с нею стали бы надеяться встретить другой случай избавления. А теперь что я ей скажу?" (LP 84).

138. "Но все-таки г-же Б. пришлось бы иметь довольно хлопот, быть может и некоторые неприятные разговоры; надобно было бы одолжаться по чужому делу людьми, услуги которых лучше приберечь для своих дел. Кто обязан и какой благоразумный человек захочет поступать не так, как г-жа Б.? мы нисколько не вправе осуждать ее" (LP 84–85).

139. Fet was somewhat close to the mark when he stated: "Even worse is the circumstance that the theory of egoism turns out to be harmful even for the circle which advocates it." See A. A. Fet, "*Chto delat'?* Iz rasskazov o novykh liudiakh. Roman N. G. Chernyshevskogo," *Literaturnoe nasledstvo* 25–26 (1936): 500.

140. "Лопухов находил, что его теория дает безошибочные средства к анализу движений человеческого сердца, и я, признаюсь, согласен с ним в этом; в те долгие годы, как я считаю ее за истину, она ни разу не ввела меня в ошибку и ни разу не отказалась легко открыть мне правду, как бы глубоко ни была затаена правда какого-нибудь человеческого дела. Правда и то, что теория эта сама-то дается не очень легко: нужно и пожить и подумать, чтоб уметь понять ее" (LP 183).

141. "убедил отца отпустить меня в Медицинскую академию, вместо того чтобы определять в чиновники. Как это произошло? Мы с отцом видели, что медики живут гораздо лучше канцелярских чиновников и столоначальников, выше которых не подняться бы мне. Вот вам причина, по которой я очутился и оставался в Академии—хороший кусок хлеба. Без этого расчета я не поступил бы в Академию и не оставался бы в ней" (LP 68).

142. "Да. Это украшение; оно и полезно для успеха дела; но дело обыкновенно бывает и без этого украшения, а без расчета не бывает. Любовь к науке была только результатом, возникавшим из дела, а не причиною его; причина была одна—выгода" (LP 69).

143. "И вот они для пользы любимой науки . . . они отказываются от богатства, даже от довольства" (LP 50).

144. Verderevskaia, p. 37, argues that, despite his disclaimers, Lopukhov sacrifices a lot because of Vera Pavlovna. See also Plimak, pp. 146–47, who argues that although the characters espouse a philosophy of egoism, in practice they act against it.

145. "Но он действительно держал себя так, как, по мнению Марьи Алексевны, мог держать себя только человек в ее собственном роде" (LP 72).

146. "Да, Марья Алексевна была права, находя много родственного себе в Лопухове" (LP 72).

147. "Я понимаю, как сильно компрометируется Лопухов в глазах просвещенной публики сочувствием Марьи Алексевны к его образу мыслей" (LP 72).

148. "Действительно, из разговора Лопухова с Верочкою обнаруживается, что образ его мыслей гораздо легче мог показаться хорош

людям вроде Марьи Алексевны, чем красноречивым партизанам разных прекрасных идей. Лопухов видел вещи в тех самых чертах, в каких представляются они всей массе рода человеческого, кроме партизанов прекрасный идей. . . . Сходство их понятий было так велико, что просвещенные и благородные романисты, журналисты и другие поучатели нашей публики давно провозгласили: «эти люди вроде Лопухова ничем не разнятся от людей вроде Марьи Алексевны». Если столь просвещенные и благородные писатели так поняли людей вроде Лопухова, то неужели мы будем осуждать Марью Алексевну за то, что она не рассмотрела в Лопухове ничего, кроме того, что поняли в людях его разряда лучшие наши писатели, мыслители и назидатели?" (LP 73).

149. "Но все это я говорю только в оправдание недосмотра Марьи Алексевны, не успевшей вовремя раскусить, что за человек Лопухов, а никак не в оправдание самому Лопухову. Лопухова оправдывать было бы нехорошо, а почему нехорошо, узришь ниже. Люди, которые, не оправдывая его, захотели бы, по человеколюбию своему, извинить его, не могли бы извинить. Например, они сказали бы в извинение ему, что он был медик и занимался естественными науками, а это располагает к материалистическому взгляду. Но такое извинение очень плохо. Мало ли какие науки располагают к такому же взгляду? . . . Стало быть, Лопухов не избавляется от своей вины" (LP 74).

150. "Сострадательные люди, не оправдывающие его, могли бы также сказать ему в извинение, что он не совершенно лишен некоторых похвальных признаков: сознательно и твердо решился отказаться от всяких житейских выгод и почетов для работы на пользу другим, находя, что наслаждение такою работою—лучшая выгода для него; на девушку, которая была так хороша, что он влюбился в нее, он смотрел таким чистым взглядом, каким не всякий брат глядит на сестру; но против этого извинения его материализму надобно сказать, что ведь и вообще нет ни одного человека, который был бы совершенно без всяких признаков чего-нибудь хорошего, и что материалисты, каковы бы там они ни были, все-таки материалисты, а этим самым уже решено и доказано, что они люди низкие и безнравственные, которых извинять нельзя, потому что извинять их значило бы потворствовать материализму. Итак, не оправдывая Лопухова, извинить его нельзя" (LP 74). This passage also clearly relates to Chernyshevskii's own personal situation. Whenever he attempted to defend the younger generation in print, he was immediately charged with endorsing and propagating materialism.

CHAPTER FOUR

1. In the rough draft the note is brought to Vera Pavlovna by one Vladimir Kopantsev in a third minichapter at the beginning of the novel.

This minichapter was later removed and the so-called foreword, which had previously been fourth, was moved into third place. For a discussion of the textual changes Chernyshevskii made, see T. I. Ornatskaia, "Roman N. G. Chernyshevskogo *Chto delat'?* (K istorii teksta)," *Russkaia literatura,* no. 3 (1977): 121. She also notes that Rakhmetov was not among those originally included in the list of personages Chernyshevskii created when beginning the novel. Rakhmetov's character is clearly an addendum.

2. Section 29 of chapter 3, specifically devoted to characterizing Rakhmetov, is about twenty pages long (fifteen pages in the LP edition). Section 30, in which he performs his one plot function is about sixteen pages long (thirteen in the LP edition). Finally, section 31, in which Rakhmetov's purpose in the novel is discussed, is about five to six pages.

3. See, for example, M. V. Teplinskii, "Avtor-povestvovatel' v romane N. G. Chernyshevskogo *Chto delat'?*" in *N. G. Chernyshevskii. Stat'i, issledovaniia i materialy* (Saratov: 1978), 8:13, who argues that not only is Rakhmetov obviously involved in some secret underground activity but so is the narrator. See also T. Iu. Dubrovina, "Bor'ba i tragicheskoe v estetike i khudozhestvennoi praktike N. G. Chernyshevskogo," in *Literaturno-kriticheskie opyty i nabliudeniia* (Kishinev: 1982), 153. Likewise, Lotman argues that in the novel, plenty of hints are given about the existence of a revolutionary organization in Russia, of which both Rakhmetov and the author are members. See L. M. Lotman, "Sotsial'nyi ideal, etika i estetika Chernyshevskogo," in *Idei sotsializma v russkoi klassicheskoi literature* (Leningrad: 1969), 226–27.

4. The concern with Rakhmetov's underground activity has led many to concentrate on the scant information provided on his activities to demonstrate his ties to the revolutionary movements of the day. Pinaev, for example, provides chronological comparisons and argues that Rakhmetov must have been a member of the secret society *Zemlia i volia.* See M. T. Pinaev, *N. G. Chernyshevskii. Khudozhestvennoe tvorchestvo (Posobie dlia studentov)* (Moscow: 1984), 69–79. See also G. Verkhovskii, *O romane N. G. Chernyshevskogo "Chto delat'?"* (Iaroslavl': 1959), 178. Verkhovskii, p. 173, borders upon the ridiculous when he argues that Rakhmetov was undoubtedly present at Chernyshevskii's dissertation defense in 1855.

5. N. P. Zhdanovskii, "Osobennosti realizma pisatelei-demokratov 60-kh godov XIX v.," in *Problemy tipologii russkogo realizma* (Moscow: 1969), 318.

6. N. V. Vodovozov, *Roman N. G. Chernyshevskogo "Chto Delat'?"* (Moscow: 1953), 23.

7. G. V. Plekhanov, "[O romane Chernyshevskogo Chto delat'?]," *Literatura i estetika* (Moscow: 1958), 2, 181.

8. See, for example, G. E. Tamarchenko, *Chernyshevskii-romanist* (Leningrad: 1976), 204–5, who argues that although Rakhmetov's role in

the *siuzhet* is minimal, ideologically he is central. P. Nikolaev, "Revoliutsionnyi roman," in *Chto delat'?* by N. G. Chernyshevskii (Moscow: 1969), 16, argues that Chernyshevskii's artistic achievement lies in his making a nonacting character into the main character. B. Riurikov, *N. G. Chernyshevskii. Kritiko-biograficheskii ocherk* (Moscow: 1961), 149, states: "Rakhmetov is the center to which all the threads of the novel converge." V. N. Shul'gin, *Ocherki zhizni i tvorchestva N. G. Chernyshevskogo* (Moscow: 1956), 112, 129, is even more emphatic, stating outright that "[t]he main character in the novel *What Is to Be Done?* is Rakhmetov" and that "[w]ithout Rakhmetov there is no novel as an authentically artistic work." See also E. I. Pokusaev, *N. G. Chernyshevskii*, 5th ed. (Moscow: 1976), 162; S. E. Shatalov and A. S. Kurilov, *Nikolai Gavrilovich Chernyshevskii* (Moscow: 1978), 52.

9. See Vodovozov, p. 24, who states: "The strength of Chernyshevskii's artistic talent is expressed in the highest degree precisely in the creation of Rakhmetov's image." See also N. A. Verderevskaia, *Stanovlenie tipa raznochintsa v russkoi realisticheskoi literature 40–60kh godov XIX veka (k probleme tipologii zhanra, siuzheta i obraza)* (Kazan', 1975), 130; Verkhovskii, p. 153.

10. M. T. Pinaev, "Izuchenie v shkole obraza Rakhmetova," in *Voprosy prepodavaniia literatury v shkole (Sbornik statei)* (Stalingrad: 1958), 14.

11. See Joseph Frank, "N. G. Chernyshevsky: A Russian Utopia," *Southern Review*, New Series 3, no. 1 (1967): 78, who states: "Chernyshevsky cannot help dwelling at some length on this revolutionary Superman—the highest exemplar of his human ideal in the present 'irrational' organization of society." Similarly, Irina Paperno, *Chernyshevsky and the Age of Realism: A Study in the Semiotics of Behavior* (Stanford: 1988), 25, argues that Rakhmetov's "appearance introduces an image of the ideal human being into the novel . . . as the reader is allowed to guess . . . [Rakhmetov is] a dedicated professional revolutionary." Charles A. Moser, *Esthetics as Nightmare: Russian Literary Theory, 1855–1870* (Princeton: 1989), 142, concurs, arguing that Chernyshevskii "presents Rakhmetov as an exemplary ideal." See also Richard Hare, *Pioneers of Russian Social Thought: Studies of Non-Marxian Formation in Nineteenth-Century Russia and of Its Partial Revival in the Soviet Union* (New York: 1951), 78; Michael R. Katz and William G. Wagner, "Introduction: Chernyshevsky, *What Is to Be Done?* and the Russian Intelligentsia," in *What Is to Be Done?* by Nikolai Chernyshevsky (Ithaca: 1989), 28.

12. See Rufus W. Mathewson Jr., *The Positive Hero in Russian Literature*, 2nd ed. (Stanford: 1975), 76, who argues that although Rakhmetov "plays a minor role in the central intrigue, . . . the entire novel, in a sense, is his vehicle." Randall questions the inordinate amount of attention paid to Rakhmetov: "It is usually assumed that Chernyshevskii thought Rakhmetov

the most admirable character in his novel, but he appears only at the crisis of the action, in two long sections out of one hundred and eight." See Francis B. Randall, *N. G. Chernyshevskii* (New York: 1967), 122.

13. Marcia A. Morris, *Saints and Revolutionaries: The Ascetic Hero in Russian Literature* (Albany, N.Y.: 1993), 136–47; N. G. O. Pereira, *The Thought and Teachings of N. G. Černyševskij* (The Hague: 1975), 80; Adam B. Ulam, *Ideologies and Illusions: Revolutionary Thought from Herzen to Solzhenitsyn* (Cambridge: 1976), 35. See also George Lukács, "Tschernyschewskijs Roman 'Was Tun?'" *Der russische Realismus in der Weltliteratur* (Berlin: 1952), 121.

14. Frank, p. 83, argues that the Bolshevik mentality comes directly from the image of Rakhmetov. He states that it is impossible to find any source in European socialism for it except in *What Is to Be Done?* See also Mathewson, p. 76; Dennis Reinhartz, "Rakhmetov in N. G. Chernyshevsky's *What Is to Be Done?* The Origins, Meaning, and Historical Impact of the Character," *Madison College Studies and Research* 29 (1971): 14.

15. Soviet scholars generally ignore the religious imagery associated with Rakhmetov, but recently Western scholars have come to stress it.

16. Ernest J. Simmons, "Part 5: Review," in *Continuity and Change in Russian and Soviet Thought* (Cambridge: 1955), 460. See also Mathewson, p. 76, who states: "It is the mood of superlatives, of course, that robs him of literary credibility, and it is the power of his will, the most important ingredient of his character, that makes him aesthetically impossible." Reinhartz disagrees, arguing that Rakhmetov was "perhaps Chernyshevsky's single most significant and lasting contribution to Russian literary tradition and revolutionary thought." See Dennis Reinhartz, "N. G. Chernyshevsky on Aesthetics and Art: The Role of the Artist in a Revolution" (Ph.D. diss., New York University, 1971), 113.

17. Abbott Gleason, *Young Russia* (Chicago: 1983), 297, 304.

18. E. L. Afanas'ev, "Roman N. G. Chernyshevskogo *Chto delat'?* i zhiznennyi ideal narodovol'tsa," in *"Chto delat'?" N. G. Chernyshevskogo. Istoriko-funktsional'noe issledovaniie* (Moscow: 1990), 158.

19. Remarks of E. N. Koval'skaia quoted in A. P. Skaftymov, "Roman *Chto delat'?*" in *N. G. Chernyshevskii. Sbornik. Neizdannye stat'i, materialy, vospominaniia* (Saratov: 1926), 137.

20. See also, for example, the remarks of an anonymous reviewer in *Knizhnyi vestnik* (1863): "Especially good is the fine analysis of Vera Pavlovna's feelings for her husband and for Kirsanov and strikingly lively is the grandiose figure of Rakhmetov." Quoted in E. Plimak, "Ispytanie vremenem," *Voprosy literatury,* no. 2 (1978): 156–57. See also the remarks of Golovin, who stated, "[The young generation] found itself an ideal in Chernyshevskii's other hero, Rakhmetov who, it is true, participates little in the course of the story, but in return is drawn in such bright strokes that he

almost left a deeper trace on the young generation than the main characters of the novel." Quoted in Vodovozov, p. 25. Randall, p. 142, notes that the sections on Rakhmetov were published separately as a pamphlet.

21. In his second report Przhetslavskii does discuss Rakhmetov somewhat and notes that he is a "higher man" and an ideal. However, Przhetslavskii's discusses Rakhmetov mainly in terms of his participation in the immorality of the three main characters. See N. A. Bukhbinder, "Tsenzura o *Chto delat'?* N. G. Chernyshevskogo," *Katorga i ssylka,* no. 44 (1928): 48–49.

22. Quoted in U. A. Gural'nik, *Nasledie N. G. Chernyshevskogo-pisatelia i sovetskoe literaturovedenie* (Moscow: 1980), 40. Tsitovich also saw Rakhmetov as a do-nothing. See P. Tsitovich, *Chto delali v romane "Chto delat'?"* 4th ed. (Odessa: 1879), 16.

23. N. N. Strakhov, "Schastlivye liudi," *Iz istorii literaturnago nigilizma. 1861–1865* (Saint Petersburg, 1890), 334.

24. N. S. Leskov, "Nikolai Gavrilovich Chernyshevskii v ego romane *Chto delat'?*" *Sobranie sochinenii* (Moscow: 1958), 10:22. This "letter" was first published in *Severnaia pchela,* no. 142 (May 31, 1863) under the signature Nikolai Gorokhov.

25. Fet's article remained unpublished for contemporaries. For a discussion, see Iu. Steklov, "Neizdannaia stat'ia A. A. Feta o romane N. G. Chernyshevskogo *Chto delat'?*" *Literaturnoe nasledstvo* 25–26 (1936): 477–84.

26. A. A. Fet, "*Chto delat'?*. Iz rasskazov o novykh liudiakh. Roman N. G. Chernyshevskogo," *Literaturnoe nasledstvo* 25–26 (1936): 515.

27. In this regard Fet treats Rakhmetov as a mere mouthpiece for Chernyshevskii's didacticism.

28. Dmitry Pisarev, "Thinking Proletariat," *Selected Philosophical, Social and Political Essays* (Moscow: 1958), 669.

29. Ibid., 671.

30. Ibid., 673–74.

31. Ibid., 675. It is important to note that Pisarev criticizes Rakhmetov himself, not Chernyshevskii's introduction of him. Pisarev argues that there is nothing improbable about Rakhmetov's asceticism and that indeed such figures do exist in real life. Thus, although Pisarev does reject Rakhmetov as a model to be followed, as an ideal, he does not condemn Chernyshevskii for drawing this portrait (672, 675). Pisarev is consistent in his rejection of Rakhmetov until the very end of his study, when he suddenly says: "If they do indeed exist, perhaps the bright future is not quite so immeasurably far from us as we are accustomed to think. Wherever Rakhmetovs appear they spread bright ideas around themselves and arouse living hopes." These comments do not at all match with his previous rejection of Rakhmetov and his course, and what he meant by this statement is

unclear (675). Looking at the same review, E. Lampert argues that Pisarev endorsed Rakhmetov as a model to be followed. See E. Lampert, *Sons against Fathers: Studies in Russian Radicalism and Revolution* (Oxford: 1965), 315, 322–23.

32. N. V. Shelgunov, "Russkie idealy, geroi i tipy," in *Shestidesiatye gody* (Moscow-Leningrad: 1940), 184.

33. Ibid.

34. Ibid., 182–83.

35. Ibid., 183–85.

36. Mathewson, 76.

37. Ziolkowski argues, in contrast, that though often unusual, Rakhmetov's behavior is rarely overtly ridiculous. See Margaret Ziolkowski, *Hagiography and Modern Russian Literature* (Princeton: 1988), 195.

38. L. M. Lotman, "Ideino-khudozhestvennye printsipy belletristiki Chernyshevskogo 1860–1870-kh godov," in *N. G. Chernyshevskii. Estetika. Literatura. Kritika* (Leningrad: 1979), 73–74; Pinaev, 1984, 86; Riurikov, 149; Shul'gin, 122; Verkhovskii, 176. Some Western scholars have also accepted this interpretation. See N. G. O. Pereira, "Chernyshevsky's *What Is to Be Done?* as a Statement of Social Utopia," *Rocky Mountain Social Science Journal* 9, no. 3 (1972): 39; Pereira, 1975, p. 80; Randall, p. 123.

39. Pinaev, 1958, 20; Shul'gin, 85. Shul'gin also argues that, by contrast, Vera Pavlovna's fourth dream was written on the eve of the first visit to Chernyshevskii by his wife. See also Lotman, 1979, p. 74, who adds that Chernyshevskii's interest in yoga may have contributed to this scene.

40. The Soviet scholar Teplinskii does argue that Rakhmetov's action is not meant for emulation and that the narrator does not agree with everything Rakhmetov says or does. See M. V. Teplinskii, *Izuchenie tvorchestva N. G. Chernyshevskogo* (Kiev: 1981), 137.

41. The a priori assumption that Rakhmetov is the hero of the text has ruined many a fine analysis. For example, N. M. Belova provides a summary of Chernyshevskii's views regarding Kant and his categorical imperative. However, by accepting Rakhmetov as the hero of *What Is to Be Done?* she is forced to conclude that Chernyshevskii turned on his former views and adopted Kant's position. See N. M. Belova, "Roman N. G. Chernyshevskogo «Chto delat'?» i prosvetitel'skaia literatura XVIII veka," *N. G. Chernyshevskii. Istoriia. Filosofiia. Literatura* (Saratov: 1994), 124.

42. According to Volodin et al., the passages where the narrator "laughs" at Rakhmetov have not been not sufficiently studied by scholars. See Volodin, A. I., Iu. F. Kariakin, and E. G. Plimak, *Chernyshevskii ili* Nechaev (Moscow: 1976), 170-71.

43. "Над теми из них, с которыми я был близок, я смеялся, когда бывал с ними наедине; они сердились или не сердились, но тоже смеялись над собою. И действительно, в них было много забавного, все

главное в них и было забавно, все то, почему они были людьми особой породы. Я люблю смеяться над такими людьми" (LP 202).

44. The narrator uses the word *smeshnoi* to describe Rakhmetov and those like him. Katz translates this word as "funny." However, that translation does not seem to capture fully the essence of the Russian word *smeshnoi,* whereas "ridiculous" or "absurd" does. Compare with Dostoevskii's *Son smeshnogo cheloveka,* usually translated as *The Dream of a Ridiculous Man.* I am indebted to Boris Norman and Vadim Liapunov for their aid regarding the finer nuances of the Russian language.

45. "Если бы тут был кто посторонний, он, каким бы чувствительным сердцем ни был одарен, не мог бы не засмеяться над торжественностью всей этой процедуры и в особенности над обрядными церемонностями этого ее финала. Смешно, это правда" (LP 218).

46. In this title the word *osobennyi* is used. Katz translates this word as "extraordinary." Though this is a fair enough translation of that word, it gives it far too positive an accent. "Peculiar" or "particular" more fully captures the nuances of the Russian original. I choose to use "peculiar," with its negative connotation, because it fits better with the context. Reinhartz, *N. G. Chernyshevsky,* p. 126, argues that Raskol'nikov in *Crime and Punishment* is Dostoevskii's response to Rakhmetov. In this regard, it is perhaps significant that instead of *osobennyi,* Raskol'nikov uses the more clear-cut word *neobyknovennyi* to refer to his "exceptional" man.

47. Elsewhere Chernyshevskii uses this word in an obviously negative sense. When describing his attitude toward August Comte, Chernyshevskii states that Comte "вздумал сделаться гением и создать философскую систему" (took it into his head to become a genius and create a philosophical system) (14:651). In a variant to his foreword to *Povesti v povesti,* Chernyshevskii again uses this term in a negative sense when describing the reaction of his "friends" to his fiction: "Этот публицист вздумал писать романы" (This publicist took it into his head to write novels) (12:681).

48. Some Soviet scholars did comment on this aspect of the text. Verderevskaia argues, for example, that it is Rakhmetov's youth that is responsible for his ridiculous behavior. She argues that the narrator's stressing of Rakhmetov's eccentricity is merely a device to make him seem more human and bring him closer to the reader (Verderevskaia, 131–32). Teplinskii argues that the narrator's sarcasm is directed not at Rakhmetov alone but at all the peculiar people. He sees the narrator's treatment as a device used by the author to keep these people lower than himself. (Teplinskii, 1978, 134–35; 1981, 136–37). Pokusaev, p. 163, argues that Chernyshevskii used the words *osobennyi chelovek* and "rigorist" merely as code words for "revolutionary." Rudenko, 1979, p. 85, notes that there is an opposition between the depiction of Rakhmetov as the positive hero and the narrator's concentration on his strangeness. Dubrovina explains the use of words such

as *smeshnoi* and *zabavnyi* as part of the dichotomy between the optimistic and the tragic that runs throughout the text. See T. Iu. Dubrovina, "Preodolenie tragicheskogo kak pafos romana *Chto delat'?* N. G. Chernyshevskogo," in *Literaturno-kriticheskie opyty i nabliudeniia* (Kishinev: 1982), 59–60. Efremov notes that the language used to describe Rakhmetov sometimes gives the impression that he is a rather strange person. He argues that this language is meant to help the reader realize that Rakhmetov is the representative of people of a different scale from ordinary people. See A. F. Efremov, "Rechevye sredstva postroeniia obraza 'osobennogo cheloveka' v romane N. G. Chernyshevskogo *Chto delat'?*" in *N. G. Chernyshevskii. Stat'i, issledovaniia i materialy* (Saratov: 1965), 4:58.

49. This choice of reading matter by Rakhmetov has been interpreted in different ways. N. L. Brodskii and N. P. Sidorov, *Kommentarii k romanu N. G. Chernyshevskogo "Chto delat'?"* (Moscow: 1933), 136, argue that by giving this book such attention, Chernyshevskii took aim at that madness, which played and plays such a big role in the worldwide historical life of human society. In short, they interpret this as Chernyshevskii's antireligious attack. Pinaev, 1984, p. 26, argues that this is a hint by Chernyshevskii at N. N. Utin, a member of *Zemlia i volia,* who worked on an article on the Apocalypse for the *Encyclopedic Dictionary.* Julia Alissandratos, "Hagiographical Commonplaces and Medieval Prototypes in N. G. Chernyshevsky's *What Is to Be Done?*" *St. Vladimir's Theological Quarterly* 26, no. 2 (1982): 113, argues that this choice is meant to associate Rakhmetov with the tradition of the holy fool. Paperno argues that this is a decisive episode in the plot, noting that this is "a book which, by blending the 'scientific' point of view with the prophetic, treats apocalyptic prophecies as predictions of future historical events." See Irina Paperno, "The Novel Myth: N. G. Chernyshevskii's *What Is to Be Done?*" in *Issues in Russian Literature before 1917* (Columbus, Ohio: 1989), 139. Morris argues that by means of this book Rakhmetov intends to study the union in one single man of two phenomena that are usually kept separate: sanity and insanity, or the rational and irrational. This concerns Rakhmetov because he, in his own mind, is the ideal embodiment of rationality, whereas society, as it exists, is a picture of irrationality (Morris, 1993, 141).

50. "Он с усердным наслаждением принялся читать книгу, которую в последние сто лет едва ли кто читал, кроме корректоров ее: читать ее для кого бы то ни было, кроме Рахметова, то же самое, что есть песок или опилки. Но ему было вкусно" (LP 202).

51. See, for example, Teplinskii, 1978, p. 134.

52. "Он вошел после меня; я был только один незнакомый ему человек в обществе. Он, как вошел, отвел Кирсанова в сторону и, указавши глазами на меня, сказал несколько слов. Кирсанов отвечал ему тоже немногими словами и был отпущен. Через минуту Рахметов сел

прямо против меня, . . . начал смотреть мне в лицо изо всей силы. Я был раздосадован" (LP 208–9).

53. *Chudak* (crank, eccentric) can be used in an affectionate manner; a negative meaning is not obligatory. However, in this context it is clearly negative. Whether interpreted as negative or not, it does contain a value judgment, clearly denoting that a person has gone beyond sensible behavior.

54. "Я тогда не любил новых знакомств, а эта навязчивость уж вовсе не нравилась мне" (LP 209).

55. "или лжец, или дрянь" (LP 209).

56. "сам был так странен, что смешно было бы обижаться, и я только мог засмеяться" (LP 210).

57. Feuer notes the possible parallel to Christ by comparing Rakhmetov's sleeping on nails to Christ's crown of thorns. See Kathryn Feuer, "What Is to Be Done about *What Is to Be Done?*" in *What Is to Be Done?* by N. G. Chernyshevsky (Ann Arbor, Mich.: 1986), x.

58. Alissandratos, 113. Ziolkowski argues, in contrast, that Rakhmetov cannot be considered a holy fool because "his strangeness has little in common with the holy fool's spirit of radical self-humiliation" (Ziolkowski, 195).

59. For a discussion of the numerous religious elements concerning Rakhmetov and the novel as a whole, see Paperno, 1989, pp. 133–49.

60. Katerina Clark, *The Soviet Novel: History as Ritual* (Chicago: 1981), 50.

61. This summary is taken from N. K. Gudzy, *History of Early Russian Literature,* trans. Susan Wilbur Jones (New York: 1949), 28–30. As Gudzii notes, the *Life of Aleksei* is typical for the biographical pattern of a saint's life: descent from pious parents of noble birth, early inclination for study, disdain for the blandishments of earthly life, strict asceticism, blissful end, and posthumous miracles. Much of this pattern is clearly relevant to Rakhmetov's story. The original text can be found in N. K. Gudzii, *Khrestomatiia po drevnei russkoi literature xi–xvii vekov,* 5th ed. (Moscow: 1952), 99–104.

62. Clark, while accurately noting the parallels, is mistaken, p. 50, when she states that Aleksei engages in mortification of the flesh. Aleksei does gladly bear the blows of the servants, but he does not subject himself to trials. Rakhmetov's sleeping on a bed of nails does follow the general hagiographical pattern, however. Compare, for example, the life of the secular saint Iuliana Lazarevskaia, who "lay on firewood with the sharp edges against her body, and she put iron keys under her ribs, and on these she took little sleep until her serfs fell asleep." See "The Life of Yuliana Lazarevsky," in *Medieval Russia's Epics, Chronicles, and Tales,* ed. Serge A. Zenkovsky (New York: 1974), 395.

63. Alissandratos, 113–16. See also Ziolkowski, pp. 191–95.

64. See also Morris, 1993, p. 142.

65. Such is the view of Morris, 1993, p. 137.

66. Nikolay Chernyshevsky, "The Anthropological Principle in Philosophy," *Selected Philosophical Essays* (Moscow: 1953), 108.

67. Ulam argues that this genealogy is an example of Chernyshevskii's snobbery. He says that although "Chernyshevsky denounces the degenerate aristocracy of the capital, . . . he cannot help describing Rakhmetov's ancient and distinguished genealogy" (Ulam, 47).

68. Compare, for example, the rather disgusting members of the gentry: Storeshnikov, Solovtsov, and even Serge in chapter 1. See also chapter 5, where Solovtsov seeks the hand of Katerina Polozova. The narrator depicts him most harshly: "It was absolutely true that it would have been better for a decent girl to die than become such a fellow's wife" (Это совершенная правда, что порядочной девушке гораздо лучше умереть, чем сделаться женою такого человека) (396; LP 305).

69. It has been argued that the narrator's proviso (274) to the contents of the second dream, in which he argues against strict determinism, provides an explanation for Rakhmetov's origin in the gentry. See Pereira, 1975, p. 76.

70. In his annotation Wagner argues that Chernyshevskii uses the reference to Speranskii to demonstrate the "enlightenment interest inherent in his superhero's family line, despite the reactionary attitudes of his father" (276).

71. For a discussion of Chernyshevskii's hostility to the Russian liberals, see N. G. O. Pereira, "N. G. Chernyshevsky as Architect of the Politics of Anti-Liberalism in Russia," *Russian Review* 32, no. 3 (1973): 264–77; Michael M. Karpovich, "N. G. Chernyshevski between Socialism and Liberalism," *Cahiers du Monde Russe et Soviétique* 1, no. 4 (1960): 569–83.

72. Chernyshevskii wrote: "Nadezhdin was a clever man, but, like Speranskii, he resisted our life and effaced himself, not knowing how to renounce the seductions of ambition. It is bitter to think about such examples" (14:319).

73. These comments regarding Speranskii appear in "Russkii reformator" which is a review of M. Korf's *Zhizn' grafa Speranskogo* (7:794–827). The brackets indicate material that did not appear in the *Sovremennik* version due to the censorship. Chernyshevskii's attitude toward Speranskii was not totally negative. He did view him as a sincere man who wanted true reforms, but who simply did not understand the forces at work in Russian society.

74. A. Lebedev, *Geroi Chernyshevskogo* (Moscow: 1962), 63–66. Lebedev argues that the fact that Vera Pavlovna's maid, Masha, does not fear Rakhmetov is evidence of his organic tie to the people.

75. Verkhovskii, 169.

76. As discussed earlier, Shelgunov argued that it was impossible for Rakhmetov to overcome his gentry origin and become one of the people. Likewise, Frederick G. Barghoorn, "The Philosophic Outlook of Chernyshevski: Materialism and Utilitarianism,"*American Slavic and East European Review* 6, nos. 18–19 (1947): 56, argues that Rakhmetov is cut off from the people by his origin in the gentry as well as his austerities.

77. Feuer states, "Rakhmetov, the revolutionary, has obtained money to work for the cause not by freeing but by *selling* most of his serfs" (xvi).

78. "он получил около 400 душ да 7000 десятин земли" (LP 203).

79. In pre-Emancipation Russia the serfs were bound to the land and were transferred with land whenever it was sold or given away. There were exceptions in that serfs could be bought for resettlement and parts of land, such as a forest or meadow, could be sold without serfs. However, in Rakhmetov's case, we are dealing with very large amounts of land: something must have happened to the serfs. The failure to mention their fate cannot be attributed to the censorship. That is, had Rakhmetov freed his serfs, there was nothing illegal or uncommon about such an act. Moreover, although Rakhmetov's dispersal of his wealth takes place before the Emancipation, the novel was written *after* it. It is also noteworthy that Pavel Bakhmetev, on whom Rakhmetov is partly based, did sell his own serfs.

80. "На другое утро хозяйка Рахметова в страшном испуге прибежала к Кирсанову: «батюшка-лекарь, не знаю, что с моим жильцом сделалось: не выходит долго из своей комнаты, дверь запер, я заглянула в щель; он лежит весь в крови; я как закричу, а он мне говорит сквозь дверь: „ничего, Аграфена Антоновна". Какое, ничего! Спаси, батюшка-лекарь, боюсь смертного случаю. Ведь он такой до себя безжалостный»" (LP 211).

81. That is, it is often claimed he is warning his radical colleagues of the need to prepare oneself to endure torture.

82. "Проба. Нужно. Неправдоподобно, конечно; однако же на всякий случай нужно. Вижу, могу" (LP 212).

83. "Кроме того, что видел Кирсанов, видно из этого также, что хозяйка, вероятно, могла бы рассказать много разного любопытного о Рахметове; но, в качестве простодушной и простоплатной, старуха была без ума от него, и уж, конечно, от нее нельзя было бы ничего добиться. Она и в этот-то раз побежала к Кирсанову потому только, что сам Рахметов дозволил ей это для ее успокоения: она слишком плакала, думая, что он хочет убить себя" (LP 212).

84. Morris, 1993, 141. Though noting these facts, Morris stills views Rakhmetov as Chernyshevskii's positive hero. She attributes Rakhmetov's deficiencies to Chernyshevskii's shortcomings as a writer.

85. это дает уважение и любовь простых людей" (LP 205).

86. "С Верою Павловною он был очень далек: она находила его очень скучным, он никогда не присоединялся к ее обществу" (LP 201).

87. "Рахметовы—это другая порода; они сливаются с общим делом так, что оно для них необходимость, наполняющая их жизнь; для них оно даже заменяет личную жизнь. А нам, Саша, недоступно это. Мы не орлы, как он. Нам необходима только личная жизнь" (LP 261).

88. Reinhartz, *N. G. Chernyshevsky*, pp. 117–18, disagrees. He argues that "in his intellectual make-up, naturally, Rakhmetov very closely reflected his creator." Reinhartz bases his argument in large part on the fact that when expressing his views on certain books, Rakhmetov's judgments sometimes coincide with Chernyshevskii's. In short, he argues, p. 115, that Rakhmetov functions as Chernyshevskii's mouthpiece. Reinhartz is correct to some degree regarding the overlap in judgments. However, as will be demonstrated later, this overlap is limited to assessments of authors. Moreover, the fact that a character may function as the mouthpiece of the author is by no means sufficient to make the character a positive hero or ideal. Compare, for example, Dostoevskii's Underground Man.

89. "Я не прикасаюсь к женщине" (LP 206).

90. "вы видите, что такие люди, как я, не имеют права связывать чью-нибудь судьбу с своею" (LP 213).

91. Rakhmetov's views on this matter were a major reason that Pisarev rejects him as a positive hero. Pisarev states: "This argumentation of Rakhmetov's [*sic*] is worthless as far as logic goes. If I prove that full enjoyment of life is necessary for human beings I have no reason whatsoever to undermine my proof by the example of my own life. To consider oneself as an exception and place oneself above human demands and outside physiological laws is, in any case, irrational." He further argues: "In general a man's life and his teaching must be in as complete agreement as possible: the ascetic who preaches enjoyment of life is in his way just as absurd and monstrous as the popes of the Middle Ages who indulged in drunkenness, luxury and debauchery and preached fasting, poverty and mortification. People are prevented from enjoying themselves either by their own prejudices or by external circumstances. To overcome prejudice one must use conviction and example, so that Rakhmetov's personal asceticism could only be harmful in the struggle against prejudice." As a contrast to Rakhmetov, Pisarev cites the example of Martin Luther, who, in preaching against monasticism, married a nun. See Pisarev, pp. 671–72.

92. For further discussion see Paperno, 1988, pp. 90–91. Regarding marriage she states that for the new men "the idea of marriage was combined with dreams of social service and with the whole complex of ideas that associated the liberation of women with the liberation of humanity, and equated the rearrangement of the marital relationship with the reorganiza-

tion of the social order." See also her article "The Myth of Reality in N. G. Černyševskij's Works and Life," in *Myth in Literature* (Columbus, Ohio: 1985), 155, where she argues that Chernyshevskii "treats woman as a symbol of life" and that "marriage is treated as the ultimate form of contact with woman. Marriage is a symbolic act of coming to terms with reality."

93. Chernyshevskii's is reported to have said: "All of us here, it can be said, reject marriage in the form in which it now exists; and yet it is impossible not to get married." See S. G. Stakhevich, "Sredi politicheskikh prestupnikov. Nikolai Gavrilovich Chernyshevskii," in *N. G. Chernyshevskii, 1828–1928. Sbornik statei, dokumentov i vospominanii* (Moscow: 1928), 82.

94. One need only look at the chapter titles to get some idea. Chapter 2 is titled "First Love and Legal Marriage;" chapter 3 is titled "Marriage and Second Love;" chapter 4 is titled "Second Marriage."

95. Feuer, xxix. Soviet scholars dealt with this issue in various ways. Verkhovskii, p. 109, argues that though it is difficult to live without love and family, it is possible. But without revolutionary struggle, it is impossible and this is what the image of Rakhmetov teaches us. Pinaev takes a more aggressive approach, arguing that Rakhmetov's renunciation of love is linked to the dislike Chernyshevskii expressed over the attention paid to the love theme in art in his dissertation (2:83–84) and to a passage in "The Anthropological Principle" (7:285), where he notes that Newton denied himself in his quest. Pinaev argues that Chernyshevskii felt that to be great, man had to renounce the love of a woman (1984, 95–96). Lebedev, p. 111, argues that the lack of a personal life for Rakhmetov is indeed a serious failing but places the blame not on Rakhmetov but on Chernyshevskii. Tamarchenko, p. 158, merely concedes that Rakhmetov is a bad expert in questions of love. He does note, however, that in chapter 5, the Lady in Black polemicizes with the ascetic mentality, defending the right to love (Tamarchenko, 220). Teplinskii, 1981, p. 137, is the most original, arguing that there is no support in the novel for Rakhmetov's views on the necessity of denying oneself love and that in the section with the Lady in Black, there is a direct disavowal of his views.

96. "Нет, и этого я не могу принять. . . . я должен подавить в себе любовь: любовь к вам связывала бы мне руки, они и так нескоро развяжутся у меня,—уж связаны. Но развяжу. Я не должен любить" (LP 213).

97. Paperno, 1988, 128–31. Paperno does argue that Chernyshevskii had an ambivalent attitude toward male sexual activity. Some scholars see Chernyshevskii as a man with sexual inadequacies that he never overcame and argue that this profoundly influenced his thinking. For example, see Pereira, 1975, pp. 93–110.

98. See the discussion in "Chernyshevskii and the Question of Asceticism" later in this chapter.

99. Naumova, proceeding from the assumption that Rakhmetov is unquestionably the positive hero, argues that his three references to the co-op demonstrate that it is the prototype for the future and that they must develop as a revolutionary force. See N. Naumova, *Roman N. G. Chernyshevskogo "Chto delat'?"* (Leningrad: 1972), 43–44.

100. "А тут требуется способность довольно редкая. Десять шансов против одного, что вас некому было заменить и что ваш отъезд губил мастерскую. Хорошо ли это? Вы подвергали почти верной, почти неизбежной гибели благосостояние пятидесяти человек. И из-за чего? Из-за маленького удобства себе. Хорошо ли это? Какая нежная заботливость к ничтожнейшему облегчению для себя—и какое бесчувствие к судьбе других! Как вам нравится эта сторона вашего дела" (LP 220). Note in this quotation that Rakhmetov also expresses the concepts of sacrifice and debt, something that Chernyshevskii did not approve of.

101. Franco Venturi, *Roots of Revolution* (New York: 1960), 179. During his youth Chernyshevskii was attracted to the ideas of the French utopian socialists. However, by the time he wrote *What Is to Be Done?* he was quite hostile to their ideas. This problem will be discussed further in the next chapter.

102. "вы подавали аргумент против святых ваших принципов защитникам мрака и зла. Теперь я не говорю уже о том, что вы разрушали благосостояние 50 человек,—что значит 50 человек!—вы вредили делу человечества, изменяли делу прогресса. Это, Вера Павловна, то, что на церковном языке называется грехом против духа святого" (LP 222–23).

103. "Вообще видишь невеселые вещи; как же тут не будешь мрачным чудовищем? Только, Вера Павловна, если уж случилось вам видеть меня в таком духе, в каком я был бы рад быть всегда, и дошло у нас до таких откровенностей,—пусть это будет секрет, что я не по своей охоте мрачное чудовище. Мне легче исполнять мою обязанность, когда не замечают, что мне самому хотелось бы не только исполнять мою обязанность, но и радоваться жизнью; теперь меня уж и не стараются развлекать, не отнимают у меня времени на отнекивание от зазывов" (LP 222).

104. Naumova, p. 41, argues otherwise. She states that the participation of Rakhmetov in the personal affairs of the heroes shows that the significance of those affairs goes far beyond the boundaries of private interests, that they are not "petty affairs." Naumova is correct to some degree. However, Rakhmetov clearly disregards the personal life of the heroes as important in and of itself.

105. Contemporaries believed that Rakhmetov might be modeled on Chernyshevskii's colleague Dobroliubov or on the Pole S. Sierakowski. See Riurikov, p. 152. The writer V. G. Korolenko, who knew Chernyshevskii personally, felt that Rakhmetov was based on the revolutionary P. D. Ballod. See

his *Sobranie sochinenii v desiati tomakh* (Moscow: 1955), 8:326. In addition to Bakhmetev and Sierakowski, Brodskii and Sidorov, p. 147, also suggest V. A. Obruchev and V. I. Kel'siev. Reinhartz, *N. G. Chernyshevsky,* p. 117, suggests that "the most important real life model for Rakhmetov was probably Bakunin; the physical and temperamental similarities are especially striking." Lanshchikov disputes the notion that Bakhmetev was the model for Rakhmetov. He does concede that Chernyshevskii gave his character the name to honor Bakhmetev's feats. However, he argues that Chernyshevskii himself, as he would have liked to have been, is the model. See Anatolii Lanshchikov, *N. G. Chernyshevskii,* 2nd ed. (Moscow: 1987), 296. Pinaev, 1984, p. 26, simply argues that there is no specific model, that Rakhmetov is a generalized image. Plimak, p. 155, argues that Rakhmetov is a composite image based on the great men of history (Cromwell, Napoleon). Finally, Lampert, pp. 207–8, argues for Speshnev, a member of the Petrashevskii circle, as a direct model of Rakhmetov.

As a literary model Scanlan suggests Rousseau's Wolmar (*The New Héloise*). See James P. Scanlan, "Chernyshevsky and Rousseau," in *Western Philosophical Systems in Russian Literature: A Collection of Critical Studies* (Los Angeles: 1979), 107. Reinhartz, *N. G. Chernyshevsky,* p. 116, suggests both Herzen's *Who Is to Blame?* and Insarov in Turgenev's *On the Eve.* Eidelman suggests Laraviniere in George Sand's *Horace.* See Dawn Diane Eidelman, "George Sandism and the Woman Question in Nineteenth-Century Russia" (Ph.D. diss., Emory University, 1990), 76.

106. This information is taken from S. A. Reiser's commentary, which appears on pp. 848–49 of the LP edition. The original sources for information on Bakhmetev are as follows: a letter of E. N. Pypina to her parents (April 23, 1863) published in *Nikolai Gavrilovich Chernyshevskii. 1828–1928. Neizdannye teksty, materialy i stat'i* (Saratov: 1928), 307; P. A. Bakhmetev, "(Pis'mo k Gertsenu)," *Literaturnoe nasledstvo* 41–42 (1941): 526–28; A. I. Gertsen, *Sobranie sochinenii v tridtsati tomakh* (Moscow: 1957), 9:344–48 (*My Past and Thoughts,* part 8, chapter 3); and Stakhevich, 104. For secondary literature, see S. A. Reiser, "'Osobennyi chelovek' P. A. Bakhmetev," *Russkaia literatura,* no. 1 (1963): 173–77; N. Ia. Eidel'man, "Pavel Aleksandrovich Bakhmetev," in *Revoliutsionnaia situatsiia v Rossii v 1859–1861 gg.* (Moscow: 1965), 387–98; N. Ia. Eidel'man, "Po sledam Rakhmetova," *Voprosy i otvety,* no. 8 (1973): 53–60.

107. For those who have reproached Chernyshevskii for creating totally unbelievable characters, Bakhmetev's very existence should serve as an object lesson. Such characters did have some resonance in the Russian reality of the time.

108. Pypina, 307.

109. In a variant to his memoirs, *My Past and Thoughts,* Herzen notes that Chernyshevskii used the story of the fund left by Bakhmetev, with some changes in *What Is to Be Done?* See Gertsen, 9:622.

110. Stakhevich, 104.

111. Ibid. Herzen's description of Bakhmetev is likewise less than adulatory. See Alexander Herzen, *My Past and Thoughts* (Berkeley: 1973), 557–61. Riurikov, p. 152, is suspicious of Bakhmetev as a model for Rakhmetov because of those descriptions.

112. Brodskii and Sidorov, p. 142, argue, in contrast, that by means of Rakhmetov, Chernyshevskii showed that the only hope for the nobleman was a complete break with his class and its lifestyle. The nobleman must give himself over to the *narod* totally. Verkhovskii, pp. 153, 167–69, views Chernyshevskii's introduction of the penitent nobleman into the novel as an attempt to be true to the Russian reality of the time. Pokusaev, p. 164, takes a similar view when he notes that apostates from the gentry were common enough and Chernyshevskii was familiar with this.

113. See, for example, Chernyshevskii's remarks on liberal philanthropy and "salon heroes" (7:185). Many scholars have noted that Chernyshevskii was opposed to the concepts of self-sacrifice and debt, but the figure of Rakhmetov presents a problem in that he has totally sacrificed himself for a cause. For example, Zhdanovskii, p. 316, argues that Chernyshevskii battles false Christian morality in the novel, especially the abstract principle of debt (*dolg*). He then argues, p. 318, however, that Chernyshevskii propounds the idea of revolutionary duty, of selfless devotion to the interests of the masses. This problem has often been dealt with by arguing that Rakhmetov is not truly making a sacrifice because he has come to identify totally with the cause of the people, to make the personal merge with the social. See Zhdanovskii, p. 319, for example. In large part, this argument is based on Vera Pavlovna's description of Rakhmetov as having come to identify with the common cause so much that it has replaced his personal life (343). Naumova, pp. 53–54, argues that Chernyshevskii was opposed to the principle of philanthropy, with its emphasis on sacrifice and the concept of "debt" (*dolg*), as a "senseless and harmful lie." She argues, in contrast, that Chernyshevskii believed that one's own interests must coincide with those of the people. See also Edward Wasiolek, *Fathers and Sons: Russia at the Crossroads* (New York: 1993), pp. 36–37, who argues that Chernyshevskii wanted not a self-sacrifice that denied oneself for the purpose of serving someone else but a self-sacrifice that was at the same time self-fulfillment.

114. Venturi notes that Chernyshevskii had a very skeptical attitude toward this type of revolutionary. Chernyshevskii did try to influence them in the realm of ideas, but avoided any involvement with them (Venturi, 169–71).

115. Stakhevich, 82. Mitrofan Danilovich Muravskii (1838–79), a revolutionary born of the gentry, was a cofounder of the Kharkov–Kiev Secret Society of 1856. See the *Great Soviet Encyclopedia* (New York: 1978) 17:239. Perhaps also relevant here are Chernyshevskii's remarks on "enthusiasts"

expressed in a letter of 1873: "I have always laughed at any enthusiasm when I did not see a particular necessity to exchange laughter with serious reprimands. Enthusiasts [*entuziasty*] are idiots, idiots who are unbearably stupid boys in grown-up bodies. The majority are good souls and because of this one ought to be indulgent to them; but [they are] children, tiny children, spending time in buffoonery unbecoming to adults" (14:551).

116. "ведь вы знаете, про таких людей, как мы с вами, говорят, что для нас нет ничего святого. Ведь мы способны на всякие насилия и злодейства" (LP 225).

117. "Вот какую штуку устроил Лопухов, а Рахметов был только его орудием. Видишь ли, государь мой, проницательный читатель, какие хитрецы благородные-то люди, и как играет в них эгоизм-то: не так, как в тебе, государь мой, потому что удовольствие-то находят они не в том, в чем ты, государь мой; они, видишь ли, высшее свое наслаждение находят в том, чтобы люди, которых они уважают, думали о них как о благородных людях, и для этого, государь мой, они хлопочут и придумывают всякие штуки не менее усердно, чем ты для своих целей, только цели-то у вас различные, потому и штуки придумываются неодинаковые тобою и ими: ты придумываешь дрянные, вредные для других, а они придумывают честные, полезные для других" (LP 230).

118. "Мало их, но ими расцветает жизнь всех; без них она заглохла бы, прокисла бы; мало их, но они дают всем людям дышать, без них люди задохнулись бы. Велика масса честных и добрых людей, а таких людей мало; но они в ней—теин в чаю, букет в благородном вине; от них ее сила и аромат; это цвет лучших людей, это двигатели двигателей, это соль соли земли" (LP 215).

119. "Так видишь ли, проницательный читатель, это я не для тебя, а для другой части публики говорю, что такие люди, как Рахметов, смешны. А тебе, проницательный читатель, я скажу, что это недурные люди; а то ведь ты, пожалуй, и не поймешь сам-то; да, недурные люди. Мало их, но ими расцветает жизнь всех" (LP 215).

120. "Да, смешные это люди, как Рахметов, очень забавны. Это я для них самих говорю, что они смешны, говорю потому, что мне жалко их; это я для тех благородных людей говорю, которые очаровываются ими: не следуйте за ними, благородные люди, говорю я, потому что скуден личными радостями путь, на который они зовут вас; но благородные люди не слушают меня и говорят: нет, не скуден, очень богат, а хоть бы и был скуден в ином месте, так не длинно же оно, у нас достанет силы пройти это место, выйти на богатые радостью, бесконечные места" (LP 215). In this quotation the narrator continues his mocking of Rakhmetov, using both the terms "ridiculous" (*smeshnoi*) and "amusing" (*zabavnyi*) to refer to him. Again, I substitute "ridiculous" for "funny" in the quotation.

121. "Поднимайтесь из вашей трущобы, друзья мои, поднимайтесь, это не так трудно, выходите на вольный белый свет, славно жить, на нем, и путь легок и заманчив, попробуйте: развитие, развитие. Наблюдайте, думайте, читайте тех, которые говорят вам о чистом наслаждении жизнью, о том, что человеку можно быть добрым и счастливым. Читайте их—их книги радуют сердце, наблюдайте жизнь—наблюдать ее интересно, думайте—думать завлекательно. Только и всего. Жертв не требуется, лишений не спрашивается—их не нужно. Желайте быть счастливыми—только, только это желание нужно" (LP 233). This passage comes in the long monologue where the narrator says that he will speak seriously with the public. I argue later that this passage cannot be taken too literally, that it must be treated critically. However, I do detect a change of tone after the narrator stops talking about aesthetic norms and begins speaking in general. This last part of the paragraph has ceased to be a part of his polemic with conventional literature and he is speaking in earnest. Freeborn sees this passage as an "emotional, impassioned and genuine summons to make the pursuit of happiness the true aim of life." See Richard Freeborn, *The Russian Revolutionary Novel: Turgenev to Pasternak* (Cambridge: 1982), 26.

122. This passage has given rise to some of the worst of reductionist criticism. Soviet scholars were obsessed with identifying exactly who these eight people were. See Brodskii and Sidorov, pp.136–37.

123. "Это мы узнали после" (LP 203).

124. ". . . никто из нас не знал" (LP 204).

125. "Да, особенный человек был этот господин, экземпляр очень редкой породы. И не за тем описывается мною так подробно один экземпляр этой очень редкой породы, чтобы научить тебя, проницательный читатель, приличному (неизвестному тебе) обращению с людьми этой породы: тебе ни одного такого человека не видать; твои глаза, проницательный читатель, не так устроены, чтобы видеть таких людей; для тебя они невидимы; их видят только честные и смелые глаза; а для того тебе служит описание такого человека, чтобы ты хоть понаслышке знал, какие люди есть на свете" (LP 214).

126. "К чему оно служит для читательниц и простых читателей, это они сами знают" (LP 214).

127. "Зачем же он введен в роман и так подробно описан? Вот попробуй, проницательный читатель, угадаешь ли ты это? А это будет сказано тебе на следующих страницах, тотчас же после разговора Рахметова с Верою Павловною; как только он уйдет, так это я и скажу тебе в конце главы" (LP 215). Gary Saul Morson, *The Boundaries of Genre: Dostoevsky's Diary of a Writer and the Traditions of Literary Utopia* (Austin: 1981), 103–4, interprets this challenge differently. He states: "The answer to the narrator's question is that Rakhmetov, who is evidently a revolutionary conspirator, is the hero of the work's *real* story, the one it cannot

tell: the subtitle of Chernyshevsky's work is '*From* Stories about New People.' This answer was so obvious to Chernyshevsky's actual readers that a harder question is why the censor ever let it pass."

128. "угадать нетрудно, если ты имеешь хоть малейшее понятие о художественности, о которой ты так любишь толковать,—да куда тебе! Ну, я подскажу больше чем половину разгадки: Рахметов выведен для исполнения главнейшего, самого коренного требования художественности, исключительно только для удовлетворения ему; ну ну, угадай хоть теперь, хоть теперь-то угадай, какое это требование, и что нужно было сделать для его удовлетворения, и каким образом оно удовлетворено через то, что показана тебе фигура Рахметова, остающаяся без всякого влияния и участия в ходе рассказа; ну-ко, угадай. Читательница и простой читатель, не толкующие о художественности, они знают это, а попробуй-ко угадать ты, мудрец. Для того и дается тебе время, и ставится собственно для этого длинная и толстая черта между строк: видишь, как я пекусь о тебе. Остановись-ко на ней, да и подумай, не отгадаешь ли" (LP 215–16).

129. "Скажи же, о проницательный читатель, зачем выведен Рахметов, который вот теперь ушел и больше не явится в моем рассказе? Ты уж знаешь от меня, что это фигура, не участвующая в действии . . .

—Неправда,—перебивает меня проницательный читатель:—Рахметов действующее лицо: ведь он принес записку, от которой . . .

—Уж очень плох ты, государь мой, в эстетических рассуждениях, которые так любишь,—перебиваю я его:—после этого, по-твоему, и Маша действующее лицо? Ведь она в самом начале рассказа тоже принесла письмо, от которого пришла в ужас Вера Павловна. И Рахель действующее лицо? ведь она дала за вещи деньги, без которых не могла бы Вера Павловна уехать. И профессор N действующее лицо, потому что рекомендовал Веру Павловну в гувернантки г-же Б., без чего не вышло бы сцены возвращения с Конногвардейского бульвара? Может быть, и Конногвардейский бульвар—действующее лицо? потому что ведь без него не было бы сцены свидания на нем и возвращения с него?" (LP 228).

130. V. G. Odinokov, *Khudozhestvennaia sistemnost' russkogo klassicheskogo romana* (Novosibirsk: 1976), 153–54, provides a similar discussion.

131. "О, да как же ты плох, государь мой! Как раз наоборот понимаешь дело. Разве нужно было выводить особого человека затем, чтоб он высказал свое мнение о других лицах? По этаким надобностям, может быть, выводят и уводят людей в своих произведениях твои великие художники, а я, хоть и плохой писатель, а все-таки несколько получше понимаю условия художественности. Нет, государь мой, Рахметов вовсе не был нужен для этого. Сколько раз сама Вера Павловна, Лопухов, Кирсанов выражают сами свое мнение о своих поступках и отношениях? Они люди не глупые, они сами могут рассудить, что хорошо, что дурно, на это им не нужно суфлера" (LP 228–29). This pas-

sage also quite clearly shows that the numerous statements by the narrator about his lack of talent are given tongue-in-cheek. In addition, Chernyshevskii is clearly playing with the "reasoner" tradition in literature.

132. "Понимаешь ли ты теперь, что если я сообщаю тебе не мысли Лопухова и Веры Павловны, а разговор Рахметова с Верою Павловною, то нужно сообщить не те только мысли, которые составляли сущность разговора, но именно разговор? Зачем же нужно сообщать тебе именно этот разговор? Затем, что он разговор Рахметова с Верою Павловною; понимаешь ли хоть теперь? Все еще нет? Хорош же, однако, ты. Плох по части смысла-то, плох" (LP 230).

133. "Понял ли ты теперь, проницательный читатель, что хотя много страниц употреблено на прямое описание того, какой человек был Рахметов, но что в сущности еще гораздо больше страниц посвящено всё исключительно тому же, чтобы познакомить тебя все с тем же лицом, которое вовсе не действующее лицо в романе? Скажи же мне теперь, зачем выставлена и так подробно описана эта фигура?" (LP 231).

134. See, for example, S. M. Shibaev, "Moral'nyi oblik 'obyknovennykh liudei' N. G. Chernyshevskogo," in *Roman N. G. Chernyshevskogo "Chto delat'?" (K 100-letiiu vykhoda v svet). Sbornik statei* (Shakhty: 1963), 60; Henry Gifford, *The Hero of His Time: A Theme in Russian Literature* (London: 1950), 190; Katz and Wagner, p. 28; Lukács, p. 119; Pereira, 1972, p. 40; Ziolkowski, p. 192.

135. Nicolas Berdyaev, *The Origin of Russian Communism* (Ann Arbor, Mich.: 1960), 52.

136. "и все-таки, лишь опомнится, находит, что она не имеет своей воли, должна угождать, принуждать себя, что это очень тяжело" (LP 60).

137. "что ж странного, что тебе хочется быть вольным и счастливым человеком! Ведь это желание—не бог знает какое головоломное открытие, не бог знает какой лодвиг геройства" (LP 60).

138. "А вот что странно, Верочка, что есть такие же люди, у которых нет этого желания, у которых совсем другие желания, и им, пожалуй, покажется странно, с какими мыслями ты, мой друг, засыпаешь в первый вечер твоей любви, что от мысли о себе, о своем милом, о своей любви ты перешла к мыслям, что всем людям надобно быть счастливыми и что надобно помогать этому скорее прийти. А ты не знаешь, что это странно, а я знаю, что это не странно, что это одно и натурально, одно и по-человечески: просто по-человечески,—«я чувствую радость и счастье»—значит «мне хочется чтобы все люди стали радостны и счастливы»—по-человечески, Верочка, эти обе мысли одно" (LP 60–61).

139. P. Reifman, *N. G. Chernyshevskii* (Tartu:1973), 88–89, argues: "Chernyshevskii's book is directed against any sort of asceticism or self-

denial. The author of *What Is to Be Done?* enters into a polemic with those who have proclaimed the lot of man as a renunciation of happiness in the name of duty." He is not quite consistent in his statements, however. For example, regarding Rakhmetov's asceticism, he later states on p. 99: "The author of *What Is to Be Done?* sings an authentic dithyramb to such people who are selflessly devoted to the cause of the revolution, seeing in selfless service to it not only their duty but also their happiness."

140. In his autobiography, Chernyshevskii relates his attitude toward the religious ascetics who occasionally appeared in Saratov: "Ascetics were understood by my elders and by all the sensible people of Saratov as people playing, making fools of themselves, making merry, as people frivolous or pitiable, stupid or bad" (12:498). Incidentally, the treatment of this text by Soviet scholars amply demonstrates how untrustworthy the *PSS* can be. At first glance, the quotation seems to come from Chernyshevskii's unfinished novel, *Povesti v povesti.* However, upon closer inspection, this passage appears within the bounds of this work due to a gross violation by *PSS*'s Soviet editors. What appears as chapter 3 in the novel is actually a shortened version of the autobiography Chernyshevskii wrote in the summer of 1863. The Soviet editors argue that Chernyshevskii intended for this variant to be used as chapter 3 and cite a correspondence in pages as proof (see 12:696). Although there may be some basis for this argument, particularly the narrative commentary attached to the autobiographical variant, it should not have been placed in volume 12 as part of *Povesti v povesti,* but rather in volume 1 as a second variant to the autobiography. The fact that chapter 3 is left blank within the manuscript version is a clear argument for leaving it blank in the published version.

141. Chernyshevskii distinguishes between Jesuit-type preaching of asceticism and the teachings of those who preached asceticism as a corrective against the destructiveness and debauchery of the upper classes. Although he makes this distinction, however, he does not endorse asceticism in any way.

142. Wasiolek, 36–37. Wasiolek bases his arguments on Chernyshevskii's "The Anthropological Principle in Philosophy." Wasiolek further states that, according to Chernyshevskii, "Man was not born to deny himself but to fulfill himself. He was not born for self-sacrifice and self-denial." Brodskii and Sidorov, p. 79, express a similar opinion about *What Is to Be Done?* and argue that the life-loving tone of the novel is directed at the false teachings of Christian ascetic morality. They further hint, p. 160, that Boccaccio's name is introduced into the novel because Chernyshevskii valued him as the defender of healthy thought against the ascetic hypocrisy and moral dissoluteness of the Catholic clergy.

143. See Barghoorn, p. 50.

144. The issue of asceticism is tied to the strict sexual dichotomy that runs throughout the novel. Rakhmetov's asceticism is, of course, the ulti-

mate extreme in the novel, the absurd result of the male characters' fascination with theory, with abstraction. The fact that Rakhmetov is male is more than sufficient reason for rejecting him as the positive hero.

145. "больше, разумеется, не слушали, даже обрызгали водою Лопухова и Алексея Петровича, когда они уже очень восхитились великою важностью минерального удобрения; но Алексей Петрович и Лопухов толковали о своих ученостях непоколебимо. Кирсанов плохо помогал им, был больше, даже вовсе на стороне дам, и они втроем играли, пели, хохотали до глубокой ночи, когда, уставши, развели, наконец, и непоколебимых ревнителей серьезного разговора" (LP 123).

146. "Вольная, просторная, деятельная жизнь, и не без некоторого сибаритства: лежанья нежась в своей теплой, мягкой постельке, сливок и печений со сливками,—она очень нравится Вере Павловне" (LP 142).

147. "Бывает ли лучше жизнь на свете? Вере Павловне еще кажется: нет. Да, в начале молодости едва ли бывает" (LP 142).

148. "да, к стыду Верочки, надобно сказать, что она была обыкновенная девушка, любившая танцовать" (LP 55).

149. The narrator does make some comments in regard to Vera Pavlovna's habits: "Without feeling the least bit ashamed, I've compromised Vera Pavlovna many times from a poetical standpoint. For example, I haven't concealed the fact that she dines every day, generally with a hearty appetite, and besides that, she takes tea twice a day" (Я, нисколько не совестясь, уж очень много компрометировал Веру Павловну со стороны поэтичности; например, не скрывал того, что она каждый день обедала, и вообще с аппетитом, а кроме того, по два раза в день пила чай) (348; LP 265). However, as is obvious from this passage, such comments form a part of the polemic with conventional aesthetics and are in no way directed at Vera Pavlovna herself.

150. "Но как хорошо каждый день поутру брать ванну; сначала вода самая теплая, потом теплый кран завертывается, открывается кран, по которому стекает вода, а кран с холодной водой остается открыт, и вода в ванне незаметно, незаметно свежеет, свежеет, как это хорошо! Полчаса, иногда больше, иногда целый час не хочется расставаться с ванною" (LP 267).

151. "А во всяком случае милый взял на себя неизменную обязанность хозяйничать за утренним чаем.

Да и нельзя было бы иначе, Саша совершенно прав, что этому так следовало устроиться, потому что пить утренний чай, то есть почти только сливки, разгоряченные не очень большою прибавкою очень густого чаю, что пить его в постели чрезвычайно приятно. Саша уходит за прибором,—да, это чаще, чем то, что он прямо входит с чайным прибором,—и хозяйничает, а она все нежится и, напившись чаю, все еще полулежит уж не в постельке, а на диванчике, таком широком, но, главное достоинство его, таком мягком, будто пуховик, полулежит до 10, до 11 часов" (LP 267–68).

152. The other female characters in the novel also lead anything but an ascetic lifestyle. If they limit themselves, it is due to difficult circumstances, not any sort of preconceived ascetic philosophy. For example, Chernyshevskii's positive female characters visit the opera often and are not at all condemned for it. Their outings to the opera are described with the evident approval of the narrator (196, 231).

153. E. H. Carr is particularly harsh in his appraisal of Chernyshevskii. He states that Chernyshevskii was a Victorian in that he "veiled the physical relations between the sexes in a cloud of prudery." He further states: "In a book which is constantly—one might almost say, primarily—concerned with the relation, and specifically the marital relation, between men and women, he dismisses the physical aspect of that relation as unessential and not seriously worth discussion." See E. H. Carr, introduction to *What Is to Be Done?* by N. G. Chernyshevsky (New York: 1961), xiii–xiv. As Katz notes, Carr obviously read only the abridged edition for which he was writing and not the original Russian text. See Michael R. Katz, "English Translations of *What Is to Be Done?*" *Slavic Review* 46, no. 1 (1987): 126.

154. See Reinhartz, *N. G. Chernyshevsky*, pp. 106–7. See also Pereira, 1972, p. 37, who, in effect, argues that Chernyshevskii meant this passionless marriage to be taken as a positive model of marriage. See also Carr, p. xiv, who argues that we have no reason to believe that Vera has physical relations with Lopukhov.

155. Naumova, 33. She calls attention to this scene as it appears in the rough draft, arguing that here more love, emotion is displayed between Vera and Lopukhov (9:420, 724, 725).

156. "В это утро Дмитрий Сергеич не идет звать жену пить чай; она здесь, прижавшись к нему" (LP 176).

157. Naumova, 34.

158. In fictitious marriages most of the participants did not even live together and, indeed, might never see each other again after the wedding. For a discussion of fictitious marriages in Russian society, see Richard Stites, *The Women's Liberation Movement in Russia: Feminism, Nihilism, and Bolshevism* (Princeton: 1978), 89–114. Naumova, p. 29, traces the genesis of the interpretation of Vera Pavlovna's first marriage as fictitious to Tsitovich.

159. Naumova, 32. It is true that Lopukhov has had some sort of affair before his involvement with Vera Pavlovna, but Naumova obviously does not consider this love.

160. Stites takes issue with the traditional interpretation of *What Is to Be Done?* as a novel that preaches sexual asceticism. He states: "What of sex itself? Does Chernyshevsky ignore it, as some commentaries and abridged translations would lead us to believe? Was the puritanical Rakhmetov, who

eschewed wine and women, the *alter ego* of Chernyshevsky? Hardly so" (Stites, 95). The twentieth-century interpretation of Chernyshevskii and his novel as excessively prudish is somewhat surprising, especially in light of the contemporary reaction to the novel. Hostile contemporaries accused Chernyshevskii of advocating free love, debauchery, and so forth.

161. A rather skewed view of *What Is to Be Done?* has been common because of the censored editions of the novel that have appeared in English, in which all the references to sexual activity were deleted. For further discussion, see Stites, p. 95; Katz, 1987, p. 126.

162. "—Саша, а ведь ты не дал мне договорить о деле,—начала Вера Павловна, когда они часа через два сидели за чаем.

—Я тебе не дал договорить? Я виноват?

—Конечно, ты.

—Кто начал дурачиться?

—И не совестно тебе это?

—Что?

—Что я начала дурачиться. Фи, так компрометировать скромную женщину своею флегматичностью!

—Будто? А я верил тому, что ты толкуешь о равенстве; если равенство, то и равенство инициативы.

—Ха, ха, ха! Какое ученое слово! Но неужели ты меня обвинишь в непоследовательности? Разве я не стараюсь иметь равенства в инициативе? Но, Саша, я теперь беру иницативу продолжать серьезный разговор, о котором мы забыли.

—Бери, но я отказываюсь следовать за тобою. Я теперь возьму инициативу продолжать забывать. Дай руку.

—Саша, но надобно же договорить.

—Завтра успеем. Теперь меня, ты видишь, слишком заинтересовало исследование этой руки" (LP 262).

163. Stites, p. 96, argues that Chernyshevskii's views on sex were closer to those of Aleksandra Kollontai than to those of Lenin, with whom he is so often linked.

164. "но больше, больше всего—это моя тайна. Ты видела в зале, как горят щеки, как блистают глаза; ты видела, они уходили, они приходили; они уходили—это я увлекала их, здесь комната каждого и каждой—мой приют, в них мои тайны ненарушимы, занавесы дверей, роскошные ковры, поглощающие звук, там тишина, там тайна; они возвращались—это я возвращала их из царства моих тайн на легкое веселье. Здесь царствую я" (LP 290).

165. One must be careful with this reference, occurring as it does in Vera Pavlovna's dream. See the discussion in the next chapter. However, this passage does fit in with the numerous other references to sex. Commenting on this passage, Stites notes, p. 96, that there were limits to Chernyshevskii's views: "Chernyshevsky would not have dreamed of allowing the

communitarian couples of Vera's fourth dream to emerge from their connubial alcoves in order to change partners."

CHAPTER FIVE

1. The term "utopian socialist" is generally used to refer to the Frenchmen Henri-Claude Saint-Simon, Charles Fourier, Pierre Leroux, Victor Considérant, and Louis Blanc, and the Englishman Robert Owen. Although Pierre-Joseph Proudhon is usually regarded as an anarchist, he is included in the discussion because Chernyshevskii speaks of him in the same breath as the utopian socialists. For a general discussion, see Leo Loubere, *Utopian Socialism: Its History since 1800* (Cambridge: 1974); Joyce Oramel Hertzler, *The History of Utopian Thought* (New York: 1965); Frank E. Manuel and Fritzie P. Manuel, *Utopian Thought in the Western World* (Cambridge: 1979). The term "utopian" or "utopian socialist" was first used in connection with these men in the nineteenth century. See Frederick Engels's famous essay "Socialism: Utopian and Scientific," which first appeared in 1880. The Russian public was acquainted with both the term "utopian" and the content of utopian teachings in the second half of the nineteenth century. See P. A. Bibikov's essay "Sovremennye Utopisty. Izlozhenie i kriticheskii razbor teorii Fur'e" (written 1859), which appeared in *Kriticheskie etiudy P. A. Bibikova* (Saint Petersburg: 1865), 9–100.

2. N. G. O. Pereira, *The Thought and Teachings of N. G. Černyševskij* (The Hague: 1975), 50. See also L. M. Lotman, "Sotsial'nyi ideal, etika i estetika Chernyshevskogo," in *Idei sotsializma v russkoi klassicheskoi literature* (Leningrad: 1969), 184–85, who discusses Chernyshevskii's debt to the utopian socialists.

3. Leonard Schapiro, *Russian Studies* (London: 1986), 215.

4. Lotman overstates her case when she argues that *What Is to Be Done?* has not been given a special consideration as a literary monument of utopian socialism (Lotman, 196–97).

5. A. P. Skaftymov, "Roman *Chto delat'?*" in *N. G. Chernyshevskii. Sbornik. Neizdannye stat'i, materialy, vospominaniia* (Saratov: 1926), 111. Skaftymov also views Chernyshevskii as borrowing the idea of women's emancipation from Fourier and Considérant (in addition to the influence of George Sand). Lukács concurs with Skaftymov, arguing that Chernyshevskii's views on the women's question are influenced by Fourier. See George Lukács, "Tschernyschewskijs Roman 'Was Tun?'" *Der russische Realismus in der Weltliteratur* (Berlin: 1952), 111–12. Sand was often closely associated with the utopian socialists, especially Pierre Leroux. For further discussion see Emily Klenin, "On the Ideological Sources of *Čto delat'?*: Sand, Družinin, Leroux," *Zeitschrift für slavische Philologie* 51, no. 2 (1991): 370.

6. N. L. Brodskii and N. P. Sidorov, *Kommentarii k romanu N. G. Chernyshevskogo "Chto delat'?"* (Moscow: 1933), 167–77. See also Leland Fetzer,

Pre-Revolutionary Russian Science Fiction: An Anthology (Seven Utopias and a Dream) (Ann Arbor, Mich.: 1982), 55–56; Joseph Frank, "N. G. Chernyshevsky: A Russian Utopia," *Southern Review,* New Series 3, no. 1 (1967): 80; Michael R. Katz, "Vera Pavlovna's Dreams in Chernyshevskii's *What Is to be Done?*" in *Issues in Russian Literature Before 1917* (Columbus, Ohio: 1989), 158; Charles A. Moser, *Antinihilism in the Russian Novel of the 1860's* (The Hague: 1964), 39–41; Irina Paperno, "The Novel Myth: N. G. Chernyshevskii's *What is to be Done?*" in *Issues in Russian Literature Before 1917* (Columbus, Ohio: 1989), 134; G. V. Plekhanov, "[O romane Chernyshevskogo Chto delat'?]" *Literatura i estetika* (Moscow: 1958), 2:179; P. Reifman, *N. G. Chernyshevskii* (Tartu: 1973), 104; Richard Hare, *Pioneers of Russian Social Thought: Studies of Non-Marxian Formation in Nineteenth-Century Russia and of Its Partial Revival in the Soviet Union* (New York: 1951), 195.

7. Richard Stites, *Revolutionary Daydreams* (New York: 1989), 26–27. Pereira also notes that the fourth dream is described in Fourierist exactitude and argues that Chernyshevskii "was not talking metaphorically" in presenting such a vision. See N. G. O. Pereira, "Chernyshevsky's *What Is to Be Done?* as a Statement of Social Utopia," *Rocky Mountain Social Science Journal* 9, no. 3 (1972): 41. See also Pereira, 1975, p. 82.

8. An exception is Venturi, who argues that the socialist ideas expounded in the novel are those of Chernyshevskii's youth and not those to which he subscribed at the time he wrote the novel. See Franco Venturi, *Roots of Revolution* (New York: 1960), 179.

9. Klenin, 370.

10. Adam B. Ulam, *Ideologies and Illusions; Revolutionary Thought from Herzen to Solzhenitsyn* (Cambridge: 1976), 45. See also William F. Woehrlin, *Chernyshevskii: The Man and the Journalist* (Cambridge: 1971), 55. Soviet scholars generally follow this line of interpretation, although there are exceptions. See, for example, B. Riurikov, *N. G. Chernyshevskii. Kritiko-biograficheskii ocherk* (Moscow: 1961), p. 147, who argues that Chernyshevskii differed from the utopians of the West.

11. See Venturi, pp. 161–62, for further discussion.

12. N. G. Chernyshevsky, "The Anthropological Principle in Philosophy," *Selected Philosophical Essays* (Moscow: 1953), 67.

13. Ibid., 68.

14. Ibid., 69.

15. See also the discussion provided by Venturi, p. 161, on Chernyshevskii's attitude toward the followers of Saint-Simon. Venturi notes that Chernyshevskii rejected the Saint-Simonians because they had no real political program, but merely enthusiasm for a sentimental or religious revival. See also Woehrlin, p. 226, who argues that Chernyshevskii criticized the Saint-Simonians because they appealed to a brotherhood based on love rather than self-interest.

16. Chernyshevskii also states that Fourier's arguments are not so strange as they seemed at first. However, he also states "I have little curiosity now, whereas before there was quite a lot, and I do not intend to take great interest in his system" (1:189, 191).

17. Chernyshevskii does stress that Fourier does have some new ideas that may seem absurd but are intelligent. However, Chernyshevskii views the intelligent ideas espoused by Fourier as belonging to the entire leftist tradition, not just to Fourier, and contends that Fourier took those ideas from his predecessors. See Venturi, p. 138, who states that on one level, Chernyshevskii appreciated Fourier as a psychologist but that on the political plane, Chernyshevskii's rationalist spirit was inevitably prompted to criticism. The principle of association seemed to Chernyshevskii the only solid kernel, and he saw this as belonging to the whole socialist tradition, not just to Fourier. See also Woehrlin, p. 55, who notes that in his first reading of Fourier Chernyshevskii did not seem overly impressed. "He showed sympathy for Fourier's general ideas on associations and on the need to harmonize human passions, but he seems to have responded to Fourier as much for his challenge to religious convictions as for his teachings on socialism." Despite those early reservations, however, Woehrlin implicitly argues that Chernyshevskii had a positive view of Fourier at the time he wrote *What Is to Be Done?*

18. Recounted in S. G. Stakhevich, "Sredi politicheskikh prestupnikov. Nikolai Gavrilovich Chernyshevskii," in *N. G. Chernyshevskii. 1828–1928 Sbornik statei, dokumentov i vospominanii* (Moscow: 1928), 95.

19. G. Verkhovskii, *O romane N. G. Chernyshevskogo "Chto delat'?"* (Iaroslavl': 1959), 146, argues that several elements of Lopukhov's biography correspond to Owen's biography: marrying the daughter of a rich businessman, going to America to put socialist ideals in practice, and so forth. Pereira, 1972, p. 36, argues that Owen was a major influence on Chernyshevskii, citing Lopukhov's portrait of Owen as explicit evidence. However, Chernyshevskii's attitude toward Robert Owen is not entirely certain. His colleague Nikolai Dobroliubov did write an article on him for *Sovremennik* (no. 1, 1859) but Chernyshevskii mentions him only infrequently. Of the few references to Owen in Chernyshevskii's *PSS*, several occur only in quotations of the works of others. It is clear that Chernyshevskii regards Owen as a "truly great thinker" (7:30) or as one "of the first-class thinkers" (9:355). In another reference, Chernyshevskii seems to distinguish Owen from the utopians, whom he clearly regards negatively (5:606). Yet despite the positive remarks made in passing, Chernyshevskii never provides an extended discussion of Owen and his experiments. A hint of Chernyshevskii's attitude can be found when he states that people of all political persuasions encouraged Owen (4:742). That is, Chernyshevskii does not view Owen as a revolutionary and, similar to his attitude toward Fourier, though he approves of

the principle of association propounded by Owen, he views that principle as belonging to the leftist movement as a whole, not exclusively to Owen. In short, Chernyshevskii is not hostile to Owen and respects his intelligence, but it is difficult to consider Chernyshevskii a follower of Owen or an avid proponent of his thought.

20. In the rough draft, Fourier is also mentioned when Beaumont/Lopukhov states to Katerina Polozova: "Which poet had a stronger imagination than Fourier? The most vivid pictures of the great poets are hardly as lively and distinct as his descriptions. But, nevertheless, he wrote theoretical discourses and not fictional stories." (LP 708).

21. See, for example, Venturi, p. 179, who states: "The answers to the question *What is to be done?* lay in student 'communes'. . . and in cooperatives of production. . . . In the last chapter Chernyshevsky pointed out—in veiled terms, obscure to those who knew nothing of him, but clear enough to those who understood his aims—the revolutionary outcome of these ventures of self-education and social activity." See also V. V. Kuleshov, "Velikii russkii revoliutsioner-demokrat N. G. Chernyshevskii i nekotorye sotsial'no-ekonomicheskie problemy v ego romane *Chto delat'?*" in *Roman N. G. Chernyshevskogo "Chto delat'?" (K 100-letiiu vykhoda v svet). Sbornik statei* (Shakhty: 1963), 13; N. Naumova, *Roman N. G. Chernyshevskogo "Chto delat'?"* (Leningrad: 1972), 44; Moser, pp. 39–41.

22. G. E. Tamarchenko, *Chernyshevskii-romanist* (Leningrad: 1976), 162–63; Schapiro, 215. Scholarly opinion is not unanimous on this point. Vodovozov, for examples, claims that Chernyshevskii was trying to depict the unsoundness (*nesostoiatel'nost'*) of co-ops. See N. V. Vodovozov, *Roman N. G. Chernyshevskogo "Chto Delat'?"* (Moscow: 1953), 23.

23. G. Žekulin, "Forerunner of Socialist Realism: The Novel 'What to do?' by N. G. Chernyshevsky," *Slavonic and East European Review* 41 (1963): 476, 483. Other criticisms of this part of the novel come from scholars who view the whole affair as unrealistic. It is noted that the affair is consummated with far too much ease, that Vera Pavlovna so easily overcomes all obstacles, that the whole thing is so unbelievable. It is argued that, despite his realist principles, Chernyshevskii has abandoned all verisimilitude and is preaching what should be, not what is. As evidence to this fact, many authors have noted the numerous attempts to form co-operatives that followed the publication of the novel and that those were all miserable failures. See, for example, Moser, p. 41, and Pereira, 1975, p. 79, who states, "But in the more flexible world of literature, thieves and harlots can be transformed overnight into paragons of virtue, propriety and industriousness." See also Rufus W. Mathewson Jr., *The Positive Hero in Russian Literature*, 2nd ed. (Stanford: 1975), 75; Francis B. Randall, *N. G. Chernyshevskii* (New York: 1967), 116. I deal with the question of Chernyshevskii's realist aesthetics in chapter 1, particularly the notion that he advocated and demanded

the exact imitation of reality. It should also be noted that the description of the co-op is not so unrealistic as has often been alleged: attempts at cooperative ventures had existed before *What Is to Be Done?* appeared. See Vodovozov, p. 23.

24. Skaftymov, 1926, 111.

25. Aleksandr Pavlovich Skaftymov, *Zhizn' i deiatel'nost' N. G. Chernyshevskogo,* 2nd ed. (Saratov: 1947), 63–64.

26. Following Lenin's formulation, which applied to Chernyshevskii's defense of the peasant commune, Skaftymov argues that this shortcoming was understandable because Chernyshevskii lived in an age before the revolutionary role of the proletariat was evident (Skaftymov, 1947, 64).

27. "«Я не требую ничего трудного, ты знаешь. Ты кое-что делаешь по-моему, для меня,—разве это трудно?» «Нет».—«Конечно, нет. Вспомни же свою мастерскую, разве у вас было много средств? разве больше, чем у других?»—«Нет, какие ж у нас были средства?» «А ведь твои швеи имеют в десять раз больше удобств, в двадцать раз больше радостей жизни, во сто раз меньше испытывают неприятного, чем другие, с такими же средствами, какие были у вас. Ты сама доказала, что и в твое время люди могут жить очень привольно. Нужно только быть рассудительными, уметь хорошо устроиться, узнать, как выгоднее употреблять средства».—«Так, так; я это знаю».—«Иди же еще посмотреть немножко, как живут люди через несколько времени после того, как стали понимать то, что давно понимала ты»" (LP 288).

28. See, for example, A. P. Skaftymov, "Khudozhestvennye proizvedeniia Chernyshevskogo, napisannye v Petropavlovskoi kreposti," *Nravstvennye iskaniia russkikh pisatelei. Stat'i i issledovaniia o russkikh klassikakh* (Moscow: 1972), 258.

29. Mathewson, 75. See also T. Iu. Dubrovina, "Khronotop v romane N. G. Chernyshevskogo *Chto delat'?*" in *Iz istorii russkoi literatury i literaturnoi kritiki* (Kishinev: 1984), 57; E. A. Podshivalova, "O khudozhestvennom khronotope v romane N. G. Chernyshevskogo *Chto delat'?*" in *Problema avtora v khudozhestvennoi literature. Mezhvuzovskii sbornik nauchnykh trudov* (Izhevsk: 1983), 66.

30. See, for example, Randall, p. 116, who states that the section on Vera Pavlovna's sewing co-op clearly constitutes a strikingly didactic section of the novel.

31. "Мастерская—разве это моя личная жизнь? Это дело—не мое дело, чужое. Я занимаюсь им не для себя, а для других; пожалуй, и для моих убеждений" (LP 261).

32. "Вера Павловна чувствовала едва ли не самую приятную из всех своих радостей от мастерской, когда объясняла кому-нибудь, что весь этот порядок устроен и держится самими девушками; этими

объяснениями она старалась убедить саму себя в том, что ей хотелось думать: что мастерская могла бы идти без нее, что могут явиться совершенно самостоятельно другие такие же мастерские и даже—почему же нет? вот было бы хорошо!—это было бы лучше всего!—даже без всякого руководства со стороны кого-нибудь не из разряда швей, а исключительно мыслью и уменьем самих швей; это была самая любимая мечта Веры Павловны" (LP 139).

33. "уже мечтали в своих разговорах, что года через два вместо двух швейных будет четыре, пять, а там скоро и десять, и двадцать" (LP 291).

34. "Тут Катя уж и вовсе отдохнула, ей стал полный простор в доме. А простор для нее значил тогда то, чтобы ей не мешали читать и мечтать. Подруг у ней было немного, две-три близких, искателей руки—без числа: ведь одна дочь у Полозова, страшно сказать: 4 милиона.

Но Катя читала мечтала, а искатели руки оставались в отчаянии. А Кате уж было 17 лет. Так, читала и мечтала, и не влюблялась" (LP 299)

35. "Катерина Васильевна влюбилась в Соловцова за его письма; она умирала от любви, основывавшейся только на ее мечтах. Уж из этого видно, что она была тогда настроена очень романически. А шумная жизнь пошлого общества, наполнявшего дом Полозовых, вовсе не располагала к экзальтированной идеальности. Значит, эта черта происходила из собственной ее натуры. Ее давно тяготил шум; она любила читать и мечтать" (LP 314).

36. "Она была мечтательница, но мечты ее были тихи, как ее характер, и в них было так же мало блеска, как в ней самой. Ее любимым поэтом был Жорж Занд; но она не воображала себя не Лелиею, ни Индианою, ни Кавальканти, ни даже Консуэло, она в своих мечтах была Жанною, но чаще всего Женевьевою. Женевьева была ее любимая героиня" (LP 314).

37. C. Corbet, "Réminiscences sandiennes dans *Que faire?* de Černyševskij," *Revue des études slaves* 43 (1964): 17–33; Klenin, 388.

38. "Но она любила мечтать о том, как завидна судьба мисс Найтенгель, . . . и по окончании войны, вернувшись на родину с сотнями спасенных ею, продолжает заботиться о больных. . . Это были мечты, исполнения которых желала бы Катерина Васильевна. Дальше мыслей о Женевьеве и мисс Найтенгель не уносила ее фантазия. Можно ли сказать, что у ней была фантазия? и можно ли назвать ее мечтательницею?" (LP 314–15).

39. Naumova, in contrast, argues that the theme of the co-op is a subtext of the depiction of the future society; that the details are seen by Vera Pavlovna and can be dreamed only by her. Because she is so involved in the affairs of the co-op, it is only natural that it colors her dream of the future (Naumova, 48–49).

40. See the discussions of the history of the preface. See also T. I. Ornatskaia, "Roman N. G. Chernyshevskogo *Chto delat'?* (K istorii teksta)," *Russkaia literatura,* no. 3 (1977): 115–27, for further discussion.

41. Henry Gifford is an exception among Western scholars in this regard. He states: "Many of Chernyshevsky's readers supposed that the *artel* was the way out for Russia, and Vera Pavlovna's workshop was imitated, but without success. However, Chernyshevsky had no illusions himself about the *artel,* which by itself was powerless to alter society. This is made perfectly clear in the original (censored) version of Chapter IV, section xvii." See Henry Gifford, *The Hero of His Time; A Theme in Russian Literature* (London: 1950), 186.

42. "Месяца через три по открытии магазина приехал к Кирсанову один отчасти знакомый, а больше незнакомый собрат его по медицине, много рассказывал о разных медицинских казусах, . . . а в заключение всего сказал, что один из его знакомых желает познакомиться с Кирсановым.

Кирсанов исполнил желание; знакомство было приятное, был разговор о многом, между прочим о магазине. Объяснил, что магазин открыт, собственно, со торговою целью; долго говорили о вывеске магазина, хорошо ли, что на вывеске написано travail. Кирсанов говорил, что travail значит труд, Au bon travail—магазин, хорошо исполняющий заказы; рассуждали о том, не лучше ли было бы заменить такой девиз фамилиею. Кирсанов стал говорить, что русская фамилия его жены наделает коммерческого убытка; наконец придумал такое средство: его жену зовут «Вера»—по-французски вера—foi, если бы на вывеске можно было написать вместо Au bon travail—A la bonne foi, то не было ли бы достаточно этого?—Это бы имело самый невинный смысл—«добросовестный магазин», и имя хозяйки было бы на вывеске; рассудивши, увидели, что это можно. Кирсанов с особенным усердием обращал разговор на такие вопросы и вообще успевал в этом, так что возвратился домой очень довольный" (LP 291).

A. Fet argued that the new name is still subversive because in the new title the letter *f* is not capitalized. Thus, it cannot represent Vera Pavlovna's name. Fet argues that, instead, this signifies that the store is primarily an organ of new faith. See A. A. Fet, "*Chto delat'?* Iz rasskazov o novykh liudiakh. Roman N. G. Chernyshevskogo," *Literaturnoe nasledstvo* 25–26 (1936): 523.

43. Žekulin, p. 479, states of this scene: "A hilariously funny scene, worthy of Saltykov-Shchedrin or even Gogol', is the conversation between Kirsanov and the 'enlightened official' about the shop opened by Vera Pavlovna in Nevsky Prospect, a conversation which finishes in Chernyshevsky's bitterly-humorous 'lyrical aside' on police surveillance." As part of his critique of the novel, Žekulin views this scene, which he labels first-rate, as the dismissal of a potential conflict (that between Vera Pavlovna and the

government authorities) from the novel. Žekulin seems to forget that Chernyshevskii wrote this novel while in prison in conditions of strict censorship. Developing such a conflict in the novel was something he could not do.

44. “Новое знакомство Кирсанова продолжалось и приносило ему много удовольствия” (LP 291).

45. “—Будем говорить прямо, Александр Матвеевич, к чему людям просвещенным не быть между собою вполне откровенными? Я сам в душе социалист и читаю Прудона с наслаждением. Но . . .”

46. “—Позвольте сказать несколько слов, чтобы не оставалось между нами недоразумений. Вы сказали: «тоже социалист». Это «тоже», вероятно, относится ко мне. Почему я, вы думаете, социалист? Может быть, вовсе нет,—кроме социалистов, есть протекционисты, есть последователи Сэ, есть последователи исторических воззрений Рау, есть последователи множества различных других направлений в политической экономии. Для причисления человека к последователям одного из них надобно иметь какие-нибудь основания.”

47. “—Это устройство позволяют последователи всех направлений, когда они говорят серьезно. Некоторые из них—и теперь уж очень немногие—нападают на него, когда ведут полемику против последователей какого-нибудь другого направления, смотря по надобности. Но нападают только тогда, когда ведут полемику. В спокойном, чисто ученом изложении не отваживается не признавать его безопасность и полезность для общества решительно никто из пишущих о политической экономии. Если я говорю неправильно, прошу вас указать мне хоть один пример противного.”

48. This statement, although Kirsanov’s own and given in a verbal duel with the authorities, does show that Chernyshevskii realized that cooperative ventures were not essentially revolutionary and did not really threaten the existing order. Chernyshevskii sounded a similar note in 1857, when he stated: “Our Aleksandr I and his ally the Prussian king, unlimited monarchs, the English king, a constitutional monarch, his brother, the Duke of Kent, the aristocratic ministers of England who were then striving for the restoration of oligarchy and the destruction of the public laws of England, the North American democrats, all alike approved of Robert Owen. In its very essence, the principle of association is a purely economic matter, not at all a political one” (4:741–42).

49. Sivovolov agrees with the enlightened man. He argues that the name of the store (Au bon travail: Magasin de Nouveautés) is revolutionary, socialist, and that by means of the word *travail* Chernyshevskii was hinting at the slogan of the French socialists, *droit au travail*, in the title of Louis Blanc’s book *Le socialisme, droit au travail* (Paris: 1848). See B. M. Sivovolov, “Roman N. G. Chernyshevskogo *Chto delat’?* v sotsial’noi praktike sovremennikov (O zhenskom trude po memuarnym istochnikam),” in

Roman N. G. Chernyshevskogo "Chto delat'?" (K 100-letiiu vykhoda v svet). Sbornik statei (Shakhty: 1963), 103.

50. "—Г-н Кирсанов, мы здесь не для ученых споров. Вы согласитесь, что мне некогда ими заниматься. Магазин г-жи Кирсановой имеет вредное направление, и я бы советовал ей, и в особенности вам, быть осторожнее.

—Если он вреден, то его надобно закрыть, а нас отдать под суд. Но мне любопытно было бы знать, в чем же состоит его вред?

—Да во всем. Начнем хотя с вывески. Что это такое «Au bon travail»?—это прямо революционный лозунг.

—В переводе это будет означать: «магазин хорошей работы»; какой тут революционный смысл, что модный магазин обещает хорошо исполнять заказы, я не понимаю.

—Смысл этих слов не тот. Они означают, что надобно все магазины так устроить, тогда только будет хорошо рабочему сословию. И само слово travail—это ясно—взято из социалистов, это революционный лозунг."

51. "—Мне приходит в голову вот что. В вывеске представляется неудобным словом travail, оно должно быть заменено именем моей жены. В этом состоит требование общественной пользы?

—Да.

—Я нахожу возможным исполнить это требование, важность оснований которого я вполне ценю, избегнув № 2 из двух невыгод—страшного удара, который нанесло бы магазину выставленное на нем имя с окончанием—off. Имя моей жены Вера. Можно передать это на французский язык словом Foi,—если оставить слово bon, ограничив эту перемену только размером необходимости, относящейся собственно к слову travail, то новая вывеска была бы: «A la bonne foi»—собственно «добросовестный магазин», но во французской надписи будет даже оттенок консервативного смысла: foi—Вера, как бы в противоположность тенденциям отрицательного характера."

52. "Довольно долго Вера Павловна и муж находили себе источник частого удовольствия в размышлениях о том, как общество,—можно сказать, общественное благоустройство,—было спасено от опасности заменою слова travail словом foi и соответственною тому переменою в роде прилагательного имени на одной из многих тысяч вывесок Невского проспекта."

53. "Мерцалова и Вера Павловна уже мечтали в своих разговорах, что года через два вместо двух швейных будет четыре, пять, а там скоро и десять, и двадцать" (LP 291).

54. "Но в сущности дело было вовсе не шуточное. Магазин отделался на этот раз очень легко; конечно, так; а все-таки ясно было, что надобно поприжаться и поприжаться, заставить забыть о себе, что теперь—по крайней мере надолго—нечего уж думать о развитии предприятия, которое так и просилось идти вперед; что высшее возможное счастье надолго должно будет состоять в том, чтобы продолжать

существовать, отказавшись на многие месяцы, вероятно не на один год, от расширения дела. Это было, конечно, тяжело. Но ведь и то сказать, разве это не предвиделось? Хорошо и то, что дело успело без помех развиться хоть настолько,—помехи могли явиться гораздо раньше; хорошо и то, что помехи проявились только в останавливающем, а не в разрушительном характере,—ведь можно было ждать и разрушения."

55. This aspect of the text is routinely stressed by those Soviet scholars. Sivovolov, pp. 102–3, for example, argues that this entire passage was very clear to readers raised on the Aesopian language of *Sovremennik.* It all leads to the conclusion that only an annihilation of the autocratic police order, only a fundamental break of existing social relations, would give the possibility of bringing about the "theory of the laborers." See also Naumova, p. 51; Brodskii and Sidorov, p. 180; Reifman, p. 106; Vodovozov, p. 23; P. Nikolaev, "Revoliutsionnyi roman," in N. G. Chernyshevskii, *Chto delat'?* (Moscow: 1969), 10; V. N. Shul'gin, *Ocherki zhizni i tvorchestva N. G. Chernyshevskogo* (Moscow: 1956), 110–11.

56. "Я пропускаю множество подробностей, потому что не описываю мастерскую, а только говорю о ней лишь в той степени, в какой это нужно для обрисовки деятельности Веры Павловны. Если я упоминаю о некоторых частностях, то единственно затем, чтобы видно было, как поступала Вера Павловна, как она вела дело шаг за шагом, и терпеливо, и неутомимо, и как твердо выдерживала свое правило: не распоряжаться ничем, а только советовать, объяснять, предлагать свое содействие, помогать исполнению решенного ее компаниею" (LP 134).

57. "Есть в рассказе еще одна черта, придуманная мною: это—мастерская. На самом деле Вера Павловна хлопотала над устройством не мастерской; и таких мастерских, какую я описал, я не знал: их нет в нашем любезном отечестве. На самом деле она <являлась> чем-нибудь вроде воскресной школы или—ближе к подлинной правде—вроде ежедневной бесплатной школы, не для детей, а для взрослых,—но для хода самого рассказа ведь это все равно, а мне показалось, что <лучше> вместо дела, более или менее известного, описать такое, которое очень мало известно у нас."

58. Moreover, most well-educated Russians of the time would have recognized the obvious utopian socialist principles underlying Vera Pavlovna's co-op. As Plekhanov states, Fourierism was already known in Russia in the 1840s and Chernyshevskii was offering the reader nothing new (Plekhanov, 179).

59. Tamarchenko, pp. 233–34, interprets the meta-narrative commentary on the co-op differently. He does argue that a direct recommendation and model for imitation was not what Chernyshevskii had in mind with Vera's co-op. It was not a direct answer to the question of what to do. However, he does view Chernyshevskii as using it for propaganda for

socialist ideas. Verkhovskii, p. 135, seems to offer an alternative explanation for this passage by arguing that the co-op, to a certain extent, is really a cover for the Sunday schools that the intelligentsia was setting up at the time, and that had been banned by the government in 1862.

60. His oft-quoted statement is: "But even more important is its internal construction which proceeds in four zones: the vulgar people, the new people, the higher people and dreams." See A. V. Lunacharskii, "N. G. Chernyshevskii kak pisatel'," *Stat'i o Chernyshevskom* (Moscow: 1958), 70.

61. See, for example, Stites, pp. 26–27; see also Fetzer, pp. 55–56; Vodovozov, p. 15.

62. Tamarchenko, 237.

63. Katz, 150. Irina Paperno, *Chernyshevsky and the Age of Realism: A Study in the Semiotics of Behavior* (Stanford: 1988), 26, also views Vera Pavlovna's dreams as allegories that illustrate the main points of Chernyshevskii's philosophical, ethical, and social doctrine. See also Tamarchenko, p. 235. Not all scholars take this point of view. Pinaev, for example, argues that Vera Pavlovna's dreams are not mere political allegory, but are very important for interpreting the *siuzhet.* See M. T. Pinaev, *N. G. Chernyshevskii. Khudozhestvennoe tvorchestvo (Posobie dlia studentov)* (Moscow: 1984), 30. See also Naumova, p. 48.

64. Woehrlin, 317. See also G. F. Samosiuk, "Utopicheskie idei romana *Chto delat'?* v otsenkakh *Sovremennika,*" in *N. G. Chernyshevskii. Stat'i, issledovaniia i materialy* (Saratov: 1978), 8:137–47, for a discussion of some contemporary reactions to the fourth dream. Saltykov-Shchedrin, for example, took a negative view of the dreams because he was opposed to the attempt to predict in detail the form of the future society. His comments in this regard helped in large part to engender a split in the radical camp. Writing in the early 1890s, Plekhanov noted that many of Chernyshevskii's supporters merely "shrugged their shoulders" at the dreams, seeing in them a naive vision or daydream (*mechta*). Plekhanov further states that it was said, even by those calling themselves socialists, that Chernyshevskii should have dealt with something closer and more practical. Plekhanov, who is far from uncritical of Chernyshevskii, defends him from those particular charges (Plekhanov, 179). Aleksei N. Tveritinov, who translated *What Is to Be Done?* into Western European languages, apparently disapproved of the fourth dream because he left it out in his translations. See Anatolii Lanshchikov, *N. G. Chernyshevskii,* 2nd ed. (Moscow: 1987), 327. Although there were those who had their reservations about the dreams, the evidence is that most were quite enthusiastic over Chernyshevskii's dreams. I. E. Repin, for example, stated: "Within educated circles young life seethed with Chernyshevskii's ideas. [News of] his exile flew like a hurricane from end to end through the universities. Everything intellectual secretly seethed, secretly lived by the uncompromising ideas of the

future and believed piously in the third [*sic*] dream of Vera Pavlovna (*What Is to Be Done?*)." Quoted in P. A. Nikolaev, "'. . . chtoby chitali vse. . . ,'" in *"Chto delat'?" N. G. Chernyshevskogo. Istoriko-funktsional'noe issledovanie* (Moscow: 1990), 9.

65. A. I. Volodin and B. M. Shakhmatov, "Utopicheskii sotsializm v Rossii. 1833–1883," in *Utopicheskii sotsializm v Rossii. Khrestomatiia* (Moscow: 1985), 61.

66. See Reifman, p. 106. Feuer argues that the novel is so full of optimism because those were comforting fantasies to a man confined in a dark, damp cell. See Kathryn Feuer, "What Is to Be Done about *What Is to Be Done?*" in *What Is to Be Done?* by N. G. Chernyshevsky (Ann Arbor, Mich.:1986), x. Riurikov uses this as an opportunity to praise Chernyshevskii's genius. He argues that it was a great accomplishment on Chernyshevskii's part to create the strong inspirational image of the fourth dream while a prisoner in the dark and damp Peter and Paul Fortress (Riurikov, 135–36). Smolitskii sees a connection between the fact that Chernyshevskii began to work on the fourth dream shortly after his wife was allowed to visit him for the first time. See V. G. Smolitskii, *Iz ravelina. O sud'be romana N. G. Chernyshevskogo "Chto delat'?"* 2nd ed. (Moscow: 1977), 46. Ulam, 1977, p. 138, traces the tendency to engage in utopia to Chernyshevskii's personality: "the almost continuous revelry in his postrevolutionary utopia is again a compensatory dream of a bookworm whose only diversion was his work." Verderevskaia takes a different strategy, arguing that utopian pictures of the future are *artistically* necessary: without them there is not a separate perspective, without which the meaning and the goal of all activity would be lost. See N. A. Verderevskaia, *Roman N. G. Chernyshevskogo "Chto delat'?" Posobie dlia uchashchikhsia* (Moscow: 1982), 50.

67. Katz, 151. Skaftymov, 1926, p. 124, takes a similar view, arguing that for Chernyshevskii, a dream is only an allegory. See also Nikolaev, 1969, p. 19, who argues that the dreams are a mere conventional device; there is no need to search for a psychological basis to them. This is not consistent with his view, expressed on the same page, that the third dream shows that Chernyshevskii is a master of psychological analysis. Brodskii and Sidorov take a similar stance, arguing that dreams in *What Is to Be Done?* are not used so much for depicting the psychology of the heroes as for allegory. For example, they view the second dream as an exposition of Chernyshevskii's anthropological principle. See Brodskii and Sidorov, pp. 98, 113.

68. Katz, 152.

69. "на третий день уже вдвое несноснее прежнего стал казаться ей «подвал», как она выражалась" (LP 102).

70. Skaftymov, 1926, p. 121, argues that Chernyshevskii shows nothing of the individual worlds of his characters, his portraits being devoid of individual significance. In contrast, Naumova, p. 48, argues for a more lit-

erary interpretation of the dreams, noting that each one corresponds to a different stage in Vera Pavlovna's development. Likewise, Pinaev, p. 30, argues that the dreams are far from mere political allegories: they are essential for interpreting the *siuzhet.* Among Western scholars, Randall is unique in that he does argue that the first dream is an allegory, but he also argues that "at the same time [it is] as genuinely dreamlike as Raskolnikov's dreams" (Randall, 111).

71. "А ведь я до двух часов не спала от радости, мой друг. А когда уснула, какой сон видела! Будто я освобождаюсь из душного подвала, будто я была в параличе и выздоровела, и выбежала в поле и со мной выбежало много подруг, тоже, как я, вырвавшихся из подвалов, выздоровевших от паралича, и нам было так весело, так весело бегать по просторному полю! Не сбылся сон! А я думала, что уж не ворочусь домой" (LP 85).

72. "движение есть реальность"; "движение—это жизнь" (LP 124).

73. Randall, 115. See also Katz, pp. 153–54, who links the content of the second dream to elements of Chernyshevskii's article "The Anthropological Principle in Philosophy" and to his interest in Justus Liebig's theories on agronomy. Katz views Chernyshevskii as trying to cope with the determinism inherent in a materialist worldview. Paperno argues that the allegory of Vera Pavlovna's second dream is an important symbolic representation of the main idea of the novel and in it Chernyshevskii provides a key to his new technique of treating reality: transfiguration. See Irina Paperno, "The Myth of Reality in N. G. Černyševskij's Works and Life," in *Myth in Literature* (Columbus, Ohio: 1985), 166.

74. See Shul'gin, pp. 100–2, for the traditional Soviet interpretation. He argues that the image of the bad soil in the dream is a symbol for rotten, corrupt society and that the only solution proposed, drainage, is a euphemism for revolution. Tamarchenko, pp. 236–37, repeats this formulation when he argues that the second dream is an expression of Chernyshevskii's sociophilosophical ideas about the influence of class inequality on the development of human characters and about the revolutionary destruction of the parasitic classes as a condition for the "healing of the soil." Verkhovskii, p. 92, argues that the image of dirt in the second dream is used to battle the philosophical and political theories of the Slavophiles and the *pochvenniki,* who wanted people to forget about class struggle. Lebedev views the second dream as Chernyshevskii's dithyramb to labor. See A. Lebedev, *Geroi Chernyshevskogo* (Moscow: 1962), 88.

75. Вера Павловна подходит к ним и говорит:

—Да полноте вам толковать о своих анализах, тожествах и антропологизмах, пожалуйста, господа, что-нибудь другое, чтоб и я могла участвовать в разговоре, или лучше давайте играть (LP 125).

76. Vera Pavlovna's comments also show that she still has not accepted and internalized the materialist philosophy of her husband.

77. This is clearly motivated by the visit to Mar'ia Aleksevna that the Lopukhovs paid the day of the dream. During that visit Vera Pavlovna wonders how she ever could have lived in such an environment (179). The dream merely continues that internal psychological struggle.

78. "Нейдут из тебя слова-то. Хорошо им жить?—спрашиваю; хороши они?—спрашиваю; такой хотела бы быть, как они?—Молчишь! рыло-то воротишь!—Слушай же ты, Верка, что я скажу. Ты ученая—на мои воровские деньги учена. Ты об добром думаешь, а как бы я не злая была, так бы ты и не знала, что такое добром называется. Понимаешь? *Всё* от меня, *моя* ты дочь, понимаешь? *Я* тебе мать.

Верочка и плачет, и дрожит, и холодеет" (LP 128).

79. In her third dream, Vera Pavlovna indicates that Mar'ia Aleksevna is right by stating (in her "diary") that Mar'ia Aleksevna tells the terrible truth in the second dream (241).

80. I believe that Chernyshevskii waits until the second dream to let the characters express their materialist views in detail precisely as a way of establishing some distance between those views and himself. The direct, quoted conversation of the characters given in the intermediary form of the dream of another character does provide a considerable amount of distance from both the narrator and the actual author. Up to this point in the novel, the narrator has consciously avoided long discussions of scientific and or materialist topics. There is little reason to attribute the materialistic, deterministic views occurring in the second dream to Chernyshevskii himself; the text simply does not bear that out.

81. Moreover, the content of this "allegory" is in conflict with Chernyshevskii's own views. For example, when Vera Pavlovna and the "Bride" converse, they express a rather naive faith in progress; that is, things are slowly getting better and one day, such vile people as Mar'ia Aleksevna will no longer be necessary (186–87). Chernyshevskii was hostile to a belief in inherent progress, and this view can in no way correspond to his own. A relevant example of Chernyshevskii's hostility to this positivist notion can be found immediately before Vera Pavlovna falls asleep for her second dream, when the narrator makes fun of the notion of the laws governing historical progress, calling it an inevitable topic of discussion in such circles (183–84). However, such naive, positivist views are quite in keeping with those of an idealistic, young woman. This dream helps to characterize Vera Pavlovna as a naive character who still has much to learn.

82. L. N. Morozenko, "O psykhologizme L. N. Tolstogo i N. G. Chernyshevskogo," *Uchenye zapiski Leningradskogo ped. instituta im. A. I. Gertsena* 414 (1971): 271–72, argues that the third dream is the only one

really forming a necessary moment in the movement of the *siuzhet.* See also Tamarchenko, pp. 170–71.

83. Katz, for example, does discuss the third dream but devotes less space to it than the others.

84. Feuer, xx; Morozenko, 270–72; Dawn Diane Eidelman, "George Sandism and the Woman Question in Nineteenth-Century Russia" (Ph.D. diss., Emory University, 1990), 90.

85. Petr Vail' and Aleksandr Genis, *Rodnaia rech'* (Tenafly, N. J.: 1990), 125–26. They also argue that this is only one of two places that Chernyshevskii reaches real heights in the description of love.

86. "А Вера Павловна? И Вера Павловна ничего не замечает. И в себе ничего не замечает? И в себе ничего не замечает Вера Павловна; только снится Вере Павловне сон" (LP 170–71).

87. This dream is referred to several times in the remainder of the novel. It obviously weighs heavily on the minds of the characters.

88. Divorce was simply not an option for the young couple. As Randall, p. 118, has noted, the novel is to some extent a loud plea for free and easy divorce.

89. One should keep in mind that Chernyshevskii was no stranger to this topic. Years before, he had analyzed and praised Tolstoi's ability to depict the human thought process, referring to it as the "dialectic of the soul." Morozenko argues that Vera Pavlovna's third dream owes much to Chernyshevskii's interest in Tolstoi's artistic method. Though stressing the value of the third dream, however, Morozenko views it as a rare exception in Chernyshevskii's fiction (Morozenko, 270–72).

90. One should note that Vail' and Genis, p. 125, argue that Chernyshevskii succeeded in spite of himself. They claim that Chernyshevskii was, in general, a weak psychologist. They attribute to Chernyshevskii a maxim that sensation is like any other chemical process. In such a worldview, they argue, there is no place for psychology: it leads to simple mechanism. In the novel, however, they argue that he got carried away and sometimes forgot his theory and, therefore, was able to give a sufficiently fine and deep psychological analysis.

91. Katz translates *iskusstvo* as "skill." This is an accurate translation, but keeping in mind Chernyshevskii's polemic with the aesthetes, "art" would perhaps be a better translation.

92. "Труден был маневр, на целые недели надобно было растянуть этот поворот налево кругом и повертываться так медленно, так ровно, как часовая стрелка: смотрите на нее, как хотите, внимательно, не увидите, что она поворачивается, а она себе исподтишка делает свое дело, идет в сторону от прежнего своего положения. Зато и какое же наслаждение было Кирсанову, как теоретику, любоваться своею ловкостью на практике. Эгоисты и материалисты, ведь они всё делают

собственно только в удовольствие себе. Да, и Кирсанов мог, положа руку на сердце, сказать, что он делает свою штуку в удовольствие себе: он радовался на свое искусство и молодечество" (LP 170).

93. Katz, 159. Pereira, 1975, p. 82, argues that the fourth dream "has justifiably placed Černyševskij in the front ranks of utopian propagandists." Ulam, 1976, p. 45, also interprets the fourth dream as evidence of Chernyshevskii's utopian socialism and argues that in his novel's vision of the future, Chernyshevskii seems to have forsaken his materialist viewpoint for this utopian, if socialist, idyll. See also Frank, pp. 80–82; Stites, pp. 26–27. Most Soviet scholars also interpret the fourth dream as a straightforward presentation by Chernyshevskii of his utopian socialist goals. For example, see Skaftymov, 1947, p. 62, who states, "The ideal of social freedom is demonstrated by Chernyshevskii in the pictures of the socialist organization depicted in Vera Pavlovna's fourth dream." Reifman, p. 104, states: "Chernyshevskii appears as a passionate propagandist of the ideas of Utopian Socialism. A society constructed in accordance with such ideas is depicted in Vera Pavlovna's fourth dream." See also Nikolaev, 1969, pp. 9–10; Tamarchenko, p. 237.

94. For example, Fetzer, p. 56, argues: "Chernyshevski's vision of the future, in a word, is his own original combination of elements drawn from a Romantic yearning for a life close to nature but based on the technological advances provided by a modern industrial society." See also Pereira, 1972, p. 41, who states: "Chernyshevsky was not talking metaphorically. Like Fourier, he believed that to achieve earthly paradise mankind only had to follow a relatively simple formula of scientific organization which would project Newton's laws into a social context, removing even the least element of chance or miscalculation, and improving weather in the bargain."

95. Vodovozov, pp. 15–16, states, "Vera Pavlovna's fourth dream is an authentic hymn to the beautiful future." Kuleshov makes a propaganda point when he states that now when Soviet society has achieved such a level of living, we can see just how brilliant and brave was Chernyshevskii's picture of the future society (Kuleshov, 11). One should also note that even Plekhanov, who is often highly critical of Chernyshevskii, commends him for this image (Plekhanov, 179).

96. See, for example, Skaftymov, 1972, p. 258, who states, "Despite all the utopianism of the individual details of these pictures, their main thesis contains a deep understanding of the sources of man's future social welfare." Riurikov, p. 161, states that there is evidence of "revolutionary romanticism" in the fourth dream, but insists that Chernyshevskii was a serious, sober revolutionary who was far from the trend of "flight from life." See also Nikolaev, 1969, p. 10; Reifman, p. 106; Verkhovskii, p. 132. Other Soviet scholars avoided the problem by simply declaring that there was nothing utopian about the fourth dream. For example, Pinaev, p. 59, inter-

prets the content of the fourth dream as Chernyshevskii's own view, but argues that there is nothing "fantastic" about it and that it was useful for the time because it helped to propagandize the principle of association. Lebedev, p. 82, though referring to the fourth dream as *romantika,* explains the existence of the fourth dream by arguing that for Chernyshevskii the concept of revolution and the concept of the beautiful are inseparable.

97. Vail' and Genis, 125.

98. In the last years of the Soviet Union, this view began to change somewhat among scholars there, as will be discussed later.

99. Rudenko argues that Chernyshevskii's historical thinking was antiutopian and kept him from any serious attempt at creating forms of the future reality. He further argues that Vera Pavlovna's fourth dream cannot be considered such an attempt. See Iu. K. Rudenko, *Roman N. G. Chernyshevskogo "Chto delat'?" Esteticheskoe svoeobrazie i khudozhestvennyi metod* (Leningrad: 1979), 83–84.

100. Kliamkin hints at this possibility when he states that Chernyshevskii the publicist wrote that it is impossible to foretell the future in all its wealth of details, but Chernyshevskii the writer seems to forget that. See I. Kliamkin, "Obraz myslei i obraz zhizni," *Literaturnoe obozrenie,* no. 7 (1978): 8.

101. "Как и многие наши обычаи и весь наш тон будут казаться грубы и грязны гораздо меньше чем через 500 лет. Но это не занимательно, я говорю о тех его рассказах, превосходных, в которых серьезно изображается страстная, высокая любовь. В них всего виднее его великий талант. Но вот что я хотела сказать, Саша: он изображает очень хорошо и сильно, судя по этому, можно сказать, что тогда не знали той неги любви, как теперь, любовь тогда не чувствовалась так сильно, хоть и говорят, что это была эпоха самого полного наслажденья любовью. Нет, как можно, они не наслаждались ею и вполовину так сильно. Их чувства были слишком поверхностны, их упоение еще слишком слабо и слишком мимолетно" (LP 274).

102. Frank, 80.

103. E. Lampert, *Sons against Fathers: Studies in Russian Radicalism and Revolution* (Oxford: 1965), 202, states regarding the fourth dream and other aspects of the novel, "Some of the answers are naïve in the extreme, showing his occasional tendency to mismatched, bizarre combinations."

104. "ты знаешь будущее. Оно светло, оно прекрасно. Говори же всем: вот что в будущем, будущее светло и прекрасно. Любите его, стремитесь к нему, работайте для него, приближайте его, переносите из него в настоящее, сколько можете перенести; настолько будет светла и добра, богата радостью и наслаждением ваша жизнь, насколько вы успеете перенести в нее из будущего. Стремитесь к нему, работайте для

него, приближайте его, переносите из него в настоящее всё, что можете перенести" (LP 290).

105. Frank, p. 80, states, "Chernyshevsky describes this Fourierist Paradise at great length and in loving detail."

106. This problem is complicated by the fact that there are undoubtedly individual elements of the dream that Chernyshevskii approved of. As discussed earlier, for example, although Chernyshevskii had little use for the utopian socialists, especially Fourier, he did approve of the principle of association that the utopian socialists used in their formulations. However, Chernyshevskii saw this principle as belonging to the leftist movement as a whole, not just to the utopian socialists.

107. Katz, p. 158, does observe the difference in narrative structure of the dream from the rest of the text by noting that to describe and interpret the futuristic scenes, an additional narrator is enlisted.

108. For a somewhat similar discussion, see Plimak, who argues that Chernyshevskii gives a dream about the radiant future to the reader as something to be used in the struggle. However, he argues, Chernyshevskii also had enough sense and tact to distance himself from that dream. Thus, it is placed in Vera Pavlovna's dream. See E. Plimak, "Ispytanie vremenem," *Voprosy literatury*, no. 2 (1978): 140–41.

109. Katz, 157.

110. Naumova, 48. She further states, p. 49, that if one takes the detail of the fourth dream as a certain authorial model of communism, then they do appear supernaive. But something else is here: the description is a reflection of those concerns, which arose during the development of the co-op. The details are seen by Vera and can be dreamed only by her. Because she is so involved in the affairs of the co-op, it is only natural that this colors her dream of the future.

111. Rudenko, 84. He further argues that this is why the dream is so Fourieristic.

112. Lanshchikov, 333. As Lanshchikov also notes, it is true that Vera Pavlovna is Chernyshevskii's favorite image and he even idealizes her, but to love one's hero is not the same as identifying him or her with oneself. See also U. A. Gural'nik, *Nasledie N. G. Chernyshevskogo-pisatelia i sovetskoe literaturovedenie* (Moscow: 1980), 222–23.

113. Lanshchikov, 334–35. Lanshchikov argues that Chernyshevskii presents Vera Pavlovna's ideas as Fourieristic to show that she is still somewhat undeveloped. He further stresses that one cannot claim that Chernyshevskii was a Fourierist based simply on the fact that Vera Pavlovna envisions the future in Fourierist terms.

114. Gural'nik and Gural'nik take a similar point of view when they argue "Vera Pavlovna's ideas about communist society are of course utopian. The naively idyllic intonations of the fourth dream, undoubtedly, tell

on the level of perception of its pathos by the contemporary reader, who is burdened by the difficult experience of twentieth-century history." See U. A. Gural'nik and Iu. U. Gural'nik, "Roman *Chto delat'?* segodnia. Opyt sovremennoi interpretatsii," in *"Chto delat'" N. G. Chernyshevskogo. Istoriko-funktsional'noe issledovanie* (Moscow: 1990), 226.

115. Verkhovskii adopts this argument in his attempt to apologize for the naïveté of the novel. He argues that Chernyshevskii depicts the younger generation as it actually is, mistakes and illusions included (Verkhovskii, 134).

CONCLUSION

1. Freeborn, in contrast, questions whether *What Is to Be Done?* is revolutionary and views it as "revolutionary" in only a limited sense, stating, "By any standards *What Is to Be Done?* can hardly be considered a dangerously subversive work, although its effect, largely due to the proscribing of it, was to prove revolutionary in several important ways." See Richard Freeborn, *The Russian Revolutionary Novel: Turgenev to Pasternak* (Cambridge: 1982), 23, 246.

2. "когда-нибудь и от этой оспы люди избавят себя, даже и средство известно, только еще не хотят принимать его, все равно как долго, очень долго не хотели принимать и средства против оспы" (LP 138).

3. As Morson, p. 102, notes in his discussion of Dostoevskii's *Diary of a Writer,* texts written under censorship always contain the possibility of a hidden meaning, which inevitably encourages readers to find such a meaning even where none is intended by the author. See Gary Saul Morson, *The Boundaries of Genre: Dostoevsky's Diary of a Writer and the Traditions of Literary Utopia* (Austin: 1981).

4. See, for example, P. S. Reifman, "Tri romana," in *Puti razvitiia russkoi literatury. Literaturovedenie* (Tartu: 1990), 92.

5. "Жюли, будь хладнокровнее. Это невозможно. Не он, так другой, все равно. Да вот, посмотри, Жан уже думает отбить ее у него, а таких Жанов тысячи, ты знаешь. От всех не убережешь, когда мать хочет торговать дочерью. Лбом стену не прошибешь, говорим мы, русские. Мы умный народ, Жюли. Видишь, как спокойно я живу, приняв этот наш русский принцип" (LP 25–26).

6. Mathewson, for example, argues that the tension between Chernyshevskii's formulation of "is" and "should be" has yielded in practice almost entirely to the second. He further argues that the desired and hoped-for not only dominate the selection of the characters, but also determine their every action and utterance. Mathewson's analysis is based largely on the assumption that Chernyshevskii meant to "write a *roman à thèse,* picturing

the future, and personifying worthy moral qualities." See Rufus W. Mathewson Jr., *The Positive Hero in Russian Literature,* 2nd ed. (Stanford: 1975), 74–75. See also Freeborn, p. 246. In a similar vein, Soviet scholars also dealt with this topic in terms of chronotope, arguing that *What Is to Be Done?* is constructed in part on the tension between two chronotopes. See T. Iu. Dubrovina, "Khronotop v romane N. G. Chernyshevskogo *Chto delat'?*" in *Iz istorii russkoi literatury i literaturnoi kritiki* (Kishinev: 1984), 54–60; E. A. Podshivalova, "O khudozhestvennom khronotope v romane N. G. Chernyshevskogo *Chto delat'?*" in *Problema avtora v khudozhestvennoi literature. Mezhvuzovskii sbornik nauchnykh trudov* (Izhevsk: 1983), 61–69.

7. Mathewson views Chernyshevskii as an important step in the creation of the positive hero. Mathewson uses this term in the sense of the "posited hero" and bases himself largely on interpreting Rakhmetov as Chernyshevskii's ideal (Mathewson, 76–77). Soviet scholars often adopted a similar approach, although, from their point of view, Chernyshevskii was to be praised for his creation of Rakhmetov. For example, see I. N. Sutiagin, "O narodnosti romana N. G. Chernyshevskogo *Chto delat'?*" in *Roman N. G. Chernyshevskogo "Chto delat'?" (K 100-letiiu vykhoda v svet). Sbornik statei* (Shakhty: 1963), 31–32.

8. See Reifman, pp. 95–99, for a recent discussion. Some of the interpretations posited by Soviet scholars bordered upon the ridiculous and were based solely on supposition, guided by the desire to make Chernyshevskii appear as a Bolshevik forerunner. For example, by positing that the winter picnic scene contains allusions to the peasant uprisings of the 1860s, Tamarchenko argues that Chernyshevskii advocates a "the worse, the better philosophy." See G. E. Tamarchenko, *Chernyshevskii-romanist* (Leningrad: 1976), 218. Such a philosophy is not consistent, however, with Chernyshevskii's activity before the Emancipation, when he fought for as good a deal as possible for the peasants. It is also not consistent with his views on the philosophy of "the end justifies the means." See also Magon, who argues that Chernyshevskii advocates a "the worse the better" philosophy in the novel. He also argues that Chernyshevskii's political program as expressed in the novel is the same as that of "Young Russia." See L. Magon, "Roman *Chto delat'?* i obshchestvenno-politicheskaia platforma *Molodoi Rossii,*" in *N. G. Chernyshevskii. Stat'i, issledovaniia i materialy* (Saratov: 1958), 1:499–513. As Pomper points out, however, the bloodthirsty character of "Young Russia" dismayed both Herzen and Chernyshevskii, who anticipated the kind of reaction it would provoke. See Philip Pomper, *The Russian Revolutionary Intelligentsia* (Arlington Heights, Ill.: 1970).

9. L. M. Lotman, "Sotsial'nyi ideal, etika i estetika Chernyshevskogo," in *Idei sotsializma v russkoi klassicheskoi literature* (Leningrad: 1969), 208. See also Iu. M. Prozorov, "N. G. Chernyshevskii," in *Istoriia*

russkoi literatury XIX veka. Vtoraia polovina (Moscow: 1987), 149, who argues that the characters are ordained for happiness and, p. 155, that the novel is a work that is optimistic and filled with hope for a quick change.

10. See, for example, Mathewson, pp. 78–80. See also N. N. Strakhov, "Schastlivye liudi," *Iz istorii literaturnago nigilizma. 1861–1865* (Saint Petersburg: 1890), 318–19.

11. Plimak provides a concise summary of this problem as it arose among Chernyshevskii's contemporaries and continued in the Soviet years. See E. Plimak, "Ispytanie vremenem," *Voprosy literatury,* no. 2 (1978): 129–34. See also Tamarchenko, p. 217, and N. A. Verderevskaia, *Stanovlenie tipa raznochintsa v russkoi realisticheskoi literature 40–60kh godov XIX veka (k probleme tipologii zhanra, siuzheta i obraza)* (Kazan': 1975), 217, who note the pessimism of the winter picnic scene.

12. "Недавно родился этот тил и быстро распложается. Он рожден временем, он знамение времени, и, сказать ли?—он исчезнет вместе с своим временем, недолгим временем. Его недавняя жизнь обречена быть и недолгою жизнью.... еще немного лет, быть может и не лет, а месяцев, и станут их проклинать, и они будут согнаны со сцены, ошиканные, срамимые.... И не останется их на сцене?—Нет" (LP 149). Plimak, 128. See also A. I. Volodin, Iu. F. Kariakin, and E. G. Plimak, *Chernyshevskii ili Nechaev* (Moscow: 1976), 175. Lotman, p. 208, takes this passage into account, arguing that Chernyshevskii is aware that the new people will not be accepted by their contemporaries, but that for the most part, he puts this tragic fact to the side. She further argues that Chernyshevskii's characters are happy because he consciously breaks with the tragic aspect of the revolutionaries' situation.

13. Plimak's analysis, first presented in A. I. Volodin et al., touched off an intense response in Soviet criticism. Dubrovina, for example, counters his assertions by linking the rejection of the traditional concept of the "tragic," formulated by Chernyshevskii in his dissertation, to the structure of the novel. She argues that there are indeed pessimistic, or tragic, elements in *What Is to Be Done?* but that the novel is constructed on the basis of the optimistic overcoming the tragic. Thus, in sum, she views the novel as optimistic. See her "Preodolenie tragicheskogo kak pafos romana *Chto delat'?* N. G. Chernyshevskogo," in *Literaturno-kriticheskie opyty i nabliudeniia* (Kishinev: 1982), 51–67. Plimak's position is succinctly stated in his 1978 article.

14. "И в самом деле, они все живут спокойно. Живут ладно и дружно, и тихо и шумно, и весело и дельно" (LP 334).

15. "Они живут весело и дружно, работают и отдыхают, и наслаждаются жизнью, и смотрят на будущее если не без забот, то с твердою и совершенно основательной уверенностью, что чем дальше, тем лучше будет" (LP 335).

16. "Но из этого еще не следует, чтобы мой рассказ о них был кончен, нет." (LP 334).

17. "Мы проживем тихо и спокойно" (LP 334).

18. "Это не зависит от моего „да" или „нет", а потому в удовольствие тебе скажу: да, мы проживем спокойно" (LP 334).

19. *What's to Be Done? A Romance,* trans. B. R. Tucker (Boston: 1886), 317. Some of Chernyshevskii's contemporaries also found this section incomprehensible. See A. A. Fet, "*Chto delat'?* Iz rasskazov o novykh liudiakh. Roman N. G. Chernyshevskogo," *Literaturnoe nasledstvo* 25–26 (1936): 525.

20. H. Carr, introduction to N. G. Chernyshevsky, *What Is to Be Done?* (New York: 1961), xiii. See also William F. Woehrlin, *Chernyshevskii: The Man and the Journalist* (Cambridge: 1971), 316, who states of this section, "The symbolism is too obscure and the suggestions too veiled to be certain what the author was trying to express in this incoherent section."

21. Katz's translation and a brief introduction appear in the *Russian Review* 41, no. 2 (April 1982): 181–96. In the same year Virago Press put out its edition of *What Is to Be Done?* using the expurgated version of Tucker's translation. For a discussion of the English translations that appeared prior to his own complete translation, see Michael R. Katz, "English Translations of *What Is to Be Done?*" *Slavic Review* 46, no. 1 (1987): 125–31.

22. See Adam B. Ulam, *Ideologies and Illusions: Revolutionary Thought from Herzen to Solzhenitsyn* (Cambridge: 1976), p. 45, who states: "To the modern reader this scene is bewildering, but to its contemporaries it was the allegory of a victorious revolution, which according to the chronological hints was to take place in 1866." See also Freeborn, p. 27; Irina Paperno, "The Novel Myth: N. G. Chernyshevskii's *What Is to Be Done?*" in *Issues in Russian Literature before 1917* (Slavica, 1989): p. 140. In his annotation (no. 312) to Katz's translation, Wagner argues that the winter picnic represents "the gathering of revolutionary forces for the final assault on the old regime" (Katz, 434).

23. See, for example, Joe Andrew, *Women in Russian Literature, 1780–1863* (London: 1988), 159. Andrew offers an excellent analysis of several aspects of the novel, but this is marred by his disregard for the conclusion of the novel. He claims that Vera Pavlovna's decision to become a doctor is the end of her development.

24. This is precisely what some English editions did. In the 1961 Vintage edition the majority of section 23 of chapter 5 and all of chapter 6 were cut so that the novel ended with the "optimistic" statements by the narrator.

25. Here Soviet scholars follow the formulation developed by Lenin, who stated "And do you remember the Lady in Black? . . . She calls Vera Pavlovna, the Kirsanovs, the Lopukhovs to the underground. In this is the

entire meaning." Quoted in N. Naumova, *Roman N. G. Chernyshevskogo "Chto delat'?"* (Leningrad: 1972), 16.

26. G. Verkhovskii, *O romane N. G. Chernyshevskogo "Chto delat'?"* (Iaroslavl': 1959), 148–50, 183; G. I. Ishchuk, "Nekotorye problemy iskusstva v romane N. G. Chernyshevskogo *Chto delat'*?" in *Roman N. G. Chernyshevskogo "Chto delat'?" (K 100-letiiu vykhoda v svet). Sbornik statei* (Shakhty: 1963), 70–71; S. M. Shibaev, "Moral'nyi oblik 'obyknovennykh liudei' N. G. Chernyshevskogo," in *Roman N. G. Chernyshevskogo "Chto delat'?" (K 100-letiiu vykhoda v svet). Sbornik statei* (Shakhty: 1963), 45–46; V. N. Shul'gin, *Ocherki zhizni i tvorchestva N. G. Chernyshevskogo* (Moscow: 1956), 118–19, 129–30; N. V. Vodovozov, *Roman N. G. Chernyshevskogo "Chto Delat'?"* (Moscow: 1953), 17–18, 25–26; Iu. K. Rudenko, *Roman N. G. Chernyshevskogo "Chto delat'?" Esteticheskoe svoeobrazie i khudozhestvennyi metod* (Leningrad: 1979), 35.

27. I will not recount the parameters of this debate in great detail. Katz, 1982, pp. 182–83, provides a short summary. The key Soviet figures in this debate were G. Tamarchenko and B. Ia. Bukhshtab. See their polemic in B. Ia. Bukhshtab, "Zapiska N. G. Chernyshevskogo o romane *Chto delat'?*" *Izvestiia Akademii Nauk SSSR. Otdelenie literatury i iazyka* 12, no. 2 (1953): 158–69; B. Ia. Bukhshtab, "K voprosy o siuzhete romana Chernyshevskogo *Chto delat'?*" *Izvestiia Akademii Nauk SSSR. Otdelenie literatury i iazyka* 15, no. 5 (1956): 444–56; G. Tamarchenko, *Romany N. G. Chernyshevskogo* (Saratov: 1954), 63–72. In his later book, Tamarchenko admits that Bukhshtab has changed his mind, but is still resistant on several issues. Tamarchenko also provides a summary of the debate up to that point. See Tamarchenko, 1976, pp. 222–25. See also M. V. Teplinskii, "Avtor-povestvovatel' v romane N. G. Chernyshevskogo *Chto delat'?*" *N. G. Chernyshevskii. Stat'i, issledovaniia i materialy* (Saratov: 1978), 8:130–31; L. M. Lotman, "Ideino-khudozhestvennye printsipy belletristiki Chernyshevskogo 1860–1870-kh godov," in *N. G. Chernyshevskii. Estetika. Literatura. Kritika* (Leningrad: 1979), 88–89; V. G. Smolitskii, *Iz ravelina. O sud'be romana N. G. Chernyshevskogo "Chto delat'?"* 2nd ed. (Moscow: 1977), 48; P. Reifman, *N. G. Chernyshevskii* (Tartu: 1973), 94; Verkhovskii, p. 148; Vodovozov, pp. 26–28.

28. Rudenko, 33. Rudenko stresses that the evidence sometimes used to support either version (the note and Chernyshevskii's diary) lies outside the bounds of the novel, whereas the text of the novel itself lends some support to both versions, with neither being obligatory.

29. In his second article, 1956, p. 446, Bukhshtab, relying on key passages found in the winter picnic scene, demonstrates that the young man of about thirty cannot be Rakhmetov. Teplinskii, p. 130, on the other hand, demonstrates that it cannot be Chernyshevskii by analyzing the ages of the various characters involved.

30. See also Naumova, p. 51, who argues that the story of the Lady in Black could be the story of any woman whose man has chosen the path of revolution. In his comments accompanying the translation of the conclusion, Katz sides with Bukhshtab, arguing that the Lady in Black and the young man of about thirty are Chernyshevskii and Ol'ga Sokratovna (Katz, 1982, 183). See also the annotations that accompany his full translation of *What Is to Be Done?*

31. I. Kliamkin, "Obraz myslei i obraz zhizni," *Literaturnoe obozrenie,* no. 7 (1978): 12–13.

32. Verderevskaia, pp. 126–127, argues that in chapter 4 everything is presented in an uplifted tone, but in the winter picnic scene a shadow falls across this. She argues that the sensation of a tragic ending arises.

33. "По крайней мере, дамы раз пять-шесть переглядывались между собою с тяжелою встревоженностью. Раза два Вера Павловна украдкою шепнула мужу: «Саша, что если это случится со мною?» Кирсанов в первый раз не нашелся, что сказать; во второй нашелся: «нет, Верочка, с тобою этого не может случиться».—«Не может? Ты уверен?»—«Да». И Катерина Васильевна раза два шепнула украдкою мужу: «со мною этого не может быть, Чарли?» В первый раз Бьюмонт только улыбнулся, не весело и не успокоительно: во второй тоже нашелся: «по всей вероятности, не может; по всей вероятности»" (LP 338). Shibaev, pp. 46–47, argues that Kirsanov and Lopukhov's slowness in answering show that the thought of giving oneself over to revolutionary activity is beginning to possess the consciousness of the regular new people.

34. N. L. Brodskii and N. P. Sidorov, *Kommentarii k romanu N. G. Chernyshevskogo "Chto delat'?"* (Moscow: 1933), 198–201, discuss these songs in detail. They argue that Chernyshevskii is attempting to remind his wife that he forewarned her about the dangers of his political activity. See also Ishchuk, pp. 67–73, who provides an extended discussion of the songs, also arguing that Chernyshevskii attempts to communicate something to his wife by means of the songs.

35. As Tamarchenko, 1976, pp. 220–21, notes, the Lady in Black polemicizes with the ascetic mentality in political activity, arguing for the right to love. He even notes that her point of view is in direct contradiction to Rakhmetov's views. However, Tamarchenko sees no contradiction and interprets Rakhmetov as Chernyshevskii's ideal, a positive model to be followed.

36. Freeborn, p. 27, in commenting on this section, argues that the image of the Lady in Black, for all its connotations of bereavement and sorrow, appears to be less that of a widow or a woman waiting for her beloved than that of a mother who sings to entertain her children. He argues that such a final image of motherhood is symbolically appropriate, underlining the fact that revolution involves giving birth to a new life.

37. "(—«Забудь, что я тебе говорила, Саша, слушай ее!»—шепчет одна и жмет руку.—«Зачем я не говорила тебе этого? Теперь буду говорить», шепчет другая)" (LP 343).

38. Consistent with the sexual dichotomy present throughout the novel, it is the female characters who first demonstrate this boldness, not the male.

39. See also Kliamkin, p. 13, who argues that until the very last pages of the novel, the main characters remain ordinary new people: their transformation is not easy and the author does not hasten it.

40. Soviet scholars often tended to see *What Is to Be Done?* as a manual on secret organizations. See Verkhovskii, p. 143; Naumova, p. 83; Lotman, 1969, pp. 226–27.

41. Soviet scholars simply rely on implication for this point. By assuming that Rakhmetov is Chernyshevskii's ideal image of a professional revolutionary, they argue that the main characters must logically adopt his path as the next stage in their development.

42. Tamarchenko argues, 1976, p. 217, that had the novel ended with the picnic scene, it would have been too gloomy, so Chernyshevskii added the sixth chapter.

43. Plimak, p. 161, argues, moreover, that Chernyshevskii urges caution. He argues that there are numerous warnings within *What Is to Be Done?* not to begin untimely attempts to start a revolution.

44. They analyze Chernyshevskii's various remarks on historical development and conclude that he was aware that "victory" in the struggle would not be immediate or a one-time thing (Volodin et al., 192–94).

45. Anatolii Lanshchikov, *N. G. Chernyshevskii,* 2nd ed. (Moscow: 1987), p. 296, argues that the question "What is to be done?" is directed not at the reader but at the author himself.

Bibliography

With regard to differing spellings of Russian surnames as they appear on the title pages of translated works: If a Russian author's name occurs in this bibliography only once, it is alphabetized according to the form in which it appears on the title page. If a Russian author's name occurs several times and in variant forms, it is alphabetized according the Library of Congress (LC) transliteration system. Significant differences from the LC system will be noted in brackets. All works in Russian are transliterated according to the LC system.

Acton, Edward. Review of *What Is to Be Done?* by Nikolai Chernyshevsky. Translated by Michael R. Katz. *Revolutionary Russia* (June 1990): 118.

Afanas'ev, E. L. "Roman N. G. Chernyshevskogo *Chto delat'?* i zhiznennyi ideal narodovol'tsa." In *"Chto delat'?" N. G. Chernyshevskogo. Istoriko-funktsional'noe issledovanie,* edited by K. N. Lomunov. Moscow: Nauka, 1990.

Alekseev, N. A., ed. *Protsess N. G. Chernyshevskogo.* Saratov: Saratovskoe oblastnoe gosudarstvennoe izdatel'stvo, 1939.

Alissandratos, Julia. "Hagiographical Commonplaces and Medieval Prototypes in N. G. Chernyshevsky's *What Is to Be Done?*" *St. Vladimir's Theological Quarterly* 26, no. 2 (1982): 103–17.

Andrew, Joe. *Russian Writers and Society in the Second Half of the Nineteenth Century.* London: Macmillan, 1982.

———. *Women in Russian Literature, 1780–1863.* London: Macmillan, 1988.

Antonova, G. N. "N. N. Strakhov o romane *Chto delat'?*" In *N. G. Chernyshevskii. Stat'i, issledovaniia i materialy,* vol. 8, edited by E. I. Pokusaev. Saratov: Izdatel'stvo Saratovskogo universiteta, 1978.

Antonovich, M. A. *Literaturno-kriticheskie stat'i.* Moscow: Gosudarstvennoe izdatel'stvo khudozhestvennoi literatury, 1961.

Bakhmetev, P. A. "(Pis'mo k Gertsenu)." *Literaturnoe nasledstvo* 41–42 (1941): 526–28.

Bakhtin, Mikhail. *The Dialogic Imagination.* Edited by Michael Holquist. Translated by Caryl Emerson and Michael Holquist. Austin: University of Texas Press, 1981.

———. *Problems of Dostoevsky's Poetics.* Edited and translated by Caryl Emerson. Minneapolis: University of Minnesota Press, 1984.

Bakhtin, M. M./P. N. Medvedev. *The Formal Method in Literary Scholarship.* Translated by Albert J. Wehrle. Cambridge: Harvard University Press, 1985.

Barghoorn, Frederick G. "The Philosophic Outlook of Chernyshevski: Materialism and Utilitarianism." *American Slavic and East European Review* 6, nos. 18–19 (December 1947): 42–56.

Barstow, Jane. "Dostoevsky's *Notes From Underground* versus Chernyshevsky's *What Is to Be Done?*" *College Literature* 5 (1978): 24–33.

Bayley, John. Introduction to *Eugene Onegin,* by Alexander Pushkin. New York: Penguin Books, 1979.

Bebel, A. "Ein idealistischer Roman." *Neue Zeit* 3 (1885).

Belova, N. M. "Roman N. G. Chernyshevskogo «Chto delat'?» i prosvetitel'skaia literatura XVIII veka." In *N. G. Chernyshevskii. Istoriia. Filosofiia. Literatura.* Saratov: Izdatel'stvo Saratovskogo universiteta, 1994.

Berdyaev, Nicolas. *The Origin of Russian Communism.* Ann Arbor: University of Michigan Press, 1960.

———. *The Russian Idea.* Westport, Conn.: Greenwood Press, 1979.

Berlin, Isaiah. Introduction to *Roots of Revolution,* by Franco Venturi. New York: Alfred A. Knopf, 1960.

———. *Russian Thinkers.* New York: Viking Press, 1978.

Berliner, G. *N. G. Chernyshevskii i ego literaturnye vragi.* Moscow-Leningrad: Gosudarstvennoe izdatel'stvo, 1930.

Bibikov, P. A. "Sovremennye Utopisty. Izlozhenie i kriticheskii razbor teorii Fur'e." *Kriticheskie etiudy P. A. Bibikova.* Saint Petersburg: 1865.

Bochkarev, N. I., ed. *Istoriia russkogo utopicheskogo sotsializma XIX veka.* Moscow: Izdatel'stvo Moskovskogo universiteta, 1985.

Bogoslovsky, Nikolai. "Great Russian Scholar and Critic." *International Literature,* no. 10 (October 1939): 41–54.

Borisov, I. "Alekseevskii ravelin v 1862–65 gg." *Russkaia starina* 108, book 12 (December 1901): 573–78.

Bowman, Herbert E. "Art and Reality in Russian 'Realist' Criticism." *Journal of Aesthetics and Art Criticism* 12, no. 3 (March, 1954): 386–92.

———. "Revolutionary Elitism in Černyševskij." *American Slavic and East European Review* 13 (1954): 185–99.

Brodskii, N. L., and N. P. Sidorov. *Kommentarii k romanu N. G. Chernyshevskogo "Chto delat'?"* Moscow: Mir, 1933.

Brown, Edward J. "So Much Depends . . . Russian Critics in Search of 'Reality.'" *Russian Review* 48 (1989): 353–81.

Brown, Richard L. "Chernyshevskii, Dostoevskii, and the Peredvizhniki: Toward a Russian Realist Aesthetic?" Ph.D. diss., Ohio University, 1980.
Bukhbinder, N. A. "Tsenzura o *Chto delat'?* N. G. Chernyshevskogo." *Katorga i ssylka,* no. 44 (1928): 43–50.
Bukhshtab, B. Ia. "K voprosy o siuzhete romana Chernyshevskogo *Chto delat'?*" *Izvestiia Akademii Nauk SSSR. Otdelenie literatury i iazyka* 15, no. 5 (September–October 1956): 444–56.
———. "Zapiska N. G. Chernyshevskogo o romane *Chto delat'?*" *Izvestiia Akademii Nauk SSSR. Otdelenie literatury i iazyka* 12, no. 2 (March–April 1953): 158–69.
Bushkanets, E. "Tsarskaia tsenzura i *Chto delat'?* Chernyshevskogo." *Ogonek,* no. 39 (September 1951): 24.
Carr, E. H. Introduction to *What Is to Be Done?* by N. G. Chernyshevsky. New York: Vintage Books, 1961.
Chernyshevskii, N. G. *Chto delat'?* Leningrad: Nauka, 1975.
———. *Izbrannye proizvedeniia v trekh tomakh.* 3 vols. Leningrad: Khudozhestvennaia literatura, 1978.
———. "L. N. Tolstoy's *Childhood* and *Boyhood* and *Military Tales.*" In *Belinsky, Chernyshevsky, and Dobrolyubov: Selected Criticism.* Edited by Ralph Matlaw. New York: Dutton, 1962.
———. *Polnoe sobranie sochinenii.* 16 vols. Moscow: Gosudarstvennoe izdatel'stvo khudozhestvennoi literatury, 1939–53.
———. *Prologue: A Novel from the Beginning of the 1860s.* Translated, annotated, and with an introduction by Michael R. Katz. Evanston, Ill.: Northwestern University Press, 1995.
———. "The Russian at the Rendez-vous." In *Belinsky, Chernyshevsky, and Dobrolyubov: Selected Criticism.* Edited by Ralph Matlaw. New York: Dutton, 1962.
———. *Selected Philosophical Essays.* Moscow: Foreign Languages Publishing House, 1953.
——— [Tchernuishevsky]. *A Vital Question; or What Is to Be Done?* Translated by Nathan Haskell Dole and S. S. Skidelsky. New York: Crowell, 1886.
——— [Tchernyshewsky]. *What's to Be Done? A Romance.* Translated by Benjamin R. Tucker. Boston, 1886.
———. *What Is to Be Done?* The Tucker translation revised and abridged by L. V. Turkevich. Introduction by E. H. Carr. New York: Vintage Books, 1961.
———. *What Is to Be Done?* The Tucker translation expanded by Cathy Porter. Introduction by E. H. Carr. New preface by Cathy Porter. London: Virago Press, 1982.
———. *What Is to Be Done?* Translated by N. Dole and S. S. Skidelsky. 1886. Reprint, with an introduction by Kathryn Feuer, Ann Arbor, Mich.: Ardis, 1986.

———. *What Is to Be Done?* Translated by Michael R. Katz. Annotated by William G. Wagner. Ithaca: Cornell University Press, 1989.

N. G. Chernyshevskii. Istoriia. Filosofiia. Literatura. Saratov: Izdatel'stvo Saratovskogo universiteta, 1994.

N. G. Chernyshevskii v obshchestvennoi mysli narodov zarubezhnykh stran. Moscow: Nauka, 1981.

Chistiakova, M. "Lev Tolstoi i Frantsiia." *Literaturnoe nasledstvo* 31–32 (1937): 981–1025.

Clark, Katerina. *The Soviet Novel: History as Ritual.* Chicago: University of Chicago Press, 1981.

Copleston, Frederick C., S. J. *Philosophy in Russia from Herzen to Lenin and Berdyaev.* Notre Dame, Ind.: University of Notre Dame Press, 1986.

Corbet, C. "Réminiscences sandiennes dans *Que faire?* de Černyševskij." *Revue des études slaves* 43 (1964): 17–33.

Demchenko, A. A. *N. G. Chernyshevskii. Nauchnaia biografiia.* 4 parts. Saratov: Izdatel'stvo Saratovskogo universiteta, 1978–94.

Dobrolyubov, N. A. *Selected Philosophical Essays.* Moscow: Foreign Languages Publishing House, 1956.

Dostoevskii, F. M. *Polnoe sobranie sochinenii v tridtsati tomakh.* 30 vols. Leningrad: Nauka, 1980.

———. *Uncle's Dream and Other Stories.* Translated by David McDuff. New York: Penguin, 1989.

F. M. Dostoevskii v vospominaniiakh sovremennikov v dvukh tomakh. 2 vols. Moscow: Khudozhestvennaia literatura, 1990.

Dubrovina, T. Iu. "Bor'ba i tragicheskoe v estetike i khudozhestvennoi praktike N. G. Chernyshevskogo." In *Literaturno-kriticheskie opyty i nabliudeniia.* Kishinev: Shtiintsa, 1982.

———. "Khronotop v romane N. G. Chernyshevskogo *Chto delat'?*" In *Iz istorii russkoi literatury i literaturnoi kritiki.* Kishinev: Shtiintsa, 1984.

———. "Preodolenie tragicheskogo kak pafos romana *Chto delat'?* N. G. Chernyshevskogo." In *Literaturno-kriticheskie opyty i nabliudeniia.* Kishinev: Shtiintsa, 1982.

Efremenko, E. L. "Publikatsiia khudozhestvennykh proizvedenii N. G. Chernyshevskogo." In *Voprosy tekstologii. Sbornik statei.* Moscow: Izdatel'stvo Akademii Nauk SSSR, 1957.

Efremov, A. F. "Rechevye sredstva postroeniia obraza 'osobennogo cheloveka' v romane N. G. Chernyshevskogo *Chto delat'?*" In *N. G. Chernyshevskii. Stat'i, issledovaniia i materialy,* vol. 4, edited by E. I. Pokusaev. Saratov: Izdatel'stvo Saratovskogo universiteta, 1965.

Eidelman, Dawn Diane. *George Sand and the Nineteenth-Century Russian Love-Triangle Novels.* Lewisburg: Bucknell University Press, 1994.

———. "George Sandism and the Woman Question in Nineteenth-Century Russia." Ph.D. diss., Emory University, 1990.

Eidel'man, N. Ia. "Pavel Aleksandrovich Bakhmetev." In *Revoliutsionnaia situatsiia v Rossii v 1859–1861 gg.*, vol. 4, edited by M. V. Nechkina. Moscow: Nauka, 1965.

———. "Po sledam Rakhmetova." *Voprosy i otvety*, no. 8 (1973): 53–60.

Engel, Barbara Alpern. *Mothers and Daughters: Women of the Intelligentsia in Nineteenth-Century Russia.* New York: Cambridge University Press, 1983.

Evgen'ev-Maksimov, V. *Sovremennik pri Chernyshevskom i Dobroliubove.* Leningrad: Khudozhestvennaia literatura, 1936.

Fanger, Donald. *The Creation of Nikolai Gogol.* Cambridge: Belknap Press of the Harvard University Press, 1979.

Fet, A. A. "*Chto delat'*? Iz rasskazov o novykh liudiakh. Roman N. G. Chernyshevskogo." *Literaturnoe nasledstvo* 25–26 (1936): 485–544.

Fetzer, Leland. *Pre-Revolutionary Russian Science Fiction: An Anthology (Seven Utopias and a Dream).* Ann Arbor, Mich.: Ardis, 1982.

Feuer, Kathryn. "*Fathers and Sons:* Fathers and Children." In *The Russian Novel from Pushkin to Pasternak,* edited by John Garrard. New Haven: Yale University Press, 1983.

________. "What Is to Be Done about *What Is to Be Done?*" In *What Is to Be Done?* by Nikolai Chernyshevsky. Ann Arbor, Mich.: Ardis, 1986.

Filina, M. A. "*Chto delat'?* Chernyshevskogo i zapadno-evropeiskaia sotsial'no-filosofskaia utopiia." In *N. G. Chernyshevskii. Estetika. Literatura. Kritika.* Leningrad: Nauka, 1979.

Frank, Joseph. *Dostoevsky: The Miraculous Years, 1865–1871.* Princeton: Princeton University Press, 1995.

———. *Dostoevsky: The Stir of Liberation, 1860–1865.* Princeton: Princeton University Press, 1986.

———. *Dostoevsky: The Years of Ordeal, 1850–1859.* Princeton: Princeton University Press, 1983.

———. "N. G. Chernyshevsky: A Russian Utopia." *Southern Review,* New Series 3, no. 1 (1967): 68–84.

———. *Through the Russian Prism.* Princeton: Princeton University Press, 1990.

Freeborn, Richard. *The Russian Revolutionary Novel: Turgenev to Pasternak.* Cambridge: Cambridge University Press, 1982.

Genereux, George. "The Crisis in Russian Literary Criticism: 1856—the Decisive Year." *Russian Literature Triquarterly,* no. 17 (1982): 117–40.

Gerstein, Linda. *Nikolai Strakhov.* Cambridge: Harvard University Press, 1971.

Gertsen, Aleksandr. *My Past and Thoughts.* Berkeley: University of California Press, 1973.

———. *Sobranie sochinenii.* 30 vols. Moscow: Izdatel'stvo Akademii Nauk SSSR, 1954–65.

Gifford, Henry. *The Hero of His Time: A Theme in Russian Literature.* London: Edward Arnold, 1950.

Gippius, Vasilii. "Chernyshevskii—stikhoved." In *N. G. Chernyshevskii. Sbornik. Neizdannye stat'i, materialy, vospominaniia.* Saratov: Izdanie nizhne-volzhskogo oblastnogo nauchnogo obshchestva kraevedeniia, 1926.

———. "Neizdannaia stat'ia Chernyshevskogo." In *Nikolai Gavrilovich Chernyshevskii 1828–1928. Neizdannye teksty, materialy i stat'i,* edited by S. Z. Katsenbogen. Saratov: 1928.

Gleason, Abbott. *Young Russia.* Chicago: Chicago University Press, 1983.

Goldman, Emma. *Living My Life.* 2 vols. New York: Dover, 1970.

Gor'kii, Maksim. *Istoriia russkoi literatury.* Moscow, 1939.

Gregory, Frederick. *Scientific Materialism in Nineteenth-Century Germany.* Boston: D. Reidel, 1977.

———. "Scientific versus Dialectical Materialism: A Clash of Ideologies in Nineteenth-Century German Radicalism." *Isis* 68, no. 242 (June 1977): 206–23.

Grigorovich, D. V. *Polnoe sobranie sochinenii v 12 tomakh.* 12 vols. Saint Petersburg, 1896.

Grigoryan, M. *N. G. Chernyshevsky's World Outlook.* Moscow: Foreign Languages Publishing House, 1954.

Gudzii, N. K. *History of Early Russian Literature.* Translated by Susan Wilbur Jones. New York: Macmillan, 1949.

———. *Khrestomatiia po drevnei russkoi literature xi–xvii vekov.* 5th ed. Moscow: Gosudarstvennoe uchebno-pedagogicheskoe izdatel'stvo ministerstva prosveshcheniia RSFSR, 1952.

Günther, H. "Turgenevs *Väter und Söhne* und Černyševskijs *Was tun?*" *Zeitschrift für Slawistik* 34, no. 5 (1989): 674–83.

Gural'nik, U. A. *Nasledie N. G. Chernyshevskogo-pisatelia i sovetskoe literaturovedenie.* Moscow: Nauka, 1980.

Gural'nik, U. A., and Iu. U. Gural'nik. "Roman *Chto delat'?* segodnia. Opyt sovremennoi interpretatsii." In *"Chto delat'" N. G. Chernyshevskogo. Istoriko-funktsional'noe issledovanie,* edited by K. N. Lomunov. Moscow: Nauka, 1990.

Hare, Richard. *Pioneers of Russian Social Thought: Studies of Non-Marxian Formation in Nineteenth-Century Russia and of Its Partial Revival in the Soviet Union.* New York: Oxford University Press, 1951.

Hecht, David. "Chernyshevsky and American Influence on Russia." *Science and Society* 9, no. 4 (Fall 1945): 318–34.

———. *Russian Radicals Look to America, 1825–1894.* Cambridge: Harvard University Press, 1947.

———. "Two Classic Russian Publicists and the United States." *American Slavic and East European Review* 4, parts 1–2 (August 1945): 1–32.

Herrmann, Lesley Singer. "George Sand and the Nineteenth-Century Russian Novel: The Quest for a Heroine." Ph.D. diss., Columbia University, 1979.

Hertzler, Joyce Oramel. *The History of Utopian Thought.* New York: Cooper Square Publishers, 1965.

Herzen: See Gertsen, A.

Ishchuk, G. I. "Nekotorye problemy iskusstva v romane N. G. Chernyshevskogo *Chto delat'?*" In *Roman N. G. Chernyshevskogo "Chto delat'?" (K 100-letiiu vykhoda v svet). Sbornik statei.* Shakhty: 1963.

[Kapnist, P.] *Sobranie materialov o napravlenii razlichnykh otraslei russkoi slovesnosti.* Saint Petersburg: Tipografiia ministerstva vnutrennikh del, 1865.

Karlinsky, Simon. "The True Father of Bolshevism." *Saturday Review,* September 4, 1976, p. 45.

———. "Vladimir Nabokov's Novel *Dar* as a Work of Literary Criticism: A Structural Analysis." *Slavic and East European Journal* 7, no. 3 (1963): 284–90.

Karp, Carole Sue. "George Sand's Reception in Russia, 1832–1881." Ph.D. diss., University of Michigan, 1976.

Karpovich, Michael M. "N. G. Chernyshevski between Socialism and Liberalism." *Cahiers du Monde Russe et Soviétique* 1, no. 4 (1960): 569–83.

Katsenbogen, S. Z., ed. *Nikolai Gavrilovich Chernyshevskii. 1828–1928. Neizdannye teksty, materialy i stat'i.* Saratov: 1928.

Katz, Michael R. "The Conclusion of *What Is to Be Done?*" *Russian Review* 41, no. 2 (April 1982): 181–96.

———. "English Translations of *What Is to Be Done?*" *Slavic Review* 46, no. 1 (Spring 1987): 125–31.

———. "Vera Pavlovna's Dreams in Chernyshevskii's *What Is to Be Done?*" In *Issues in Russian Literature before 1917,* edited by J. Douglas Clayton. Columbus, Ohio: Slavica, 1989.

Katz, Michael R., and William G. Wagner. "Introduction: Chernyshevsky, *What Is to Be Done?* and the Russian Intelligentsia." In *What Is to Be Done?* by Nikolai Chernyshevsky. Ithaca: Cornell University Press, 1989.

Kautski, K. "Tchernichewsky et Malthus." *La Revue Socialiste,* no. 10 (1880): 425–32, and no. 11 (1880): 458–65.

Klenin, Emily. "On the Ideological Sources of *Čto delat'?* Sand, Družinin, Leroux." *Zeitschrift für slavische Philologie* 51, no. 2 (1991): 367–405.

Kliamkin, I. "Obraz myslei i obraz zhizni." *Literaturnoe obozrenie,* no. 7 (1978): 7–14.

Kohn, Hans. *The Mind of Modern Russia.* New Brunswick, N.J.: Rutgers University Press, 1955.

Korolenko, V. G. *Sobranie sochinenii v desiati tomakh.* 10 vols. Moscow: Gosudarstvennoe izdatel'stvo khudozhestvennoi literatury, 1953–56.

Koz'min, B. P. *Iz istorii revoliutsionnoi mysli v Rossii.* Moscow: Izdatel'stvo Akademii Nauk SSSR, 1961.

Kropotkin, Peter. *Ideals and Realities in Russian Literature.* New York: A. A. Knopf, 1915.

Kuleshov, V. V. "Velikii russkii revoliutsioner-demokrat N. G. Chernyshevskii i nekotorye sotsial'no-ekonomicheskie problemy v ego romane *Chto delat'?*" In *Roman N. G. Chernyshevskogo "Chto delat'?" (K 100-letiiu vykhoda v svet). Sbornik statei.* Shakhty: 1963.

Lampert, Evgenii. *Sons against Fathers: Studies in Russian Radicalism and Revolution.* Oxford: Clarendon Press, 1965.

Lanshchikov, Anatolii. *N. G. Chernyshevskii.* 2nd ed. Moscow: Sovremennik, 1987.

Lebedev, A. *Geroi Chernyshevskogo.* Moscow: Sovetskii pisatel', 1962.

Leskov, N. S. "Nikolai Gavrilovich Chernyshevskii v ego romane *Chto delat'?*" *Sobranie sochinenii,* vol. 10. Moscow: Gosudarstvennoe izdatel'stvo khudozhestvennoi literatury, 1958.

Lomunov, K. N., ed. *"Chto delat'?" N. G. Chernyshevskogo. Istoriko-funktsional'noe issledovanie.* Moscow: Nauka, 1990.

Lossky, N. O. *History of Russian Philosophy.* New York: International Universities Press, 1951.

Lotman, L. M. "Ideino-khudozhestvennye printsipy belletristiki Chernyshevskogo 1860–1870-kh godov." In *N. G. Chernyshevskii. Estetika. Literatura. Kritika,* edited by V. G. Bazanov, A. N. Iezuitov, and K. I. Rovda. Leningrad: Nauka, 1979.

———. "Sotsial'nyi ideal, etika i estetika Chernyshevskogo." In *Idei sotsializma v russkoi klassicheskoi literature,* edited by N. I. Prutskov. Leningrad: Nauka, 1969.

Loubere, Leo. *Utopian Socialism: Its History since 1800.* Cambridge: Schenkman, 1974.

Lukács, George. "Tschernyschewskijs Roman *Was Tun?*" *Der russische Realismus in der Weltliteratur.* Berlin: Aufbau-Verlag, 1952.

Lunacharskii, A. V. *Stat'i o Chernyshevskom.* Moscow: Gosudarstvennoe izdatel'stvo khudozhestvennoi literatury, 1958.

Lunacharsky, Anatoly. *On Literature and Art.* Moscow: Progress Publishers, 1973.

Magon, L. "Roman *Chto delat'?* i obshchestvenno-politicheskaia platforma *Molodoi Rossii.*" In *N. G. Chernyshevskii. Stat'i, issledovaniia i materialy,* vol. 1, edited by E. I. Pokusaev. Saratov: Saratovskoe knizhnoe izdatel'stvo, 1958.

Mandelbaum, Maurice. *History, Man and Reason: A Study in Nineteenth-Century Thought.* Baltimore: Johns Hopkins University Press, 1971.

Manuel, Frank E., and Fritzie P. Manuel. *Utopian Thought in the Western World.* Cambridge: Belknap Press of Harvard University Press, 1979.

Masaryk, Thomas Garrigue. *The Spirit of Russia: Studies in History, Literature, and Philosophy.* 2 vols. New York: Macmillan, 1955.

Mathewson, Rufus W., Jr. "The Hero and Society: The Literary Definitions (1855–1865, 1934–39)." In *Continuity and Change in Russian and Soviet Thought*, edited by Ernest J. Simmons. Cambridge: Harvard University Press, 1955.

———. *The Positive Hero in Russian Literature.* 2nd ed. Stanford: Stanford University Press, 1975.

Matich, Olga. "Dialectics of Cultural Return: Zinaida Gippius' Personal Myth." In *Cultural Mythologies of Russian Modernism,* edited by Boris Gasparov, Robert P. Hughes, and Irina Paperno. Berkeley: University of California Press, 1992.

Matlaw, Ralph E., ed. *Belinsky, Chernyshevsky and Dobrolyubov: Selected Criticism.* New York: Dutton, 1962.

———. Introduction to *Notes from Underground and The Grand Inquisitor,* by Fyodor Dostoevsky. New York: Dutton, 1960.

McLean, Hugh. *Nikolai Leskov: The Man and His Art.* Cambridge: Harvard University Press, 1977.

Meshcheriakov, V. P. *D. V. Grigorovich—Pisatel' i iskusstvoved.* Leningrad: Nauka, 1985.

Morozenko, L. N. "O psykhologizme L. N. Tolstogo i N. G. Chernyshevskogo." *Uchenye zapiski Leningradskogo gosudarstvennogo pedagogicheskogo instituta imeni A. I. Gertsena* 414 (1971): 262–72.

Morris, Marcia Ann. "In Search of Perfection: The Ascetic Hero in Russian Literature." Ph.D. diss., Columbia University, 1987.

———. *Saints and Revolutionaries: The Ascetic Hero in Russian Literature.* Albany: State University of New York Press, 1993.

Morson, Gary Saul. *The Boundaries of Genre: Dostoevsky's Diary of a Writer and the Traditions of Literary Utopia.* Austin: University of Texas Press, 1981.

———. "Introduction: Literary History and the Russian Experience." In *Literature and History,* edited by Gary Saul Morson. Stanford: Stanford University Press, 1986.

Moser, Charles A. *Antinihilism in the Russian Novel of the 1860's.* The Hague: Mouton & Co., 1964.

———. *Esthetics as Nightmare: Russian Literary Theory, 1855–1870.* Princeton: Princeton University Press, 1989.

Moskos, George. "(Dis)regarding Viéra: What Is to Be Done with Chernyshevsky?" *West Virginia University Philological Papers* 38 (1992): 49–58.

Mysliakov, V. A. "*Ottsy i deti* v vospriiatii Chernyshevskogo." *Russkaia literatura,* no. 2 (1978): 36–53.

Naumova, N. *Roman N. G. Chernyshevskogo "Chto delat'?"* Leningrad: Khudozhestvennaia literatura, 1972.

Nikolaev, P. "'. . . chtoby chitali vse. . . .'" In *"Chto delat'?" N. G. Chernyshevskogo. Istoriko-funktsional'noe issledovanie,* edited by K. N. Lomunov. Moscow: Nauka, 1990.

———. "Revoliutsionnyi roman." In *Chto delat'?* by N. G. Chernyshevskii. Moscow: Khudozhestvennaia literatura, 1969.

Odinokov, V. G. *Khudozhestvennaia sistemnost' russkogo klassicheskogo romana.* Novosibirsk: Nauka, 1976.

———. *"Normativnost'* i psykhologizm v romane N. G. Chernyshevskogo *Chto delat'?*" In *Problemy literaturnykh zhanrov. Materialy vtoroi nauchnoi mezhvuzovskoi konferentsii 30 sentiabria–4 oktiabria 1975 goda.* Tomsk: Izdatel'stvo Tomskogo universiteta, 1975.

Offord, Derek. "The Causes of Crime and the Meaning of Law: *Crime and Punishment* and Contemporary Radical Thought." In *New Essays on Dostoevsky,* edited by Malcolm V. Jones and Garth M. Terry. Cambridge: Cambridge University Press, 1983.

———. "Dostoyevsky and Chernyshevsky." *Slavonic and East European Review* 57, no. 4 (October 1979): 509–30.

Oksman, Iu. G., ed. *N. G. Chernyshevskii v vospominaniiakh sovremennikov.* 2 vols. Saratov: Saratovskoe knizhnoe izdatel'stvo, 1958–59.

Ornatskaia, T. I. "Roman N. G. Chernyshevskogo *Chto delat'?* (K istorii teksta)." *Russkaia literatura,* no. 3 (1977): 115–27.

Ornatskaia, T. I., and Galina Silina. "*What Is to Be Done?* Deciphering the Manuscript." *Soviet Literature* 10 (1975): 131–33.

Panaeva, A. Ia. *Vospominaniia.* Moscow: Gosudarstvennoe izdatel'stvo khudozhestvennoi literatury, 1956.

Paperno, Irina. *Chernyshevsky and the Age of Realism: A Study in the Semiotics of Behavior.* Stanford: Stanford University Press, 1988.

———. "The Myth of Reality in N. G. Černyševskij's Works and Life." In *Myth in Literature,* edited by Andrej Kodjak, Krystyna Pomorska, and Stephen Rudy. Columbus, Ohio: Slavica, 1985.

———. "The Novel Myth: N. G. Chernyshevskii's *What Is to Be Done?*" In *Issues in Russian Literature Before 1917,* edited by J. Douglas Clayton. Columbus, Ohio: Slavica, 1989.

Pereira, N. G. O. "Chernyshevsky's *What Is to Be Done?* as a Statement of Social Utopia." *Rocky Mountain Social Science Journal* 9, no. 3 (1972): 35–44.

———. "N. G. Chernyshevsky as Architect of the Politics of Anti-Liberalism in Russia." *Russian Review* 32, no. 3 (1973): 264–77.

———. *The Thought and Teachings of N. G. Černyševskij.* The Hague: Mouton, 1975.

Pinaev, M. T. "Izuchenie v shkole obraza Rakhmetova." In *Voprosy prepodavaniia literatury v shkole (Sbornik statei).* Stalingrad: Stalingradskii gosudarstvennyi pedagogicheskii institut, 1958.

———. *N. G. Chernyshevskii. Khudozhestvennoe tvorchestvo (Posobie dlia studentov).* Moscow: Prosveshchenie, 1984.

Pisarev, D. *Selected Philosophical, Social and Political Essays.* Moscow: Foreign Languages Publishing House, 1958.

Plekhanov, G. V. *Literatura i estetika.* 2 vols. Moscow: Gosudarstvennoe izdatel'stvo khudozhestvennoi literatury, 1958.

———. *N. G. Chernyshevskii.* Saint Petersburg: Shipovnik, 1910.

Plimak, E. "Ispytanie vremenem." *Voprosy literatury,* no. 2 (1978): 127–65.

Podshivalova, E. A. "O khudozhestvennom khronotope v romane N. G. Chernyshevskogo *Chto delat'?*" In *Problema avtora v khudozhestvennoi literature. Mezhvuzovskii sbornik nauchnykh trudov.* Izhevsk: 1983.

———. "Opyt tipologicheskogo izucheniia tvorchestva N. G. Chernyshevskogo." *Problemy tipologii literaturnogo protsessa.* Perm': Permskii gosudarstvennyi universitet, 1982.

Pokusaev, E. I. *N. G. Chernyshevskii.* 5th ed. Moscow: Prosveshchenie, 1976.

———, ed. *N. G. Chernyshevskii. Stat'i, issledovaniia i materialy.* 10 vols. Saratov: Izdatel'stvo Saratovskogo universiteta, 1958–87.

Pomialovskii, N. G. *Meshchanskoe schast'e. Molotov.* Moscow: Gosudarstvennoe izdatel'stvo khudozhestvennoi literatury, 1957.

Pomper, Philip. *The Russian Revolutionary Intelligentsia.* Arlington Heights, Ill.: Harlan Davidson, 1970.

Posin, Jack Abraham. "Chernyshevsky, Dobrolyubov, and Pisarev, the Ideological Forerunners of Bolshevism." Ph.D. diss., University of California, 1939.

Prokshin, V. G. "O svoeobrazii psykhologicheskogo analiza v romanakh N. G. Chernyshevskogo." In *N. G. Chernyshevskii. Stat'i, issledovaniia i materialy,* vol. 5, edited by E. I. Pokusaev. Saratov: Izdatel'stvo Saratovskogo universiteta, 1968.

Prozorov, Iu. M. "Nikolai Gavrilovich Chernyshevskii." In *Istoriia russkoi literatury XIX veka. Vtoraia polovina,* edited by N. N. Skatov. Moscow: Prosveshchenie, 1987.

Przhetslavskii, O. A. "Vospominaniia O. A. Przhetslavskago." *Russkaia starina* 14, no. 3 (September 1875): 131–60.

Pursglove, Michael. *D. V. Grigorovich: The Man Who Discovered Chekhov.* Brookfield, Vt.: Gower, 1987.

Rampton, David. *Vladimir Nabokov: A Critical Study of the Novels.* Cambridge: Cambridge University Press, 1984.

Randall, Francis B. *N. G. Chernyshevskii.* New York: Twayne Publishers, 1967.

Reifman, P. S. *N. G. Chernyshevskii.* Tartu: Tartuskii gosudarstvennyi universitet, 1973.

———. "Predpolagaiutsia li deti?" In *Trudy po russkoi i slavianskoi filologii. XV. Literaturovedenie.* Tartu: Tartuskii gosudarstvernyi universitet, 1970.

———. "Tri romana." In *Puti razvitiia russkoi literatury. Literaturovedenie.* Tartu: Tartuskii universitet, 1990.

———. "Vremia v romane N. G. Chernyshevskogo 'Chto delat'?'" In *Literaturnyi protsess: vnutrennie zakony i vneshnie vozdeistviia.* Tartu: Tartuskii universitet, 1990.

Reinhartz, Dennis. "N. G. Chernyshevsky on Aesthetics and Art: The Role of the Artist in a Revolution." Ph.D. diss., New York University, 1971.

———. "Rakhmetov in N. G. Chernyshevsky's *What Is to Be Done?* The Origins, Meaning, and Historical Impact of the Character." *Madison College Studies and Research* 29 (1971): 5–14.

———. "Russian Nihilism and American Anarchism: A Brief Encounter." *Madison College Studies and Research* 31 (March 1972): 48–52.

Reiser, S. A. "Legenda o prototypakh *Chto delat'?* Chernyshevskogo." *Trudy Leningradskogo bibliotechnogo instituta imeni N. K. Krupskoi. Kafedra literatury* 2 (1957): 115–25.

———. "Nekotorye problemy izuchenii romana *Chto delat'?*" In *Chto delat'?* by N. G. Chernyshevskii. Leningrad: Nauka, 1975.

———. "'Osobennyi chelovek' P. A. Bakhmetev." *Russkaia literatura,* no. 1 (1963): 173–77.

Ripp, Victor. "Turgenev as a Social Novelist: The Problem of the Part and the Whole." In *Literature and Society in Imperial Russia, 1800–1914,* edited by William Mills Todd III. Stanford: Stanford University Press, 1978.

———. *Turgenev's Russia.* Ithaca: Cornell University Press, 1980.

Riurikov, B. *N. G. Chernyshevskii. Kritiko-biograficheskii ocherk.* Moscow: Gosudarstvennoe izdatel'stvo khudozhestvennoi literatury, 1961.

Rogers, James Allen. "Russian Opposition to Darwinism in the Nineteenth Century." *Isis* 65, no. 229 (December 1974): 487–505.

Rostislav, [Fedor Tolstoi,] "Lzhemudrost' geroev Chernyshevskogo." *Severnaia pchela,* no. 138, May 27, 1863.

Rudenko, Iu. K. *Chernyshevskii-romanist i literaturnye traditsii.* Leningrad: Izdatel'stvo Leningradskogo universiteta, 1989.

———. "N. G. Chernyshevskii kak khudozhnik: belletristicheskie opyty 1840-kh godov." *Russkaia literatura,* no. 1 (1970): 101–20.

———. "Printsip tsiklizatsii v khudozhestvennoi sisteme N. G. Chernyshevskogo (K postanovke voprosa)." In *Problemy poetiki russkogo realizma XIX veka,* edited by G. P. Makogonenko, V. M. Markovich, and M. Rev. Leningrad: Leningradskii universitet, 1984.

———. "Problema chitatelia v romane N. G. Chernyshevskogo *Chto delat'?*" In *Russkaia literatura XIX–XX vekov,* edited by I. G. Iampol'skii. Leningrad: Izdatel'stvo Leningradskogo universiteta, 1971.

———. *Roman N. G. Chernyshevskogo "Chto delat'?" Esteticheskoe svoeobrazie i khudozhestvennyi metod.* Leningrad: Izdatel'stvo Leningradskogo universiteta, 1979.

Saltykov-Shchedrin, M. E. *Sobranie sochinenii.* 20 vols. Moscow: Khudozhestvennaia literatura, 1965–77.

Samosiuk, G. F. "Utopicheskie idei romana *Chto delat'?* v otsenkakh *Sovremennika.*" In *N. G. Chernyshevskii. Stat'i, issledovaniia i materialy,* vol. 8, edited by E. I. Pokusaev. Saratov: Izdatel'stvo Saratovskogo universiteta, 1978.

Sazhin, M. P. *Vospominaniia.* Moscow, 1925.

Scanlan, James P. "Chernyshevsky and Rousseau." In *Western Philosophical Systems in Russian Literature: A Collection of Critical Studies,* edited by Anthony M. Mlikotin. Los Angeles: University of Southern California Press, 1979.

———. "Nicholas Chernyshevsky and Philosophical Materialism in Russia." *Journal of the History of Philosophy* 8, no. 1 (1970): 65–86.

———. "Nikolaj Černyševskij and Soviet Philosophy." *Studies in Soviet Thought* 8, no. 1 (March 1967): 1–27.

———. "Nikolaj Chernyshevsky and the Philosophy of Realism in Nineteenth-Century Russian Aesthetics." *Studies in Soviet Thought* 30 (1985): 1–14.

Schapiro, Leonard. *Russian Studies.* London: Collins Harvill, 1986.

Schedo-Ferroti, D. K. *Aus der Literatur des Nigilismus. Kritische Beleichtung des Tschernyscheffskyschen Romans "Was tun?"* Braunschweig: 1871.

Shatalov, S. E., and A. S. Kurilov. *Nikolai Gavrilovich Chernyshevskii.* Moscow: Znanie, 1978.

Shchegolev, P. *Alekseevskii ravelin.* Moscow: Kniga, 1989.

Shcheulin, V. V. "N. G. Chernyshevskii i voprosy iazyka i stilia." In *Roman N. G. Chernyshevskogo "Chto delat'?" (K 100-letiiu vykhoda v svet). Sbornik statei.* Shakhty: 1963.

Shelgunov, N. V. "Russkie idealy, geroi i tipy." In *Shestidesiatye gody,* edited by N. K. Piksanov and O. V. Tsekhnovitser. Moscow-Leningrad: Nauka, 1940.

Shestakov, V. P. "Evoliutsiia russkoi literaturnoi utopii." In *Russkaia literaturnaia utopiia,* edited by V. P. Shestakov. Moscow: Izdatel'stvo Moskovskogo universiteta, 1986.

Shibaev, S. M. "Moral'nyi oblik 'obyknovennykh liudei' N. G. Chernyshevskogo." *Roman N. G. Chernyshevskogo "Chto delat'?" (K 100-letiiu vykhoda v svet). Sbornik statei.* Shakhty: 1963.

Shul'gin, V. N. *Ocherki zhizni i tvorchestva N. G. Chernyshevskogo.* Moscow: Gosudarstvennoe izdatel'stvo khudozhestvennoi literatury, 1956.

Sigrist, A. "Fal'sifitsirovannyi Chernyshevskii: stereotipy i novatsii." *Voprosy literatury,* no. 1 (1971): 130–45.

Simmons, Ernest J. "Part V Review." In *Continuity and Change in Russian and Soviet Thought,* edited by Ernest J. Simmons. Cambridge: Harvard University Press, 1955.

Sivovolov, B. M. "Roman N. G. Chernyshevskogo *Chto delat'?* v sotsial'noi praktike sovremennikov (O zhenskom trude po memuarnym istochnikam)."

In *Roman N. G. Chernyshevskogo "Chto delat'?" (K 100-letiiu vykhoda v svet). Sbornik statei.* Shakhty: 1963.

Skaftymov, A. P. *Nravstvennye iskaniia russkikh pisatelei. Stat'i i issledovaniia o russkikh klassikakh.* Moscow: Khudozhestvennaia literatura, 1972.

———. "Roman *Chto delat'?*" In *N. G. Chernyshevskii. Sbornik. Neizdannye stat'i, materialy, vospominaniia.* Saratov: Izdanie nizhne-volzhskogo oblastnogo nauchnogo obshchestva kraevedeniia, 1926.

———. *Zhizn' i deiatel'nost' N. G. Chernyshevskogo.* 2nd ed. Saratov: OGIZ, 1947.

Skvortsov-Stepanov, I. I., ed. *Lenin o Chernyshevskom.* Moscow-Leningrad: Institut Lenina pri Ts. K. V. K. P. (b.), 1928.

Smolitskii, V. G. *Iz ravelina. O sud'be romana N. G. Chernyshevskogo "Chto delat'?"* 2nd ed. Moscow: Kniga, 1977.

Solov'ev, N. "Printsipy zhizni." *Vsemirnyi trud* 1 (1867): 137–77.

———. "Zhenshchinam." *Epokha,* no. 12 (December 1864): 15–24.

Stakhevich, S. G. "Sredi politicheskikh prestupnikov. Nikolai Gavrilovich Chernyshevskii." In *N. G. Chernyshevskii, 1828–1928. Sbornik statei, dokumentov i vospominanii.* Moscow: 1928.

Steklov, Iu. M. *N. G. Chernyshevskii. Ego zhizn' i deiatel'nost' (1828–1889).* Saint Petersburg: Obshchestvennaia pol'za, 1909.

———. *N. G. Chernyshevskii. Ego zhizn' i deiatel'nost'. 1828–1889.* 2nd ed. 2 vols. Moscow-Leningrad: Gosudarstvennoe izdatel'stvo, 1928.

———. "Neizdannaia stat'ia A. A. Feta o romane N. G. Chernyshevskogo *Chto delat'?*" *Literaturnoe nasledstvo* 25–26 (1936): 477–84.

Stites, Richard. *Revolutionary Daydreams.* New York: Oxford University Press, 1989.

———. *The Women's Liberation Movement in Russia: Feminism, Nihilism, and Bolshevism.* Princeton: Princeton University Press, 1978.

Strakhov, N. N. "Schastlivye liudi." *Iz istorii literaturnago nigilizma. 1861–1865.* Saint Petersburg: 1890. Reprint, The Hague: Europe Printing, 1967.

———. "Zametki letopistsa. Poslednie dva goda v peterburgskoi zhurnalistike." *Epokha,* no. 10 (1864): 9.

Struve, Gleb. "*Monologue Intérieur:* The Origins of the Formula and the First Statement of Its Possibilities." *PMLA* 69, no. 5 (December 1954): 1101–11.

Sutiagin, I. N. "O narodnosti romana N. G. Chernyshevskogo *Chto delat'?*" In *Roman N. G. Chernyshevskogo "Chto delat'?" (K 100-letiiu vykhoda v svet). Sbornik statei.* Shakhty: 1963.

Tamarchenko, G. E. *Chernyshevskii-romanist.* Leningrad: Khudozhestvennaia literatura, 1976.

———. *Romany N. G. Chernyshevskogo.* Saratov: Saratovskoe knizhnoe izdatel'stvo, 1954.

Tchernuishevsky, N. G.: see Chernyshevskii, N. G.

Tchernyshewsky, N. G.: see Chernyshevskii, N. G.

Teplinskii, M. V. "Avtor-povestvovatel' v romane N. G. Chernyshevskogo *Chto delat'?*" In *N. G. Chernyshevskii. Stat'i, issledovaniia i materialy*, vol. 8, edited by E. I. Pokusaev. Saratov: Izdatel'stvo Saratovskogo universiteta, 1978.

———. *Izuchenie tvorchestva N. G. Chernyshevskogo.* Kiev: Radians'ka Shkola, 1981.

Terras, Victor. *Belinskij and Russian Literary Criticism: The Heritage of Organic Aesthetics.* Madison: University of Wisconsin Press, 1974.

Todes, Daniel P. *Darwin without Malthus: The Struggle for Existence in Russian Evolutionary Thought.* New York: Oxford University Press, 1989.

Tolstoi, L. N. *The Death of Ivan Ilych and Other Stories.* Translated by J. D. Duff. New York: Signet, 1960.

———. *Polnoe sobranie sochinenii.* 90 vols. Moscow-Leningrad: Gosudarstvennoe izdatel'stvo khudozhestvennoi literatury, 1928–58.

Travushkin, N. S. *Chernyshevskii v gody katorgi i ssylki.* Moscow: Khudozhestvennaia literatura, 1978.

Troitskii, V. Iu. "Ideino-esteticheskaia bor'ba vokrug romana N. G. Chernyshevskogo *Chto delat'?* (N. G. Chernyshevskii, N. S. Leskov, I. A. Goncharov)." In *"Chto delat'?" N. G. Chernyshevskogo. Istoriko-funktsional'noe issledovanie*, edited by K. N. Lomunov. Moscow: Nauka, 1990.

Tsitovich, P. *Chto delali v romane "Chto delat'?"* 4th ed. Odessa: 1879.

Turgenev, I. S. *Pis'ma v trinadtsati tomakh.* 13 vols. Part of *Polnoe sobranie sochinenii i pisem v dvadtsati vos'mi tomakh.* 28 vols. Moscow-Leningrad: Izdatel'stvo Akademii Nauk SSSR, 1961–68.

———. *Turgenev's Letters.* Selected, translated, and edited by A. V. Knowles. New York: Charles Scribner's Sons, 1983.

———. *Turgenev's Letters.* Edited and translated by Edgar H. Lehrman. New York: Knopf, 1961.

Ulam, Adam B. *The Bolsheviks.* New York: Collier, 1965.

———. *Ideologies and Illusions: Revolutionary Thought from Herzen to Solzhenitsyn.* Cambridge: Harvard University Press, 1976.

———. *In the Name of the People.* New York: Viking Press, 1977.

———. "Party Girl." *New York Times Book Review*, January 31, 1993, p. 12.

Vail', Petr, and Aleksandr Genis. *Rodnaia rech'.* Tenafly, N.J.: Ermitazh, 1990.

Valentino, Russell Scott. "The Rise of the Russian Tendentious Novel: Generic Hybridization and Literary Change." Ph.D. diss., UCLA, 1993.

Valentinov, Nikolai. "Chernyshevskii i Lenin." *Novyi zhurnal* 26 (1951): 193–216, and 27 (1951): 225–49.

———. *Encounters with Lenin.* London: Oxford University Press, 1968.

Venturi, Franco. *Roots of Revolution.* New York: Alfred A. Knopf, 1960.

Verderevskaia, N. A. "O 'prototipicheskoi versii' v izuchenii khudozhestvennykh proizvedenii Chernyshevskogo." In *N. G. Chernyshevskii.*

Stat'i, issledovaniia i materialy, vol. 5, edited by E. I. Pokusaev. Saratov: Izdatel'stvo Saratovskogo universiteta, 1968.

———. *Roman N. G. Chernyshevskogo "Chto delat'?" Posobie dlia uchashchikhsia.* Moscow: Prosveshchenie, 1982.

———. *Russkii roman 40–60-kh godov XIX veka.* Kazan': Izdatel'stvo Kazan'skogo universiteta, 1980.

———. *Stanovlenie tipa raznochintsa v russkoi realisticheskoi literature 40–60kh godov XIX veka (k probleme tipologii zhanra, siuzheta i obraza).* Kazan': Kazan'skii gosudarstvennyi pedagogicheskii institut, 1975.

Verkhovskii, G. *O romane N. G. Chernyshevskogo "Chto delat'?"* Iaroslavl': Iaroslavskoe knizhnoe izdatel'stvo, 1959.

Viduetskaia, I. P. "Pisateli-demokraty 1860-kh—nachala 1880-kh godov i roman Chernyshevskogo *Chto delat'?*" In *"Chto delat'?" N. G. Chernyshevskogo. Istoriko-funktsional'noe issledovanie,* edited by K. N. Lomunov. Moscow: Nauka, 1990.

———. "Roman *Chto delat'?* v otsenke revoliutsionno-demokraticheskoi kritiki." In *"Chto delat'?" N. G. Chernyshevskogo. Istoriko-funktsional'noe issledovanie,* edited by K. N. Lomunov. Moscow: Nauka, 1990.

Vodovozov, N. V. *Roman N. G. Chernyshevskogo "Chto Delat'?"* Moscow: Znanie, 1953.

Vodovozova, E. N. *Na zare zhizni.* 2 vols. Moscow: Khudozhestvennaia literatura, 1964.

Volk, S. S., and V. S. Nikonenko. *Materializm N. G. Chernyshevskogo.* Leningrad: Izdatel'stvo Leningradskogo universiteta, 1979.

Volodin, A. I., Iu. F. Kariakin, and E. G. Plimak. *Chernyshevskii ili Nechaev.* Moscow: Mysl', 1976.

Volodin, A. I., and B. M. Shakhmatov. "Utopicheskii sotsializm v Rossii. 1833–1883." In *Utopicheskii sotsializm v Rossii. Khrestomatiia,* edited by A. I. Volodin. Moscow: Izdatel'stvo politicheskoi literatury, 1985.

Vucinich, Alexander. *Darwin in Russian Thought.* Berkeley: University of California Press, 1988.

———. *Social Thought in Tsarist Russia: The Quest for a General Science of Society, 1861–1917.* Chicago: University of Chicago Press, 1976.

Walicki, Andrzej. *A History of Russian Thought from the Enlightenment to Marxism.* Stanford: Stanford University Press, 1979.

Wasiolek, Edward. "Design in the Russian Novel." In *The Russian Novel from Pushkin to Pasternak,* edited by John Garrard. New Haven: Yale University Press, 1983.

———. *Fathers and Sons: Russia at the Crossroads.* New York: Twayne Publishers, 1993.

———. "Tolstoy's *The Death of Ivan Ilych* and Jamesian Fictional Imperative." *Modern Fiction Studies* 6, no. 4 (1960–61): 314–24.

Wellek, René. *A History of Modern Criticism: 1750–1950.* Vol. 4: *The Later Nineteenth Century.* New Haven: Yale University Press, 1965.

———. "Social and Aesthetic Values in Russian Nineteenth-Century Literary Criticism (Belinskii, Chernyshevskii, Dobroliubov, Pisarev)." In *Continuity and Change in Russian and Soviet Thought,* edited by Ernest J. Simmons. Cambridge: Harvard University Press, 1955.

W[est], H[enry] R. "Philosophical Schools and Doctrines." *Encyclopaedia Britannica.* 15th ed. Vol. 25.

Wiemer, Annegret J. "Corpus Ex Machina: Nikolai Chernyshevsky's *What Is to Be Done?* (1863) and Mary Bradley Lane's *Mizora* (1880–81)." *Neophilologus* 79, no. 2 (April 1995): 187–96.

Woehrlin, William F. *Chernyshevskii: The Man and the Journalist.* Cambridge: Harvard University Press, 1971.

Zaitsev, V. "Glupovtsy, popavshie v *Sovremennik.*" *Russkoe slovo,* no. 2 (1864): 34–42.

Žekulin, G. "Forerunner of Socialist Realism: the Novel 'What to do?' by N. G. Chernyshevs/ky." *Slavonic and East European Review* 41 (1963): 467–83.

Zel'dovich, M. G. "Zabytyi epizod bor'by vokrug romana N. G. Chernyshevskogo *Chto delat'?*" In *N. G. Chernyshevskii. Stat'i, issledovaniia i materialy,* vol. 2, edited by E. I. Pokusaev. Saratov: Izdatel'stvo Saratovskogo universiteta, 1961.

Zenkovsky, Serge A. *Medieval Russia's Epics, Chronicles, and Tales.* New York: Dutton, 1974.

Zenkovsky, V. V. *A History of Russian Philosophy.* 2 vols. New York: Columbia University Press, 1953.

Zhdanovskii, N. P. "Osobennosti realizma pisatelei-demokratov 60-kh godov XIX v." In *Problemy tipologii russkogo realizma,* edited by N. L. Stepanov and U. R. Fokht. Moscow: Nauka, 1969.

Ziolkowski, Margaret. *Hagiography and Modern Russian Literature.* Princeton: Princeton University Press, 1988.

Index

Names in quotation marks are those of characters in the novel.

About the Author

Andrew M. Drozd is an assistant professor of Russian at the University of Alabama.